The Shell Channel Pilot

The Shell Channel Pilot

The South Coast of England & the North Coast of France

TOM CUNLIFFE

Imray Laurie Norie & Wilson Ltd
St Ives Cambridgeshire England

Published by
Imray Laurie Norie & Wilson Ltd
Wych House, St Ives, Huntingdon,
Cambridgeshire PE17 4BT, England.
☎ +44 (0)1480 462114 *Fax* +44 (0)1480 496109
E-mail ilnw@imray.com
1997

First edition 1995
Reprint with revisions 1996
Second edition 1997

The plans and details of tidal streams are based on
information published by the British Admiralty
Hydrographic Office and the Service Hydro-
graphique et Océanographique de la Marine with
permission.

British Library Cataloguing in Publication Data.

A catalogue record for this book is available from
the British Library.

ISBN 0 85288 386 2

CAUTION
Every effort has been made to ensure the accuracy
of this book. It contains selected information and
thus is not definitive and does not include all known
information on the subject in hand; this is particularly relevant to the plans, which should not be used
for navigation. The publisher and author believe
that its selection is a useful aid to prudent navigation, but the safety of a vessel depends ultimately on
the judgement of the navigator, who should assess
all information, published or unpublished, available
to him/her.

PLANS
The plans in this guide are not to be used for navigation. They are designed to support the text and
should at all times be used with navigational charts.

The views expressed are those of the author alone
and are not necessarily shared by Shell Ltd UK.

The Shell symbol and the name 'Shell' are both
trademarks.

CORRECTIONS
The editors would be glad to receive any corrections, information or suggestions which readers may
consider would improve the book, as new impres-
sions will be required from time to time. Letters
should be addressed to the Editor, *The Shell Channel
Pilot*, care of the publishers. The more precise the
information the better, but even partial or doubtful
information is helpful, if it is made clear what the
doubts are.

CORRECTIONAL SUPPLEMENTS
Imray pilot books are amended at intervals by the
issue of correctional supplements. Supplements, if
available, are supplied free of charge with the books
when they are purchased. Further supplements are
available from the publishers. The following should
be quoted:
1. Name of book
2. Date of edition (above)
3. Date of last supplement (if applicable)
4. Name and address to which supplement should
   be sent.

The last input of technical information was April
1997.

Printed in Great Britain by Bath Press Colourbooks
Ltd, Blantyre.

Contents

Harbours marked ★ are tidally sensitive (see Tidal heights, page 3).

Foreword

Dedication

The Shell Channel Pilot is dedicated to the memory of Captain John Coote RN, a great man of the sea.

The English Channel is one of the world's finest yacht cruising grounds. It has varying coastal topography, from the granite shores of Brittany to the Solent harbour mud-flats and the chalk cliffs of Sussex. Resorts, cities, naval bases and great commercial ports line its waters, but it also offers islands and quiet anchorages. For British or French sailors there is the added spice of foreign shores anything from a few hours to a day away, while for visitors from further afield two great nations are here to be explored by yacht, which, as all cruising people know, is the best way to discover any country.

Channel tides are of major significance to any sailing or low-powered motor craft. In parts of Brittany ranges climb up to a mind-bending 12m, with streams to match. Yet this very feature, which can easily alarm, is what makes the place so exciting to work in a small boat. A yacht might sail 30 miles through the water during a 6-hour period while receiving an extra 15 miles free by courtesy of the tide. This increases the range of an average daytime passage and makes more ambitious plans possible.

Coupled with the tides, our ever-changing weather generates such a massive variation in conditions that it is true to say that for those who sail our waters no two days are ever the same.

Since 1937 *The Shell Pilot* and its immediate progenitor, *Sailing on the South Coast*, by the redoubtable K. Adlard Coles, have been guiding yachtsmen into a greater enjoyment of Channel waters. The book started in the famous 'dumpy' format, and Shell soon took up the sponsorship. The work passed through various editions with its original publishers, Faber and Faber. In due course *The Shell Pilot*, as it was now known, came under the editorship of Captain John Coote RN, a famous submariner who became equally notable as an ocean-racing navigator. Johnnie Coote was a friend to all who loved the sea. He had great influence, and yachtsmen in all areas of the sport benefited from his work. Among cruising sailors, however, he will be mainly remembered for his tireless efforts on *The Shell Pilot*. In 1985 he expanded its horizons by including a new volume (in the traditional format) which covered selected French Channel ports. In addition to the usual pilotage notes, it contained swashbuckling commentaries on the World War II Normandy landings, as well as many a useful tip on where to eat and where not to.

Johnnie Coote died in 1993, deeply mourned by his family and a host of friends, just as the old *Shell Pilot* was coming due for a new edition. Shortly before his death he handed the tiller over to me. At the same time, Faber and Faber were arranging to pass this, their one nautical title, over to Imray, who are, of course, nautical specialists. The scene was thus set for a major change in the book. People's sailing habits have altered since Adlard Coles' day and far more yachts now cross and recross the Channel as a matter of course. It has therefore been decided that while *The Shell Channel Pilot* will retain its traditional feel of uncomplicated sailing directions, clear plans and useful photographs, the original two-volume, small-sized format will be brought into line with the standard A4 publication. Both sides of the Channel can now be combined in one book; an exciting development which creates the first yachting pilot for the whole of the English Channel cruising ground. I am sure Adlard Coles would have approved.

Whilst the text of the book is almost entirely new, it is based on Johnnie Coote's work, which in turn drew its inspiration from Adlard Coles. Thus, the circle remains unbroken. Every effort has been made, both by myself and by Imray, to ensure that the information is up to date at the time of publishing. The notes on every harbour on the English side have been checked by the harbourmasters concerned or, in the absence of harbour authorities, with the local yacht club. Both official and unofficial sources have been extremely cooperative, and we acknowledge their assistance most warmly. French harbour staff have been personally visited wherever possible and, as with England, I have drawn heavily on my own experience of navigating Channel waters.

The Coote initiative of mentioning notable restaurants and other points of interest has been maintained. I have also tried to indicate the proximity of laundry facilities because, as a family yachtsman myself, I have found these of great use on trips of more than a few days' duration.

The new *Shell Channel Pilot* has aerial photographs ably taken mostly by Patrick Roach which will provide invaluable assistance when attempting to make sense of a two-dimensional chart. Most of the black-and-white photographs were shot by Johnnie Coote and have been generously made available by Mrs Coote and Faber and Faber.

I cannot end this foreword without recommending all yacht skippers to make maximum use of binoculars and to secure the services of a sharp-eyed mate. My own pilotage is frequently rendered free of impending drama by the presence of my wife, Ros, whose father was a fighter pilot and who has inherited his gimlet vision. Not content with this practical contribution, she also runs a tight ship in my study. Without her and that most equable of publishers, Willie Wilson, this new version of the *Shell Channel Pilot* might well have been blown overboard somewhere off the Needles, or swallowed up by the secret recesses of my computer.

Tom Cunliffe
March 1997

Acknowledgements

The majority of the aerial photographs in colour were taken by Patrick Roach. Pat Blenkinsop piloted the aircraft.

The index has been compiled by Elizabeth Cook.

Introduction

Warning

Users of this pilot book should be constantly aware that while every reasonable effort has been made to ensure its accuracy, experience shows that, as with all pilot books, there will remain the occasional error in the information. These generally arise due to changes in harbour arrangements and navigational aids subsequent to the date of compilation, but it is not unknown for a bearing or course either to be noted incorrectly in the first instance, or to become incorrect through errors in the typesetting or editing process. When a ship takes on a human pilot, the captain retains full responsibility for her safe passage. The same applies to yachtsmen using this book. Make sure your charts are up to date and proceed with caution.

Sailing directions

Charts

It cannot be over-stressed that, like all yachting pilots, *The Shell Channel Pilot* exists largely to expand and clarify the information on official navigational charts; these may be British Admiralty, SHOM, Imray or the Carte Guide de Navigation Cotière (Navicarte). The plans in this book are included in order to illustrate the text and are not to be used for chartwork navigation.

For planning and passage-making purposes you will require an overall Channel chart, which will cost the same as a dozen oysters and a bottle of Muscadet on the quay at St Vaast. What you buy after that will depend on how adventurous you want to be and the depth of your pocket. Some people find Admiralty charts the easiest to read. I am inclined to concur with this, but it must be said that the harbour plans and other information included on Imray's passage charts can represent a substantial saving in the number of charts to buy. French Navicarte charts are unusual in presentation, but once you are used to them they are an excellent pilotage tool. French (SHOM) charts are beautiful – some would say they are works of art. Unless you have seen them often, however, the British Admiralty offerings, while more prosaic, are far easier to read.

Datum

With the advent of accurate electronic fixing systems, it should be noted that the position reading from your GPS set may differ from that on the chart you are using. Always check the *datum* of the chart

(usually given near the title, the cautions and any other such information), compare it with that on your computer and be ready to make any necessary alterations to your apparent position. Such changes may be insignificant in terms of pre-electronic navigation, but for a navigator who takes full advantage of the pinpoint accuracy sometimes now available, they may be important.

The term 'datum' in this context should not be confused with the 'Chart Datum' from which soundings are measured.

Waypoints

The Shell Channel Pilot has resisted the temptation to give waypoints. The reason for this is that in the experience of the compiler, the position of the desired waypoint may change from day to day, depending on wind and tide. Furthermore, if the waypoint were, for example, a landfall buoy and this were moved, confusion could be doubled. It is therefore recommended that users select their own waypoints where required.

Depths

Depths are given in metres at Lowest Astronomical Tide (LAT), which is also Chart Datum level. Thus, except in exceptional circumstances, you are unlikely to experience anything less than the depth stated.

Heights

Heights of lighthouses etc. are expressed in metres above sea level at mean high water springs. They will therefore only be less than this at times of unusually high tides.

Distances

Distances at sea are stated in nautical miles and cables. A cable's length is 200 yards, one tenth of a mile or, if you prefer, one tenth of a minute of latitude. Should you be of the metric persuasion, it represents something under 200 metres.

Tidal height information

This is given for every port by reference to Dover as the standard port. The heights thus computed will sometimes perforce be approximate and skippers are strongly recommended to calculate more accurate information from the *Admiralty Tide Tables* or the almanacs. The information given in this book will prove useful for planning purposes, however.

Always bear in mind that published tidal data are only predictions. The facts on the day may be affected significantly by wind and weather.

The *double high water* phenomenon in and around the Solent is notoriously difficult to predict. The above cautions should be particularly noted in this area.

Leading lines

While leading lines are theoretically safe, they sometimes pass a danger in close proximity to the channel. Examine the chart, therefore, and be ready to 'borrow' to one side or the other to give a safety margin.

Bearings and courses

Bearings and courses are given in degrees True, to which any necessary corrections must be made for Variation and Deviation. Unless otherwise stated, all bearings of shore objects, or headings up approach channels, are given as True from seaward.

Symbols

Symbols in the text for lights, sound signals and any other charted information are generally lifted straight from the chart and apply the same conventions, thus: 'Fort Gilkicker (Oc.G.10s7M)' is read as 'Fort Gilkicker, green light, occulting once every 10 seconds, 7 miles nominal range'. The attention of readers using French charts is drawn to the English/French glossary in the Appendix.

The anchorage symbol ⚓ is used on the plans to indicate a general anchorage. Its precise location does not necessarily recommend the ideal place to let go. Skippers are expected to apply the principles of good seamanship to selecting a precise location to lay their anchors.

Buoyage

IALA System A buoyage applies throughout the English Channel.

Customs

Since the rise of the EU, few formalities have been required of yachts passing between member states. Vessels arriving in the Channel from outside the EU are, of course, subject to the usual customs and immigration requirements. They should accordingly report at a major port as soon as practicable.

Unfortunately for us Europeans, there still exists a nonsense to encumber our local cruising. British yachts bound for the Channel Islands are required to fill out *Part I* of form *C1328*, obtainable from any customs house and many harbour offices. Hand in the remaining parts as directed on your return. If you have made an unscheduled call at the Channel Islands on your way home from France, you must clear into the UK by reporting your arrival to the nearest customs house by telephone. You will then be directed as to your correct course of action. In the islands themselves, ask the harbour staff for clearance advice.

On arrival at or from the Channel Islands, you must wear a yellow 'Q' flag as soon as you are within 12 miles of the coast, keeping it up until you are cleared.

Traffic signals

No.	Lights		Main message
1	☀☀☀	Flashing	Serious emergency – all vessels to stop or divert according to instructions
2	●●●	Fixed or Slow Occulting	Vessels shall not proceed (*Note* Some ports may use an exemption signal, as in 2a below)
3	●●●		Vessels may proceed One way traffic
4	●●○		Vessels may proceed Two way traffic
5	●○●		A vessel may proceed only when she has received specific orders to do so (*Note* Some ports may use an exemption signal, as in 5a below)

Exemption signals and messages

| 2a | ○● / ● / ● | Fixed or Slow Occulting | Vessels shall not proceed, except that vessels which navigate outside the main channel need not comply with the main message |
| 5a | ○● / ○ / ● | | A vessel may proceed only when she has received specific orders to do so, except that vessels which navigate outside the main channel need not comply with the main message |

Auxiliary signals and messages

White and/or yellow lights, displayed to the right of the main lights	Local meanings, as promulgated in local port orders

Checklist for cross-Channel departure

- Passports: you may never be asked for these, but they are useful for cashing cheques and can be needed for independent return to the UK. Captain Coote advised that they might be required for credit purposes in the casinos of northern France.
- Clear customs for Channel Islands (see above) if necessary.
- Carry your ship's papers or small-craft registry documentation.
- Carry your Yachtmaster's Certificate if you have one. The Helmsman's Overseas Certificate of Competence (HOCC) issued through the RYA is sufficient if you are not a coastal skipper or yachtmaster. At the time of writing this is required only for French inland waters, but times may change.
- Always carry a British ensign, a French courtesy flag and a 'Q' flag.

VHF

It is now normal practice on approaching a British yacht harbour to call ahead on VHF to arrange a berth. Radio channels are given in the text. This may not always be convenient in France – it takes a very confident linguist to chance his arm on the radio with a French harbourmaster. Indeed, while the majority of English yacht harbours now maintain a VHF watch, at least in working hours, many French ones do not. If in doubt, tie up on the visitors' berths or reception pontoon and go to the harbour office for instructions.

French time

French time operates from the basis of 'Zone −1'. This means that you must subtract 1 hour from a French time as given in a tide table to convert that time to UT. Since an hour must then be added to UT to correct it to what a British watch says, you will realise that British Summer Time is the same as Zone −1. This simple device works for published tide times in France. It does not help you with restaurant opening times and the rest, which add an hour to Zone −1 and thus step away from the British once more.

Navigating the English Channel

I remember once returning home from a long cruise to foreign parts. I had enjoyed some excellent tropical sailing, yet as the old boat came onto soundings and I reached for my tidal stream atlas my heart gave a small skip of joy. At long last there would be more to passage-making than just pointing the boat in the right direction. I would be challenged once more, and my satisfaction would be in proportion to my success in meeting the demands of the ocean's own breathing, for in the Channel, the tide is king.

Winds can be from any quarter in the summer months, but are often westerly. This makes life easy for the south-coast sailor wanting to visit France, but highly inconvenient for a Dutchman who has it in mind to cruise the Isles of Scilly. We cannot change the weather, and where we end up in relation to the wind direction will always contain an element of lottery, but the tides are a different matter. Heights and streams are predicted years in advance to a surprising degree of accuracy, so that we have all the necessary information to allow us to work the fair stream wherever possible and avoid the worst excesses of foul tide. Occasionally there is no advantage either way, but even then the stream remains important, for without understanding its movements we cannot estimate our position. This leaves us with no hope save electronics, which, should our volts pour away down an electrical plughole, will be no hope at all.

Tidal streams

The tidal stream charts included in this book relate to the time of high water at Dover. The arrows indicating stream direction are self-explanatory. The speeds are given as two figures with a dot between them: for example, 21.42. This indicates that the neap rate at that point is 2·1 knots while the mean spring rate is 4·2. Tables are available for computing intermediate rates, but for most practical purposes an interpolation 'in your head' will prove satisfactory.

Study of the various tidal charts reveals a number of useful phenomena:

- Tides are strongest round headlands.
- In general, tides are weaker in the southwest of England than elsewhere.
- Tides run savagely around Cap de la Hague between Alderney and France (the Race of Alderney), and are generally strong on the French side of the Channel from Barfleur right down to Ouessant.
- Solent tides run hard, particularly in the West Solent and at the western entrance. They also turn an hour or so before the main Channel stream.
- Vicious tides may be encountered in the vicinity of Portland Bill. For information about these, see the chapter on 'Principal headlands'.
- As the tide floods up-Channel, with high waters progressively later the further east you go, it is possible to carry fair tide all the way from the Hamble River to Dover, given a boat speed of 7 or 8 knots, depending upon the tide. You must work the eddy down the Solent north shore, then step onto the 'gravy train' once past the Looe channel at Selsey Bill.
- Carrying a fair or neutral stream from the west Solent to Guernsey is easy, despite a distance of up to 90 miles. Take the last of the ebb down to the Needles, then make sure you arrive at the Alderney Race (60 miles on) at, or an hour or two after, HW Dover. You will then receive a push of anything from 3 to 7 knots all the way to St Peter Port. Get it wrong, and you might just as well stop off in Alderney for a night in The Diver's Bar.
- Always use your tidal atlas or charts creatively. They are your lifeline to happiness.

Tidal heights

Whilst many of the ports dealt with in *The Shell Channel Pilot* can be entered in most weathers and at any state of tide, others are tidally sensitive. These are marked ⋆ on the Contents page so that if the reader needs a decision at sea in a hurry in bad weather, he or she can see at a glance if a harbour is likely to present a problem. Those with a ⋆ will need more careful study.

A number of harbours on both sides of the Channel quite literally dry out at low water, or are only accessible via lock gates at half-tide or above. Drying harbours offer great satisfaction to boats able to

take the ground conveniently, but for any strangers, all tidal harbours require great care.

In general, because the tide floods eastwards, it is better to approach such a port from the west, carrying fair tide. This raises its own problems when you leave, because from high water onwards the stream should be running away to the west again. Happily, this is not always so clear cut, with high water not coinciding perfectly with the end of the east-going stream. Careful planning with this question in mind can yield satisfying results.

Channel crossings

Various challenges and problems attach themselves to crossing the Channel, depending upon how far east or west you happen to be. These generally revolve around large cross-tide effects, shipping and the desirability of making a dawn landfall. The last factor is less important in the narrow waters at the east end of the Channel, while for many people, electronic navigation is rendering the attraction of a look at the lighthouses before they are switched off less of a consideration on the longer passages than once it was.

Traffic Separation Schemes

These are clearly marked on the passage charts. Their purpose is to prevent big-ship collisions in areas of heavy traffic. If navigating within such a scheme, yachts must proceed in the direction indicated for traffic flow, but you are generally better advised to stay out of them if you can. You may not navigate in the separation zone which lies between the lanes. You may only cross it at right angles. If you need to cross the whole scheme, you must do so at your best speed at right angles to the flow of traffic. When the tide is strong, this means that you do not try to plot a vector course in order to traverse the zone on a ground track at right angles to the lanes. You will cross more quickly if you *steer* at right angles. You will also be complying with the regulations.

Should you require to enter a traffic lane in such a scheme, do so at a shallow angle.

In the Dover Strait, these schemes are enforced rigorously and yachts must comply on pain of considerable fines. Fortunately, if you are proceeding from one local port to another, or otherwise along the coast, you may make use of the Inshore Traffic Zones. These are set up specifically to accommodate coastal shipping and small craft. You may pass in either direction, paying particular heed to the Colregs, being always aware of the presence of the main event going on in mid-Channel.

There is a further Traffic Separation Scheme off the Casquets to the northwest of Alderney. This must be considered if your passage plan leads you into its vicinity. Although the area seems well clear of danger, it has proved to be a pressure point and you must take heed.

The only other such zone of interest to Channel yachtsmen lies between Land's End and the Isles of Scilly. This one is less crowded and you cross it at right angles anyway, unless you are going to windward, in which case, watch out!

Tidal vectors

When you are crossing the narrow part of the Channel – a trip of 4 or 5 hours perhaps – you can safely lay off a tidal offset for the whole period (diagram 1), given that you are not falling foul of a Traffic Separation Scheme. If you are crossing the central Channel, however, you must be careful. Unless your boat is extremely fast, your trip will be of over one tide's duration. You will thus be set east and west during the passage. It is a grave error to try to offset each hour's tide as in diagram 2, because if you do, you will sail considerably further each hour than you need. You may end up putting as much as 15 miles onto a 60-mile passage.

Instead, add up the total east-going and the total west-going streams for your projected time at sea. Subtract the lesser from the greater and what is left is your *net tidal vector*. Apply this to your course to steer (see plan) and you will make your fastest possible crossing. The yacht will drift off the rhumb line, but this does not matter at all, for the tide will surely drift her back again before your arrival. You must bear this in mind if using a navigation computer and, unless you are prepared to steam or sail further than you need through the water, have nothing to do with 'cross track error' until you are nearly there.

Up-tide arrivals

Always steer for a point up-tide of your destination, even if this is somewhat to leeward, except in the heaviest weather. It is the easiest thing in the world to make up a couple of miles downtide after you have identified your position. Trying to claw back from a downtide situation can be tedious in the extreme.

Sea state

Bear in mind that in windy conditions, the 'chops of the Channel' become far more boisterous when the tide is running to windward. This can be dramatic at times. I recall coming out of Cherbourg at midnight in a northeasterly gale as a man young enough to know no better. We organised our departure to give us a full 6 hours' east-going spring tide.

By the time we were an hour out from Fort de l'Ouest every oil-lamp glass on board had jumped off its brackets (which shows how long ago it was) and we had thoroughly frightened ourselves. We made ground to windward, but it was never worth it.

For all these dire warnings, however, the Channel is the most rewarding place to sail that I can imagine. Take time to plan, work wind and tide, and the rewards are beyond price.

Laying of a course each hour is not, in this case, the quickest way across the Channel.

A simple crossing in narrow waters (watch out for the Traffic Separation Scheme).

Diagram 1

Weather services

BBC Radio 4
Shipping forecasts are broadcast on BBC Radio 4 on 198kHz (1515m) 92·4-94·6MHz, and on local MF frequencies daily at 0033, 0555, 1355 and 1750 (clock times). The 0033 broadcast includes area Trafalgar.

The 0033 shipping forecast is followed by a forecast, valid until 1800, for coastal waters of Great Britain up to 12M offshore, and reports from selected stations.

The bulletins include a summary of gale warnings in force; a general synopsis of the weather for the next 24 hours and expected changes within that period; forecasts for each sea area for the next 24 hours, giving wind direction and speed, weather and visibility; and the latest reports from selected stations. For each station are given wind direction and Beaufort force, present weather, visibility, and (if available) sea-level pressure and tendency.

Gale warnings are broadcast at the earliest juncture in the BBC Radio 4 programme after receipt, and also after the next news bulletin.

BBC Radio 3 & 4 Inshore forecasts
Forecasts are given for inshore waters (12 miles) until 1800 the next day at the end of Radio 4 programmes at about 0038. The forecast is followed by the 2200 reports from stations including St Catherine's (Isle of Wight) and Land's End.

On BBC Radio 3 a forecast for Great Britain is given at 0655 on 90·2–92·4MHz.

Weather centres
To arrange a forecast ring:

Plymouth	(01752) 251860
Southampton	(01703) 228844
London	0171-696 0573 or 0171-405 4356
Birmingham	0121-717 0570
Bristol	(0117) 9279298
Jersey	(01534) 46111 Ext 2229

Marine Call
Automatic telephone forecasts are available as follows at a peak rate (and more by VHF).
In each case dial 0891 500 then the three figures as follows:

450 3/5 day UK
992 2/5 day English Channel (Dover to Land's End)
458 South West Hartland Pt to Lyme Regis)
457 Mid-Channel (Lyme Regis to Selsey Bill)
456 Channel East (Selsey Bill to North Foreland)
455 Anglia (North Foreland to The Wash)
432 Channel Islands

MetFAX
Weather maps and forecasts by FAX are available as follows:

0336-400 401   MetFAX Marine Index
01344-854 435   MetFAX ☎ helpline
01344-854 018   MetFAX facsimile helpline
0336-400 443   Beaufort scale

Net tide vector

Course to steer

Actual track of boat

This system is far more efficient.

Diagram 2

0336-400 442	Map of Shipping Areas
0336-400 441	24 hour Shipping forecast
0336-400 450	3/5 day Inshore Waters forecast UK
0336-400 444	Surface analysis chart
0336-400 445	25 hour Surface pressure forecast
0336 400 458	2 day SW Channel coastal forecast
0336 400 457	2 day Mid-Channel coastal forecast
0336-400 471	2/5 day Channel Waters forecast
0336-400 456	2 day E Channel coastal forecast
0336-400 470	2/5 day Biscay area forecast
0336-400 470	Channel Islands 2 day forecast

NAVTEX
NAVTEX services are available from Niton (S), Corsen (CROSS) (A), and Oostende (T).

FRENCH RADIO
France Inter 162kHz 1005 (Mon-Fri) 0650 (Sat-Sun) 2005 (daily)
Storm warnings, synopsis, 24 hour forecast for all French areas.
For English channel only
Brest 711kHz, 1404kHz 0655
Paris 864kHz, 0655
Lille 1377kHz 0655

Coast radio stations

UNITED KINGDOM STATIONS
Calls are made on 2182kHz. During distress working use 2191kHz and listen in on the broadcast frequency.
All times are UT.
Gale warnings are broadcast after the first silence period after receipt. They are repeated at the end of the next silence period.
Weather bulletins generally also on request.
*For autolink or manual calls

Station	Distress kHz	Transmits kHz	Receives kHz	Navigational warnings	Weather messages	Gale warnings
North Foreland (GNF) 51°22'N 01°25'E	VHF Remote Ch 16, 26*			Ch 26 0133, 0533, 0933, 1333, 1733, 2133 *Traffic lists* Ch 26 at 0133, 0303, 0533, 0733, 0903, 0933, 1333, 1503, 1733, 1933, 2103, 2133	Ch 26 0733, 1933 On request	At the end of the first silence period after receipt 0303, 0903, 1503, 2103
Hastings 50°52'N 00°37'E	VHF remote Ch 07, 16, 66*			*Traffic lists* etc as N Foreland on Ch 07		
Thames 51°20'N 00°20'E	VHF 02*, 16			As N Foreland on Ch 02		
Niton (GNI) 50°35'N 01°18'W	2182	1641, 2628	2009	0233, 1833, 0633, 1033, 1433, 1833 2233	0733, 1933 and on request	0233, 0633, 1033, 1433, 1833, 2233
	VHF 28					
				Traffic lists 1641kHz 0233, 0303, 0633, 0733, 0903, 1033, 1433, 1503, 1833, 1933, 2103, 2233		
Weymouth Bay 50°36'N 02°27'W	VHF remote Ch 05, 16			*Traffic lists* as Niton Radio on Ch 05		
Land's End (GLD) 50°07'N 06°40'W	2182	2670 2782 3610	2111(W)* 2120(X)*	0233, 0303, 0633, 0733, 0903, 1033 1433, 1503, 1833 1933, 2103, 2233	0733, 1933 and on request	0303, 0903, 1503, 2103
	VHF 16, 27, 64¹, 85, 88					
	Broadcasts on 2670kHz and Ch 27, 64			*Traffic lists* after warnings and weather messages		
1. Ch 64 directed to the Isles of Scilly						
Ilfracombe (GIL) 51°11'N 4°07'W	VHF remote Ch 05*, 16			Ch 05 0233, 0633, 1033, 1433, 1833, 2233 *Traffic lists*, etc. as Land's End	0733, 1933 On request	At end of first silence period after receipt 0303, 0903, 1503, 2103
Pendennis 50°09N 05°03'W	VHF remote Ch 16, 62*			As Ilfracombe on Ch 62 *Traffic lists*, etc. as Land's End on Ch 62		
Start Point 50°21'N 03°43'W	VHF remote Ch 16, 26, 60			As Ilfracombe on Ch 26 *Traffic lists*, etc. as Land's End on Ch 26		

St Peter Port 49°27'N 02°32'W	2182 *Replies* 1764	1662·5[1] 1764	1662·5[1] 2049 2056 2049 2056 2108 2381[2]	0133, 0533, 0933 1333, 1733, 2133	No service	No service
				Traffic lists after *Nav. warnings.* Ships called on 2182kHz and VHF Ch 16		

VHF Ch 16, 20[5], 62[3], 67[4]

Broadcasts on 1764kHz and Ch 62, 20

1. Trinity House and SAR only
2. When 2182 is distress working
3. Link calls available on Ch 62 only
4. Ch 67 available for yacht safety messages
5. For VHF services, direct calling on Ch 20

Jersey 49°11'N 02°14'W	2182 *Replies* 1659	1659	2045[2] 2048[2] 2084[3] 2534[3] 2191[6]	0433, 0645, 0745, 0833, 1245, 1633, 1845, 2033, 2245	0645, 0745, 0845, 1245, 1845, 2245 and on request	On receipt, at the end of the next silence period and at 0307, 0907, 1507, 2107

VHF Ch 16, 25, 67[5], 82[4]

Broadcasts on 1659kHz, Ch 25 and 82   *Traffic lists* after weather messages. Ships called on 2182kHz and Ch 16

1. All services 24hrs
2. Foreign vessels
3. UK vessels
4. Direct calling for UK vessels
5. Small craft distress/safety. Call on Ch 16
6. Vessels may call on 2191kHz during distress

FRENCH STATIONS

Transmit/receive VHF Ch 16. 24hrs for distress/safety only.
VHF working Chs 0700-2200 local time
All other times are UT
VHF Ch 16 for distress/safety only
Navigational and weather broadcasts are on scheduled frequency or VHF Ch after announcement on 2182kHz or Ch 16

Station	*Transmits kHz*	*Receives kHz*	*Navigational warnings*	*Weather messages*	*Gale warnings*
Boulogne (FFB) 50°43'N 01°37'E	1692[1] 1770 2744 2747 3722 3792 3795 2182 (24hr)	2045[3] 2048[3] 2051 2054 2057 2093[2] 2117[1] 3168 3314 2182 (24hr)	1692, 1770kHz on receipt. At the end of the next silence period. 0133, 0533, 0933, 1333 1733, 2133 and 0730, 1733	1692 at 0703, 1833 in French	1770 on receipt and every H+03, H+33 when storm imminent, and every odd H+03 while warning is in force. In French

VHF Ch 16, 23, 25   *Traffic lists* 1770kHz every odd H+03

1. For fishing vessels
2. For French vessels
3. For foreign vessels

Dunkerque
51°02'N 02°24'E
VHF Ch 16, 24, 61 remotely controlled from Boulogne
No traffic lists or nav. warnings. Weather bulletins Ch 61 in French 0633, 1433 local time, Belgian border to Baie de Somme

Calais
50°55'N 01°43'E
VHF Ch 16, 01, 87 remotely controlled from Boulogne
No traffic lists or nav. warnings. Weather bulletins Ch 87 in French 0633, 1433 local time, Belgian border to Baie de Somme

Dieppe
49°55'N 01°03'E
VHF Ch 02, 16, 24 remotely controlled from Boulogne
No traffic lists or nav. warnings. Weather Bulletins Ch 02 in French 0633, 1433 local time, Baie de Somme to La Hague

Fécamp
49°46'N 00°22'E
VHF Ch 16 remotely controlled from Boulogne (24hrs)
No broadcast services

Le Havre
49°31'N 00°04'E
VHF Ch 16, 23, 26, 28 remotely controlled from Boulogne
No traffic lists or nav. warnings. Weather Bulletins Ch 26 in French 0633, 1433 local time, Baie de Somme to La Hague

Port-en-Bessin
49°20'N 00°42'W
VHF Ch 03, 16 remotely controlled from Boulogne
No traffic lists or nav. warnings. Weather Bulletins Ch 03 in French 0633, 1433 local time, La Hague to Penmarc'h (47°50'N)

Cherbourg
49°38'N 01°36'W
VHF Ch 16, 27 remotely controlled from Boulogne
No traffic lists or nav. warnings. Weather Bulletins Ch 27 in French 0633, 1433 local time, La Hague to Penmarc'h (47°50'N)

Carteret
49°23'N 01°47'W
VHF Ch 16, 24 remotely controlled
No broadcast services

St-Malo
48°38'N 02°02'W
VHF Ch 01, 02, 16 remotely controlled from Saint Nazaire
No broadcast services

Paimpol
48°45'N 02°59'W
VHF Ch 16, 84 remotely controlled from Brest-le-Conquet
No broadcast services

Plougasnou
48°42'N 03°48'W
VHF Ch 16, 81 remotely controlled from Brest-le-Conquet
No broadcast services

Ouessant
48°27'N 05°05'W
VHF Ch 16, 24, 82 remotely controlled from Brest-le-Conquet

Rouen
49°27'N 01°02'E

VHF Ch 16, 25, 27 remotely controlled
from Boulogne
No broadcast services

No broadcast services

	Transmits kHz	Receives kHz		Nav. warnings kHz	Weather bulletins	Gale warnings
Brest-le-Conquet (FFU) 48°20'N 04°44'W	1635 1671[1], 2723 2726 3719 3722[1] 2182(24hr)	2045[3] 2051 2057 2096[1] 2182 3317[1]	2048[3] 2054 2060[2] 3168 (24hr)	1671, 1876, 2691 on receipt and every 4h from 0333, Brest Avurnavs in French for English Channel and approaches, and Bay of Biscay. and Pte du Raz to South	1671, 1876, 2691 3722 at 0733, 1803 in French areas 14-22. Ch 26 0733, 1533 local time in French, Le Havre to Penmarc'h and Penmarc'h to south of Vendée	1635 on receipt and every H+03, H+33 when storm imminent, and every H+03 while warning in force. In French areas 14-22

	VHF Ch 16, 26, 28		*Traffic lists* 1635kHz (Le Conquet) and 2691kHz (St Malo) ev even H+03
Located at St-Malo 48°38'N 02°02'W	2691[1] 2182 (24hr)	2182 (24hr)	
Located at Quimperlé 47°52'N 03°30'W	1876[1] 2182 (24hr)	1992[1] 2182 (24hr)	

1. For fishing vessels   2. For French vessels   3. For foreign vessels

CENTRES REGIONAUX OPERATIONNELS DE SURVEILLANCE ET DE SAUVETAGE (CROSS)

The Centres Régionaux Opérationnels de Surveillance et de Sauvetage (CROSS) are centres for marine rescue co-ordination (a CROSS is an MRCC: Maritime Rescue Co-ordination Centre; a Sous-CROSS is an MRSC: Maritime Rescue Sub-Centre).
CROSS stations broadcast weather information in French or English after a call on VHF Ch 16.

Gris-Nez (CROSS)
Dunkerque 51°03'N 2°21'E
Gris Nez 50°52'N 1°35'E
St Frieux 50°37'N 1°35'E
L'Ailly 49°55'N 0°58'E
Transmits and receives 2182kHz and Ch 16, 15, 67, 68, 73
Storm warnings Ch 79 on receipt and at every H+03, H+10 and on request. In French and English for coastal waters from Belgium border to Cap d'Antifer (49°42'N)
Weather messages
L'Ailly Ch 79 0703, 1903 LT in French and English, for Baie de Somme to Cap de la Hague
Dunkerque Ch 79 0720, 1920 LT in French and English, from the French/Belgium border to Baie de Somme
Gris-Nez Ch 79 0720 1920 LT in French and English, from the French/Belgium border to Baie de Somme
Navigational warnings Ch 79 every at every H+10. Pas de Calais (Dover Strait) bulletin in English and French.
Fog warning on Ch 79 every H+25

Jobourg (CROSS)
Antifer 49°41'N 0°09'E
Ver sur Mer 49°20'N 0°34'W
Gatteville 49°24'N 1°16'W
Jobourg 49°44'N 1°54'W
Granville 49°52'N 1°35'W
Roches Douvres 49°06'N 2°49'W

Transmits and receives 2182kHz and Ch 16, 67, 68
Storm warnings Ch 80 on receipt and at every H+03. On request. In French.
Jobourg Ch 80 on receipt and every H+10, H+50. On request. In French and English
Weather messages Granville Ch 80 at 1703, 1903 LT
Jobourg Ch 80 0715, 1915 LT. In French for Cap de la Hague to la pointe de Penmarc'h
Jobourg Ch 80 at 0733, 1933 LT
Port-en-Bessin Ch 80 at 0745, 1945 LT
Antifer Ch 80 at 0803, 2003 LT
In French for Cap de la Hague to Baie de Somme
Navigational warnings Jobourg Ch 80 at every H+20, H+50 On request. In English and French.

Corsen (CROSS)
Station does not accept public correspondence
Cap Fréhel 48°41'N 2°19'W
Bodic 48°48'N 3°05'W
Ile de Batz 48°45'N 4°02'W
Le Stiff 48°28'N 5°03'W
Corsen 48°24'N 4°47'W
Pointe du Raz 48°02'N 4°43'W
Transmits and receives on VHF Ch 16, 15, 67, 68, 73
Storm warnings Le Stiff Ch 79 on receipt and every H+10, H+40
Cap Fréhel, Bodic, Ile de Batz, Corsen, Pointe du Raz Ch 79 On receipt and every H+03. Gale warnings in French for coastal waters from La Hague to Pointe de Penmarc'h. Storm warnings in French and English in summer and French in winter.
Weather messages Le Stiff Ch 79 at 0150, 0450, 0750, 1050, 1350, 1650, 1950, 2250 and on request. In English
Pointe du Raz Ch 79 at 0433, 0703, 1903 LT
Ile de Batz Ch 79 at 0445, 0715, 1915 Lt
Cap Fréhel Ch 79 at 0450, 0733, 1933 LT
All on request in French for coastal waters from La Hague to Pointe de Penmarc'h
Navigation warnings Ch 79 on request (Le Stiff and every H+10, H+40). In English and French

I. The English Coast
Ramsgate to the Isles of Scilly

Principal headlands

NORTH FORELAND

Tidal streams 3·2 miles 141° from headland
North-going −0120 Dover
South-going +0440 Dover
Spring rate 2¾ knots

Conspicuous 26m white eight-sided light tower (Fl(5)WR.20s57m19/15M) set on dramatic, nearly perpendicular chalk cliffs.

North Foreland.

SOUTH FORELAND

Tidal streams between South Foreland and Deal
North-going approx −0145 Dover
South-going approx +0415 Dover
Spring rate 2¼ knots

The headland is an irregular chalk cliff over 90m high with two disused lighthouses at its summit. The western structure is a 21m square white castellated tower, 114m above sea level.

DUNGENESS

Tidal stream at position 2·4M 140° from Dungeness High lighthouse
East-going stream begins −2000 Dover
West-going stream +0400 Dover

Spring rate up to 2 knots, maybe more close inshore. These stream times are approximate as Dungeness is a sort of tidal watershed, experiencing some confusion as North Sea tides slop through into the Channel via Dover Strait.

A low promontory with a redundant lighthouse, and a nuclear power station to its west. There is a steep beach at its southeast end. The prominent lighthouse (Fl.10s40m27M Horn(3)60s) is a black round tower with white bands. The light also shows F.R sectors indicating comparatively shoal water inshore, but these are of little interest to the average small vessel.
  Uneasy anchorage can be found in the roads on either side of Dungeness, according to direction of wind.

BEACHY HEAD

Tidal streams 2 miles south of the lighthouse
East-going begins −0520 Dover; spring rate 2·6 knots
West-going begins +0015 Dover; spring rate 2 knots

An extremely prominent chalk headland with a disused lighthouse about a mile west of the head. The current lighthouse (Fl(2)20s31m25M Horn 30s) is immediately to seaward of Beachy Head on a shelf of rock. To the southeast of Beachy Head are the rocks known as Head Ledge extending some half a mile from the cliffs. The white lighthouse has a broad red band and an elevation of 43m. Beachy Head should be given a berth of 2 miles in heavy weather as there are overfalls and rough water to the south of it.
  7 miles east of Beachy Head are the Royal Sovereign shoals with 3·5m least water. They can create a nasty sea, and are marked on the south side by a very conspicuous light tower (Fl.20s28m12M Horn(2)30s).

Beachy Head. White tower with red band and lantern 31m high, seen from the southwest.

St Catherine's Point. White octagonal castellated tower 36m above sea level. Not very conspicuous by day.

ST CATHERINE'S POINT

Tidal streams between St Catherine's Point and Dunnose
East +0515 Dover
West −0015 Dover
Maximum spring rate can achieve 5 knots immediately off the point, but is somewhat weaker to seaward.

St Catherine's Point is at the southern extremity of the Isle of Wight. It stands low at the foot of the hill which forms one of the highest parts of the island. The lighthouse is a 26m octagonal castellated tower standing at the back of a very low cliff; its light is Fl.5s41m27M. It also has a F.R light (099°-vis-116°) shining over Rocken End which lurks only 2 cables west of the Point.

Owing to the uneven bottom and the strong streams there are significant tidal overfalls off St Catherine's. These should be avoided, particularly under wind-against-tide conditions, and may be dangerous in bad weather. The race varies according to wind, tide and swell and is sometimes rougher or calmer than may be anticipated from the conditions.

There are also lesser overfalls to the east of St Catherine's off Dunnose, with a number of isolated tide rips and whirlpools which may be almost as rough as St Catherine's race in small areas.

SELSEY BILL AND THE OWERS

Tidal streams in the Looe channel
East +0445 Dover
West −0120 Dover
Spring rate 2·6 knots, but faster between the Malt Owers and the Boulder bank. There are local variations in the directions of the streams 3 miles south of the Owers light buoy:
East-northeast +0540 Dover
West-southwest −0050 Dover
2½ to 3 knots at springs

Selsey Bill is a low point which is difficult to locate in poor visibility. There is a conspicuous hotel on the west side of the point. South of the Bill lie groups of rocks and ledges, between which passes the Looe Channel. The Owers pillar light buoy with ⚑ topmark (Q(6)+LFl.15s Whis) is 7M southeast of Selsey Bill. By keeping south of the light buoy danger is avoided, but in clear weather and moderate winds the Looe channel, which is marked by buoys, affords a short cut, with the aid of a large-scale chart. The buoys are not easy to spot from a distance, so proceed with caution and do not lose heart too soon.

THE NEEDLES ROCKS

It is important to refer to tidal stream charts as you approach the Solent from the west, as streams are strong.

Tidal streams off Hurst Point
Northeast begins +0505 Dover
Southwest −0055 Dover
4 to 5 knots at springs

Off the Needles the streams tend to be earlier.

In the Needles Channel streams set strongly in both directions across the Shingles, so care is needed not to be set into danger.

Main flood stream divides at the Needles. The stronger flood stream runs northeast into the Needles Channel, while further south the stream runs east to southeast off the Isle of Wight coast. Conversely, on the ebb the local streams join west

of the Needles and set west-southwest towards Durlston Head.

The sharp, white Needles stacks, with the light-house (white tower with red band, Oc(2)WRG.20s 24m17/14M Horn(2)30s) at their seaward end, are unmistakable, but they are by no means conspicu-ous from west or southwest in hazy weather. From these directions, the high white cliffs above Scratchell's Bay, immediately southeast of the Needles, appear first, together with the high down 3 miles east on which stands Tennyson's Cross.

In heavy weather or fog, the western end of the Isle of Wight should be avoided if possible. Southwest winds make matters worse, if late on the tide with the ebb well underway. Entry to the Solent under such conditions should only be attempted via the North Channel, which lies north of the Shingles. If you must, this is a realistic option despite the proximity of the lee shore approaching Hurst Castle, but in gales it is safer to make for Poole or remain in harbour.

HENGISTBURY HEAD

Tidal streams are fairly strong at springs in the vicinity, and there are modest overfalls on the ebb tide over the ledges. The streams within Christ-church Bay itself are comparatively weak.

This unlit point, shaped like a long, low wedge of cheese, 5 miles east of Bournemouth pier and 1 mile southwest of the entrance to Christchurch harbour is the only headland between the Needles and Handfast Point south of Poole. It is conspicuous from seaward, being dark, reddish ironstone, though it may look yellowish from seaward.

There are ledges off the headland, and comparatively shoal water as far as Christchurch Ledge, which runs out to 2½ miles southeast. Watch out for pots in this vicinity, particularly after dark. One way and another, you are better off passing to the south of it.

PEVERIL POINT TO ST ALBAN'S HEAD

There are two official tidal races in this area: a small but vicious one off Peveril Point, and the larger race off St Alban's Head. There are also local tide rips, and under certain conditions patches of broken water may be found practically the whole way from Handfast Point and Old Harry Rocks to St Alban's.

PEVERIL LEDGES

Tidal streams 3 cables east of Peveril Point
North-northeast +0500 Dover <1½ knots
South-southwest −0215 Dover <3 knots
Rates of tide may be greater on a spring ebb.

In bad weather, Peveril Race extends from the Point to seaward of its buoy, especially to the southeast of it during the west-going stream.

The Ledges extend about 3 cables from the low, rocky Peveril Point on the south side of Swanage Bay. The depths on the ledges gradually deepen to seaward and the end of the reefs is marked by an unlit red can buoy.

DURLSTON HEAD

Tidal streams
Northeast-going begins +0530 Dover
Southwest −0030 Dover
Up to 3 knots at springs

A rough, steep-sided headland of a characteristic shape, readily identified by the castellated building on its summit.

Inshore eddy
Extending westward from Durlston Head along the Dorset coast to beyond Lulworth there is an early turn of the tide – sometimes up to 90 minutes early – close inshore contrary to the main stream further seaward.

Hengistbury Head from southeast. Entrance to Christchurch on right.

Anvil Point lighthouse. White tower and squat buildings 12m high, set 45m above sea level. Durlstone Head to the right.

St Alban's Head from SSE. No conspicuous buildings, except a tiny lookout hut.

ANVIL POINT

Just half a mile or so southwest of Durlston, Anvil Point is easily located by the conspicuous white lighthouse and white wall round its enclosure, which stands in the green grass above the headland (Fl.10s45m24M). It also has a VHF lighthouse.

ST ALBAN'S HEAD

Tidal streams 1½ miles off the Head
East-going begins approx +0545 Dover
West-going −0015 Dover
Over 3 knots at springs

Instantly recognisable by its 'hanging cliff', where the near-vertical seaward face near the summit is falling steadily away onto rocks at its base.

There is a considerable tidal race which lies eastward of the Head on the flood and westward on the ebb. The race varies considerably in its position and its severity. It extends some 3 miles seaward except during southerly winds when it lies closer inshore. It may be avoided by giving the land a berth of 3 miles. There is a passage of nearly half a mile between St Alban's Head and the race, but it varies and may be less during onshore winds, and is not entirely immune from tidal disturbance. After prolonged heavy onshore winds the whole area can be 'wall-to-wall breakers', but in reasonable weather vessels can avoid the worst of the overfalls by keeping inshore in the deep water close to the headland. The inshore passage enjoys the early fair eddy, and it should be noted that a local eddy runs to the southeast nearly continuously down the west side of St Alban's promontory.

PORTLAND BILL AND RACE

From the east or the west, Portland looks like an island, high on its northern end against the low Chesil Beach, sloping down towards the southern extremity, where the round lighthouse tower with a white and red band (Fl(4)20s43m25M Dia 30s) is situated. A F.R.13M (271°-vis-291°) covers the Shambles shoals for vessels approaching from the east. There is also a disused light tower standing 4 cables to the north-northeast.

Portland Race is the most dangerous extended area of broken water in the English Channel. Quite substantial vessels drawn into it have been known to disappear without trace. It lies south of Portland Bill, a little to the west during the ebb, and to the east during the flood, occurring as a result of an uneven bottom in conjunction with two strong south-going streams which roar down either side of the Bill for 10 hours out of every 12, to hit each other at the Race. Here, they meet the main east or west-going Channel tide. In bad weather there is confused and dangerous water as far as the eastern end of the Shambles.

The worst part of the Race extends over 2 miles from the Bill and is well defined by the overfalls. At spring tides the Race can exceed 7 knots, but for details of the speed and probable direction of the stream, consult the Admiralty tidal charts.

Portland Bill lighthouse from the southwest. White tower, red band, 43m high.

Portland Bill from the east. Note wedge shape. The Varne at right. At great range, Portland appears as an island, separated from the mainland.

During the west-going stream there is a northerly set into West Bay from southwest of the Bill, which at times is strong.

When rounding Portland Bill the navigator has two principal options to choose between. The easier one is to pass outside the Race, about 3 miles off the Bill in calm weather or 5 miles off in bad, especially at spring tides if the wind is against streams. Even out here you will experience rough water.

The alternative is to use the 'inside passage'. This is a channel about a quarter of a mile wide (varying with direction of wind) lying between the Bill and the Race. This channel should not be used at night, and by day only under suitable conditions, for although the water is comparatively smooth, the streams are strong and the overfalls are not entirely avoided either off Grove Point or immediately west of the Bill, according to wind direction. There are also numerous lobster pots close inshore, some of whose buoys can be towed under by the stream. The correct timing of the passage is a matter of the utmost importance.

When bound westward, round the Bill between 1 hour before and 2 hours after HW Dover. When bound eastward, round the Bill between 5 hours after and 4 hours before HW Dover, though towards the end of this period you will find a foul set down the east side of the Bill.

Whether bound west or east through the inside passage, it is important to close with Portland at least a mile to the north of the Bill to be sure of not being set south into the Race. You can then work southward with a fair tide to arrive off the Bill at the correct time.

GOLDEN CAP

A useful landmark 3½ miles east of Lyme Regis and 3 miles west of Bridport. The point rises to Golden Cap, a conical hill 187m high which has pronounced yellow cliffs at its summit. With the sun on them, these can be conspicuous from a long distance even in hazy weather. Inshore streams are weak.

BEER HEAD

Tidal streams
East-going approx +0600 Dover
West-going begins at HW Dover
Inshore streams are weak.

This 130m-high chalk headland is the last white cliff on the coast before chalk gives way to the red cliffs of Devon. It is surprisingly conspicuous when one is crossing Lyme Bay well offshore.

BERRY HEAD

Tidal streams
North +0540 Dover
South −0100 Dover
1½ knots maximum

Bold, steep-ended limestone headland with a long, flat top, falling at about 45° to the sea. White lighthouse on summit with an elevation of 58m (Fl(2) 15s58m14M).

START POINT

Tidal streams 3 miles south of the Point
East-northeast +0455 Dover
West-southwest −0120 Dover
2 knots at springs
Inshore, the streams are about an hour earlier, reaching 4 knots at springs, irregular at neaps.

A long, sharp-ridged headland, with 28m round white lighthouse (Fl(3)10s62m25M Horn 60s) which is unmistakable. A F.R.55m light covers the Skerries bank on 210° to 255°. There are rocks off the Start which are awash at HW and extend nearly 3 cables south of the Point. The Start race extends nearly a mile seaward of the Point; its severity depends much on the conditions of wind, tide and swell. The overfalls can be avoided in daylight by passing close to the rocks, but there is an outlying one to the south, so care is needed. It is safer for strangers to give the Point a berth of at least a mile.

Berry Head from the south. Note coastguard station near right-hand edge.

Start Point from the southwest with unmarked off-lying rocks and Berry Head beyond. White tower 28m high, 62m above sea level.

Prawle Point from the southeast. Prominent old coastguard hut on cliff top 50m above sea level. Bolt Head beyond (left).

Bolt Head from the southwest with Starehole Bay on the right.

Bolt Tail from the southwest with Hope Cove on left.

PRAWLE POINT

Lies 3½ miles west of Start Point to the southeast of Salcombe Bar and has a prominent white coastguard station at its summit.

BOLT HEAD AND BOLT TAIL

Bolt Head stands on the west side of the entrance to Salcombe. Its spiky outline is unique in the Channel, and the ridge of dark, rugged cliffs extending to Bolt Tail is conspicuous. The sea is often rough between the two heads up to a mile or two offshore.

Rame Head from the southeast outside Plymouth Sound, 102m high with ruined chapel on summit. Rame Head is conspicuous from well out at sea because of its symmetrical shape.

Dodman Point from SSW. Stone cross on summit 111m above sea level. No lighthouse. The Dodman often appears dark from seawards.

St Anthony Head marking the eastern side of entrance to Falmouth. White octagonal tower 19m high.

RAME HEAD

This is a classic, breast-shaped hill with a ruined chapel on the summit, conspicuous when one is approaching Plymouth Sound.

DODMAN POINT

This is a notable unlit headland standing about half-way between Fowey and Falmouth. It is 110m high, and precipitous, with a stone cross near its south-west extremity. The off-lying bottom is irregular, and as a result tide rips may extend 1½ miles to seaward.

ST ANTHONY HEAD

Lies 9 miles southwest of the Dodman, at the western side of the entrance to Falmouth. Its white octagonal tower light is Oc.WR.15s22m22/20M, and its horn sounds every 30s in fog. Immediately east-southeast of the headland stands Zone Point where there is a disused coastguard station.

LIZARD POINT

The Lizard is the most westerly of the conspicuous headlands on the south coast of England. It is a dividing line in the sense that west of it there is only limited shelter in Penzance Bay, but eastward there are many harbours available in bad weather.

Tidal streams at the Lizard
East-going starts at +0330 Dover
West-going starts at −0245 Dover

Lizard Point lighthouse. Octagonal white tower 19m high at eastern end of buildings, 70m above sea level with off-lying dangers unmarked.

Spring rates are 2 and 3 knots respectively, and at times stronger.

The Lizard is a bold headland with a classically conspicuous lighthouse compound near its summit. This consists of white buildings with a white wall round their enclosure. The octagonal tower of the white lighthouse (Fl.3s70m25M Siren Mo(N)60s) is situated at the eastern end of the buildings. Six cables eastward there is a coastguard station and Lloyd's signal station.

The group of rocks known as Stag Rocks, some of which are above water while others dry 4 to 5m, extends over half a mile south of the Lizard. These are visible at most states of the tide in daylight, but a mile east of Lizard Point off Bass Point lie the Vrogue Rocks, which have less than 2m over them at LW. The Craggan Rocks, with 1·5m over them, lie north-northeast of Bass Point, but these dangers will be avoided by vessels proceeding east or west. The Lizard Race extends 2 to 3 miles to seaward, and at times there is a race southeast of the head. The state of the seas varies considerably according to tide and wind direction, and things may get very rough with strong westerly winds against the down-Channel stream. In rough weather, or when a swell is running, especially with wind against a spring tide, vessels should keep at least 3 miles off Lizard Point.

The Boa race, which also breaks in bad weather, lies about 3 miles west-northwest of Lizard Point.

LAND'S END

Tidal streams
The ebb tide sets northwest immediately off the point for 9½ hours, starting at HW Dover −0300, and runs at up to 2½ knots. The east-going flood turns 6 hours before HW Dover and only runs for 3 hours.

Situated 20 miles west-northwest of the Lizard, Land's End is higher but less conspicuous, having no lighthouse. The unlit Gwennap Head is at its southernmost extension, with the dangerous Runnel Stone Rocks a mile offshore. These are marked by a lit south cardinal buoy which has been known to drag off-station in severe weather. In calm weather and with local knowledge it is said to be possible to cut inside, but the distance saved will not be worth the ulcers.

The Longships lighthouse, a mile or so to the west of Land's End (Iso.WR.10s35m19/15M Horn 10s), marks the westernmost point of England, excepting the Scilly Isles 20 miles further west. There are always confused seas around the menacing group of rocks marked by Longships, and yachts on passage should keep at least a mile to seaward.

Harbour pilotage

Ramsgate

Tides

HW +0020 Dover

MHWS	MLWS	MHWN	MLWN
4·9m	0·4m	3·8m	1·2m

Streams

Streams run fast across Ramsgate entrance channel. North-northeast set runs from an hour before HW Dover for 6 hours; south-southwest set from 5 hours after HW Dover until 1 hour before the next HW. The lighthouse on the end of West Pier at the entrance to Royal Harbour shows a fixed red light when depth in the entrance is more than 3m above chart datum. When less than 3m, the light turns green.

Depths

The entrance channel is dredged to 7·5m, the outer ferry harbour to 6·5m. There is a least depth of 2·5m in the dredged entrance to Royal Harbour, though the best water is usually to the west side. West Gully (visitors' pontoons) has 2·1m LAT, which is also the dredged depth of Royal Harbour (see plan) and its visitors' pontoons near the east side of the lock. The new marina which will replace these latter berths (in 1995) will be dredged to 3m. The inner non-tidal harbour has a maintained depth of 3m except in certain corners indicated on the plan.

General

Ramsgate is a tactically important harbour of refuge for all vessels on passage from the English Channel to the Thames, or the North Sea. Royal Harbour is well sheltered, though not always comfortable, and can be entered in almost any weather short of storms from the east. Unusually for this corner of Britain, entry for most yachts is not subject to tidal restrictions. Ramsgate's history is colourful, and includes being a major port for the evacuation of Dunkerque in 1940 and the embarkation of Wellington's army before Waterloo. The artificial harbour was built in recognition of the site's importance to the fleets of sailing ships which used to lie up in the Downs awaiting fair winds for either 'Down Channel' or 'Up Thames'.

Today Ramsgate's importance centres on the frequent movements of ferries and jetfoils, as a result of which mariners are advised to proceed with caution at all times. Notwithstanding this, yachts are welcomed actively by the harbour authorities.

Approach

The crucial feature of approaching Ramsgate is that at some stage you must join the dredged entry channel which leads in due west from the *Gull* east cardinal buoy (VQ(3)5s), 3·7 miles slightly north of east from the harbour entrance. This channel is clearly marked with buoys (see plan), and is made entirely unambiguous by the leading lights (rear

Ramsgate Harbour.

Oc.5s, front DirOc.WRG.10s5M). By day, the leading marks are: rear – black and white ▾; front – black ▴ with white stripe.

A recommended yacht track has been established immediately to the south of the main channel, running parallel to it and passing north of Quern Bank and its guarding north cardinal buoy (Q).

Arriving from the north, you should cross the main channel at right angles west of *No. 3* green buoy (Fl.G.2·5s), then turn to starboard and follow the recommended yacht track, entering the harbour as shown on the plan.

Approach from the east presents no difficulty, as the recommended yacht track may be joined in the vicinity of the fourth red can out (Fl.R.5s).

Coming up from the south, you will be in the proximity of the Gull Stream buoys. There is no need to follow these as far as *Brake* (red can, Fl(4)R.15s Bell), but so long as you pass within half a mile or so of it, you will be comfortably clear of Brake shoal. From here you can shape a course towards Ramsgate entrance channel, taking care to leave the unlit beacon tower to the east of Quern Bank well to port. This can safely be achieved by keeping the third red buoy out from the entrance (Fl(2)R.10s) in transit with North Foreland lighthouse (Fl(5)WR.20s), which shows white from this bearing.

Entrance

If you are equipped with VHF, always call Ramsgate Port Control on Ch 14 when in the offing, to receive authority to proceed either to the holding area (see below) or to the Royal Harbour. There are traffic lights exhibited on West Pier just inshore of the lighthouse. Three vertical green lights – enter or leave port, or enter channel from seaward. Three vertical reds – no entry to channel, nobody to enter or leave port.

There is a small-craft holding area (see plan) to the south of the eastern part of the South Breakwater and another north of *No. 3* green buoy.

There is enough space in the outer harbour for any yacht under 27·4m (90ft) to round up and lower her canvas. This can be useful, as there is often a lumpy sea outside.

The outer breakwaters have a red and white and a green and white beacon, each 10m high, lit with a VQ.R to port, Q.G to starboard. Enter between these beacons, keeping to the north side of the channel, then look for the small green buoy (Q.G) situated one cable west-northwest of the North Breakwater head. Leave this to starboard and swing round to about 015° to enter Royal Harbour. Note the East and West Banks, indicated on the plan.

Berthing

Once inside Royal Harbour, all but the largest yachts have three main options. You can head for the visitors' pontoons in West Gully, where you are allowed to lie for 24 hours on payment of dues. You may have to raft up here; under occasional circumstances, you may be allowed a longer stay.

Ramsgate. (A) East breakwater head with entrance to Royal Harbour. (B) RoRo berth.

Ramsgate. (A) Entrance to marina, bridge open, lock gate shut. (B) Lock-master. (C) Royal Temple Yacht Club.

If you wish to enter the marina, but the gates are closed, you could berth on the waiting pontoons (April to October) immediately to the east of the gates, or in the new marina if this is available.

The first two of these berths may be subject to surge. The best choice, for anything other than a brief stop-over to await the tide or to let a blow go through, is to enter the lock into the inner harbour, where the marina is to be found. The lock opens ±2 hours HW. There are traffic lights at the entrance operating the same code as those on West Pier.

In the lock entrance you will be allocated a berth (otherwise call VHF Ch 14) which will probably be in the west end of the dock. Quite large vessels can be accommodated in here by arrangement, but if you wish to stay outside and are too big for the pontoons, ask if you may lie on the inside of the West Pier.

Charges are realistic in Ramsgate Marina, and it is perfectly sheltered, so it is an excellent place to leave a boat for a few weeks. Do not expect quiet nights on board, however. The trucks of all Europe thunder by through the night, bound for the ferries and exotic destinations. Their exhausts and under-carriages roar and crash to the echo from the high brick walls.

Facilities

Fuel from the barge in West Gully, seven days a week, 0830–1730. If unattended, call *Foy Boat* on VHF Ch 14, or ☎ 01843 592662. Fresh water in marina and on pontoons outside. Chandlery and full technical back-up (*Camping Gaz* and *Calor Gas*). Repairs and engineers. Diver. Showers, toilets and launderette close by marina are open to all. Harbour Board maintain a number of slipways. Full domestic and entertainment facilities at hand as the harbour is right in the town centre.

Royal Temple Yacht Club has a fine view overlooking the harbour (☎ 01843 591766).

Rabies control

Note that the harbour will not tolerate animals aboard yachts at any price, even if they stay aboard.

Sandwich

Tides

HW at Bar +0015 Dover

HW at Sandwich +0100 Dover

Tidal heights for the lower River Stour are:

MHWS	MLWS	MHWN	MLWN
3·3m	0·1m	2·6m	0·3m

Streams

These can be very strong in the river at springs. Note that HW at Sandwich comes 45 minutes later than at the bar. The end of the flood can be surprisingly vigorous, perhaps because its duration is between 3 and 5 hours, depending upon the tide and the fresh water content of the river. The ebb, correspondingly, runs for anything up to 9 hours.

Depths

Bar dries 0·3 to 0·9m LAT. Depths in the river are variable, generally between 0·5 and 1m LAT. Craft of 2m draught can certainly reach Sandwich on mean spring tides.

General

Sandwich, one of the original Cinque Ports charged with the defence of the realm against invaders since Norman times, lies 4½ miles from the mouth of the meandering River Stour. Before it silted up, it was the jump-off point for great fleets of warships. Nowadays yachts lie alongside the Town Quay.

In the 18th century the local earl launched the fast-food business with sandwiches devoured during nonstop sessions at the gaming tables. In our times, Sandwich's golf links gave Ian Fleming the inspiration for some of James Bond's rougher matches.

Approach

The approach to the River Stour and Sandwich really begins some distance offshore on an approximate transit of the 135m chimney inland in Pegwell Bay with the left hand one of the three adjacent cooling towers. These items are all so conspicuous that in any visibility worthy of the name they cannot be missed. Stay on this transit on a course of around 260° until you arrive in the

Mouth of River Stour. (A) Commercial berths. (B) Channel beacons with topmarks.

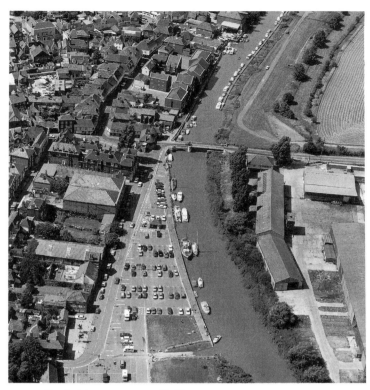
Sandwich town quay and bridge.

vicinity of the first pair of channel buoys which are a red and green conical. Pass between these and follow the next pairs down to the southwest until you come to the only lit channel mark. This is a spindly structure bearing a Fl.R.10s light. Its opposite number is a post with a lattice green triangular topmark. From here to the mouth of the river at Shell Ness, the channel is marked by posts – red square topmarks to port, green triangles to starboard. It is now trending in a westerly direction and the best water tends to lie on its northern side. In due course you will discern Shell Ness, but it is not conspicuous, so this may seem a long time coming.

Follow the posts into the river; when in doubt, keep central until the upper end of Richborough New Wharf. Thereafter, the best water is usually to be found nearer the west bank, when the river is wide enough to offer a realistic choice. Pass the tiny Sandwich Marina and press on the final half-mile to Sandwich.

It cannot be over-stressed that, for the stranger, it is prudent to navigate the Stour on a rising tide, and that night entry without local knowledge is not recommended.

Berthing

Anchoring in the Stour is impractical. Berth alongside the quay at Sandwich, then go to the newsagent at No. 4 Quay Street, where you will find the berthing master, Mr Grout. He will give any advice necessary.

Deep-keeled yachts should dry against the wall (thin layer of mud over chalk), towards the upper end of the quay. Bilgekeelers can settle into soft mud at the downstream end. Further downstream, Sandwich Marina (max LOA 18m, draught 2·1m) may have room for visitors.

Facilities

Fresh water and toilets at Sandwich Quay. Fuel in cans from nearby garage. Early closing Wednesdays. Yacht yard above bridge with chandlery, *Calor Gas* and engineering facilities. Other utilities, such as pubs, restaurants and banks, in the town. Yacht club: Sandwich Sailing and Motor Boat Club.

Dover

Tides

MHWS	MLWS	MHWN	MLWN
6·7m	0·8m	5·3m	2m

Note Irregular, depending on wind conditions.

Streams
Streams off the harbour vary considerably, with a maximum spring rate of 3 knots. The flood sets northeast at HW −1hr to HW +3hr.

Depths

The outer harbour is generally deep, but shoals gradually to its landward boundary. Note the large, isolated bank just north of centre. Depths in the Inner Harbour are generally 9m, shoaling to 4m on the west side of Prince of Wales Pier and to 3m on close approach to the Hoverport ramp. The approach channel from the Inner Harbour to the Tidal Basin between the North and South Piers has an average dredged depth of 5m below chart datum. A dredged channel (1·5m) leads from here up to Wellington Dock and its waiting pontoon. The locked dock itself has 4·5m at springs, and 3·3m at neaps. Granville Dock, into which larger yachts may occasionally be directed, is deeper. The dock sill is at chart datum, or 1·83m lower than that of the Wellington Dock.

General

Dover is the busiest port in England, and its primary commercial importance is known to every mariner. The outer harbour is often exposed in a small-craft context, and Wellington Dock Marina locks in and out only at ±1½hr HW. Nevertheless, in recent years Dover Harbour has gone out of its way to become a yacht-friendly port. In settled weather it is perfectly possible to anchor in the outer harbour to wait for a tide. When it blows hard, or for longer stays, Wellington Dock promises complete shelter with all manner of facilities.

Approach and entrance

Dover Harbour is some two miles southwest of the South Foreland. By day, the long breakwaters overlooked by the famous castle make the harbour

Dover. The marina lies beyond the bridge. Note the tidal harbour dead centre.

DOVER

N

Dover Castle
114

DOVER

Car Ferry Terminal

Castle

Pier D
Pier C
Pier B
Pier A

Q.R.
Siren(2)10s
Oc.R.5s
Fl(2)R.5s
Siren 5s

Q(6)+LFL.15s
Siren(3)20s

Eastern Arm

51°N
7'.5

Royal
Cinque Ports
YC

Mont

See Inset

Northampton
Quay

Groynes

Yacht Moorings

1₇
2₆
7₉

Foul Ground

*Wellington
Dock
Marina*

Port Control Stn
SS (Traffic)
Storm Sigs

Fl.G.5s12m5M
Horn(2)30s

12

Eastern Entrance

1₇

Outer Harbour

B
Fl(4)Y.6s

Crosswall Quay

Lock   Clock Tr

Fl.R.2·5s11m5M

*Granville
Dock*

Custom Ho.
Quay

QG

0₈

Commercial anchorage

9₄

Fl(4)WR.10s15m15/23M

Oc.G

3FG

Clarence Quay

Hoverport

C
Fl.Y.4s

6₉

Fairway

Rail Ferries

Iso.G

QG+Fl.Y

Q
BY

*Foul
Ground*

Iso.R   QR

Inner Harbour

VQ.G.14m4M
+Fl.Y.1.5s(Occas)

1₇

Southern Breakwater

Bulwark Rk

Marine
Station

5₅

Oc.R.30s21m18M

7₃   *Foul
Ground*

Western Entrance

2FR
FR

2FR(vert)

FR

Extension

Admiralty Pier

Fl.7·5s21m20M
Horn 10s
SS (Traffic)

11

15

INSET:

Wellington
Dock Marina

7'

Commercial Quay

3₆

Swing
Bridge

1₆

*Granville
Dock*

F.WR

Tidal
Harbour

1₄

Hoverport
Oc.

51°
07'
N

2F.R

5

3F G

1°18'·8E

Depths in Metres

19'

1°20'E

21'

28

easy to identify. At night, the breakwater lights are as follows: the west entrance has Oc.R.30s21m18M on the south breakwater and Fl.7·5s21m20M Horn 10s at the seaward end of Admiralty Pier; this also displays the port movement lights. Towards the east entrance, the Knuckle light on the southern breakwater is Fl(4)WR.10s15m15/13M, with a Fl.R.2·5s 11m5M at the entrance.

The Eastern Arm has Port Control, Horn(2)30s and a Fl.G.5s12m5M light. Lights inside the harbour are shown on the plan.

In southwesterly gales a very confused and steep swell may develop off the western entrance. Exercise extreme caution during these periods, especially if they coincide with HW springs.

Yachts may use either entrance, although a careful lookout should be kept for the entry signals. Permission to enter may also be requested by Aldis lamp using International Code signals (SV – I wish to enter, SW – I wish to leave); yachts with VHF call *Dover Port Control* on Ch 74 or 16 to establish a working frequency (usually Ch 12). A series of short flashes from Port Control at the end of the Eastern Arm, or from the Harbour Patrol launch, indicates 'STOP. WAIT'.

In order to leave room for bigger ships to manoeuvre, yachts should keep well clear of the entrances until they receive their entry or exit signals.

Enter under power if possible and look out for the Harbour Patrol launches, which are always ready with friendly advice for yachts. Do not hesitate to call Dover Port Control on VHF if you are in any doubt, or need advice on movement in or near the port.

Traffic signals

Lights covering both entrances are exhibited at the ends of the Eastern Arm and Admiralty Pier. All traffic is regulated by day or night by IALA port signals, using directional high intensity lights beamed to seaward or inshore as relevant. Signals are vertically displayed as follows:

RRR flashing – Emergency; entrance closed
RRR fixed – Entry or exit prohibited from the direction indicated
GWG – Ships may proceed to or from direction indicated

Navigation in Outer Harbour

If in doubt, call Harbour Control, or speak with the Harbour Patrol launch (flashing blue light at night), which will advise you.

Dover. Waiting area outside Wellington Dock. (A) Dockmaster's office. (B) Waiting pontoon. (C) Lock open, bridge lowered.

Dover. Wellington Dock – mostly long-term berth-holders. (A) Dover Harbour Board offices. Since the date of this photograph, many more pontoon berths have been added.

Yachts should beware of hovercraft and Seacats which may use either entrance at 40 knots. They must also keep well clear of Channel ferries and cargo ships manoeuvring in the fairway.

The best anchorage for yachts lies east of Prince of Wales Pier, and west or northwest of the Fl.Y spherical buoy marking the western limit of the dredged anchorage for commercial craft (see plan). There is plenty of room here, and the shelter is the best you'll get, but be ready with earplugs for the hovercraft limbering up on the other side of the pier. Alternatively, visitors may make use of the white mooring buoys north of the commercial anchorage, where craft may be left unattended. At no time may anchored craft be so left.

Inner Harbour

Having been given permission to enter, the Inner Harbour is quite straightforward. It is well lit (for lights, see plan), but note that anchoring is strictly prohibited within its walls. As noted above, there is a dredged channel to the reception pontoon outside Wellington Dock. At LW, it is important to head straight for the Granville Dock gates. There is a sectored leading light (324°-330°) which affords safe access from the main channel to the waiting pontoon.

You will be allocated a berth either inside Wellington Dock if appropriate; otherwise in the newly dredged marina in the tidal harbour. For Wellington Dock, an amber flashing light and a bell warn of the opening of the lock. Traffic lights now control your movements, with 3F.R stopping traffic and GWG giving the all-clear. Generally, outbound traffic clears the lock first.

Departures

All yachts must report to marina staff prior to departure. If bound east, you will usually leave on the first bridge opening so as to take full advantage of the favourable tide. If you are going west, the marina may allow you to wait on the reception pontoon until the stream serves. Whichever way you intend to turn at the breakwater entrance, you must report to Harbour Control for instructions before leaving the Inner Harbour. As likely as not, you will then be escorted seawards by the patrol launch.

Facilities

Harbour Office (☎ 01304 240400). Marina (☎ 01304 241663). Customs (☎ 01304 202441). Water, showers, toilets, launderette and small shop at Wellington Dock. Showers and toilets also by courtesy of yacht club, which offers temporary membership to visiting yachts. Chandlery and stores available. Launderette in town centre. *Calor Gas* and *Camping Gaz* from chandlery. Diver. Sailmaker. Full repair facilities at Dover Yacht Company. Diesel from barge moored east of Prince of Wales Pier; also from pump just outside Granville Dock gates. Petrol in cans from garage. Water taxi available to anchored yachts via Harbour Patrol

(contact Port Control, VHF Ch 74). All town facilities, including provisions, banks, fine restaurants, transport cafés and fish and chips.

Folkestone

Tides

HW −0010 Dover

MHWS	MLWS	MHWN	MLWN
7·1m	0·7m	5·7m	2m

Streams

Tidal streams run at up to 2 knots off the pier head as follows: east-northeast from 2 hours before HW Dover; setting west-southwest from 3½ hours after HW Dover. There is an eddy on the east-going stream.

Depths

The Outer Harbour is dredged to a least depth of 4·5m and is formed by the breakwater, which extends into deep water. In the entrance to the Inner Harbour there is 5·5m at MHWS; there is 3·3m to 4·2m MHWS within the harbour. At neaps there is at least 1m less. At LW it dries everywhere.

General

Folkestone is a busy commerical port, operating a freight and Seacat service to Boulogne. The Inner Harbour is only suitable for yachts with legs, or those prepared to dry out by the wall at the South Quay. It is not a good refuge in bad weather, and yachts are only welcome for occasional overnight moorings, as the whole Inner Harbour is full. The Inner Harbour faces east, but the entrance itself receives extra protection from the west from a long breakwater (built for railway ferries) which forms the Outer Harbour. The Inner Harbour is mostly used by fishing boats equipped with legs. The town itself has all the usual urban facilities.

Folkestone Harbour at low water. The shoal area outside the dredged zone shows clearly inside the breakwater.

Approach and entrance

The Port of Folkestone operates on VHF Ch 15, and should at all times be contacted before entering or leaving. The harbour is busier than ever and Port Control emphasises the importance of this requirement.

Folkestone is about 5½ miles west of Dover. It is a large town and is thus easy to recognise. The harbour lies nearer its eastern end, behind the conspicuous outer breakwater.

There are rocky ledges to the west of the breakwater and east of the Inner Harbour entrance. Of these, the Mole Head Rocks less than two cables east of the inner end of the outer breakwater, together with the ledges off Copt Point, are the more dangerous. To clear all these when approaching from the east, keep the South Foreland well open of the Dover cliffs. When the south end of the East Pier of the Inner Harbour (Q.G) bears 305°, alter course leaving the outer breakwater close to port.

Make allowance for the fact that the bottom begins to shoal about 2 cables off the Inner Harbour, shelving gradually to 1m drying at the entrance. For depths within the harbour, see 'Anchorage and harbour', below.

Traffic signals

Leading lights (occasional) F.G behind F.R at 295° on ferry terminal.

Entry and leaving signals are exhibited as follows from a trellis mast adjacent to the lighthouse at the pier head: three vertical green lights indicate permission to enter and three vertical red lights show that the port is closed.

When leaving, three vertical green lights give permission to leave, and three vertical red lights indicate that departure is prohibited.

For entry to the Inner Harbour, a single red light indicates that the Inner Harbour is closed while a single green light shows permission to enter. For departure, green is 'go' and red means that the harbour entrance is closed.

Anchorage and harbour

Anchoring outside the Inner Harbour is inadvisable owing to the ferry traffic and the risk of fouling the ground moorings used for winching off the ferries. It is also exposed and has indifferent holding ground. No yacht may ever moor alongside the ferry pier except in the direst emergency.

Yachts may lie in the Inner Harbour if there is room, either inside East Pier on legs or alongside South Quay. At LAT the harbour dries 1m at the entrance, about 2·2m in the centre and up to 3·7m at the northern end of East Pier. Yachtsmen must calculate the tide level by reference to the heights above datum (see under 'Tides', above), but boats of up to 2·5m draught can enter 3 hours either side of HW.

The swing bridge at the western end of the Inner Harbour is permanently fixed, and the shallow inner basin can be entered only by boats able to pass below it.

Wherever you berth, if you have not already contacted the harbour authorities on VHF Ch 15 you should check with them that your selection is suitable.

Folkestone. Inner Harbour at low water.

Facilities

Water at quay. Good shopping centre. Station. Buses to all parts. Yacht club: Folkestone Yacht and Motor Boat Club (☎ 01303 251574) near slipway in Inner Harbour offers showers when clubhouse is open. Bosun's Locker chandlery. Harbourmaster's ☎ 01303 220544. Diesel by pump from the Stade at HW.

Rye

Tides

HW +0002 Dover

Rye Harbour

MHWS	MLWS	MHWN	MLWN
5·3m	Dries	3·6m	Dries

Approaches

MHWS	MHWN	No LW data
7·7m	6·0m	

Depths

The bar dries 1·5m LAT, and the River Rother has little more than a foot of fresh water at MLWS, though this may increase after heavy rain. Tides are big, however, and the visitors' berths at Strand Quay have around 4m at MHWS, and 2·3m at MHWN.

General

Rye is an ancient harbour whose history dates back to the Iron Age. Shingle drift along the coast has moved its entrance many times, but the harbour has not lost its commercial significance, even in the face of a drying bar and a river channel now reduced to half a metre of fresh water at LW springs. An average of 50 vessel visits per year maintains the harbour's vitality. There is also a fishing fleet of moderate proportions, and a number of yachts sail from here on a regular basis.

Shelter is superb, once inside, and although all the berths dry, there is a warm welcome for visitors. The town, which is a Cinque Port, is picturesque in the extreme, standing proudly on its hill and beckoning the brave, as it has done for a very long time indeed.

Given an offshore wind, fair weather and the right state of tide, strangers should not find the well marked entrance difficult. An onshore breeze of Force 5 is uncomfortable, however, and probably too much for a first attempt. Power is desirable, as the tide runs very hard in the narrow channel – the flood is stronger than the ebb, which is unusual in rivers.

Approach and entrance

Rye Harbour entrance lies at the apex of Rye Bay, which is a shoal bight to the west of Dungeness. Apart from Tower Knoll 2½ miles to the west (2·2m), and Boulder Banks (3m), there are no dangers in the offing, save the generally shoal nature of the bay. Its sand bottom holds no shocks, however, so a prudent eye on depth will suffice to keep you out of danger.

The *Rye Fairway* buoy (L.Fl.10s) lies about 5° south of west from Dungeness, distance 7 miles. From the west the most prominent landmark, around 5 miles down the coast, is Fairlight Church, which (under its older name) has the distinction of a mention in the great sea song *Spanish Ladies*: 'We bore away up-Channel past Fairlee and Dungeness...' From here you may have to take note of Boulder Banks or Tower Knoll (see above).

From the *Fairway* buoy it is 1·8 miles on a track of 329° to the conspicuous west pier with its characteristic red-painted tripod beacon (Fl.R.5s7m6M). Note that the three horizontal timbers of this beacon form a unique tide gauge. The central one shows 3m; the upper member gives you 4·5m above datum.

The entrance to the channel, which is from 30m to 45m wide, lies between the east and west piers. On the west side a long training wall has a groyne which extends to seaward of the entrance. This training wall is covered between half-tide and high water (depths above 2·4m). It is marked by a series of pole beacons with red cage topmarks, some on top of dolphins; there are three Q.R lights at irregular intervals along the walls as far as Rye Harbour, and further lights at the bend beyond it.

Rye Harbour approach. Note training walls which cover at HW.

The east pier is also long, though it does not extend as far seaward as its counterpart; at its end there is an unusual square, four-legged green tower (Q(9)15s5M). Two cables northwest, where the east bank begins, is a Q.G light. At MHWS the upper parts of this east pier are awash, but it is marked by posts with green conical topmarks.

Vessels making for Rye should head up towards the *Rye Fairway* buoy, then alter course to around 328° so as to leave the tripod of the west pier open on the port bow. There is always an easterly set across the harbour entrance, especially on the flood tide. Once inside, a mid-channel course is generally best, although the deeper water is on the west side. Care must be taken on the flood, when side currents flowing across the training wall may affect steering. The cage beacons marking the training wall are fixed to its inside edge, except for one off the harbourmaster's office. This is a prominent solitary house on the east bank of the Rother opposite the lifeboat slip. The harbour office is adjacent the harbourmaster's house with timber constructed moorings below. Visiting vessels are requested to stop at these reception moorings and report to the harbourmaster who will provide up-river chartlets and berthing instructions for Rye.

The entrance should not be approached by vessels with a draught of 2m earlier than 3 hours before HW; the best time to enter is around 1 hour before HW. The best time to leave is not later than 1 hour after HW, but for yachts of moderate draught 2½ hours either side is possible with care at springs. A conventional tide gauge is fitted to the seaward end of the eastern training wall.

By night, a directional Oc.WG indicates the safe water into the inner channel. White is on 326° through 331°. Green is on either side. The eastern pier end has a fog horn (7s).

Just below the village of Rye Harbour the well marked training wall on the west side of the entrance channel gives way to the River Rother, which is also clearly marked all the way up to the town of Rye.

A mile upstream of Rye Harbour village, the Rock Channel branches off to the west. North of here, the river is navigable for a short distance only. Watch out for the 2F.R lights which you will see unexpectedly on the north side of the Rock Channel entrance. Look for the small red and green buoys in the channel, but do not turn to port until they are well open, as the inside of the bend shoals. Now maintain a course in the centre of the channel for almost ½ mile until you reach the sluicegate of the River Brede on your port hand. Keep very close to the moored yachts to port of you in this vicinity, as the opposite side of the river is very shallow indeed. After completing your starboard turn, go back to the centre of the channel up to Strand Quay and choose a berth on the town side, on your starboard hand. Some of the bottom is deep, soft mud, but other areas have a layer of mud over shingle. In the absence of advice, be prepared to lean on the pilings if you have a deep keel.

Firing range
The army firing range at Lydd has a Sea Danger Area extending 2M offshore and stretching east from *Rye Fairway* buoy to a north/south line approximately 1·5M west of Dungeness lighthouse. Firing takes place on about 300 days per annum from 0830–1630 LT (occasionally to 2300). Red flags or red lights are displayed ashore when the range is in use, and a range safety craft may be on station.

Further details via VHF Ch 13 or 73 (☎ 01679 20203 or 01303 249541 ext 8518).

RYE HARBOUR

Rye

Fish Market

Rye Yacht Centre

River Rother

Moorings

2F.R(vert)

Q.R   Q.G

Boat Yards

Martello Tower

Rock Channel *(moorings)*

R. Rother

River Brede

Channel

Q.G

marked

Q.R

Q.G

Q.G

by

beacons

Q.R

Q.R

Admiralty Jetty

Commercial Quay

Q.R

WC

Golf Course

Q.R

Q.R

Oc.WG.4s3m7/6M

Rye Harbour

Q.G

Q.R

Q.G

Training Wall marked by beacons (covers at HW)

Q.G

Training wall marked by beacons (covers at HW)

Q.R

5₄

Camber Sands

4̲₅

Q.R

Q(9)15s7m5M
Horn 7s

1̲₇

1̲₃

2̲₇

Fl.R.5s7m6M

1₂

1₃

0̲₃

The Nook

0̲₉

0₇

Oc.G

1₂

Groynes

1̲₈

0₃

Oc.W

2

50° 55' N

2̲

0̲₄

Oc.G

1₅

2₈

329°

Rye Bay

Winchelsea Beach

1̲₄

0

1₁

2₅

4₃

4₁

1̲₁

0₇

3₂

0°47'E

5 **48'**

44'   **45'**   **46'**

57'

56'

Rye. West pier and tripod beacon from the southeast at low water.

Rye. Admiralty jetty.

Rye. The tripod beacon at the end of the breakwater.

Rye. The fairway buoy.

Traffic signals

International three-light traffic signals are exhibited from the harbour office during times of commercial shipping movement, usually at or near HW. These must be obeyed.

Berthing procedure

With sufficient rise of tide, all visiting yachts should moor initially at special berths provided alongside the piles at Rye Harbour village, about a mile from the entrance on the east side of the river, just beyond the harbourmaster's office. This is about 2 miles from Rye town. The berths are lighted at night. Double mooring is not allowed. Care should be taken when turning at Rye Harbour village at springs.

The large range of tide calls for careful mooring, but yachts will lie afloat for about 4 hours, then take the bottom, which is hard muddy shingle. Always consult the harbourmaster, who can be contacted on VHF Ch 14 or 16, or at the harbour office.

Lying at Admiralty Jetty holds little potential for a long stay. Up-river the charms of Rye await, but first you must report to the harbour office, where you will be instructed in how to work up to Strand Quay. You will also be invited to pay your dues, and will be given a most useful and informative booklet about the port and town of Rye. If you are in a multihull, you may be denied access to Strand Quay.

Facilities

Showers and toilets at Strand Quay and at the harbour office by Admiralty Jetty. Diesel from Sandrock Marina in Rock Channel at HW. Diesel is now also available from a 24-hour unmanned pontoon, tide permitting. Discs for pump operation may be purchased from the harbourmaster. Garage at Strand Quay. There is a bunkering barge on the west bank of the river.

Fresh water by hose at Admiralty Jetty and Strand Quay or by can from taps at Strand Quay. Chandlery at Rye (Rock Channel) with *Calor Gas/Camping Gaz* exchange. Repairs from Phillips Yard in Rock Channel, including electronics. There is a slipway (HW ±2/3hr) at Rye Harbour village, with road access. Excellent town facilities of all types in Rye itself.

Communications

Rye Harbour (a dinghy trip from Admiralty Jetty) connects by regular buses to Rye itself, whence rail and bus connections to all parts.

Eastbourne (Sovereign Yacht Harbour)

Tides

HW −0005 Dover

MHWS	MLWS	MHWN	MLWN
7·4m	0·7m	5·5m	2·2m

Depths

Maximum 2·4m in the dredged channel and the outer harbour, with half a metre more on the lock sill and inside.

General

Sovereign Harbour is a modern, artificial development of large proportions situated at the southwest end of Pevensey Bay, about two miles northeast of Eastbourne Pier. Visitors are welcome. All berths are inside the locked inner harbour and are thus perfectly sheltered. The entrance channel is dredged and well marked so that in most conditions it presents no difficulties. In a hard blow from east-northeast through to east-southeast, however, it could be unwise for a stranger to attempt it.

The pleasures of Eastbourne, a short cab ride away, are many and varied, but for pure relaxation a stroll along the Edwardian promenade followed by an hour's snooze in a deckchair by the bandstand is hard to beat. The gulls cry, the sun seems always to shine, while elderly gentlemen in panama hats and linen jackets tap their fingers gently to the stirring strains of *Soldiers of the Queen*.

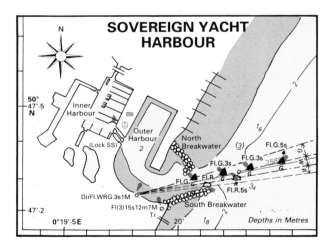

Approach and entrance

From east or southeast the only dangers, except the inshore rocks of Bexhill Reef, Oyster Reef and Codheath Shoals, 4 miles up-Channel, are the tide rips set up under certain conditions on Royal Sovereign Shoals and the Horse of Willingdon. Fortunately, these can readily be given a wide berth with sensible pilotage.

From the west, clear the shore by a mile or so after rounding Beachy Head. This will keep you outside Holywell Bank and any small craft or swimmers ambitious enough to cross your track.

Call *Sovereign Harbour* on Ch 15 (or 16) from a mile or two out if you have VHF.

The Martello tower at Langney Point now serves as a lighthouse indicating the position of Sovereign Harbour. The xenon light (Fl(3)15s) is visible in daylight, so identification is easy.

The start of the entrance channel is marked by a red and white vertically striped fairway buoy (LFl.10s) about 4·5 cables east-northeast of the breakwaters. The outside channel is clearly buoyed with four lit green buoys and two lit reds and is crystal clear at night by virtue of the single point leading light (Dir.Fl.WRG.5s) whose white sector leads in on 258°. If it shows red turn to starboard, if green swing to port. The first two lit green buoys (Fl.G.3s) to starboard keep you clear of a wreck.

Come off the leading line at the third red buoy and head up for the locks, making sure to leave the final red buoy (Fl.R.3s) to port. There is plenty of room to round up and drop sails in the outer harbour.

The locks monitor VHF Ch 17 24 hours a day. Call them for instructions and note the international traffic signals. Rig fenders on both sides and stand by with warps before entering. Inside the locks, which are 150ft long by 50ft wide, secure to the convenient floating pontoons as far down the lock as possible. Spring lines are advisable and be prepared for the fact that the lock pontoons have 1·2m freeboard. Once inside the harbour, you will be allocated a berth via a computerised management system. Report to the harbourmaster's office once you are secured, to register and receive security access cards, etc.

Facilities

Langney Marine Services can deal with repairs of most sorts on site. There is a 50-ton lift. DIY fuel pontoon (1·2m freeboard) open 24 hours a day, with discounts available for bulk purchases of diesel. Fresh water at berths. Excellent showers, toilets and launderettes. Asda superstore with breakfast bar and cashpoint so you can pay for your coddled eggs. Multiscreen cinema, chandlery, pizzeria, hairdressers, a pharmacy – even dry cleaners and a pump-out facility for holding tanks.

A berth-holders' yacht club is planned to open in May 1997.

Communications

Cab to Eastbourne, thence by train to London Victoria (85 mins) via Gatwick Airport (45 mins).

Eastbourne. Sovereign Harbour.

Newhaven Harbour. Note large shoal area in the bight formed by
the breakwater (see plan).

Newhaven

Tides

HW +0004 Dover

MHWS	MLWS	MHWN	MLWN
6·7m	0·4m	5·1m	2·0m

Depths

Entrance and harbour dredged to 5·5m as far as Sleeper's Hole. There is 3m up to the lifeboat stage, and not less than 1·2m to bridge leading to River Ouse. A nominal 1·5m alongside the visitors' pontoon in the marina, but this may vary according to state of dredging. The bottom is soft. Silting and dredging continually occurring.

Approach and entrance

Newhaven is a traditional port of refuge about halfway between the Solent and Dover.

The town of Seaford is 5 miles west of Beachy Head; at the western end of the low and shingly Seaford Bay stands Burrow Head. Immediately to the east, at the foot of this, lies Newhaven. The big breakwater at the entrance, with its fine classic lighthouse, is conspicuous and makes an easily recognisable landmark.

From the east, stand well away from Seaford Head and steer for a position off Burrow Head. Alter course for the entrance when it bears north, steering in towards the eastern pier, which is some 3 cables inshore of its western partner. In bad weather, with an onshore wind, there is an awkward sea off the entrance south of the breakwater. Steer mid-channel, noting signals as described below.

From the west, keep at least half a mile off Burrow Head. Do not come close to the end of the breakwater in strong onshore winds, for very rough conditions may be experienced.

Within half a mile of the shore, a weak west-going stream starts about 1½ to 2 hours before HW. In the entrance the stream reaches 2 knots at springs, running with ebb and flood into the harbour.

Signals

Harbour Control is located inside the breakwater at the western entrance to the port. Traffic is controlled by signals:

Entry permitted
By day Red triangle over red ball
By night Green all-round

Departure permitted
By day Red ball over red triangle
By night Red all-round

Vessels under 15m free to move in or out
By day Red ball
By night Green light over red

No movement permitted
By day Red ball over red triangle over red ball
By night Lights RGR(vertical)

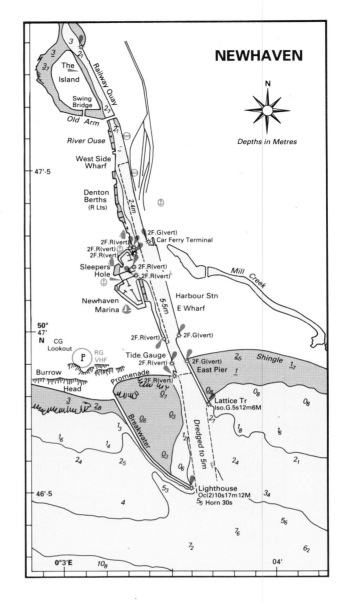

River Ouse Swing Bridge traffic signals
Fl.G Bridge moving
F.R Ships may proceed downstream
F.G Ships may proceed upstream

Anchorage and berths

All yachts entering the harbour should seek instructions from Harbour Control on VHF Ch 16 or 12. Space is limited.

Berthing is usually available in the 355-berth marina in Sleeper's Hole, 3 cables within entrance on port-hand side. Call the marina watchhouse on Ch 37 or 80. The former is to be preferred, as Dover Coastguard is frequently using Ch 80.

Facilities

Fuel and water from marina. All repairs, including sails. Electronics (☎ 01273 586179) close to marina. Early closing Wednesday. Yacht yard, gridirons and scrubbing hard. Divers (contact marina). Hauling-out facilities at marina.

Good selection of restaurants, from fish and chips upwards. Café by marina patronised by fishermen. Launching site at Sleeper's Hole on application to marina office. Yacht club: Newhaven and Seaford Sailing Club. Customs. A convenient port for opera-lovers on course for Glyndebourne.

Communications

Railway station and numerous buses to all parts.

Brighton

Tides

HW approx +0004 Dover

MHWS	MLWS	MHWN	MLWN
6·6m	0·5m	5·0m	2·0m

Depths

At least 2·7m in the immediate offing. The entrance is dredged to 2·5m. Inside the tidal basin berths vary from 3m to 1·6m on some of the inner pontoons. The locked inner harbour has 2·7m.

General

Brighton Marina, situated approximately 1 mile east of Palace Pier, is a most useful stop-over for yachts on passage up or down the Channel. The harbour is entirely artificial, and was built to seaward of what had always been known as Black Rock. It was opened by the Queen in 1979. It provides berths for almost 2,000 boats, even though a substantial part of the inner basin has been filled in to supply land for further housing, a leisure centre and a superstore.

The harbour is formed by a long, curving eastern breakwater and a shorter western one, extending to seaward. Together with a wave screen and Spending Beach, they form a double entrance which kills the sea almost completely. Shelter inside is excellent.

Approach and entrance

When coming from the west there are no notable dangers except for Palace Pier (2F.R) itself, which would be hard not to see in any but the thickest visibility. From the east, if you are well inshore, watch out for the heavily used lobster grounds to the north of the Fl.Y.5s buoy marking the sewer outfall off Portobello. These are particularly insidious at night under power.

The best final approach from offshore is to line up the high-rise hospital featuring a white stripe down its seaward side with the light (Q.R.7M) on the red and white horizontally striped beacon at the head of the western breakwater. These form a transit of 330°. Do not come too close to either breakwater as you enter, because wave backlash can be considerable and there may be shoaling. On the eastern breakwater is a white and green pillar (Fl(4)WR.20s 10/8M) with a smaller pillar (Q.G) at the extreme end. The sectored light shows white from 100°–295°. Coming from the east, if you see the red you are closer inshore than you might care to be.

Immediately inside the eastern breakwater the channel swings to starboard, well marked with 3 red and 3 green buoys. The first and last red buoys flash every 3 seconds, the first green likewise. The inner breakwaters have 2F.R and 2F.G marking their positions at night. There is room inside for all but the largest craft to round up and lower canvas.

The reception pontoon lies to port. If you have not been allocated a berth, tie up here and enquire with the berthing master. It is preferable, however, to telephone (☎ 01273 693636) or to call on VHF Ch 11, 37 or 80 shortly before you arrive. The harbour office is manned 24 hours. There are berths with depths from 1·6 to 3·0m for vessels up to 30m long. There is always room for visitors.

Brighton Marina entrance is difficult in strong onshore winds and can be virtually impassable in a southeasterly gale. In such conditions the harbour should not be considered. Newhaven would offer a safer, though still extremely lively, alternative.

Brighton. Approach from the southeast. Note vertical white stripe on high-rise hospital building and red-and-white light structure on western breakwater (extreme left).

BRIGHTON MARINA

Inner Harbour

2·7m

Boat Yard

Hoist·

Black Rock Ledge

YC

WC

Spending Beach

Harbour Control

WC

48'·8

Groyne

Fl.R.3s
R

Western Breakwater

Fl.R.3s

2F.R(vert)

2F.G(vert)

South Quay

Fl.G.3s

Fl.(4)WR.20s 16m10/8M

Q.G.8m7M

2₅

3

1₆

2₂

3

1₆

2₂

2₂

2₅

Waiting Pontoon

Scrubbing Grid

50° 48'·5 N

Q.R.10m7M Horn(2)30s

RC

White

2

3

Red

Outer Harbour

2₂

2₂

2₅

Eastern Breakwater

N

Depths in Metres

6'·5

0°6'W

5'·5

Brighton Marina.

Fog signal

The western breakwater has an excellent fog signal (Horn(2)30s), and the 10M range radiobeacon can be a great comfort (*BM* 294·50 kHz).

Facilities

Fresh water and power on the pontoons. Fuel (also *Calor Gas* and *Camping Gaz*) near the lock to the inner basin, where there is a boatyard and a travel-hoist. Full repair facilities on site, as well as a diver. Smart restaurants and a fishermen's café in the marina complex, plus a hypermarket where you could provision for a world voyage. There is a cash-point at the hypermarket which opens seven days a week in season.

Within the breakwaters there is also a scrubbing grid where boats can make use of the big tidal ranges. Waste oil disposal tank behind the services workshop.

Brighton Marina Yacht Club (☎ 01273 697049) welcomes visitors, both to its shore-based facilities and to its competitive racing.

The town centre of Brighton with its numerous attractions is a mile or so along the front. The main line station has regular fast trains to London and connects with other South Coast stations.

Shoreham

Tides

HW +0010 Dover

MHWS	MLWS	MHWN	MLWN
6·3m	0·6m	4·9m	2·0m

Streams

Off the entrance the west-going stream starts about 2hr before HW and the east-going 6hr later. During the west-going stream there is a southwest set across the entrance from the east breakwater towards the west breakwater, where part of it is deflected into the entrance. This run of tide bends round to the northeast towards the end of the east pier. The eddy is strongest ±1hr HW.

The maximum rate of the main stream at the harbour entrance is about 3 knots, but the river which makes up the Western Arm of the harbour can attain 4 knots at the flood, with an ebb of 5 knots in some parts at springs. In the Eastern Arm there is practically no stream, but a yacht should be piloted with caution in the vicinity of the division off the middle pier.

Depths

The approach shoals to a least depth of 1·7m, with 2·1m in the entrance. The harbour is mostly dredged, with depths shown on the plan. Note that the berths available to visitors in the Western Arm of the harbour dry. The Eastern Arm of the harbour has 2m.

Inside the lock, Southwick Canal is deep enough for commercial coasting vessels, with depths in the order of 5 to 7m.

General

Shoreham Harbour consists of the well sheltered Western Arm, which is the mouth of the River Adur, and the short Eastern Arm leading through lock gates to the Southwick Canal. Shoreham has few attractions for visiting yachtsmen unless a berth inside the locks is available. This is best arranged by calling the harbourmaster on VHF Ch 16 or 14, or ☎ 01273 592366. There is considerable commercial traffic (timber, seaborne aggregates, stone and steel) whose movements take priority and which uses up most of the wharf frontage along the north bank of the River Adur.

Approach and entrance

Shoreham Harbour entrance is about 4 miles west of Brighton Palace Pier. It is conspicuous from seaward by virtue of the enormous chimney (marked at night by red lights) about a mile east-northeast of the entrance. The entrance itself lies between two conspicuous concrete breakwaters. An unlit south cardinal buoy nearly 3 cables east-southeast of the entrance marks the outer end of a sewer outfall.

The shallowing water in the approach off the entrance can be very rough in strong onshore winds and may be dangerous, particularly on the ebb tide.

SHOREHAM-BY-SEA

Sussex YC (Shoreham)
Tarmac Wharf
Free Wharf
Fishermans Wharf
Lennards Wharf
Egypt Wharf
Railway Wharf
Kingston-by-Sea
R Lts (49)
High Light Fl.10s13m15M
Lady Bee Marina
Sussex YC (Southwick)
R Adur
Western Arm
2F.G(vert)
Lock
The Canal
Sussex Wharf
Soldiers Pt
2F.G(vert)
Eastern Arm
Power Station Site
Oc.5s8m10M
Horn 20s
SS (INT)
Training Wall
E Pier
F.WG
East Breakwater
Shoreham Beach
Groynes
F.WR
West Breakwater
Fl.R.5s7M
Fl.G.5s8M
Siren 120s
Y8
50° 49'·5 N
50°
N
Ldg Lts 355°
16'
0°15'W
14'
Depths in Metres

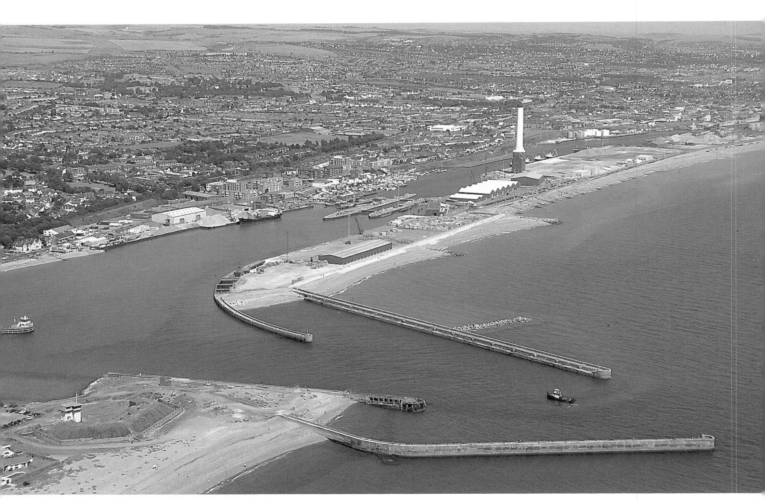

Shoreham entrance from the southwest.

Newhaven is generally a better port of refuge, as is Brighton in suitable conditions.

The entrance lies between the two concrete breakwaters (Fl.R.5s7M and Fl.G.5s8M), within which are the west and east piers (F.WR.6m and F.WG). Further north is the 'middle pier', on the fork of the Western and Eastern arms of the harbour.

The leading lights consist of a lower light (Oc.5s10M) on the watch hut at the end of the middle pier and a higher one (Fl.10s13m15M) from a grey lighthouse beyond. The structures are conspicuous by day, and approach to the harbour is best made on their transit at 355°. A radio mast (red lights, 49m) is just to the left of the transit.

The Western Arm is only suitable for visiting yachts able to take the ground. The channel in the Eastern Arm is dredged, and leads via locks into the Southwick Canal. Traffic signals, given below, must be observed. Depending upon the tide, the locks are manned from about 4 hours before HW to about 3 hours after, and open about once an hour for traffic in each direction.

A small-craft lock has been established, employing a single sector gate at either end of the Prince George Lock. It offers improved access for small craft, but is restricted to vessels of less than 20ft beam.

Traffic control signals

From lock
3F.R(vert) – do not approach lock entrance
GWG(vert) – vessels may approach lock

Middle Pier Control Station

Oc.Or.3s – No vessel shall enter the port for the purpose of proceeding to the Eastern or Western Arm, and no vessel outside the port entrance shall be navigated in such a way as to hinder the passage of vessels leaving the port.

Lifeboat House (focusing over Eastern Arm)

Oc.R.3s – No vessel shall proceed along the Eastern Arm for the purpose of leaving the port, moving to another berth in the Eastern Arm, or passing into the Western Arm of the port.

Lifeboat House (focusing over Western Arm)

Oc.R.3s – No vessel shall proceed along the Western Arm for the purpose of leaving the port, moving to another berth in the Western Arm, or passing into the Eastern Arm of the port.

Fog signals

East breakwater – Siren 120s.
Middle pier – Horn 20s. This is only sounded when ships are approaching.

Anchorages and berths

Anchor outside clear of the fairway in offshore winds and settled weather; the bottom is mostly sand over clay or chalk. Anchoring is not permitted within the harbour.

Directions for berthing inside the harbour may be obtained from the duty officer at the locks, where the Port Control building is situated.

All the available berths along the Western Arm (River Adur) dry out and there are many houseboats already there. The Shoreham clubhouse of the Sussex Yacht Club will be found on the N side.

Waiting for the locks: yachts are usually directed to secure temporarily to the north of the fairway.

Inside the locks visitors of up to 30m LOA can often be accommodated at the Lady Bee Marina (VHF Ch 80, ☎ 01273 593801) or the new Aldrington Quay Marina at the eastern end of the canal. The Sussex Yacht Club have floating pontoons inside the locks above the Lady Bee Marina. Occasionally they may have a space (☎ 01273 494868).

Except to approach Aldrington Marina, yachts may not proceed east of the Southwick clubhouse of the Sussex Yacht Club without the explicit permission of the harbourmaster, to whom you must report on the day of arrival. The harbour office and customs house are both within a few minutes' walk of the marinas.

Facilities

Toilets and showers at both marinas and the Sussex YC. There is a launderette in Shoreham High Street.

Water may be obtained at the marinas. Fuel at the local garage at Southwick, with diesel from the pump at Corral's (Mon–Fri 0700–1730, −3hr to +2hr HW) in the Western Arm.

Chandlery at Muggeridge Ltd, 378 Brighton Road, and at Lady Bee Marina, which also supplies *Calor Gas* and *Camping Gaz*. Southwick Hardware still sells paraffin. Banks and provision stores in the town, with an off-licence and general store near to the marinas. Most repairs can be taken care of through Lady Bee Marina, but if in doubt ask at the Sussex Yacht Club.

Pubs and restaurants in Shoreham. The charming Shoreham clubhouse of the Sussex Yacht Club serves lunches through the week, except Mondays, and dinners on Friday and Saturday nights.

Communications

Shoreham has excellent communications by rail or bus to Brighton and London. It also has the distinction of having its own airport, with scheduled flights to France and the Channel Islands as well as charter services.

Littlehampton

Littlehampton entrance.

Tides

HW at entrance +0015 Dover

Height at entrance

MHWS	MLWS	MHWN	MLWN
5·9m	0·4m	4·5m	1·8m

(MLWS 0·8m at Norfolk Wharf)

Streams

These can be fierce in the entrance, up to 6 knots on the spring ebb. In the offing, the stream turns west nearly 2 hours before HW. Be prepared for a strong contrary eddy inside the training wall.

Depths

The bar theoretically dries 0·8m, but LW heights are such that in practice it is virtually always covered. Nevertheless, tidal height calculations must be worked from this figure. Inside, depths in the river vary between a metre or so and 2·4m as far as the opening footbridge. This has a height of 3·6m at MHWS, and only opens for visitors who 'book' it by 1630 the previous day. If you can pass under this, however, there are only two further low bridges (the old road bridge in the town has a clearance of only 1·7m at MHWS) between you and Arundel, with depths of at least 1·3m at MLWS the whole way. The new road bridge just short of Arundel is considerably higher, and exceedingly satisfactory dinghy trips into the hinterland above this historic town have been reported (1994).

General

Littlehampton is a convenient harbour for yachts, with a relaxed, friendly atmosphere and berthing facilities handy for all the pleasures of the town. It is the home of the famous building yard of Hillyard and, at the right state of tide, can offer a realistic stop-over for yachts bound either up or down the Channel. Shelter is good except in strong southerly and southeasterly weather, which can send a swell up the harbour.

Approach and entrance

Littlehampton is readily identifiable from seaward, but if in doubt note the isolated high-rise building and the funfair immediately to the east of the entrance. Approaching from the west through the Looe channel, do not turn to port too soon after the *Mixon* beacon. There is grief aplenty still available inshore. It is therefore prudent to stand on for a mile or so, then steer a track of 065° until you either pick up the leading marks for Littlehampton or bring the head of the 275m-long West Pier onto a bearing of 346°. The West Pier head consists of a large 'cage' of piles. Closer in, the structures supporting its 2F.R lights will be seen.

The bar extends 3 cables to seaward of West Pier. Leading marks for the best water across it on 346° are as follows: a white pepper-mill-shaped lighthouse (Oc.WY.7·5s9m10M) at the inshore end of the east breakwater, and in front of it a black steel column (F.G.6m7M) at the seaward end of the breakwater. The black column is hard to spot by day until it comes 'on' with the white lighthouse, but for all practical purposes you will be safe if you steer across the bar on this sort of heading, then between the West Pier head and *East* beacon, with its green ▲ topmark. The east breakwater is continued seaward in the form of a training wall which covers at 3m height of tide. When it is submerged, it can still be identified by a line of perches which then mark the east side of the channel inshore of the *East* beacon.

There is a tide gauge on the West Pier head giving height in metres above chart datum. This gauge can be read from seaward by sharp eyes equipped with good binoculars.

If approaching from the east, maintain a sensible offing until the bar is reached.

Littlehampton entrance can be dangerous in strong onshore winds, and should not be attempted in these conditions when the tide is ebbing hard.

Bylaws

Keep clear of all commercial traffic, particularly if a ship signals one long and two short blasts. Traffic passing up and down the harbour has right of way over anything crossing the river, with the exception of the ferry, which takes precedence over everyone. Vessels proceeding against the stream keep clear of those moving with the tide.

Berthing

Anchoring is prohibited inside the harbour. Visiting yachts may secure temporarily alongside Town Quay, immediately above the ferry. The harbour-master's office is here (a well marked portakabin) and the wharf is also identified by a grey tripod crane. There are pontoon berths on the wharf. You should now report to the harbour office and ask to be allocated a berth.

Do not secure to a pontoon berth on the west bank. These are privately owned, many by members of the adjacent Arun Yacht Club. Occasionally one of these berths may be available to craft under 8·5m LOA, but you should check first with the club – ☎ 01903 714533 (members), or 716016 (secretary). The harbourmaster's number is ☎ 01903 721215. Littlehampton Marina, which listens on VHF Ch 37, but has Ch 80 also available (☎ 01903 713553), maintains 30 visitors' berths for craft of up to 2·5m draught and 18m LOA, but note the restrictions imposed by the footbridge (see above).

Facilities

Fuel, water and repairs at any of the three boatyards on the river, or at the marina, which has a slip, a lift and a chandlery. All shopping, banks, etc. in town. Showers, toilets on Town Quay and at the marina.

Littlehampton. Entrance showing submerged training wall beacons on starboard hand. Note that the topmark is now a green triangle.

Littlehampton. Unusual lighthouse on east bank near entrance. Note funfair, conspicuous from seaward.

Chichester

Tides

HW +0027 Dover

Entrance

MHWS	MLWS	MHWN	MLWN
4·9m	0·9m	4·0m	1·9m

Minor differences inside the harbour, but none are greater than the LW figures for Itchenor, where neaps are 0·2m lower than at the entrance.

Depths

Various shoal areas in the approaches to the bar, with the least depth of 0·3m southwest by south from the *Bar* beacon. Drying areas to east and west. The bar is dredged to 1·5m, though depths may vary after severe weather. Further in, depths increase rapidly into the entrance where there is a pool of 26m. Thereafter, there is at least 2·4m as far as Emsworth south cardinal beacon and the same up to Itchenor. Further up the harbour depths diminish in both channels – see plan for details. It should be understood that Chichester Bar, like many others, has a tendency to shoal. In 1996 its LAT depth was reported as down to 1m in places, leading to dredging in spring '97 to re-establish the charted depth. There is an automatic tide gauge on the bar beacon.

The *Bar* beacon.

Chichester harbour entrance.

General

Chichester Harbour is an ideal dinghy-sailing area, with extensive deep-water channels usable by deep-draughted yachts. Over 10,000 craft upwards of 3m LOA are based here, with 2,000 yachts on marina berths. Bosham, Emsworth, Birdham and Itchenor are all attractive villages, and the anchorage at East Head is a delight when not too crowded. Generally speaking, the area is low-lying and the shores are muddy and reedy, though there are also some beautiful sand and shingle beaches. The harbour's commercial past goes back to Roman times but is now almost completely consigned to the history books. As a leisure centre, however, these waters have few equals.

The harbour is controlled by Chichester Harbour Conservancy through a manager/harbourmaster based at Itchenor (☎ 01243 512301). His call sign is *Chichester Harbour Radio* on VHF Ch 14, and his launch *Regnum* also listens on VHF Ch 14. Watch is kept during office hours; his staff will be pleased to advise you about berthing or any other problems you may have.

Policing is strict on the 8-knot speed limit and also on Rule of the Road. If you are motorsailing, even motoring with a sail idling in calm weather, hoist your motorsailing cone, point downwards.

Hayling Island Sailing Club and Sandy Point, beyond which the channel to Sparke's Yacht Harbour leads westwards.

CHICHESTER HARBOUR

N

49'

50°
48'
N

47'

46'

P CG

Hayling
Island

Sunshine
Holiday Village

Saltings

Saltings

Jetty

Mengham
Rythe SC

Sandy Pt
Hayling Island SC

Sparkes Yacht
Harbour

Hospital

Eastoke Pt

Bn
Q.R

West

Pole

Red

White

Chi Spit
(Apr-Nov)

Chi

Depths in Metres

Bay

Chichester Bar
Fl.WR.5s14m7.5M &
Fl(2)R.10s7m2M
RW

CHICHESTER
BAR

58'   57'   56'

NE Hayling
Fl(2)R.10s

Emsworth Bn
Q(6)+LFl.15s   See continuation

Emsworth
Channel

Marker Pt

Marker
Fl(2)G.10s

Oar Rythe

Verner
Fl.R.10s

Mill Rythe

(Marked by Bns)

(marked by Bns)

Mill
Rythe
G

Dip Rythe

N Pilsey
G

NW Pilsey
Fl.G.5s

Fishery
Q(6)+LFl.15s
YB

Tide gauge

BYB

N Winner
Fl(2)G.10s

NW Winner
Fl.G.10s

W Winner
Q.G

26

EMSWORTH

50°
50'.5
N

Conigar Pt

Northney
Fl(4)R.10s
R

Sweare Deep
Fl(3)R.10s
R

Northney
Marina

Northney
Holiday Village

Fowley I.

Emsworth SC

Echo
Fl(3)G.10s

Tarquin
Yacht
Harbour

Small
Craft
Moorings

Little
Deep

Fisherman's Bn
Fl(3)R.10s
R

Mooring Piles

Sweare Deep

Emsworth Bn
Q(6)+LFl.15s
Y

Great
Deep

50'

1°57'W   56'

THORNEY
ISLAND

Longmere Pt

CHICHESTER

HARBOUR

Pilsey I.

Pilsey
Sands

Stocker's Sands

Copyhold
R

Stocker
Fl(3)R.10s
R

NE Winner

Mid Winner
Fl(3)G.10s

Sandhead
Fl(4)R.10s
R

NE Sandhead
Fl(4)R.10s
R

East Head
Fl(4)G.10s

East Head

The   Winner

West
Wittering

Thorney
Channel
(marked by Bns)

Awash at
HW Springs

Broken Piles

Thorney
Fl.G.5s
G

Pilsey I.
Fl(2)R.10s
G

Camber
Q(6)+LFl.15s
YB

Rookwood

Ella Nore

Target
(3) BY

East

Pole

Sands

Target
(3) BY

1°55'W   54'

CHICHESTER HARBOUR

Depths in Metres

Fishbourne **CHICHESTER**

Apuldram

Dell Quay Sailing Club

Fishbourne Channel (marked by buoys)

Small Craft Moorings

Moorings

Copperas Pt

Chichester Yacht Basin

Canal

Chichester YC

Lake

Chichester

Birdham YC

Lock

Birdham Pool

Birdham

Oldpark Wood

CYB Fl.G.5s

Birdham Bn Fl(4)G.10s

Longmore Pt

Hard

Bosham Hoe

N

Bosham

Spire

Bosham Sailing Club

Quay

Boatyard

Moorings

Chidham Creek

Moorings

Bosham Channel

Clump of trees to N limit

Hard Wks

Bosham SC

Boatyard

Jetties

Jetties

Ferry (Summer only)

Itchenor Sailing Club

Itchenor

Itchenor Reach

Jetty

Jetties

2F.G (vert)

2F.G (vert)

Fairway Fl(3)G.10s

Deep End

Main Channel Bn

Cobnor Pt

Chalkdock Pt

Wear Pt

Roman Transit Bn

Chalkdock Bn Fl(2)G.10s

Chichester Channel

Bns in line 032°

Chidham Pt

Nutbourne Channel (marked)

Nutbourne

Marshes

Saltings

Saltings

Oaze Rythe

Broken Piles

Rookwood

Thorney Channel

Thorney Bn

Fl.G.5s

Broken Piles

Camber Bn Q(6)+Fl.15s

Pilsey Bn Fl(2)R.10s

NE Sandhead Fl.R.10s

Ella Nore

Prinsted Channel (marked)

Prinsted Pt

Andrews Boatyard

Stanbury Pt

Thorney Island Sailing Club

Thorney

MOD

Dish Aerial

Longmere Pt

Pilsey Island

Pilsey Sands

Stocker's Sands

Sandhead Fl(4)R.10s

Copyhold

East Head Bn Fl(4)G.10s

East Head

NE Winner

1000 Metres

0

1°54'W

50°48'N

49'

50'

51'

52'

53'

49'

59

Itchenor.

Approach and entrance

Chichester Harbour entrance lies some 7 miles west of Selsey Bill. Sands extend seaward on both sides of the approach, namely the West Pole, the Middle Pole and the East Pole. Chichester Bar claims victims nearly every year from amongst those foolish enough to chance their luck. The ebb runs hard, the waters are shoal and exposed from southwest through to southeast, with southeast being the worst wind direction. Do not even think of entering the harbour after half-ebb in a strong onshore wind. In an onshore gale, don't do it at all. These cautions cannot be over-stressed.

Approaching from the east, either from the Looe channel or from the Outer Owers, do not turn in too soon. The conspicuous low *Bar* beacon is a large four-legged dolphin surmounted by a white lattice tower. The safest approach is to put this on a bearing of around 005° from a mile or more offshore, then shape up to leave it a few boat's-lengths to port, noting as you pass the height of *tide* on the gauge on one of its legs (add 1·5m to find the *depth* on the bar). You may also notice the seasonal red can buoy *Chi Spit* about 2 cables south of the beacon. Whatever happens, leave this to port. It marks the position of the drying West Pole sands which creep ever southwards.

If you cannot discern the *Bar* beacon from the offing, it is a good policy to place the very conspicuous Nab Tower on a back bearing of 184° and run in on this until you pick up the beacon.

The East Pole Sands stretch well to seaward of the beacon and are only really cleared by a bearing on the beacon of 325° or more, so if you head in early and find your course for the beacon is less than this, clear out, steer to seawards and think again. This bearing is covered by the red sector of the *Bar* light (Fl.WR.5s7/5M and Fl(2)R.10s2M). The secondary Fl(2)R light covers the West Pole.

Approaching from the southwest, you may find yourself seeing the Fl(2)R as well as the safe white sector of the bar light. Steer to starboard until the red goes out on a bearing of 020°. In daylight, keep *Chi Spit* buoy to port (or in winter, when it is not there, approach the *Bar* beacon for a heading of 020° or less) in order to clear the West Pole.

A track of 013° from a point about half a cable east of the beacon will now lead you to the harbour entrance in rapidly deepening water. Leave the red *Eastoke* beacon (Q.R) to port and, 2½ cables further on, the *W Winner* green beacon (Q.G) to starboard, taking care to leave the small unlit red posts on the ends of the groynes round Eastoke Point to port. Streams in this channel can reach extremes of over 6 knots on a big spring ebb. Run in parallel with the steep shingle beach on your port hand until you are between the Hayling Island Sailing Club clubhouse on Sandy Point to port and the green *NW Winner* buoy (Fl.G.10s) to starboard. You now have two choices: Emsworth Channel to the north and Chichester Channel to the east.

Emsworth Channel

Steering about 335° from the Sandy Point/*NW Winner* entrance, leave the lit *Fishery* south cardinal well to starboard, followed by the *NW Pilsey* (Fl.G.5s) green buoy. The channel is now well marked and adequately lit up the almost straight 2-mile leg northward which culminates in the lit south cardinal *Emsworth* beacon and the red (Fl(2)R.10s) *NE Hayling* beacon. If you are bound up Sweare Deep towards Northney Marina, you will leave *NE Hayling* to port and follow red piles up the channel, keeping them on your port hand on a northwesterly heading as far as *Sweare Deep* beacon (Fl(3)R.10s).

Leave this to port and a heading of around 290° will take you up to *Northney* (Fl(4)R.10s) beacon. Swing round this and to the southwest you will see the red and green piles at the marina entrance. Boats drawing up to 2m can work into the marina on a mean tide.

The other channel from *Emsworth* beacon leads up to the village itself and the Tarquin Yacht Harbour, once known as Emsworth Yacht Harbour. The lower part of the channel as far as the red *Fisherman's* beacon (Fl(3)R.10s) is set with pile moorings. Above here, a series of red piles is left to port, following the drying (0·5m) channel a little east of north until at the first lit green pile (Fl(3)G. 10s) the channel swings to starboard between a second green and further red piles up to the marina, where a sill maintains a depth of 1·5m. This marina is only accessible to shoal-draught boats for an hour or two either side of HW.

There are various other channels in the vicinity of Emsworth, all of which dry, some being marked with piles and withies.

Chichester Channel

This leads to Thorney Channel, Bosham Channel, Itchenor and thence to Birdham Pool, Chichester Yacht Basin, and drying 'points beyond'.

After passing Hayling Island Sailing Club, bear to the east to leave to starboard the *NW Winner* (Fl.G. 10s), the green conical *N Winner* (Fl(2)G.10s), the *Mid Winner* (Fl(3)G.10s) conical buoys and the *East Head* beacon (Fl(4)G.10s) with its tide gauge.

Leave to port *Stocker* (Fl(3)R.10s), *Copyhold* (unlit) and *Sandhead* (Fl(4)R.10s), all of which are red can buoys.

Do not take any chances with the Winner. Cutting corners here can lead to long and gravelly waits for the tide. If the wind kicks in hard while you are stranded, your position may become hazardous. The bank is well marked, so there should be no difficulty.

After leaving *NE Sandhead* (Fl.R.10s) to port, the channel bears to the northeast, onto the distant *Roman Transit* beacon (red port-hand daymark) in line with the so-called *Main Channel* beacon (white rectangular daymark) on the shore at 032°. Both line up with Stoke Clump, a conspicuous group of trees on the distant downs. If visibility shuts out these markers, do not concern yourself, for the channel is clearly marked on the port hand by the lit south cardinal *Camber* beacon at the entrance of the Thorney Channel, and by the unlit green *Rookwood* buoy (leave to starboard). There are also a number of perches, but these are situated high up on the mud and should be given a wide berth near low water.

After passing the *Chalkdock* beacon (Fl(2)G.10s), come to starboard and shape up for the green conical starboard-hand *Fairway* buoy (Fl(3)G.10s) at the junction of the Bosham and Chichester Channels. Close to the northeast is the *Deep End* south cardinal beacon, which is an unlit starboard-hand mark for the Bosham Channel and a port-hand one for the Itchenor Reach. The latter is deep

Birdham Pool.

Bosham.

almost to Longmore Point, getting on for a mile east of Itchenor. Hereafter the channel shallows, but is marked by buoys. Access to Birdham Pool and the Chichester Yacht Basin is dependent on some rise of tide.

Birdham Pool is entered by following a series of green piles, after rounding *Birdham* beacon (Fl(4)G. 10s), then passing through a lock manned for 3 hours either side of HW in winter and from 0700 to 2200 in season. Yachts of up to 2m draught can get there, tide permitting, but the approaches dry at least one metre, so proceed with caution.

Chichester Yacht Basin's beacon (*CYB* Fl.G.5s) lies a couple of cables east-northeast of Birdham's. From it, a line of green piles leads east-southeast down a channel which has approximately half a metre of water (LAT) up to the locks. These are manned in summer from 0700 to 2359 weekends and 0700 to 2100 Mondays to Thursdays; in winter, from 0800 to 1700.

Bosham Channel carries 1·8m to within 2 cables of the quay at the village and is marked by red and green perches. It is possible for craft drawing 1·8m to lie alongside the quay, and to dry out at moderate spring tides.

Thorney Channel is entered by leaving the lit south cardinal *Camber* beacon to starboard, and then leaving *Pilsey Island* red beacon (Fl(2)R.10s) to port and a green perch to starboard; neither should be passed close to. Now pass between a pair of beacons, beyond which the channel is straight and marked by red and green perches. Depths range from 3·7m down to 1·8m to the northeast of Stanbury Point. The upper channel contains moorings.

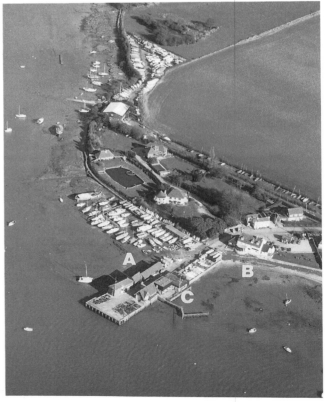

Dell Quay. (A) Public slip. (B) Pub. (C) Sailing Club.

Anchorages and berthing

North of Sandy Point, just inside the entrance on the west side, there is a large clutch of moorings. The occasional one may be free for a lunch stop. Hayling Island Sailing Club maintain a jetty to the west of their dinghy launching area whose outer end is fully intertidal. This is available for 'picking-up and putting-down' stays up to a maximum of twenty minutes.

East Head Beyond the beacon there is a pleasant anchorage on a sandy bottom. It is fine in settled weather, but very crowded in summer and rather exposed except from south and east. A shallow creek marked by perches leads to the Roman Landing and West Wittering Sailing Club.

Itchenor There is a pontoon at the end of a long low jetty below the harbour office. Lie here for 15 minutes *only* to take on water and load stores or bodies. Upstream are 6 large visitors' moorings where you may be invited to raft up to six abreast. Still further upstream is a visitors' pontoon on the south side of the channel. If in doubt, call the harbourmaster on VHF Ch 14. A pretty village with few domestic facilities, save a pub. There is, however, a boatyard and a small chandlery.

Birdham Pool Approach as described above (see 'Approach and entrance'). Birdham can accommodate yachts up to 15m long and 2m draught. The place has great charm, a shipyard with full repair facilities, showers, toilets, fuel, sailmaker, chandler and electrical engineer. Shops are a 25-minute walk. Do not call on VHF. They are not listening. Just come up on the tide.

Chichester Yacht Basin Call on VHF Ch 37. Access from two hours either side of LW, depending upon draught and tide rise.

Traffic signals
Q.R – <1m of water in channel
Q.Y – gates open
Lock signals
R – wait
G – enter

Take care in the lock during free flow periods. The tide can swirl in and out at great speed. Visitors are welcome up to 20m LOA and 1·8m draught. The surroundings are pleasant and the facilities all you would expect in a major modern marina, including a launderette. Provisions/newsagent, chandler, bar/restaurant, riggers, sailmakers and engineers are all on site. The Chichester Yacht Club welcomes visitors to all its facilities.

Thorney Channel is a beautiful and well sheltered anchorage when you can find space, of which there is often plenty off Pilsey Island. You can 'dinghy' ashore onto a spit but, thankfully some would say, there are no facilities.

Northney Marina usually has space for visitors drawing up to 2m. Call on VHF Ch 80, or ☎ 01705 466321. All facilities, but shops are 15 minutes' walk.

Tarquin Yacht Harbour maintains only four visitors' berths, but may have more due to berth-holders' absence.

Call on VHF Ch 37 or 80; this is highly advisable as space is limited. Facilities are water, toilets, showers and a payphone, but Emsworth Shipyard next door can solve most problems. 10 minutes' walk brings you to the town of Emsworth with shops, pubs, bistros, etc. Emsworth Slipper Sailing Club and Emsworth Sailing Club welcome visitors.

Emsworth Channel There are a number of pile moorings for craft up to 12m in the channel. They are the first five you come to and have 2m of water at LAT. A new jetty in Emsworth, established 1997 and exact position unknown at the time of going to print, will be available at HW±4. A two-hour stay is free. There is fresh water, rubbish disposal, and Emsworth shops and pubs are convenient.

Sparke's Yacht Harbour, with 400 pontoon berths and all the facilities of an active yacht yard, lies immediately west of Sandy Point, the home of the Hayling Island Sailing Club, at the end of its own 2m dredged channel. Leave the unlit east cardinal beacon to port, swinging to port out of the main channel, and follow the yellow 'x' leading marks to the westward until the red and green channel posts leading to the conveniently sited marina open up on your port hand. Berths have depth up to 2·5m afloat at MLWS. Contact on VHF Ch 37 or ☎ 01705 463572. Excellent facilities including fuel, repairs, showers, laundry room, bar/restaurant, chandler with *Calor Gas/Camping Gaz* exchange, and some provisions.

Bosham It is possible to dry out alongside Bosham quay, in depths/heights noted above (see 'Approach and entrance – Chichester Channel'). Village facilities only, with pleasant walks, two pubs and a yacht club. This is an excellent scrubbing berth, with a firm bottom and a freshwater stream running beneath the wall to sluice off with. It is also one of the prettiest berths on the South Coast. Leave the west cardinal beacon below the quay well to starboard. There is a south cardinal mark by the end of a wooden breakwater/training wall which runs parallel and close to the quay. Leave the mark to starboard and keep close to the piled quay wall. Tie up and enjoy the summer's day.

Launching sites in Chichester The harbour is a small-craft paradise, so it is not surprising that it is well equipped with launching places. Some are as follows:

1. From public hards at the ends of roads at Itchenor, Bosham, Dell Quay, Thornham and Emsworth, with car parks nearby.
2. Near HW on the northeast side of Hayling Bridge at the slipway administered by the Langstone Sailing Club, and also at Birdham Yacht Club and Dell Quay.
3. At Sandy Point, with the permission of the Hayling Island Sailing Club.
4. At Emsworth, from the public hard or Tarquin Yacht Harbour.

Approach to Tarquin Yacht Harbour.

Yacht clubs

Birdham Yacht Club, Bosham Sailing Club, Chichester Cruising Club (Itchenor), Chichester Yacht Club (Birdham), Dell Quay Sailing Club, Emsworth Sailing Club, Hayling Island Sailing Club, Itchenor Sailing Club, Langstone Sailing Club, Mengham Rythe Sailing Club, West Wittering Sailing Club, Thorney Island Sailing Club.

Tarquin Yacht Harbour.

Langstone Harbour

Tides

Similar to Portsmouth
HW +0014 Dover

MHWS	MLWS	MHWN	MLWN
4·8m	0·8m	3·9m	1·9m

Streams

Streams run extremely strongly at springs in the vicinity of the entrance – beware of mooring buoys towed under by the tide.

Depths

With prudent pilotage, a least depth of 2·1m LAT may be found on the bar. A large proportion of the harbour dries, but the main channels offer well over 2m for much of their length. The short channel up to Langstone Marina virtually dries. The automatic sill 'opens' when there is 1·6m of water above it, giving access to the marina where 2·4m is available in its deepest part. The waiting pontoon outside has 2·5m at LAT.

General

It could be said that Langstone Harbour lacks the natural beauty of Chichester to the east, or the historic fascination of Portsmouth on its western flank. Nonetheless, this large expanse of mud and tide-controlled water possesses a distinct charm of its own. It has been called bleak, but some enjoy its gutsy, outpost feel in a region where many places have been tooth-combed almost to the extinction of their natural character.

Approach and entrance

The entrance to Langstone Harbour is identified by a tall chimney on its west bank. As at Chichester, the channel into the harbour is bounded on both sides by dangerous banks of shingle and sand, in this case the West and East Winner.

If arriving from the east, it is prudent to leave the south cardinal *Winner* buoy (unlit) to starboard, then hold a course of due west until the red and white fairway buoy comes into transit with the inner end of the west side of the entrance. The buoy is set in the deepest available water, and even if the banks shift, this approach should keep you off them. From the fairway buoy steer for the entrance, taking note of the transit (353°) of the red entrance dolphin (with port-hand topmark on the end of an outfall)

Langstone Harbour entrance. *Portsmouth City Council*

LANGSTONE HARBOUR

Depths in Metres

Eastney Cruising Association clubhouse on west side of entrance.

East side of Langstone Harbour entrance.

Langstone fairway buoy.

and the edge of the land on the west side of the entrance. As you approach the entrance itself, any cross set will be replaced by a potentially very strong stream running straight in or out. This can kick up a bad sea, especially towards the end of a spring ebb in strong onshore winds.

Coming from the southwest, bring Horse Sand Fort onto a stern transit (235°) with No Man's Land Fort. This will lead to the vicinity of the black/red/black isolated danger beacon with ⦙ topmark marking Roway Wreck. Before you reach the beacon, you will have identified the red and white *Langstone* fairway buoy fine on your starboard bow. Steer towards this, being mindful of a 1·3m (LAT) patch just to the north of your track. Outside the line of the beacon and the buoy is a least depth of 1·8m, which at MLWS gives you 2·6m of water.

Approaching from the west, you may opt for the gap in the submerged barrier joining Horse Sand Fort with the Hampshire shore. The passage lies almost a mile south of Lumps Fort on the beach and is marked by a dolphin (Q.R) on its south side, whose light is exceedingly feeble. Keep close to the dolphin, in 1·2m (LAT), then steer east until the two forts come in line as described above.

Once inside the harbour, navigate to your chosen berth, but be ready for powerful streams in the lower part of the main channel.

Fraser Gunnery Range

In occasional use Mon–Fri (0800–1800) as notified by Radio Solent, or by telephone (☎ 01705 822351). The range area is a circle of 1 mile radius centred on 50°47'·03N 01°01'·09W. There is also a sector 120°–155° ranging out to 9 miles. The range is marked when in use by two red flags, and at night by 2F.R and an Oc(2)Y.10s light exhibited just to the west of the harbour entrance.

Berthing

No anchoring is allowed in the harbour without the permission of the harbourmaster, who maintains a watch on VHF Ch 16 and 12. Call *Langstone Harbour Radio* during working hours, including weekends. The favoured anchorage for deep-draught craft is on the north side of Langstone Channel on a clean, sandy bottom. The berth is, however, exposed and a long way from any shoreside comforts.

There are a number of visitors' moorings in the main run of the entrance. Those on the west side are maintained by the Eastney Cruising Association (☎ 01705 734103). To the east of the fairway are the Harbour Board moorings. The harbourmaster's office can be reached on ☎ 01705 463419, or call *Langstone Harbour Radio*. It should be noted that at springs the tide past these moorings reaches prodigious velocities, and that as a result the greatest care should be taken over dinghy work. Anyone unfortunate enough to fall from a moored yacht during the height of the ebb on a dark night could very well be lost. Despite these gloomy observations, should you opt for one of these berths, Hayling Ferry will provide a 'get-you-ashore' service. Call *Pride of Hayling* on VHF Ch 10.

The deep-water moorings inside the entrance are private, and those outside the channels mainly dry.

Langstone Marina has 30 visitors' berths. Enter the narrow channel by passing close north of the western pontoon and the point on your port hand, immediately inside the harbour entrance. Watch out for cross set. The channel is now marked with red and green piles, the salient ones being lit. It appears tortuous, but as you work along its half-mile length it becomes plain enough. There is a waiting pontoon with shore access immediately outside the sill. The sill itself is automatically operated by water pressure, so that when 1·6m stands above it a balance weight folds it down flat, allowing access. As this happens, the red lights turn to green and boats drawing 1·6m or less may enter. If your draught is greater, observe the gauge near the gate, which indicates depth on the sill. Vessels outward bound have right of way in the 7m-wide entrance.

Langstone Marina keeps a 24-hour watch on VHF Ch 80 and can be called on ☎ 01705 822719.

Facilities
Hayling Island Phone, diesel and fresh water from Hayling pontoon near to the harbourmaster's office. Water here is deep, but this is a very busy berth, so no vessels should be left without sufficient crew to move them except with specific permission from the harbour office, and then only in the designated berth. If you ignore this warning, you are liable to be towed away and billed.

Ferry Boat Inn with bar meals, a café and a modest general store. Launching site at slip. Summer bus service to Hayling Island and Havant. Ferry to Eastney all year round, thence to Portsmouth by bus, or bracing walk.

Eastney Cruising Association is a hospitable organisation whose fine clubhouse contains showers, a bar and a restaurant. Visitors are welcome and the members are a friendly, able group whose numbers have included none other than Sir Alec Rose.

Southsea Marina has fuel, water, showers and a chandlery. Basic provisions. Visitors are granted access to the marina clubhouse with balcony, bar and good meals. Launderette and first-class provision shop at caravan park after an easy walk.

Communications
Bus to Portsmouth.

Portsmouth

Tides
HW +0029 Dover

MHWS	MLWS	MHWN	MLWN
4·7m	0·8m	3·8m	1·9m

Depths
The entrance and main channels are deep, as are the approaches to Camper and Nicholson's Marina (Gosport) and Haslar Marina. Portchester Lake shoals towards the top, but is dredged 1·5m up to the Port Solent lock. The main branch of Fareham Lake has depths of over 5m for much of its length, but depths reduce to 3m off Wicor Hard. Above here the creek shoals up to Fareham, where it dries 0·9m off the Lower Quay, with greater drying heights towards the undeveloped edges. The outer Camber Dock has 2·2m, with around 1·6m on the Town Quay itself (but see 'Approach, entrance and navigation', below).

General
Portsmouth is inextricably tied up with the Royal Navy's history. Wherever you look, the Senior Service has made its mark. HMS *Victory* towers over the Royal Dockyard. HMS *Warrior* soars over HMS *Victory*, while the remains of Henry VIII's *Mary Rose* are no less important, for all their comparative modesty. Across the water at Haslar is a submarine museum, with HMS *Alliance* on blocks above the tide. Ships of today's navy are much in evidence, both active and mothballed, and naval buildings abound.

As the battle fleets decline, the economy of the town is bolstered to some extent by the cross-Channel ferries which berth in Fountain Lake, immediately off the M27 spur road.

The upper reaches of Portsmouth Harbour are a great place for dinghy sailors, or Yachtmaster Examiners in search of challenges for their customers on 'green' water. Many sailors will be pleased to learn that water-skiing is forbidden within the domain of QHM (Queen's Harbour Master) Portsmouth, who runs this great port with surprisingly little fuss.

Approach, entrance and navigation
Boat Channel
Vessels under 20m LOA entering harbour should either use the Boat Channel, on the west side of the entrance, or stay close inshore on the east side. Such craft should leave *only* by the Boat Channel. If you have an engine, you must use it between red *No. 4* buoy (Q.R, the last port-hand mark before the entrance) and the red *Ballast* buoy (Fl.R.2·5s), the first red you come to a cable or so inside. The Boat Channel is situated immediately outside the main channel until the entrance is reached, at which point vessels making use of it must stay as close as they dare to the two red posts with topmarks a few metres off the bank.

PORTSMOUTH HARBOUR

N

Mud

Porchester Lake

LFl.G

Fl(2)G

Fl(3)G

Fl(3)R.5s ☆

Moorings

Whale Island

Mud

Mud

Mud

Infilled 1996
Works in progress 1996

Continental Ferry
Terminal

Fl.R ☆

Q(9)15s ☆

2 F.R ☆

2 F.R ☆

8·0m.

Infilled 1996

Moorings

FOUNTAIN LAKE

2 F.G.

Q.(6) + L.Fl.15s.

8·5m.

2 F.R.

2 F.R.

Mud

2 F.R.

HARDWAY

Priddy's
Hard

2 F.R.

North Corner

Middle
Ship
Jetty

Basin No.3

8·0m.

Forton Lake

Burrow I.

Mud

HM Dockyard

CHY
(36)

Mary Rose Ship Hall

HMS
Victory

LANDPORT

Royal Clarence
Victualling Yard

Weevil
Lake

4·0m.

9·0m.

2 F.R.

Semaphore Tower

Mary Rose

CENTRAL SS
(Traffic) HMS
Warrior

PORTSEA

BLDG
(63)

TOWER

GOSPORT

Cold Harbour

2 F.R(vert)
Dir.W.R.G.2m.1M.

Fl.G.

2 F.G.

Harbour Stn

BLDG
(56)

Gosport
Marina

Ferry

F.Y.

2 F.R.
2 F.R.

2 F.G.

CHY
(38)

PORTSMOUTH

Ballast
Fl.R.2·5s.

2 F.G.
2 F.G.

TOWER   BLDGS
(37)

(51)

Q.G.

The Camber

Q.G.

I.of W. Ferry
Terminal

Haslar
Marina

Mud

2 F.G.
2 F.R.

Ft Blockhouse

2 F.G.

Portsmouth S.C.

TOWER   Cupola

OLD PORTSMOUTH

Dir.W.R.G 13·5M.

2 F.R.
2 F.R.

Oc.G.15s
2 F.G.

2 F.R

RN   TOWER
Submarine   (43)
Museum

SPIRE

East
Sand

Clarence Pier (Grn Lts)

Flats

Royal Naval
Hospital

F.Y.+   Hovercraft
Oc.WR Terminal
G.3M

HASLAR

Haslar Bank

S.G

No.3
Q.G.

No.4
Q.R.

Al.W.R

Al.W.G

Iso.R.

SOUTHSEA

WAR MEM.

SS(Southsea Y.C.)

BLDG

Hamilton
Bank

G.cS

(Apr-Oct)Y

No.1
Fl.(3)G.10s

Southsea Castle
Iso.2s.16m.11M.
Dir.W.R.G 11m
13·5M.

Fort Monckton

Monckton
Patch

No.2
Fl.(3)R.10s

Al.W.G

Oc.G

April-Oct
Y

Castle
Fl.(2)G.6s.

Harrow Bank

M.G

SPIT   SAND

Ridge
Fl.(2)R.6s.

Oc.R

Fort Gilkicker
Oc.G.10s.7M.

Mussel
Patch

(Apr-Oct)

Spit Bank

9·5m.

Gilkicker Pt

M

Numerous small obstructions

M

Spit Sand Fort
Fl.R.5s.18m.7M.

The Ridge

April-Oct
Y

Spit Refuge
Fl.R.5s
Bell

Boyne
Fl.G.5s.

Iso.W

Al.W.R   Al.W.G

War Mem. S.Side of flats 049°

April-Oct
Y

F.R   F.W. C03°   Al.W.G   F.G.

War memorial transit 049°.

In the Boat Channel: leaving *No. 4* buoy close to starboard heading to pass close to Fort Blockhouse.

Portsmouth. Entrance between Fort Blockhouse on the left and Old Portsmouth on the right. Small Boat Channel is on the extreme left-hand side, leaving red beacons close to port.

Red beacons off Fort Blockhouse which must be left close outside by small craft.

Approach to Gosport Marina, with fuel barge at the end of wave baffles.

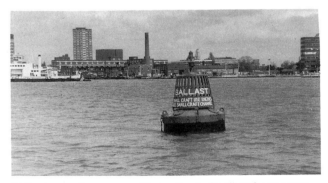

Ballast buoy off entrance to Haslar Creek. Small craft must pass to the west of it.

The approach from eastward simply follows the buoyed channel from Horse Sand and No Man's Land Forts past *Saddle* (VQ.G), *Horse Sand* (Fl.G. 2·5s) and so on to the Boat Channel. It is important to maintain a good lookout. Yachts should be ready to leave the channel for the navigable water outside it well before the arrival of any commercial vessel. Approaching along the coast from the direction of Langstone and Chichester Harbour, you may opt for the passage through the Horse Sand submerged barrier, given a sufficient rise of tide.

From the west, leave Fort Gilkicker (Oc.G.10s 7M) a cable to port. You now have 3 choices. You can steer about 110° towards *Outer Spit* south cardinal, and so join the main channel, turning to port south of Spit Sand Fort as your draught dictates, but bearing in mind that south of the fort there is always at least 2·1m of water. This route is, however, time-consuming and devious. The preferred course is to cross Spit Sand with a minimum of 1·8m on the transit (049°) of the War

Memorial on Southsea front in line with the right-hand side of the yellow apartment building behind it. Watch your echo sounder as you cross the sand, and as soon as the bottom falls away to 5m or more, turn in towards the harbour entrance, keeping the red main channel buoys close to starboard.

To the northwest of this transit lies Hamilton Bank, the inshore end of which dries 0·6m. There is a channel inside the drying patch with a depth of 0·5m which is forbidden to vessels over 20m LOA and is only recommended to navigators with local knowledge. However, a yacht drawing 1·8m or less can make use of it subject to a sensible tide rise. Use the chart, and keep within a cable of the wall for the final 2 cables before the harbour mouth (once past the white tower 100m behind the wall), closing to 100m or less at the corner itself. This will keep you off Hamilton Bank. It should be noted that the bank does shift. A transit is being considered that will lead in through this channel. In the meantime, it should be used with the greatest caution.

Both these latter approaches are unlit, so should only be used at night with caution, or a more than ample rise of tide. If you do opt to cross Spit Sand or Hamilton Bank after dark, watch out for unlit buoys.

By night, note the sectored light on Fort Blockhouse, on the western entrance. Occulting white (fixed when on 320°) puts you squarely in the centre of the channel as far as *No. 4* buoy. Oc.G says you are on the starboard side of the channel, red places you to port. If you see Al.WG, or Al.WR, it tells you that you are straying out to that side.

From *No. 4* buoy, the lead in is taken over by a directional light set up half a mile inside the entrance by Camper and Nicholson's Marina. This takes you onto about 335° and shows isophase white in the central channel, with Al.WR to port, and Al.WG to starboard. If you see isophase white, you are neither in the Boat Channel nor close enough to the east side. Take action accordingly.

Tides in the entrance run very hard, up to a maximum of 5 knots on spring ebb. There may be counter-currents on the flood, particularly on the west edge of the channel just inside the entrance. Once inside, proceed as follows:

The Camber

The Camber entrance lies immediately north of the peninsula of Old Portsmouth, with its conspicuous pubs, which is on your starboard hand as you enter the harbour. Unless you have arrived along the east side, however, do not turn to starboard until you reach *Ballast* buoy. Leave the Isle of Wight ferry terminal to port and follow the dock round.

Haslar Creek

Haslar Creek, running southwest from the immediate vicinity of the main harbour entrance, has long been the home of HMS *Hornet* and the Joint Services Sailing Club. Their marina on the south side, well up the creek, is private. For the public Haslar Marina, see 'Marinas', below.

Old Portsmouth. Entrance to the Camber. Ferry terminal on left. Proceed ahead to where fishing boat is lying, then swing to starboard into dock.

Some yacht berths are available on the right after rounding the Bridge Tavern.

Fareham Lake

Fareham Lake is the western channel of the two into which the upper harbour divides about 1½ miles inside the entrance. The lower part of the channel is defined by big-ship moorings and mothballed warships. These peter out above Bomb Ketch and Spider Lakes, which are largely filled with private moorings. From here on, the channel is marked by green and red posts, some of which are lit.

Do not be distracted by the red pile (*No. 57*, Fl(3)R.5s) on your starboard hand at the lower end of the channel. This marks the entrance to Portchester Lake, for which it is a port-hand marker.

Yachts drawing 2m can navigate up to the drying Fareham Quay for two hours either side of HW, but note that you will have to pass under power cables with a height of 12m.

Portchester Lake

This begins as described above, between red *No. 57* pile and green *No. 95*. The channel is sufficiently lit to permit night entry with care. By day it presents no problems until, after turning north-northeast at Brick Kiln Lake, the channel takes a dive to the northwest at green *No. 85* pile. Do not confuse piles *No. 83* (red) and *No. 84* (green) with Portchester channel markers. They indicate the entrance to Tipner Lake.

When Portchester Castle comes abeam to port, you are entering the dredged (1·5m) channel which leads via lit green piles and unlit reds – except for *No. 72*, which is Fl(3)R.10s – up to the lock at Port Solent Marina.

Portsmouth marinas. Haslar (above) and (below) the entrance to
Port Solent.

Fountain Lake

This is the main eastern arm of the big-ship harbour; the cross-Channel ferries operate from the eastern end. Yachting is discouraged except for boats bound to or from the Naval Sailing Centre at Whale Island.

Moorings and anchorage

Gosport Cruising Club, Weevil Lake

Some moorings may be temporarily available.

Hardway Sailing Club

Half a mile due west of the junction of Portchester and Fareham Lakes, Hardway Sailing Club has a number of piles painted red with orange tops which may be used by visitors whose length does not exceed 10·6m (35ft). The club is very active and has the usual shore facilities. Provisions can be bought nearby, as can chandlery and *Calor Gas/Camping Gaz* refills. The club has a restaurant, and the streets behind hold further possibilities for the adventurous diner, including a Chinese takeaway.

Wicormarine

Further up Fareham Lake, still in well over 3m LAT, is Wicormarine. Here, a well equipped and friendly yard welcomes you to use any spare moorings and to avail yourself of the shower facilities. Chandlery with *Calor Gas/Camping Gaz* exchange. All repair services. Water and diesel (HW ±3 hours).

The Camber

Tie up alongside the wall in the vicinity of the Bridge Tavern which, although face-lifted and given new furnishings, is far from being the pub it once was. The wall has a number of wicked girders and pilings, so berth with care.

Anchoring

Portsmouth Harbour presents an unattractive anchoring prospect, unless your yacht can dry out upright in mud. In this case, no doubt an independent spirit would find a quiet corner full of interest.

Marinas

Haslar Marina

Magnificent marina with excellent shelter and deep water. This is the company which started the move back to realistic marina prices on the central South Coast. Their big visitors' berths can accommodate anyone who turns up, even a 45m yacht.

Approach is easy up Haslar Creek in 8m of water and more. Call on VHF Ch 80 as you approach. The office is manned 24 hours a day. Facilities are first class, with toilet, wash basin and shower in each ensuite cubicle. Laundry, ice, public phone and a proper chandlery (not a boutique with a few small shackles) which will open at any hour in order to get you on your way. Divers on site, as well as diesel and outboard engineers.

The marina maintains a light vessel where the Royal Albert Yacht Club have a bar and restaurant to which visitors are welcome.

The berthing masters are skilled in directing you to the better and often lesser-known pubs in the immediate vicinity. Gosport itself and the Portsmouth Ferry are two minutes' walk.

Gosport Marina

No problem with pilotage here. Call them up on VHF Ch 37 or 80 (24-hour watch, call sign *Camper Base*). Beware of tides running through the berths. Depths vary, but there are plenty with deep draught. Advise the berthing master of your length and draught when you call.

Camper and Nicholson's, to which the marina is attached, can hoist 180 tons, and can cope with all repairs and emergencies. There is also a scrubbing grid, chandlery, diesel, fresh water, launderette and marina club with all the usual facilities.

The outer berths at Gosport Marina can be subject to wash and some surge.

Port Solent Marina

Large, modern locked marina development at the top of Portchester Creek, at the upper end of the 1·5m dredged channel. Call *Port Solent* VHF Ch 37, or 80, for the lock-keeper. The locks work 24 hours a day, with some free flow around HW. All the usual marina facilities await you inside, plus many shops and an on-site supermarket, open 0800–2200 every day. Yacht Club open to visiting sailors. 40-ton hoist, various repair companies.

Communications

Isle of Wight car ferries. Cross-channel ferries. Railway station with trains to all parts.

Bembridge

Tides

Long stand at HW, the beginning of which is approx +0014 Dover

Range

MHWS	MLWS	MHWN	MLWN
3·1m	0·2m	2·3m	0·5m

Depths

The entrance channel may dry in the vicinity of red buoys *No. 6* and *No. 6a* through to *No. 10*, but the tide gauge beacon at its entrance indicates depth of water at its shallowest part. Much of the harbour itself also dries, but within the channels there is more than enough water to accommodate any craft which can pass the bar. Vessels drawing 1·8m can

Bembridge beacon. Tide gauge shows depth at shallowest part of the channel.

Bembridge Point. Sign post has been removed since the date of this photograph. Bembridge Sailing Club to the left.

Fairway in Brading Haven towards St Helen's Quay and Marina (far right).

lie afloat on visitors' pontoons at LAT. Deeper water than this exists in the pool just inside the entrance, where moorings may occasionally be available by arrangement with Attrill's or Coombes' boatyards.

General

Brading Haven, with Bembridge at its seaward end and St Helen's at the other, was once a busy Roman port. It has long since silted up, however, leaving only limited access and mooring areas for yachts. Since Elizabethan days St Helen's Roads outside have provided shelter, so long as westerlies predominate. This anchorage is still good today, though considerable quantities of kelp may necessitate more than one 'try' before you are confident your hook is holding.

St Helen's Fort, which stands ¾ mile northeast of the entrance, was built by Palmerston in 1860 to guard against a French invasion which never materialised. A second prominent navigational feature, which has even less social relevance nowadays, is the conspicuous whitewashed seamark on the Duver foreshore south of Node's Point. This is the remains of a 13th-century church, most of which slid into the sea in 1550. Stones from its ruins were widely used for scouring wooden decks, hence, according to local folklore, their being known as 'holystones'.

Access to Bembridge is limited by the nature of the entrance channel, whose depth and whereabouts are modified, apparently at random, by the shifting sands. Buoyage is maintained, however, so a stranger may enter with confidence, given a rising tide, a sensible clearance and seamanlike caution.

Approach and entrance

From the west, make for the yellow tide gauge beacon (Fl.Y.2s). Beware of the shoals and extending rocks off Nettlestone and Horestone Points. Coming from the east, leave St Helen's Fort at least a cable to port before heading up for the tide gauge. From the northeast, open the transit between the right-hand edge of St Helen's Fort and the white daymark, then steer for the yellow beacon. Night entry into Bembridge is not recommended without local knowledge, as the channel itself is unlit and may be tortuous. The yellow light is also very feeble.

From the beacon, enter between green and red buoys *Nos 01* and *02*. Now follow the buoys implicitly. On first seeing them from seaward they may present a confusing image, but so long as you work through the numbers in order and have read the tide gauge to your satisfaction, all will be well.

Once inside the entrance, look for *Nos 11A* and *13* green cones. Swing round to starboard past the moorings, keeping red cans *10A* and *12* to port. Now proceed in a westerly direction, past the visitors' pontoons to the east of green *No. 15*, between buoys *16* (red) and *17* (green) until you reach Bembridge Marina.

Berthing

No anchoring is allowed in the harbour (nor, incidentally, within 200m of St Helen's Fort), with the exception of the sandy beach in front of Bembridge Sailing Club and the harbourmaster's office. Here shoal-draught yachts may moor fore and aft and dry out.

Deep-water berthing (not less than 1·5m LAT) is available at Bembridge Marina (VHF Ch 80 at HW ±3 hours during daylight). The visitors' berths are on the first and second pontoons (Nos 5 and 6). Before departing, check the marina tide gauge which indicates the least depth in the entrance channel.

Berths are also available for visitors on the detached pontoons west of *No. 15* buoy, up to three abreast on the south side.

Facilities

Brading Haven Yacht Club (☎ 01983 872289) immediately east of the marina is an active sailing club with 1,500 members. The club welcomes visiting yachtsmen and provides hot meals, generous bar hours, showers and toilet facilities. Its private pier can be used for landing by dinghy.

Bembridge Marina has its own car park, toilets, fresh water, showers and rubbish skips.

Bembridge Sailing Club, with its fleet on private moorings occupies the southwest corner of the harbour. Visitors by invitation.

Fuel and repairs at Attrill's Yard, opposite *No. 13* buoy (☎ 01983 872319), or at Stratton's, near *No. 17* buoy.

Chandlery, marine engineer and sailmaker near the Bembridge Sailing Club (☎ 01983 872686). Bembridge village has all facilities including two restaurants and a pub offering meals, but it is a long walk from the marina. A ten-minute stroll up to St Helen's Green brings you to The Vine, a supermarket and two further restaurants. Even closer to the marina is the Old Mill Caravan Shop which meets most daily requirements including milk and newspapers. Open forenoons and late afternoons, seven days a week.

Excellent swimming from the safe, sandy beach on the seaward side of the harbour. Many first-class walks. Fishermen's Wharf features Captain Stan, who sells fish and seafood fresh out of the boats from his own doughty craft.

Communications

Buses to Sandown and Ryde, whence you can cross to Southsea by catamaran or hovercraft. Taxis from Bembridge Harbour Taxis (☎ 01983 874132).

Bembridge with the tide well down, showing the necessity of following the buoyed channel.

Ryde

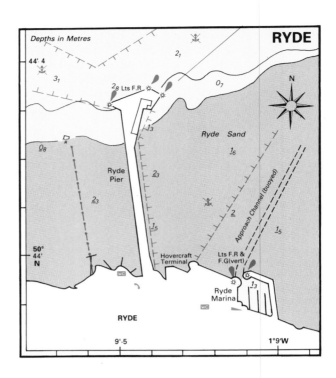

Tides

Similar to Portsmouth
HW Dover + 0015

MHWS	MLWS	MHWN	MLWN
4·5m	0·9m	3·7m	1·9m

Depths

The harbour dries 1·3m above chart datum. The buoyed channel shoals to a similar height, with a 1·5m drying patch near the entrance.

General

Ever since paddle-wheel ferries from Southsea linked the main railway network to all parts of the Isle of Wight, Ryde has been its largest town. The community's winter population is 34,000, swollen by swarms of summer visitors.

Ryde now has its own artificial 150-berth yacht harbour, enclosed by a substantial breakwater, approximately 2 cables east of Ryde pier. The harbour dries completely at LW, leaving a sandy bottom on which suitable craft may take the ground with confidence. It is well sheltered from all directions except northwest, when strong conditions may bring in some surge at the top of the tide.

Successful rallies have been organised at Ryde. These began in 1993; the harbourmaster will be pleased to supply details (☎ 01983 613879).

Approach

Ryde Harbour is identified from seaward by the ice rink and the ten-pin bowling building. It lies immediately east of these. Maintaining an awareness of the extent of Ryde Sands, proceed to a point 600m east of Ryde pier head. On the edge of the 1m contour, pick up the first of the small, unlit R and G channel buoys on course 197°. From here it is under half a mile to the small northwest-facing entrance. A single directional amber light shining seawards indicates 1m depths inside; a second light above it means not less than 1·5m. There is also a tide gauge. 2F.R are mounted on the breakwater, with 2F.G on your starboard side at the entrance. Night entry is assisted by a floodlight, directed shorewards, mounted on the end of the breakwater.

Visitors should realise that the buoyed channel is not dredged. It exists to keep yachts clear of hovercraft manoeuvring to and from their terminal close by. Keep in the channel and you have rights. Stray from it and you may be deemed responsible for any resulting difficulties involving hovercraft.

Berths

There are up to 70 visitors' berths in the harbour. Tie up either alongside the eastern arm of the breakwater or on the nearest pontoon to it. There is a slipway at the southwest corner. Deep-keeled yachts can dry out on firm sand against the wooden piles mounted on the inner side of the breakwater.

Fender boards provided. The harbourmaster's office is in a portacabin at the southeast corner. Contact him on ☎ 01983 613879, or on VHF Ch 80 – call sign *Ryde Harbour*. Be sure not to call 'Ryde Marina', as this has led to confusion with nearby 'Hythe Marina' in the past.

On no account pump heads or bilges whilst in the harbour.

Facilities

Fresh water, toilets, showers, car parking and garbage disposal.

No fuel or repair facilities at the harbour, and generally speaking, Ryde is light on technical support for yachts. Diesel and petrol are, however, available from a garage within walking distance, and there are numerous pubs, bars, restaurants, hotels, B&Bs, banks and all the other comforts of a large town.

Communications

By catamaran to Portsmouth Station and the main line, or hovercraft to Southsea. Buses to all parts of the Island. Railway to Shanklin.

Fishbourne – Wootton Creek

Tides

Long stand at HW
HW approx +0014 Dover
Range

MHWS	MLWS	MHWN	MLWN
4·5m	0·7m	3·7m	1·9m

Depths

3m in the dredged fairway as far as the ferry terminal. Thereafter the creek dries, except for a channel of 0·3–0·6m and a 2m dredged pool at Fishbourne Quay.

General

Fishbourne has considerable natural beauty and offers attractive amenities ashore. It has limited room for visiting deep-keeled yachts, although it provides excellent shelter for shoal-draught craft and those able to take the ground. The east bank of the entrance to Wootton Creek is largely given over to the busy terminal for RoRo ferries linking the Island to Old Portsmouth.

Approach and entrance

Whether you approach Wootton from east or west, watch for off-lying dangers. From the east, keep outside the line from Ryde pier head to the north cardinal *Wootton* beacon (Q.1M), which lies 1½ miles west of Ryde pier and ½ mile offshore, and marks the seaward end of the 3m dredged fairway. From the west, avoid Peel Wreck, marked by an unlit red can and, close to the entrance, Wootton Rocks, whose position is indicated by a post or withy with a topmark.

The 224° fairway is clearly marked by four beacons on its starboard hand and two to port: *No. 1* Fl(2)G.5s, *No. 2* Fl.R.5s, *No. 3* Fl.G.3s, *No. 4* Fl.R.2·5s, *No. 5* Fl.G.2·5s and *No. 7* Q.G. A directional Oc.WRG.10s light inshore of the ferry ramp shows a narrow 1·5° white sector when you are on course; green means you are off to starboard, red indicates straying port of the line. 2F.R lights are exhibited from the end of the jetty at the east side of the ferry berth. There is very little water either side of the fairway inshore of beacons *2* and *3*, so do not use the channel during a ferry movement. In fog, a bell is rung from the ferry jetty.

WOOTTON CREEK

Just beyond *No. 7* beacon, work round to starboard onto a westerly heading, bringing the two triangular leading marks on the western bank into line. These indicate the run of the best water through the pool and into the creek, though it is also worth taking note of the lie of the moorings. If continuing further, watch for a small green buoy off a jetty exhibiting a speed limit sign, and leave it very close to starboard. This will keep you clear of the gravel spit extending out into the creek on your port side. The small red buoy following it must be left to port, as must a line of old piles, after which Fishbourne Quay is immediately at hand. To proceed beyond this point, keep to the starboard side and follow the line of moored boats for the best water in the fairway.

Berths and moorings

Anchorage (no charge) can be found on the north side of the fairway opposite the yacht club. You will probably dry out at half-ebb – as you will if you anchor further up the creek – but the bottom is soft mud. Do not anchor in the fairway. Wherever you bring up, an anchor buoy is advisable.

Apart from privately owned moorings, the Royal Victoria Yacht Club (☎ 01983 882325) has some buoys and four piles for visitors to secure between, fore and aft. These also dry. The boatyard at Fishbourne Quay makes available to visitors its own floating pontoons in a 2m dredged pool. These can

be reached by deep-draught yachts around the top of the tide, but do not expect to arrive or leave at less than half-tide.

There is a public landing at Wootton Bridge, accessible to dinghies.

Facilities

Before the war the Royal Victoria Yacht Club had imposing premises on the front at Ryde, from which it conducted racing for all classes, including the J-boats. Its more modest clubhouse in Wootton Creek is still most hospitable to visitors from other clubs and offers full facilities. There are two pubs in the vicinity, both of which provide substantial food: The Fishbourne Inn, close to the ferry, and The Sloop, at Wootton Bridge.

The boatyard has full repair facilities as well as toilets, fuel, fresh water, telephone and a chandlery. In addition to the Sloop Inn, two supermarkets are located near Wootton Bridge. All of these are best visited by dinghy on the tide, unless you enjoy a long walk.

Communications

Depending upon season, the car ferry to Portsmouth leaves on the hour – sometimes the half-hour – from first light until midnight.

Buses from Wootton Bridge go to Ryde and Newport.

Taxis on ☎ 01983 884345 or 883421.

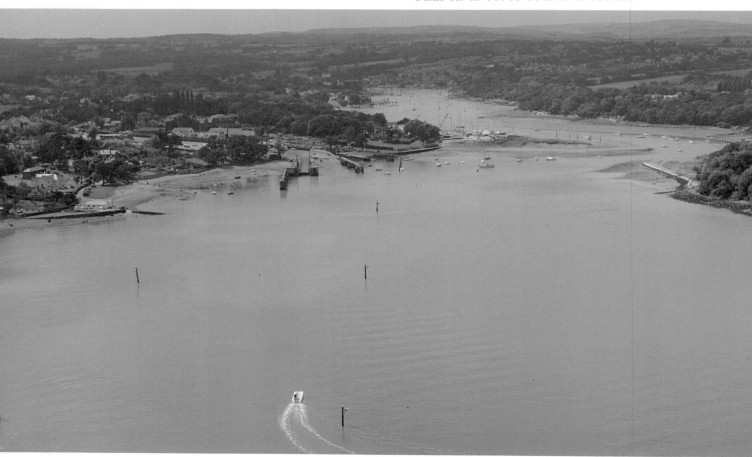

Wootton Creek fairway.

Cowes

Tides

Double HW at springs, otherwise a 2-hour stand.
HW approx +0021 Dover

MHWS	MLWS	MHWN	MLWN
4·2m	0·8m	5m	1·8m

Depths

A minimum of 2·2m (LAT) in the fairway, continuing to one cable south of the chain ferry (known locally as the floating bridge), though 2m has been reported (1997) immediately N of here. After a shallow patch which still leaves 1·5m at LAT, deeper water of at least 2·5m extends up-river to within half a mile of The Folly Inn. From this point, at least 1·2m LAT will be found as far as *Medham* beacon, with a minimum of approximately 1m as far as *South Folly* beacon, two cables above the pub. Thereafter, the river shoals gently into the 'drying mode', giving depths on the visitors' pontoons at Newport of at least 2·5m at MHWS, and a minimum of 1·7m at MHWN. It should be noted that the apparently shoal water leading up to The Folly Inn poses little problem in practice to most yachts; even at MLWS a vessel drawing 1·5m can creep up with caution. Deeper-draughted craft whose skippers have been over-ambitious will suffer little worse than a brief sojourn with their keels in soft mud.

General

Cowes lies at the mouth of the Medina River which, on favourable tides, is navigable for 4 miles up to the Island's capital, Newport. Cowes itself is sheltered in all but north or northeast winds, but when the weather kicks in from these directions, visitors in the outer harbour can seek shelter above the chain ferry.

Cowes is justly known as England's leading yacht-racing centre. Clubs and facilities of all types abound, and the Castle at the western entrance has been the home of the Royal Yacht Squadron since mid-Victorian days. Full back-up facilities, but do not expect too much at weekends.

Cowes is a community of great character, but is not what the uninformed visitor generally expects. The main street was smartened up during the late 1980s, and fascinating sights abound for the observer with a sharp eye. Nonetheless, the town grew up around ship and yacht yards with a large working population. This meant streets lined with houses more suited to Victorian tradesmen than to the yachtsmen they ultimately served. Do not be dismayed by this. Spend time here and you will begin to discover the rich essence of the place. If you still can't cope with the workaday atmosphere, walk round past the Castle to Cowes Green, where the gentlemen had their villas. It is a different world, and you might run into the ghost of Uffa Fox, watching critically as a latecomer barges on the Squadron Line.

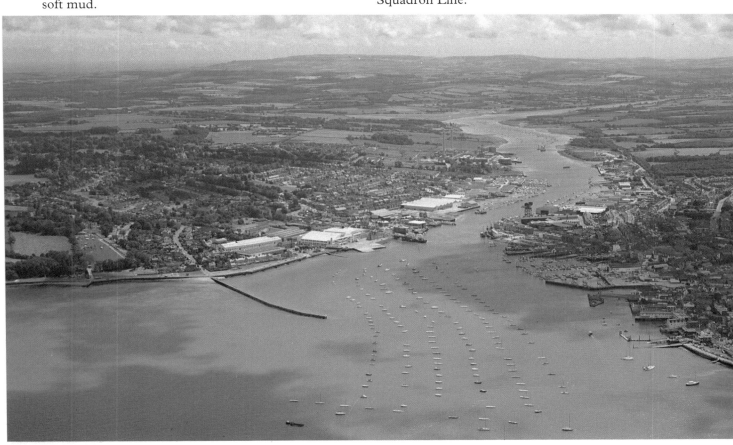

Cowes, East and West and the River Medina.

COWES

UPPER MEDINA

NOTES

The chains of the ferry (floating bridge) lie at least 0.6m above the bottom of the channel.

Cables cross the river immediately above and below the floating bridge

The Castle is the home of the Royal Yacht Squadron.

Medina river looking downstream. (A) Cowes Yacht Haven. (B) Souter's yard. (C) Cowes Marina. (D) UK Sailing Centre. (E) Chain ferry. (F) East Cowes breakwater. (G) Fore-and-aft pile moorings and Squadron pontoons.

Approach

From whichever direction you head for Cowes, remember that the Solent tides run fast in this vicinity. Coming from the west, rocks lurk close offshore either side of Egypt Point. The Shrape mud-flats catch many a navigator taking the most direct course from Old Castle Point in the east, and whatever the state of the tide, never cut through the closely packed moorings for racing keelboats which extend both sides of the breakwater.

One of Britain's busiest shipping lanes runs past Cowes Harbour entrance. Solent bylaws give commercial craft right of way over all yachts at all times, besides which, to impede the progress of a supertanker setting up to make the tight turn round the Bramble Bank could have the gravest ecological consequences. The harbour itself is also subject to commercial traffic, with coasters running up to Medina Wharf and beyond. Add car ferries to this, as well as high-speed passenger transport, and the necessity of keeping a good lookout both ahead and astern will be clear. Listen on VHF Ch 69 – the port working frequency.

The most prominent seamark off Cowes is the north cardinal *Prince Consort* buoy (VQ) 4 cables northeast of the red can *No. 4* fairway buoy (Q.R). This pairs with the green conical *No. 3* buoy (Fl.G. 3s), and between them lies the 164° leading line with its two Iso.2s lights. The front one is white, on a pile off the slip by the customs watch-house, downstream from the Island Sailing Club pontoon; the rear one is red, on another pile by the Jubilee ferry pontoon. Each has a tide gauge showing water above chart datum in the fairway. You may not notice these during a daytime entry, but the river is so straightforward in daylight that failing to spot them will not trouble you.

Proceeding up the fairway, there are two red can buoys on the port hand. *No. 6* (Fl(2)R.5s) is followed, close to the East Cowes ferry terminal, by *No. 8* (Fl(2)R.5s). Jubilee Pier, the West Cowes catamaran terminal, next to the Old Town Quay, is marked by 2F.G(vertical) at each end, as are the limits of the Cowes Yacht Haven. The breakwater off East Cowes Point has a Fl.R.3s3M light.

The river above *No. 8* buoy has plenty of water (subject to depths given above) as far as the Folly Inn. If in doubt, stay in the middle. Although there is not a great deal in the way of lit navigational marks above the chain ferry, night entry is easy enough because of the essentially straightforward character of the river and the ambient light from shore establishments, though these peter out above Medina Wharf.

Note that tides run very hard through the chain ferry, particularly the spring ebb. Large yachts which may experience difficulty manoeuvring under these circumstances should call the chain ferry on Ch 69 and advise.

The speed limit is 6 knots over the ground.

Berths and moorings

Cowes is well stocked with berthing facilities, as it needs to be during Cowes Week or on the weekend set aside in early June for the Round the Island Race, which often sees 1,500 yachts on the starting line.

Berths may be allocated by the harbourmaster from his launch or his office, situated between the Jubilee Pier and Cowes Yacht Haven. Contact him on VHF Ch 69 or by phone (☎ 01983 293952), manned during working hours. There are five visitors' buoys just downstream of the Island Sailing Club, and a short-stay pontoon at Thetis Wharf, near the chain ferry, with walkway access to the shore. The harbourmaster also has fore-and-aft pontoon berths further upstream. Those which are owned by clubs are clearly marked. Other moorings are privately controlled.

Anchoring is prohibited in Cowes Harbour itself. It is permitted out of the fairway up-river south of the last of the moorings, but is likely to be impractical unless you want to dry out.

Visitors are also accommodated on pontoons off the famous Folly Inn, 1½ miles up-river of the chain ferry. The Folly may not be everyone's ideal of a bijou pub but, like Cowes itself, the place grows upon those who frequent it. Now renovated and extended, the Folly retains its unique character and offers good facilities as well as fine ales to the weary sailor.

The Cowes harbourmaster's jurisdiction extends two miles upstream as far as the Folly Inn. Beyond that, Isle of Wight Council's Marine Authority controls all the berths in the river. There is a small harbour office at the head of the pier next to The Folly Inn. Call *Folly Launch* on Ch 69, or ☎ 01983 295722.

Newport offers alongside drying-out berths at the Odessa Yard on the west bank, and at the Town Quay opposite, close to the end of navigable water. The harbourmaster listens on Ch 69, or can be reached on ☎ 01983 525994.

Marinas

Cowes Yacht Haven (formerly Groves and Gutteridge, Ancasta and West Cowes Marina) is now dredged to 3m near the fairway and 2·5m close inshore within the south basin. It has 220 pontoon berths, a high proportion of them for visitors. During peak periods you may find yourself rafted up on the river side of the long pontoon, exposed to the wash of passing traffic and onshore winds. Call *Cowes Yacht Haven* on VHF Ch 80.

Shepard's Wharf, downstream from the chain ferry, has some pontoon berths. Contact ☎ 01983 297821.

UK Sailing Academy (the old National Sailing Centre) maintains a small marina on the west bank a little under 3 cables above the chain ferry. A limited number of visitors' berths are available on a first-come, first-served basis. No VHF watch is kept, but the berth is a snug one in all conditions. Showers and toilets. Shore access via Arctic Road, with a 15-minute walk to Cowes centre. Fish and chips from the Arctic Fisheries two hundred yards up Arctic Road, with good provisions and bonded stores from the corner shop just across the road.

East Cowes Marina has 300 berths for boats drawing up to 4m. Contact on Ch 80, or ☎ 01983 293983. Excellent shelter, but shoreside amenities are limited and less accessible than those in West Cowes, which can only be reached by water taxi or a considerable walk on either side of the floating bridge.

Island Harbour (formerly Medina Marina), half a mile upstream from the Folly, is a 180-berth locked harbour for boats up to 15·2m (50ft) LOA. It is accessible at the top half of the tide by way of a clearly marked buoyed channel off the fairway. Movements through the locks are ordered from a prominent white control tower by red or green traffic lights. Full marina facilities include the Skipper licensed restaurant and the nearby converted paddle-wheel ferry *Ryde Queen*. Contact on VHF Ch 80, or ☎ 01983 526020. There is a waiting pontoon immediately outside the lock-gate.

Facilities

Cowes offers yachtsmen every facility they may require. There are cranes at Thetis Wharf and Souter's, and a travel-hoist at Cowes Yacht Haven, whilst Lallow's slip can handle all but the largest boats. Groves and Gutteridge (or their successors) and Shepard's Wharf are amongst several who can tackle most engineering, electronic and structural problems. The latter hires tools for owners to carry out their own work.

Yacht clubs: Island Sailing Club, Cowes Corinthian, Royal Corinthian, Royal London and the Royal Yacht Squadron.

There are restaurants and pubs to suit all tastes and pockets.

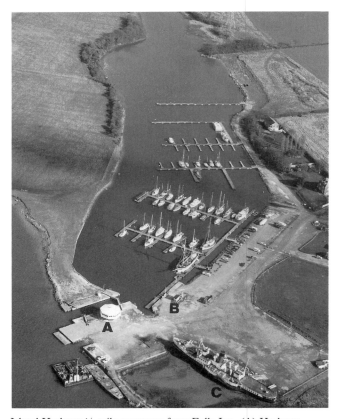

Island Harbour ½ mile upstream from Folly Inn. (A) Harbour office. (B) Fuel berth. (C) Medway Queen restaurant.

Fuel is obtainable outside the Yacht Haven, at Lallow's pier and from the bunkering barge operated by Marine Support Bunkering off Souter's; they also have *Calor Gas*. Island Harbour has its own fuelling point inside.

Various chandlers, including Pascall Atkey right in the middle of town.

Customs are in the watch-house next to the Island Sailing Club. ☎ 01983 293132. Out of hours ☎ 01703 827350.

Communications

Car ferries run regularly from East Cowes terminal. Catamarans to Southampton from Jubilee Pier, every half-hour from 0630–2230 (2330 Fri/Sat). Both have connecting bus services to Southampton main line railway station with services to Waterloo and the West.

Frequent buses to Newport with connections to the rest of the Island.

Taxi stands at each ferry terminal, or call Tony's Taxi on ☎ 01836 248679 or Russell's on 01983 292083.

Hamble River

Tides

Double HW
First HW springs approx Dover −0020

MHWS	MLWS	MHWN	MLWN
4·5m	0·8m	3·8m	2·0m

Depths

Over 3m LAT as far as Port Hamble. At least 2·8m from there up to *Crableck* beacon above Mercury Yacht Harbour. Half a cable above *Crableck* beacon, depths fall fractionally below 2m for a few yards, then 2m and more will be encountered as far as the Elephant Boatyard. Between the Elephant and Bursledon Bridge, depths may shoal to 1·5m LAT.

General

The Hamble offers all-weather shelter except to vessels moored close to the entrance in strong winds from south through southwest. Enough visitors' berths are available to encourage an interesting stop-over. The density of the Hamble's private moorings and marinas and the diversity of craft occupying them make the river a must for the sailing enthusiast. Night entry is possible with care on a first visit, at least as far as Port Hamble.

The charm that the river and its banks must have exhibited before the yachting revolution is not now always easy to spot, though extensive mud-flats and sedge still contrive to avoid the developers' dredgers. Hamble village itself has a tumbly main street with pubs and other temptations. Warsash offers little to the pleasure-seeker. At Old Bursledon, however, connoisseurs of great yards will discover the Elephant Boatyard still purveying traditional skills

alongside the best of the modern. They will also discover interesting walks, good pubs and fascinating views. The mighty Swanwick Marina across the river gives inspiration to those who would bring nature under control, but down-river on the east bank the Crableck supplies a haven of unspoilt delight. No shareholders' group has ever contrived to concrete these meadows by floating a new share issue. Here, the birds still sing, and a poor man may yet moor his yacht in the ancient, accommodating mud of Hampshire.

Approach and entrance

Coming in from the West Solent, make tracks for *Hamble Point* south cardinal buoy (Q(6)+LFl.15s), taking care not to impede commercial traffic passing up and down from Southampton and the huge Fawley oil jetties. From the East Solent, head for the same point, watching out for anchored coasters lying between Hook (green) and Coronation (yellow) buoys. Despite the generally shoal water on your starboard hand, the bottom is as flat as a billiard table in this vicinity, so you can avoid unpleasantness by reading your chart, then keeping an eye on your echo sounder in the confidence that at least nothing sudden will happen.

Approaching from Southampton, do not cut inside the 'spit pile' (*No. 2* east cardinal Q(3)10s 3M). There is a least depth of 0·8m between here and *Hamble Point* buoy, with over 2·5m for the 100m nearest the buoy, so time your turn accordingly.

Once inside the entrance, follow the channel, clearly marked with red and green piles (noting that *No. 6* (red) is marking a dogleg), as far as Warsash and Hamble Point Marina. Above here, although there are a number of lit navigational piles, you will do best by sticking to the centre of the river between the moorings. The density of the mooring piles suddenly thins out above Mercury Marina, and here it is important to identify *Crableck* beacon with its tide gauge, and give it a robust clearance to starboard. To the east of it the river shoals rapidly.

Now follow between the piles once more in a northeasterly direction past Crableck and Universal yards on your starboard hand. At the head of this reach, take care to keep the red pile to port and the green to starboard as you swing to port towards Bursledon. After making the turn you will see two sets of trots ahead. Pass between these and the marina, then follow the centre of the river up to the Jolly Sailor and the Elephant Boatyard pontoons on your port hand.

Bursledon Bridge is the effective head of navigation of sailing craft, though if your air draught enables you to pass under its 4m height you will also clear the railway and motorway bridges immediately upstream of it. You then enter a different world, where fields and woodland hold sway, and the water off the Horse and Jockey at Curbridge may float the shoalest of craft for long enough to permit a swift lunch-time session on a brewer's (in this case, spring) tide.

The River Hamble entrance.

By night, enter the river on the 345° transit of *No. 6* pile (Oc(2)R.12s4m2M) and *Hamble* beacon ashore behind it (Q.R.12m). Before you arrive at *No. 6* pile, bring on the second leading lights (Q.G and Iso.G.6s) on 026°. These are not so easy to spot amongst the shore lights. Do not lose heart, however; when they are nearly 'on' they become clear enough. Once inside the river, look out for moored craft and follow the various red and green lights implicitly. If you are proposing to venture north of Port Hamble, moonlight and caution are strongly recommended if you have not seen the river in daylight.

Berthing

Anchoring in the river is impractical except for shoal-draught craft prepared to dry out beyond the fairway.

For the harbourmaster's visitors' berths apply to his launch, or call him at Warsash on VHF Ch 68, or ☎ 01489 576387. Visitors may land at his pontoon in front of the Rising Sun at Warsash for advice, or at the public landing at Hamble, which is administered in a similar way to the pontoon at Warsash. You may be directed to the mid-stream pontoons, clearly marked 'visitors', in deep water just upstream of the harbourmaster's pontoon. Further upstream, just above Port Hamble, are more well marked visitors' piles (Nos 9–16), with 2·0m LAT. These are comparatively convenient for Hamble village.

It is also sometimes possible to find a berth at The Elephant Boatyard or at Universal Shipyard, on the east bank above Crableck, both by arrangement.

Marinas

Much of the Hamble River berthing is now given over to large marinas which offer the usual facilities. All maintain a number of visitors' berths and monitor VHF Ch 80.

Hamble Point Marina Some depth restrictions here for deeper-draught vessels. If in doubt, check with berthing master. Not the easiest marina for the visiting yachtsman anxious to sample the fleshpots but unwilling to take a cab.

Port Hamble Deep water. Well situated for Hamble village.

Mercury Yacht Harbour Quiet marina a considerable distance from the village.

Swanwick Marina Large marina attached to Moody's Yard. Launderette. Direct access to railway and to the main A27 Road. A very short dinghy trip to The Jolly Sailor pub on the waterfront at Old Bursledon. If you don't want to launch your boat, you can walk round in about 20 minutes.

Facilities

All possible facilities are available around the river. Numerous repair yards, some with travel-hoists capable of lifting maxis. Most marinas support chandlery shops. Fuel at various obvious sites, fresh water from marinas or harbourmaster's pontoon. Customs office at Port Hamble. Warsash Nautical Bookshop, one of the nation's finest, is sited up the hill by the crossroads, 10 minutes' walk from the Public Hard. Pubs in Warsash are disappointing, though the Rising Sun can be a godsend to the mariner who, having dried out his yacht on the piles

RIVER HAMBLE
Depths in Metres

N

BURSLEDON
Elephant Boatyard

Stn
Bursledon Br. (4·0m.)
Swanwick Marina
Boatyard
Jolly Sailor Hard
Public Hard
Bn
Fl.R.2s
Fl G 2s
Shipyard
Fl.R 2s
Badnam Creek
Outfall Bns
Badnam Bn
Crableck Bn
Fl.G.2s
Tide Gauge
Mercury Yacht Harbour
Piles
Piles
Fl.R 2s
Bn
Piles
Fl.G 2s
Port Hamble Marina
Piles
R.A.F. Y.C.
R.Southern Y.C.
Tide gauge
Fl.G.2s
HAMBLE
Bn
Hard
F.R
F R
RED ROOF
Hamble S.C.
Hard
Hard
Bn R
Tanks
Fl.R 2s
Tr + FS
Sailing Club Bn
Iso.G.6s
Warsash S.C.
WARSASH
Hamble Point Marina
Hamble Bn
Q.R.
Cougar Marine
2F.R (vert)
Warsash Shore Bn
Q.G.
2 F.G.
Shell Mex Jetty
No.10
Fl(2)R.5s
Warsash Jetty
Mud
HAMBLE SPIT
No.8
Fl.R.3s
Tide Gauge
No.9
Fl(2)G.5s
Newtown
School of Navigation
Cathead
(Mar.-Oct)
Oc.(2)R.12s
No.6
No.7
Fl.G.3s
Southampton Water
No.5
Fl(3)G.10s
No.4
Q.R
No.3
Fl(2)G.5s
Esso Marine Terminal
No.2
Q(3)10s
No.1
Fl.G.3s
Warsash Bn
Or.
Mud
Hamble Point
Q.(6)+L.Fl.15s
Lts F R

Note - Lights
Certain mooring piles on the E side
of the main fairway carry Q.G. lights
while others, on the W side carry Q.R.
lights. Many of the jetties and pontoons
are marked by 2 F. lights, displayed
vertically, green on the E side, red on
the W side.

345°
026°

1.18′W

at Warsash Public Hard, discovers himself faint from his labours. Hamble, on the other hand, is well supplied. Go right up the street past the square to find the White Hart. The King and Queen halfway up the High Street has a launderette in the basement especially for yachtsmen.

At Bursledon, the famous Jolly Sailor sells excellent beer and good pub food. Eat on the terrace when you can.

Scrubbing berths on piles at Warsash Public Hard below the Rising Sun Inn. Also at Land's End Hard opposite Swanwick Marina and at Mercury. Launching ramps at Warsash Public Hard, Hamble Public Hard, Swanwick Shore Public Hard, and Land's End Hard (no car park) at Bursledon.

Banks at Warsash and Hamble.

The Royal Southern Yacht Club, RAF Yacht Club, Hamble River Sailing Club and Warsash Sailing Club are all based in the river.

Communications

The Hamble River is not notably well served by public transport, but it is by no means cut off. Buses run from Hamble, Warsash and Swanwick. There is a railway station at Bursledon, with trains to Southampton or Portsmouth. Hamble Station (same line as Bursledon) is a cab ride from the village or the marinas.

Southampton

Tides
Double HW
First HW springs approx −0013 Dover
Stand halfway up the flood (the 'young flood stand') beginning at approximately LW +1½ hours and ending at approximately LW +3 hours.

MHWS	MLWS	MHWN	MLWN
4·5m	0·5m	3·7m	1·8m

Depths
Southampton Water main fairway is dredged to 10m.

The River Itchen has 6m or more as far as Ocean Village, then shoals to a minimum of 2m (LAT) up to Shamrock Quay.

There is at least 2·5m up to and inside Town Quay Marina, with greater depths on the Town Quay Pier itself.

Apart from shoaling areas on its southern bank, and the well marked shoal off Marchwood, the River Test is dredged to 10·2m as far as the swinging ground at the top end of the container berths. Above this point the river shoals rapidly and dries up to Eling Channel and the well sheltered Eling Basin.

General
Southampton lies at the head of the 6-mile-long Southampton Water. The port could be said to have been founded by the Roman Emperor Vespasian in AD50, when he ordered a fortified settlement on the River Itchen. After Rome fell, the town pursued the usual track of prosperity followed by minor sackings until the French did a thorough job on the place in 1338. Some say that this deplorable event occurred while the inhabitants were in church instead of watching their backs. The Pilgrim Fathers sailed from here aboard the *Mayflower* in 1620. The great ocean liners saw their finest hours along Southampton's wharves, and in 1944 over 3 million troops were embarked for the Normandy landings.

So long as there has been popular yachting, Southampton has been a centre for local enthusiasts, but only in recent years has this great port really opened up for visitors. It now boasts four major marinas, providing excellent shelter, all-tide access and full though varying facilities.

The city of Southampton, like many other ports, lost much of its innate character to the bombing in World War II, but the local watermen were not blitzed out and the essential spirit of the place lives on in the yards and creeks of the Test and Itchen. There is literally nothing that you cannot have done for your boat in this buzzing hive of seafaring.

Approaches
At all times, yachts navigating within the Port of Southampton, which includes Southampton Water and its approaches, should be aware of the priority

Port Signal and Radar Station at the division of Southampton Water. River Test to left, Itchen to right.

given to any commercial traffic. Whenever possible, it is good policy to operate in the mainly navigable waters outside the buoyed shipping channels. Pay particular note to the manoeuvring requirements of large vessels approaching Southampton from the east and leaving the Bramble Bank in mid-Solent to starboard. The need to keep very well clear of these ships in the area between *Prince Consort* north cardinal buoy (off Cowes) and Calshot cannot be overstated. Do not insist on your right of way under sail. Under local bylaws you do not have any.

Traffic is controlled by Vessel Traffic Services (*VTS*, VHF Ch 12). They will be pleased to help with any problems you may experience in general navigation of Southampton Harbour. Look out for their blue harbour launches with a yellow strip across the bows (blue light at night). If you are manoeuvring too close to a ship, you may receive a visit from a harbour launch, which will invite you to clear the way.

Southampton Water is entered between *Calshot Spit* light float (Fl.5s) and *Calshot* north cardinal (VQ) bell buoy. Note Calshot Castle and its conspicuous radar tower.

Running up Southampton Water there are good depths available on both sides of the dredged fairway as far as Western Shelf. Above the two conspicuous beacons 6 cables northwest of Hamble bunkering jetty the northeast shore is generally shoal, but this presents no difficulties to the navigator because a series of green buoys is established in the vicinity of the 5m contour, outside the main channel. If you are on this side of the fairway, care is needed as you approach *Western Shelf* (Fl(3)G.15s) and *No. 1* (Oc.G.4s) buoys. Shoal water extends much closer to these than to the green main channel buoys lower down Southampton Water.

Entrance

River Itchen

The Itchen is clearly marked. Enter between the conspicuous Port Signal and Radar Station, at the junction of the two channels, and the *Swinging Ground No. 1* green buoy (Oc.G.4s). Now keep the docks (steep-to) to port and the series of large lit green beacons to starboard. Ocean Village Marina is opposite *No. 4* beacon (Q.G) and is clearly identified by its new, red-roofed 'developer houses'.

Above Ocean Village, favour the east side of the river until you have passed under the Itchen Bridge (height 24·4m), then swing back to the middle, leaving the green *Chapel* beacon (Fl.G.3s) to starboard.

The east bank is now shoal, but presents no problems if you keep to the west of the numerous mid-stream moorings. The wharves on the west side are mainly steep-to until you reach Shamrock Quay Marina opposite *No. 5* pile (Fl.G.3s). Above Shamrock Quay depths continue in the region of 2m to Northam Bridge (height 4·7m), which may be regarded as the head of normal yacht navigation.

River Test

Leave the Port Signal and Radar Station to starboard, then steer about 325°, keeping the dock walls to starboard and the large red navigation buoys to port.

Pass Town Quay (white building complex with grey roofs) and Royal Pier (Red Funnel Terminal for Isle of Wight car ferries) on your starboard hand. The main channel continues with plenty of water up to the head of the container berths.

If you are proceeding to Marchwood Basin, enter Marchwood Channel between *No. 2* red buoy (Oc.R.4s) and *Crackmore* buoy (Oc.R.8s). Steer towards a daymark triangle on a dolphin (labelled 'Marchwood YC') on 298°. This mark used to be the front mark of a transit, but at the time of going to print (early 1997) the rear mark was disestablished. The depth on this bearing is 2·4m to within half a cable of the dolphin. Close to starboard is a shoal. On the port hand, the water shoals almost as far as Husband's Jetty, after which it deepens to at least 2m for 3 cables. Observing a north cardinal buoy (Q) close southwest of *No. 2* buoy will keep you in the channel.

Moorings abound hereabouts. Note the shoal water in the Marchwood Channel from about ½ cable southeast of the first beacon nearly as far as the rear beacon; both beacons should be left close to port. There are many small-craft moorings in the area, in depths of 0·5m to 0·9m. Immediately after passing the rear beacon a vessel is back in the deep water of the main channel, dredged to 10·2m. This now leads past the container berths and Swinging Ground.

The Eling Channel, which is very narrow and dries out, is entered close south of the northwest *Swinging Ground* (Eling) buoy. It is marked by beacons with triangle topmarks on the starboard hand, except at the junction with the Redbridge Channel, which is marked by a south cardinal beacon. Near the entrance of Eling Channel there are two port-hand beacons, south of which are small-craft moorings in 0·3m. Power cables cross the channel; height 36m.

SOUTHAMPTON WATER

N

Bursledon

Swanwick Marina

R. Itchen

Silos

No. 1
Oc.G.4s

Hythe
Knock
Fl.R.3s

Weston
Shelf
Fl(3)G.15s

Netley

Moorhead

Hovercraft
Testing
Area

NW
Netley
Fl.G.7s

Deans
Elbow
Oc.R.4s

MOD
Moorings

Netley
Fl.G.3s

Southampton
Water

Hythe
Marina
Village

Hythe Pier

Red
Lts

Hythe

Hound
Fl(3)G.10s

Lains
Lake
Fl(2)R.4s

Deans
Lake

After
Barn

Lts
Fl.2s

LFl.Y.5M

Mercury
Yacht
Harbour

Port
Hamble

Hamble

Hamble Point
Marina

Warsash

Newtown

Greenland
IQ.G.10s

Cadland
Fl.R.3s

BP
Hamble
Terminal

Hamble
Pt

Hamble
Pt
Oc(2)R

Q.R

River Hamble

Esso
Terminal

Esso
Oil
Refinery

Fawley

Q(3)10s
Fl.G.3s

Hamble Pt
Q(6)+LFl.15s

Chilling

Fawley

Ashlett
Creek

Fawley
Power
Station

Q.R

Fl.G
Fl(2)R

Fl.R.3s

Bald Head
Q.G
Bell

Hook
Q.G
Bell

Calshot Reach

345

Corination
Fl.Y.5s

Reach

Castle
Tower
(34)

Black
Jack
Fl(2)R.4s

Reach
Fl(3)G.10s

Ch marked by
lit buoys

Q.R

Calshot

Castle
Pt
IQ.R.10s

North Channel

Calshot
VQ
Bell(1)30s

Outfall

Iso.R.10s5M
+4F.R
Horn 20s

Calshot
Spit
Fl.5s12m11M
Horn(2)

N Thorn
Q.G

E Knoll
G

Bourne Gap
Fl.R.3s

Thorn Reach

W Knoll
G

Bramble Bank

Thorn Knoll
Fl.G.5s

Bramble Bn
Restricted Area

W Bramble
VQ(9)10s
Bell

Stansore Pt

NE Gurnard
Fl(3)R.10s

Western Approach Channel

S Bramble
Fl.G.2·5s

Calshot

50°
48'
N

1°18' W

Approach to Hythe Marina Village. Lock gate shut.

River Itchen leading towards entrance to Ocean Village Marina just right of yacht under sail.

Anchorage and moorings

Because of the scale of the area, anchoring or mooring may be less than comfortable in all but the fairest weather. Nonetheless, it is possible to anchor in Southampton Water so long as one keeps clear of prohibited areas, moorings, fairways, docks and their approaches. Moorings may also be found and used by arrangement in a number of places.

Behind Calshot Castle Occasionally, a mooring may be available here. Good shelter from the southwest. If you anchor, use a tripping line.

Hythe Large yachts can anchor south of Hythe pier. Smaller craft apply at the yacht yard or club for moorings. (Yacht yard, shops, banks, fuel, etc. Early closing Wednesday. Ferry to Southampton from Hythe Pier.)

Southampton Off Royal Pier are one or two Harbour Board moorings for large yachts.

Marchwood Moorings south of Marchwood Channel. Enquire at Husband's Yard or the hospitable Marchwood Yacht Club (fuel and water at shipyard jetty. Launch service to Southampton Town Quay).

Eling Channel Anchorage possible just outside the container-ship swinging ground at neaps.

River Itchen A few Harbour Board large yacht moorings. It is possible to anchor on the east side of the river, out of the fairway, giving due care to the depth of water.

Entrance to Ocean Village Marina from River Itchen. Signals: RRR – Stop; GGW – Free flow.

Netley Anchorage in calm weather only, or offshore (northeast) winds.

Marinas

By far the most usual way to visit Southampton is to make use of one of its excellent marinas.

Town Quay Marina Town Quay Marina will be found, after Ocean Dock, by leaving the end of the Quay itself (F.Y) to port. You will now see a wave breaker ahead, with an overlapping entrance near its eastern end.

The marina is relatively small, but visitors are welcome and the place is certainly convenient for Southampton city centre and all its facilities. You can phone to reserve a berth (☎ 01703 234397) or try Ch 80, but except at peak times you will often be lucky if you just turn up. Yachts over 15m, or 2·5m

Shamrock Quay on west bank of Itchen River.

draught, should definitely make contact first, however. Town Quay has showers, toilet, launderette and 24-hour security.

Hythe Marina Village This is entered via a short, straight channel, dredged to 2m and well marked by red and green piles. The outer beacon, to be left to starboard, is an east cardinal (Q(3)10s), while on your port hand is a beacon with a red ■ topmark. Like Ocean Village, Hythe Marina Village is made conspicuous by the characteristic nature of its architecture. Visitors are welcome, and can lock in at any state of the tide into a dredged basin with control depth of 2·5m. Call on VHF Ch 80, or ☎ 01703 207073, especially if your boat is over 16m LOA.

Fuel, water, electricity, showers, toilets, launderette, etc. Also restaurant and on-site pub. Hythe is close by, with further excellent facilities, as well as the regular ferry service to Southampton Town Quay.

The lock works 24 hours a day. It exhibits 2F.R lights to port and 2F.G to starboard. Note the following traffic signals at the control tower:

3 fixed red – wait
3 flashing red – all traffic stop
3 fixed green – go ahead
2 fixed green over one white – free flow in the lock (around HW except dead neaps).

There is a useful waiting pontoon (2F.R at outer end) outside the lock which is linked to the shore.

Ocean Village Marina

Conspicuous by its houses and its large sign. Ocean Village Marina welcomes visitors, but try to book ahead at peak times as it gets very busy (VHF Ch 80 or ☎ 01703 229385). Toilets and showers, plus the Royal Southampton Yacht Club. Convenient for city centre, well sheltered and excellently staffed by people who care about you and your boat. Note the traffic lights on the northern approach wall: 3F.R – all stop, 2 greens over a white – free flow.

Shamrock Quay

Named after *Shamrock V*, one of the Lipton *America*'s Cup challengers built by Camper and Nicholson's, whose yard this once was, Shamrock Quay has every repair facility. Major yachts are still refitted here, as are small ones and everything in between. Visitors' berths are available, but if the tide is running dock with the greatest care if you are allotted an inside berth. The streams can be vicious, particularly on the spring ebb. Good chandlery and toilets, showers and laundry. Excellent 'transport-style' café, the Yellow Welly. If the on-site pub doesn't suit your taste, walk a hundred yards outside the gate to fetch the Cooper's Arms, a fine traditional dock-side watering hole. Central Southampton is a cab-ride away.

Fuel

Diesel is available from mobile barges in the Southampton area. Notable amongst these is 'Mr Diesel'. Call him on VHF Ch 8 and he will come alongside in the best-handled small tugboat in the south. A charming man, with fuel at the right price.

Launching sites

- Foreshore north of Hythe pier
- Ramp at head of Ashlett Creek, south of oil refineries
- Hard on north shore of Eling Creek
- Itchen River: at Woolston hard on east side, or at either marina
- Public hard, Netley

Yacht clubs

Royal Southampton Yacht Club, Southampton Sailing Club, Eling Sailing Club, Weston Sailing Club, Hythe Sailing Club, Marchwood Yacht Club, Esso Sailing Club, Netley Cliff Sailing Club.

Communications

Car ferries or fast catamaran to Cowes, Isle of Wight.

Main line trains to Waterloo and the West (70 minutes to London).

The Beaulieu River

Tides

Double HW. First HW springs at entrance approximately −0030 Dover

Range

MHWS	MLWS	MHWN	MLWN
3·7m	0·6m	3·1m	1·6m

Streams

There is a general slackening of the flood stream from 2 hours after LW lasting until about 4 hours after. This is more noticeable at springs, and is known as the 'young flood stand'. The usual mid-Solent HW stand is also experienced, and the ebb does not run hard until its final 3½ hours. All these effects are much gentler during neap tides.

Depths

The Beaulieu River has a bar on which the depth varies from year to year, but 0·9m at LAT is a good assumption, always bearing in mind that prolonged winds from the north or east can depress Solent tidal heights. Allow generous clearance two hours either side of LW if the wind is blowing in. Inside, a least depth of 1·8m will be found as far as Buckler's Hard, except for a 1·2m patch opposite a small boathouse 3 cables downstream of the marina. Navigable water exists up to Beaulieu at HW, but drying heights of up to 2·6m may be found in the upper reaches, outside the stream bed.

General

The Beaulieu River runs up into the New Forest and is undoubtedly the most beautiful harbour on the mainland side of the Solent. Anchoring inside Gull Island on a moonlit night offers an intimacy with nature not easy to discover in these crowded waters. Above Gins Farm oak woods close in, from which ships of Nelson's navy were built, many of them at the upstream village of Buckler's Hard. The whole river, including its bed, is owned by Lord Montagu, whose careful custody has made it pay while avoiding any hint of over-exploitation.

Approach and entrance

The old passage across the bar is marked by the transit of two orange lattice boards in line on 341°. The front one has a triangular top and is sited on the first port-hand pile (*No. 2*) inside the entrance dolphin. The rear board, which has a vertical black bar in its centre, is sited high in the pine trees on the low cliff to the north of the river. At the time of writing, as for some years prior to this, the deepest water lies on the transit of the left hand side of Lepe House and R pile No. 2. There are no surprises here, with the bottom shoaling fairly smoothly.

Approaching from the east, keep the three red beacons (Q.R) off Stansore Point to starboard, then steer about WSW until in the vicinity of a yellow spherical racing buoy which lies conveniently to the east of the transit before turning in to the mouth of

Entrance to Beaulieu River. Note dolphin 'bar' beacon and dogleg course around Beaulieu Spit. Shoals off Stone Point in the foreground.

the river. If the buoy, which is seasonal, is not there, make your turn well before the transit closes, bringing the bathing huts on Gurnard (IOW) beach right aft. The shallowest part of the bar lies in the area up to 2 cables to seaward of the RW dolphin. Thereafter, if you have succeeded in getting this far without touching, you will float up to Buckler's Hard, unless you are proceeding very slowly against the last of a strong ebb.

From the west, keep well off the mudbanks of Beaulieu Spit and Warren Flat. You will recognise the entrance by the conspicuous white boathouse and a cottage, also picked out in white, at the west end of a row of old coastguard houses. As when coming from the east, place yourself east of the transit before turning in. At night, keep the dolphin (Fl.R.5s3M) bearing about 315° until you are in the entrance.

Once in the river, proceed between the red and green beacons until they run out above Needs Ore Point. Thereafter, the channel is marked by withies which stand at or near the low water mark. The moorings make the channel easy to spot, but a first-time entry at night requires plenty of moon and the greatest caution if you are not to suffer an expensive collision with a moored yacht. After dark, the lit piles provide an adequate safe passage as far as the first moorings; all the piles carry reflectors. There-after you are on your own, except for a lit green pile marking a mudbank opposite the marina.

Take note of the shoals charted on the north side of the long 'sea reach'. They have temporarily stopped many a homeward bounder creeping into the river near the bottom of the tide.

Berthing

Anchoring is welcomed in the lower reaches below Needs Ore. Small yachts can bring up in the bight formed by the causeway linking Gull Island to the mainland, otherwise anchor on the south side of the channel. Holding is good in mud, with fine shelter in westerly weather. You will lie safely enough in an easterly, but strong winds from this quarter can bring in a scend which disagrees with a spring ebb. Anchoring elsewhere is impractical for all but the smallest yacht because of the danger of foul-berthing moored craft.

The river is well stocked with harbour moorings, both above and below Buckler's Hard, which are let to berth holders. Any suitable buoy can be picked up, given the usual regard to courtesies if the owner should return. Visitors' berths off the village are between piles. When these are full, a further group of trots is available just above the marina. The marina itself welcomes visitors when berths are clear, and vessels of up to 23m (75ft) can be accom-modated. Whoever you are and wherever you berth, the harbour staff will come to direct you and to gather dues. The harbourmaster does not monitor any public radio channel.

Facilities

Beaulieu may not be cheap, but its facilities are top class. Water and fuel, telephone, excellent showers and a launderette are available at the yacht harbour, with the Agamemnon Boatyard and Chandlery close by. Buckler's Hard Garage offers excellent outboard repair facilities, open seven days a week in summer.

There is a scrubbing pad at Buckler's Hard capable of floating boats up to 2m draught at MHWS. There is also a launching site with a communal car park.

The Royal Southampton YC maintains a station at Gins Farm, welcoming members of affiliated clubs when open.

Customs visit regularly. There are excellent walks from the marina up to Beaulieu, where the National Motor Museum is situated. Buckler's Hard has a useful licensed village store, open daily in season, and the Master Builder's House provides both public bar and restaurant services. Taxis are available, but otherwise public transport is poor, with Beaulieu Road and Brockenhurst rail stations six miles distant.

Newtown River

Tides

Double HW. First HW springs approximately −0030 Dover

Range

MHWS	MLWS	MHWN	MLWN
3·4m	0·5m	2·8m	1·5m

Streams

7 hours flood tide. Approximately 2-hour stand at HW. A vigorous ebb for the remainder of the period.

Depths

1·5m LAT on the bar. Deep water in entrance. Up to 2·5m on visitors' moorings in Newtown River, depending upon swing. 1·8m anchoring depths at lower end of Clamerkin Lake.

Newtown River with Shalfleet Quay in clear view. The dozen or so yachts immediately inside the entrance are on visitors' moorings.

General

The uninformed visitor to Newtown River would never for a moment imagine the depth and length of its history. Said to date back to Roman times, the port of Newtown was sufficiently prosperous in 1001 to warrant sacking by Vikings. By the mid-14th century the borough was assessed at twice the value of Newport, and in 1377 the French took full advantage by helping themselves to its riches, leaving the town in flames.

Now, overgrown tracks are all that remain of busy streets, and nature with her oak woods and saltings reigns unchallenged. Over 150 species of bird pass here as the year turns, including rare little terns and migrant ospreys.

Newtown River is owned and administered by the National Trust. A visit out of season reveals a paradise for those who love the wild foreshore. On summer weekends, you may occasionally find your patience stretched by the proximity of your fellow-humans.

Approach and entrance

The entrance to Newtown River is narrow and not conspicuous from seaward. Coming in from the west, however, if you look carefully east-southeast from the green conical *Hamstead Ledge* buoy you should make out its buoys and leading marks. From the east, keep roughly on a line joining the green buoys *Salt Mead* and *Hamstead Ledge* until the Rowridge TV mast bears about 150°. This mast is the closer of the two you may see well inshore on the Island. Look below it with your binoculars and you will discern the entry marks.

There is shoal water on both sides of the approach, but if you keep to the excellent leading marks (a white and black circular 'target' kept snug in the 'V' of the 'Y'-shaped marker in front of it) on 130° you will find a least depth of 1·5m LAT. The transit will carry you close to a small red spherical buoy, difficult to spot from the offing. This must be left to port unless there is a suitable rise of tide. Continue down the transit until you have left a small green buoy with a green pile alongside it to starboard, then steer straight through the middle of the entrance. This is scoured out by the strong stream to a considerable depth. To starboard the shingle bank is steep-to with mud beyond. To port, Fishhouse Point also shoals rapidly.

Once inside, note carefully the colour and rough-hewn topmarks of the many withies. It is easy to go astray, particularly as the weather can do away with the colours on the woodwork. It is therefore important to familiarise yourself with the lie of the water before entering.

The channel's first swing is to port. Do not make the turn into Clamerkin Lake too soon; or if you are proceeding towards Shalfleet, watch out for the drying bank to starboard. Once these dangers have been negotiated, a careful eye on marks, moorings and echo sounder will reveal the rest.

Anchorage and moorings

Any vacant mooring that appears to be of suitable size may be picked up by a visitor. The large white buoys in the main run-up towards Shalfleet Creek, as well as those inside Clamerkin Lake, are official. All others are private, but this need not mean they are unavailable. The berthing master will advise.

Now that most of the best water is taken up with moorings, the principal anchorages are to be found in Clamerkin Lake. You can lie in 1·8m LAT between the entrance and the first moorings. Subject to tide and swinging room, it is also possible to find a snug berth between the moorings and the oyster beds further up. These latter are clearly marked and must on no account be disturbed.

Holding ground is good in mud, and the whole complex of creeks is well sheltered, save for the outer regions, which become uncomfortable in strong northerlies. If the anchorage is crowded, the weather unsettled and spring tides upon you, be ready to take the Newtown Pyjama Party in jovial spirit...

Landing

Newtown Quay (tidal) gives access to the ancient town hall and numerous fine walks. Shalfleet Quay is found at the boatyard in the creek of the same name. The yard is served by an unmetalled lane leading to the village, about 10 minutes' walk away. Do not land on the spit leading to Fish House Point (April to September). It is a bird sanctuary.

Facilities

Water from tap at the south end of the footbridge by Newtown Quay; also at Lower Hamstead Farm. Fuel from Shalfleet Service Station, just to the east of the village on the main road. Provisions from Eddy's Farm Shop at Shalfleet (up lane beside church and left turn at Warlands Lane) – closed Sunday pm, Wednesday pm and every lunchtime. Excellent seafood and good beer at the New Inn, Shalfleet, but organise your run ashore so that if your dinghy is going to dry out, you have another pint or two as it re-floats.

Yarmouth Harbour

Tides

Long stand at HW. First HW springs approximately −0050 Dover

Range

MHWS	MLWS	MHWN	MLWN
3·1m	0·8m	2·5m	1·5m

Streams

Streams in the harbour run with the state of tide, and this must be borne in mind when manoeuvring. Pay particular attention to the spring ebb in the vicinity of the entrance.

Depths

The harbour is dredged to 2m below chart datum from the entrance to the bridge, though draughts in excess of this figure can be accommodated in places. There is a minimum of 2m in the entrance, and more on the transit in the approach.

General

Yarmouth is an extremely useful passage port, lying as it does immediately inside the tide-swept Needles Channel. It is also a favoured destination for many of the numerous yachts enjoying the sheltered Solent scene. It is well equipped with convivial hostelries, pretty, and snugly sheltered from all but northeasterly weather.

The town is a car ferry port for the Isle of Wight, but this has not spoiled its atmosphere. Indeed, the bustle it lends to the summer months adds to the fun of what can be a very busy little harbour. Do not be disappointed to be turned away if you arrive in late afternoon during a holiday weekend. Berthing is plentiful, but not endless which, alas, sometimes seems to be the condition of the stream of yachts.

Approach and entrance

Yarmouth is easy to spot from seaward. By day its pier and church tower are unmistakable, while by night the lights of the town, the ferry dock, and specifically the 2F.R lights on the end of the pier, show the way. Approaching from the west, keep outside the only danger, Black Rock, with its unlit G buoy. If you are arriving from east of the pier, look out for the large, unlit mooring buoys which, fortunately, are clearly charted. In the more immediate offing is a further mooring buoy lit Fl.Y, but whose light is readily missed.

Tides run very hard in the Solent outside Yarmouth, so care is needed not to become disorientated, particularly on night approaches.

Yarmouth entrance lies immediately west of the pier. Note the leading marks on 187° (white diamonds with two horizontal black lines, each with F.G light). These are not always clear on a first entry. If you are unable to discern them, keep ½ cable or so west of the pier head and steer in towards the centre of the entrance on about 185°.

Yarmouth Harbour. Road bridge on extreme right-hand side.
Ferry moored at terminal. Visitors' moorings this side of pier
head. More visitors inside.

There you will see a dolphin (Fl.G.5s1M) on the end of the breakwater. On the port hand is the short ferry jetty (2F.R at end). Immediately inside this are public steps (for landing only – no dinghies to be left here) used by the water taxi. The steps are followed by the Town Quay wall, against which yachts may lie. Note the tide gauges on Town Quay and on pile *A1*. These indicate the height of tide above chart datum. In the entrance, beware of the wash from ferry propellers which may turn constantly, even when the ship is loading.

Once clear of the dolphin, bear to starboard towards the rows of mooring piles, unless you are intending to berth on the Town Quay. The piles can present a bewildering spectacle to the inexperienced, but the harbourmaster or his staff are usually on hand in a dory to direct visitors to a berth. Be aware that Yarmouth is an important lifeboat station, and take care not to berth so as to impede the boat.

Do not even consider sailing into Yarmouth in any but the smallest and handiest of yachts. There is no room to manoeuvre under canvas.

If the harbour is full, a red flag is flown at the pier head, and an illuminated board is shown at the entrance, bearing the dismal legend, 'Harbour Full'.

At night, after the 2F.R on the end of Yarmouth pier, where an additional high intensity F.W is shown in fog, look for the green light on the dolphin and the 2F.R on the car ferry terminal. When this latter is abeam, you can begin swinging to starboard. Note that the jetty on the east side of the ferry terminal carries F.R.4m2M and an additional high intensity F.Y in fog. The entrance is brightly lit by the arc lights from the terminal, which helps a lot, but always remember the cross set in the offing. After dark, it can be especially deceptive.

Berthing

First come, first served. The harbourmaster does not keep a VHF watch, but vessels over 15m LOA or 2·4m draught should telephone before arrival (☎ 01983 760321).

Berth between piles (all numbered and lettered), as directed by the harbourmaster. Raft up as necessary, always leaving room in the 'fairways' between the trots. Berthing is also possible alongside the Town Quay, which is dredged for its entire length as an emergency ferry berth, but in northeasterly winds this can become uncomfortable. The road bridge to the upper Yar opens, but visitors are not allowed above it.

When the harbour is full, you may pick up one of the twelve visitors' moorings laid on the 3m contour outside the breakwater. Here, rafting is not permitted owing to the surge and occasional wash from shipping. A riding light is a sensible precaution.

Anchorage for deep-draught yachts is possible to seaward of the visitors' moorings, but it is an uncomfortable berth in all but the fairest weather. Inside the moorings, depths shoal rapidly.

Facilities

Three yacht yards, including Harold Hayles, who have a slipway, an engineer, and where most jobs can be undertaken. The harbourmaster maintains a DIY 5-ton crane on the South Quay. His staff will assist visitors to lift their yachts at £1 per foot, and will hire them a pressure washer for a further £10. Many yachts of up to 9·7m (32ft) fall within the weight limit and can make use of this unusual facility.

First-class showers with launderette on the South Quay.

Excellent chandlery in the town square. First-class pubs, a good hotel and the finest puff pastry in the West at The Wheatsheaf (reported 1993). Provisions from various sources. EC Wednesday. Fuel and water on South Quay. Water only on Town Quay. Launching from slips at quay or from ferry slip by arrangement with the harbourmaster. Water taxi. Royal Solent YC. Buses to Newport.

Lymington

Tides

Double HW at springs, otherwise a long HW stand
HW approx Dover −0045 springs, +0010 neaps

MHWS	MLWS	MHWN	MLWN
3·0m	0·7m	2·6m	1·4m

Depths

2·4m minimum at chart datum up to Lymington Yacht Haven. 2·2m minimum to Berthon's Lymington Marina. Thereafter, no less than 1·1m up to the Town Quay, which has alongside depth of 1·5m.

General

Lymington is an attractive town on the edge of the New Forest. Its 1½-mile river is dominated by frequent car ferries to Yarmouth, operating from the railhead on the east bank, and by two of the largest marinas in the Solent area, on the west bank. It boasts a comprehensive back-up for yachts and powerboats: designers, electronic and marine engineers, sailmakers, builders and repair yards.

The river mouth is only 2½ miles from the Needles Channel, gateway to the open sea.

Approach

There are no dangers in the immediate vicinity of the Lymington River. Note, however, that shoal waters extend on both sides. From a distance the first landmark you will see, apart from the veritable forest of masts up-river, is the club starting platform. This takes the form of a shed on stilts, standing immediately to the east of the channel.

LYMINGTON

Yachts should keep clear of the ferry vessels
which have right of way in the narrow channel

Anchoring is prohibited in the river without
permission from the harbourmaster

N

Walhampton

Railway

Town Quay
45'5
Obstns

Railway
Pier
Station

Bampton Farm

Elmers Court
Country Park

Lisle Court

Car Ferry
Terminal

Lymington
Marina

LYMINGTON

Fortuna
Pontoon

F.R.17m8M

2F.R(vert)

Pier Pile
No13

Landing
Stage

Horn
Reach

Royal
Lymington Y.C.

Public Pontoon

Marsh

Waterford

Lymington
Town S.C.

F.R.12m8M

No.11
G. Fl.G.2s

Short Reach

Nash Pt

Wk

Harper's
Post
BYB

2F.G(vert)
2LdgF.Y.

Harper's
Post S

No.10
R

Cage Boom
Fl.G.2s
BW
2DirF

Pyewell Lake
craft moorings

50°45'N

Cocked Hat
Fl.R.2s

BW

Enticott
Fl.G.2s

Lymington Yacht
Haven
(dredged to 2·4m)

Bag of
Halfpence
R

Marshes

Leading Lts 007·30

187·30

Pylewell Boom

Awash at
HW Springs

Marsh

Seymours
Post
Fl.R.2s
R

Tar Barrel
Fl.G.2s

RW

Cutters Lake

RW
2DirF

No 7
Fl.G.2s
GNB

No 5
G

Eight Acre Pond

44'5

No 6
R

Long Reach

Small Craft Moorings

Lymington River

Lower West Lake

Awash at
HW Springs

Marsh

Yacht starting
platform

No.4
Fl.R.2s
R

No 1
Fl.G.2s
G

No 3
Fl.G.2s
G

No 2
Cross Boom
Fl.R.2s
R

Oxey Marsh

Jack in the Basket
Fl.R.2s
R

Oxey Lake

Bn

32'

1°31'W

Depths in Metres

On closer approach, identify the red *Jack in the Basket* beacon (Fl.R.2s9m). This is highly conspicuous by virtue of its black 'basket' topmark. Its name, according to one source, comes from fishermen's wives leaving their hard-worked husbands' jack, or lunch, in a basket attached to the outer pile. I prefer the more robust explanation that malefactors were once immured in a cage on the pile as an alternative to the town stocks. There they could be pelted with fish offal, or other suitable reminders of their misdemeanours. Leave *Jack* to port, and pick up the 319° leading line. This is marked by two metal columns. Their F.R.8M lights are readily identifiable by night, but entry in daylight is simply a matter of following the prominent red and green beacons marking the channel from its seaward end between *No. 2* (Fl.R.2s) with a rectangular red topmark and *No. 1* (Fl.G.2s) with a triangular green topmark. Do not confuse the latter with the nearby starting platform.

Half a mile upstream, with the green *Tar Barrel* beacon (Fl.G.2s) abeam, alter to starboard to 007° and pick up the black and white leading marks (DirF) for inward-bound ferries at the end of the next short reach. When departing, the corresponding red and white leading marks (DirF) on 187° are in the mud-flats south of the red *Seymour's Post* beacon (Fl.R.2s).

At *No. 10* red beacon, opposite the green *No. 9 Cage Boom* mark (Fl.G.2s), the fairway swings to the left, facing the clearly marked entrance to Lymington Yacht Haven on a heading of about 282°.

From the east cardinal *Harper's Post* beacon (Q(3)10s), carry on past the prominent Royal Lymington Yacht Club (with its own landing and pontoon berths) towards the ferry terminal, leaving the Lymington Marina and Berthon yard to port. In addition to all the pontoons, there are pile berths opposite the marina fuel dock. These can be safely negotiated on either hand. Thereafter, the river shoals gradually as you approach the Town Quay.

At night, the dogleg in the outer river has led to many a moonlit tryst on the mud. Note that all the lit piles show similar light characteristics (Fl.R.2s or Fl.G.2s). Keep your wits about you to avoid an early end to your entry.

The speed limit is 6 knots, and the ferries have absolute right of way. There is nearly always room

Lymington. (A) Town Quay. (B) Berthon Boat Co. & Marina.
(C) Lymington Yacht Haven. (D) Royal Lymington YC.
(E) Ferry – ¾ inch to its left is the 'starting box'.

to give the ferries clear water and stay afloat yourself. Bear in mind, however, that at LW springs, the ferry's displacement wave may leave a deep-draught yacht temporarily embarrassed – fortunately in soft mud.

Berths and moorings

Anchoring anywhere in the river is prohibited.

The Harbour Commissioners have in their gift 200 berths, mostly up-river. Under favourable tidal conditions, boats drawing less than 2m should head for the Town Quay if marina prices fail to appeal. (At peak holiday periods it could well be full, even though it is permissible to lie six abreast on the pontoon.) Alternatively, the harbourmaster (☎ 01590 672014), who is usually on hand in his launch, may direct a visitor to a buoy. Not only is berthing at the Town Quay about half the price of the marinas, but you step off the boat into a cobbled lane between traditional waterfront cottages and shops leading straight to the High Street.

Be sure all the boats lying outside you are aware of your intended ETD well in advance.

Lymington Yacht Haven has 600 pontoon berths. Call Ch 80 or 37 (M), or ☎ 01590 677071. To enter, leave the east cardinal *Harper's Post* beacon close to starboard and an artificial breakwater to port. The leading transit is on 244°: by day two red triangles on poles, by night a F.Y on each. Follow the 'visitors' signs to C pontoon, near the fuelling point and marina office. Berthing here entitles one to access to the hospitable Lymington Town Sailing Club nearby.

Berthon's Lymington Marina is opposite the car ferry terminal and can handle boats of all sizes. Call on VHF Ch 80 or 37 (M), or ☎ 01590 673312.

Both marinas have full facilities.

Facilities

The Royal Lymington Yacht Club welcomes guests by invitation. Lymington Town Sailing Club is open to all bona fide yachtsmen. Both provide hospitality and views across the Solent of a high order.

Numerous pubs and restaurants to suit all tastes, nationalities and pockets. The Ship Inn, by the Town Quay, offers showers and man-sized breakfasts, in addition to other meals. The Railings Restaurant in Stanwell House Hotel rates two crossed knives and forks in the Michelin guide.

The High Street has all the shops, banks, etc. you would expect to find in a prosperous country town of 36,000 inhabitants. First-class market in the High Street on Saturdays.

Fuel and fresh water at both marinas. Fresh water only at the Town Quay, where a public scrubbing berth is situated.

Communications

The ferry to Yarmouth sails at regular intervals from early morning until late evening, depending upon the time of year.

Trains to Brockenhurst, where there are main line connections.

Keyhaven

Tides

Long stand at HW (double HW at springs)
First HW springs −0055 Dover
HW neaps +10m Dover

MHWS	MLWS	MHWN	MLWN
2·7m	0·7m	2·3m	1·4m

Depths

0·3m LAT in the shallowest part of the entrance, in the vicinity of the red buoy. 6m immediately inside the entrance, then just under 3m in the anchorage west of the main part of North Point. About 1·5m off Mount Lake. Thereafter the water shoals to 0·2m at the quay, with much of the creek drying outside the stream bed.

General

Keyhaven entrance is exposed to easterly winds, but in normal conditions the creek gives a pleasant though somewhat crowded haven for small craft.

Approach and entrance

Keyhaven lies on the north side of the Solent, 4 cables north-northwest of Hurst Point. On your approach, allow for strong tidal streams. These run southerly from −1hr to +5hr HW Dover, at a maximum of 2½ knots.

The entrance to Keyhaven lies at North Point, which is conspicuous, standing out as a low sand and shingle promontory against a background of mud-flats. There are two rather inconspicuous leading marks on the flats, each with a red and white vertical topmark. They form a transit of 283°. There are no lights.

Shape a course for a position something over a quarter of a mile northeast of the old pier near Hurst High Light, then pick up the leading marks. A little under a cable east of the entrance there is a small green buoy to be left to starboard, and a red buoy to port. Proceed from this pair to round a red port-hand buoy 15m north-northwest of North Point, after which you must leave the series of spherical green buoys to starboard, taking care to steer along the bows of the moored boats, the mooring buoys in a single line being in the deepest water.

The channel at first bears to the southwest, clearly marked by the starboard-hand buoys in the first reach, then continues around the bend to the northwest as far as Mount Lake. Above that, 3 cables short of Keyhaven where the channel turns northwards, there is a green spherical buoy at the end of Long Reach. The trend of the channel can be judged by the line of yachts on moorings in the centre or, further upstream where it is very shallow, by a double line of smaller craft.

Near HW it is possible to enter through Hawkers Lake, keeping close to the line of boat moorings.

Keyhaven entrance.

Keyhaven, looking eastwards out towards the Solent. (A) Hurst Point high light. (B) Watch hut. (C) North Point. (D) First of succession of green buoys.

Leading marks on 283°. Shown bold on photograph but normally inconspicuous. Topmarks may vary from year to year.

Anchorage

The only anchorage inside Keyhaven Lake lies between North Point and the first of the private moorings which occupy the whole river further up. Contact the river warden next to the yacht club (☎ 01590 645695) for temporary moorings.

Immediately outside Keyhaven, off the old pier near Hurst High Light, is an open roadstead which is sheltered in moderate SW–NE winds. The quietest water is found just S of the transit of Hurst High and Low Lights, 50yds or so off the beach. To the north of this the water soon begins to shoal. You may roll somewhat in disturbed conditions and a big tide, but you will be safe.

Facilities

Landing steps can be found at the end of Keyhaven Old Quay. There are others at New Quay, beyond the yacht club, but these are shallow at LWS. West Solent boat builders for repairs and laying-up services. There is a hard for scrubbing with 1·8m at MHWS.

Water, fuel and some chandlery from the boatyard. Hospitable Gun Inn at Keyhaven.

At Milford-on-Sea, 1 mile distant, are the usual facilities of a small seaside town. Early closing Wednesday.

Launching sites at Keyhaven hards with car park adjacent.

Yacht clubs: Hurst Castle Sailing Club on North Point; Keyhaven Yacht Club at the head of the lake is friendly (☎ 01590 642165).

Christchurch

Tides

HW springs −0210 Dover
HW neaps −0140 Dover

Entrance

MHWS	MLWS	MHWN	MLWN
1·8m	0·6m	1·4m	0·7m

Tuckton

MHWS	MLWS	MHWN	MLWN
1·7m	0·9m	1·3m	0·9m

Note that Christchurch has a double high water and that the heights predicted here relate to the highest rise. At neaps, the flood is a slow rise to second HW, which is the higher of the two. River water is a significant factor on depths inside, and the ebb stream can run up to 4½ knots at a high spring, particularly at the entrance.

Depths

0·1m on the bar, but this may be less in prolonged easterly winds. 2m off Mudeford Quay. The channel up to Christchurch varies greatly in depth, from 0·1m to 3m. Generally speaking, boats drawing up to 1·37m can creep in at HW springs, but only shoal-draught yachts drawing 1·12m or less can proceed up the harbour.

General

Christchurch Harbour is an interesting place to visit, if your draught permits. The town has many facilities, as well as being the home of a fine old priory with its surrounding gardens and ruins, and the environment of the harbour is surprisingly unspoilt, with salt marsh, reefs, dunes and woodland, and the river winding up to the confluence of the Stour and the Avon at Christchurch Quay.

Approach and entrance

Christchurch Harbour entrance lies about a mile north of the unmistakable promontory of Hengistbury Head. From the east, approach with the conspicuous priory tower well open to the right of Hengistbury on about 285° until, in steadily shoaling water, a series of small red and green entrance channel buoys appears ahead of you. It is impossible to be specific about these because their

Keyhaven. Hurst Point and, below, Christchurch harbour
entrance. Mudeford on left, looking out to sea.

position changes frequently, as do the direction and depths of the channel itself.

These buoys, and those inside the harbour, are maintained by the local fishermen's association, supported by a voluntary group representing all those concerned with navigating these waters.

Proceed across the bar and up the channel, keeping red buoys to port, green to starboard, until you enter the Run. This is 250m wide and is formed by Mudeford Quay on the north side and a shingle spit to the south. Do not be alarmed if the entrance buoys take you very close to the wall of the quay before you turn sharply to port. Tides run so strongly here that this is well scoured out and remains steep-to. The channel is unlit, save for 2F.G (vertical) on the seaward end of Mudeford Quay.

Christchurch approach from seaward. Initially course tends towards right-hand edge of Mudeford Haven Quay – channel is now buoyed.

Once inside the Run, turn to port and follow the sand spit (with a prominent black house and beach huts on it), leaving green buoys and some small boat moorings to starboard. Now follow the red and green buoys (reds to port, greens to starboard) as far

Christchurch. The Run with Hengistbury Head beyond. Yachts at anchor inside.

up as you wish to proceed, all the way to Christchurch if required. The plan indicates the general lie of the channel which, like the entrance, may be subject to shifting. Outside the buoys, the harbour mostly dries anything up to 1m.

The channel swings to starboard off a floating jetty 300 metres past the black house. Follow the green buoys to starboard, leaving a triple trot of moorings to port. From halfway up this reach you can feel your way with caution into the isolated hole with 0·5m which lies due north of Hengistbury Head.

Approach from the west is hampered by the unmarked Beerpan Rocks, which lie one cable to the south-southeast of the beacon immediately off Hengistbury Head, as well as by a further rock and various shoals of up to 1·2m further east and up to 6 cables offshore. In settled weather, with enough tide to cross Christchurch Bar, you may feel you can sail over all these except Beerpan, but with any sea running in from the southwest this would be imprudent. It is safer to give the headland at least a mile clearance until its left-hand edge bears south of west before working up towards the entrance.

Moorings and anchorage

Anchor anywhere you can on the limit of the buoyed channel, but do not expect an easy ride. Finding space to anchor is not easy, owing to the narrowness of the channel and the closeness of the moorings.

Apart from the hole behind Hengistbury Head, where you should anchor inside the moorings (about 1m at low water neaps), there is another likely spot clear of the single visitor's mooring opposite Grimbury Point just to the north of the final port-hand buoy. Another is 200 metres to the northwest of Grimbury Point, close to the western bank.

Christchurch Sailing Club (☎ 01202 483150) maintain a pontoon where visitors may lie, and they may also have a buoy to spare. Rossiter Yachts in the right-hand arm of the River Avon keep a pair of moorings available to visitors (☎ 01202 483250).

Facilities

Three yacht yards. Fuel and fresh water available at Rossiter Yachts jetty. Christchurch is a thriving town with all shops, hotel and banking facilities.

Launching sites

Slipways At Christchurch Quay; at the Sailing Club by permission; at one of the yacht yards.

From the beach on the harbour side of Mudeford Quay, where there is convenient car parking.

Communications

Frequent buses and main line trains. Hurn Airport nearby.

Poole

Tides

Tides in Poole Harbour are small in range but highly significant to navigation. Streams run particularly fast in the narrow entrance, where an ebb rate of 4½ knots can be found at springs. Times are difficult to predict, and those using tide tables will note that only the times of LW are confirmed. The long double HW stand is best predicted by reference to its height (in the tide tables) and the tidal curve. Heights are approximately as follows:

Entrance

MHWS	MLWS	MHWN	MLWN
2·0m	0·3m	1·6m	1·1m

Town Quay

MHWS	MLWS	MHWN	MLWN
2·1m	0·6m	1·6m	1·2m

Wareham

MHWS	MLWS	MHWN	MLWN
2·2m	0·9m	1·7m	1·2m

Old Harry (Handfast Point) ¾ mile southwest of *Fairway* buoy – conspicuous.

POOLE HARBOUR

Lytchett Bay

Rockley Point

HAMWORTHY

Holes Bay

Rockley Channel (marked by beacons)

Wood Bar Looe

Moriconum Quay

2F.G (vert)

2F.G(vert)
2F.G(vert)
Q(6)+LFl.15s

No.75 Lake
Fl.G.5s

No.77

No.76

Moorings

Holton Mere

No.74
Fl.R.5s

No.73

Poole YC Marina

Fl.G.10s

Fl(3)10s
Fl.G.5s
No.67
Fl.G.3s

No.78

Russel Quay

W Transit
Q.Y

E Transit
Q.Y

No.69

No.70

Wareham Channel

Keyworth Point

No.80

No.82
Fl.R.5s

No.84

See continuation

Marked by beacons

Gigger's Island

Hydes Quay

Bower Pt

No.71

No.72
Fl.R.5s

Patchins Point

Poole Harbour

Arne Bay

Shipstal Pt

ARNE
(25)

Ch marked by stakes

Upper Wych Channel

Long Island
(Private)

Round Island
(Private)

Middlebere Lake

Wych Lake

Fitzworm Pt

Nath Point

Ower Bay

Cleavel Pt

N

CONTINUATION TO WAREHAM

N

R Trent

Swineham Point

Marked by beacons

Turners Cove

Bower Pt

River Frome

Wareham

Quay

Catwalk

Slip

Ridge wharf
Yacht Centre

Redcliffe YC

Obstn

2°5'W

43'

42'

50°
41'
N

50°
41'·5
N

50°
40'

6'

4'

3'

2'

2°1'W

2°

POOLE HARBOUR AND ENTRANCE

POOLE

PARKSTONE

POOLE TOWN QUAY AND COBBS QUAY

Continuation to Cobbs Quay

STUDLAND

Depths

The deep-water fairway from the bar up the Swash Channel, through the Middle Ship Channel and up to the ferry berths is dredged to 6·2m. The Middle Ship small-craft channel is dredged to 2·0m, but may be only 1·5m near the stakes. However, the old Main Channel (now the North Channel) is still available and has a minimum of 3·6m. The least depth at Poole Quay is 3·5m and there is about 2·5m, plus tide, up to Poole Yacht Club Yacht Haven. The channel up to Wareham has a least depth of 0·1m below chart datum, giving over 1m of water at MLWN. Holes Bay has a minimum of 0·3m going up to Cobb's Quay.

General

Poole is a very large natural harbour which can be entered by day or night and at all states of tide. Much of its area is shoal, but there is nonetheless ample deep water for ships and yachts in great numbers. It is a main RoRo terminal for cross-channel ferries. There are a number of yacht clubs and every facility for the yachtsman. There is also a choice of berth types from marina, through the piled Town Quay, down to swinging moorings and anchorages. For the shoal-draught cruiser, the possibilities for taking the ground for a quiet night in an interesting spot are considerable, subject always to the ubiquitous small-craft moorings.

Approach and entrance

Swash Channel The Swash Channel is the main entry to Poole Harbour and runs largely between a training bank on its western side and the Hook Sand to the east. While some yachts may be able to cross the outer end of Hook Sand at HW, the bank should be treated with the greatest respect. Whether you are approaching from the east or the south, your most prominent landmark will be the white chalk stacks of Old Harry Rocks off Handfast Point, where the water cuts up in strong winds against the fast-flowing tide. *Poole Fairway* buoy (red and white, LFl.10s) lies 6½ cables northeast of these stacks. The *Bar No. 1* buoy (Q.G) is found ½ mile north-northeast of the *Fairway* buoy, with the Swash Channel starting off at 335° from between this and *No. 2* red can buoy (Fl.R.2s). The channel is well buoyed and lit (see plan), but after dark you must be on the lookout for unlit buoys.

You will see a buoy (Q.R) at the end of the training bank (marked by red beacons when submerged) on your port side before arriving at red *No. 10* buoy (Fl.R.4s) and green *No. 9* buoy (Fl.G.5s). Here the channel begins to swing to port towards the red can *Channel No. 12* (Fl.R.2s) and *Hook Sand No. 11* green buoy (Fl.G.3s). As you pass between this pair, alter to 315° for the harbour entrance, with its chain ferry and the conspicuous Haven Hotel on the northeast shore. Be careful of the chain ferry, which has a difficult time in a busy entrance where streams run extremely hard. It shows a white strobe light forward to indicate motion.

The channel divides inside the entrance, the main arm swinging to starboard around a lit west cardinal beacon off North Haven Point, and a second channel running off hard to port around *No. 18* red can buoy (Fl.R.5s). It should be noted that streams can be of major significance all up and down the Swash Channel and that on the ebb tide in southeasterly gales a bad sea is set up in the vicinity of Poole Bar. If there is any significant commercial traffic in the offing, small craft drawing up to 3m should use the small-craft channel which lies immediately west of the buoyed ship channel.

East Looe Channel

If arriving from the east, this is an attractive alternative to the long slog down to the bar and

Poole approach. View from the vicinity of the outer end of the training bank.

Poole entrance. (A) Chain ferry. (B) Brownsea Island. (C) Sandbanks Hotel. East Looe Channel runs close inshore in front of this.

Poole harbour entrance looking northwest.

Salterns Marina.

Poole Town Quay.

Cobbs Quay Marina.

back, particularly if the tide is ebbing hard down the Swash Channel. There is a least depth of 1·6m a cable or so east-southeast of *East Looe* buoy (Q.R). This is situated 2 cables offshore and a little over 4 cables somewhat north of east of the Haven Hotel. To use the channel, approach the buoy so as to be well off Hook Sand, leave it close to port, then steer about 260°, leaving an unlit north cardinal beacon to port. Thereafter, you run parallel to the beach in deeper water until you join the Swash Channel at the harbour entrance. The East Looe is not recommended to strangers after dark.

Channels within the harbour
If proceeding up towards the Town Quay, head first for the lit east cardinal *Brownsea* buoy, then alter north-northeast towards the lit south cardinal *No. 20* bell buoy. This marks the division of the two main channels.

The Middle Ship Channel
This well marked and well lit channel (see plan) takes you up to *Aunt Betty* east cardinal buoy, where you swing round into the straight mile run on 293° up to *Stakes* lit south cardinal buoy. Note the small-craft channel on your port side, which craft drawing 1·5m or less are obliged to use as necessary. From *Stakes*, if proceeding to the Quay, steer 343° up the Little Channel past two unlit green piles and *Oyster Bank* beacon (Fl(2)G.5s) until the Quay opens to the west. Berth on the north side.

The North Channel
Also well marked and lit, this was the main channel before the Middle Ship Channel was dredged in the late 1980s. It leads to Salterns Marina and Park-stone Bay. Salterns Marina is entered beyond *No. 29* green buoy (Fl.G.5s) and the unlit *No. 31* green buoy. The marina entrance channel runs at 033°, past a small unlit red buoy (leave to port) and three small green buoys to starboard. The entrance now opens on your port hand, with 2F.R lights to port and 2F.G lights to starboard. If continuing beyond the marina, stay in the buoyed North Channel until you rejoin the Ship Channel at *Diver* west cardinal buoy.

Poole Yacht Club Yacht Haven.

Wych Channel
The Wych begins in the vicinity of the fuel barge moored near *Aunt Betty* buoy and runs close parallel to the north shore of Brownsea Island. It is marked by red and green posts with topmarks. The channel swings round the west end of the island, carrying at least 2·2m of water as far as Pottery Pier. There is a shoal channel called Wills Cut marked by an east cardinal beacon on the north side of the Wych. This channel runs a degree or two west of north up to another east cardinal beacon, soon after which the deep water of the Little Channel up to Poole Quay is regained. The Upper Wych Channel swings round a south cardinal beacon and winds away into the marshes behind Round Island. It is marked all the way and does not dry, though depths vary considerably.

River Frome looking downstream. Last bend before Wareham (Redcliffe Yacht Club), bottom centre and Ridge Wharf Marina (top). Note boats secured fore-and-aft along left bank.

South Deep

South Deep runs southwest from *No. 18* red can (Fl.R.5s) and *No. 1* green pile (Fl.G.5s). It is lit (see plan) as far as the oil workings on Furzey Island, above which it is marked by less ostentatious beacons and piles. South Deep connects up with the Wych Channel via Ramshorn Lake, joining it at the only west cardinal beacon in the vicinity.

Wareham Channel

To enter the channel, ignore the Little Channel at *Stakes* buoy and continue west past the ferry terminals (note the transit of two Q.Y lights), then proceed between red and green buoys as per the plan. Beyond Lake Pier there are a number of big-ship mooring buoys to be left to port. Upstream of these, there are a number of seasonal red buoys before the channel becomes defined by red and green posts with topmarks. These wind southwest, south, then swing around to the northwest past Bower Point. Here they peter out, but you should steer about 325° from the last one, heading immediately west of Swineham Point. As the point approaches and the river proper opens up, turn into it and keep in the middle, favouring the outside of the bends. The shallowest part (0·1m LAT) is off Redcliffe, where the bottom can be uncomfortably hard. Thence, on to Wareham.

Holes Bay

Access through Poole Town Bridge above the Quay, opening approximately every 2 hours from 0730 until 2130 at weekends and 0930 to 2130 weekdays.

Light signals:

Red – bridge closed

Green – bridge open

Fl.G – bridge opening: proceed with caution

Keep to the east bank past the Sunseekers Marina until you reach Backwater Channel leading off to the northwest for 3 cables, marked by red and green piles. At the east cardinal post, swing sharply to port with the channel straight to Cobb's Quay Marina, leaving the post on your starboard hand.

Anchorages and berths

Studland Bay is an excellent anchorage with good holding and fine shelter in west and southwest winds. There are lovely views and a small village about ¼ mile inshore with a grocer's shop, a hotel and a post office. Early closing Thursdays. Studland is one of the south coast's most popular anchorages, and can be approached without difficulty. Sound in to find a suitable depth. The holding is good.

Off Brownsea Island Anchor in the entrance to South Deep clear of the fairway, or off Goathorn Point clear of moorings, or in one of the deep pools further up. Beware of the clearly marked oyster beds and do not anchor near these. There are some moorings off Goathorn Point which may be vacant. The best anchorage is probably in the pool to the southwest of Green Island in 3m, clear of underwater pipes, cables and oyster beds. Careful pilotage on a good rise of tide will be needed to get you there.

North of South Middle Ground buoy (No. 20) to the east of the Middle Ship Channel are numerous moorings, some of which are sometimes vacant.

Salterns Marina (300 berths) usually has room for a visitor. Manoeuvring space is tight; if you have not called ahead on VHF Ch 80 or 37, tie up on the hammerhead of B pontoon for instructions. There are all marina facilities, including a laundry and use of the fine bar premises of the Poole Harbour Yacht Club. There is also a chandlery which changes *Calor Gas/Camping Gaz* bottles, but you are some distance from town, with little option save a cab ride.

Town Quay 100 berths rafted up. Call on VHF Ch 14, *Poole Quay*, or *Poole Harbour Control* out of hours. If less than 12·5m LOA, a call is unnecessary. Just stand off the conspicuous marina office until they notice, or tie up to a suitable berth, or raft up to a similar-sized boat. The quay wall is clearly marked to indicate berths allocated to craft of varying LOA. Rafting up to six deep is permitted. Beware of the strong current around the bridge.

There are pay showers near the bridge, with public toilets at the east and west ends of the quay.

Cobb's Quay Marina has 600 berths, with depths of 1·2m at MLWS. The bottom is soft mud, so owners of keels need not despair. Bridge openings are described above. Call VHF Ch 80.

Poole Yacht Club Yacht Haven is private, but welcomes visiting yachtsmen from recognised clubs arriving by boat. The facilities are excellent, but the visitors' berths cannot be reserved, being allocated on a first-come basis. ☎ 01202 672687, or call *Pike* on VHF Ch 80 and 37 (May to September 0800–2200). Yachts up to 11·5m LOA and 2·5m draught can be accommodated.

River Frome Shallow berths at Wareham Quay (0·2m MLWS), where all town facilities are available. Ridge Wharf Yacht Centre, on the south bank a little over half a mile upstream of Swineham Point, has a surprising number of facilities and usually has room for visitors. Generally speaking, strangers whose yachts draw more than 1·3m are not recommended to attempt Wareham.

Facilities

Yacht yards with repair facilities at Sandbanks, Parkstone, Cobb's Quay, Salterns Marina and many other places. Fuel from barge by *Aunt Betty* buoy; call *Poole Bay Fuels*, VHF Ch 37 working hours. Diesel from Corral's (opposite Town Quay) during working hours. Fresh water from marinas, and at the Town Quay by hose on application to the berthing office.

Salterns Marina and Cobb's Quay have fuel facilities, as do Ridge Wharf Yacht Centre, Dorset Yacht Co. and Sandbanks Yacht Centre. There are a number of chandlers, including good ones at Poole Quay and Salterns Marina. Sundry pubs and restaurants, first-class shopping, various sailmakers, and numerous launching sites, including the slipway at Baites, east of Fishermen's Dock, Lilliput Yacht Services, Sandbanks Road, Cobb's Quay, Poole Harbour Yacht Club, Ridge Wharf Yacht Centre and Sunseekers Marina.

Communications

Main line trains to London Waterloo.

Swanage

Tides

HW springs −0235 Dover
HW neaps +0120 Dover
These time differences should be considered very approximate.

MHWS	MLWS	MHWN	MLWN
2·0m	0·5m	1·6m	1·2m

Streams
The tide swirls about in Swanage Bay, so expect to swing. Beware of the race at Peveril Point (up to 3 knots at springs) – see below.

General

Swanage offers a pleasant if somewhat insecure anchorage in the right weather conditions. The bay is sheltered from north-northwest to south-south-west, but if the wind blows in with any force it soon becomes untenable.

Holding is not good, with a thin layer of sand over rock, with some weed patches adding to the fun, but the aspect is amenable, and in settled weather the anchorage is an excellent afternoon-tea stop. Unless you are sure of your anchor and the wind direction, an easier overnight berth can be had in Studland Bay (see Poole), which has better shelter and superior holding, and is closer to Poole Harbour, your final bolt hole in the event of unexpected easterlies.

Entry from the east is simple. From the north, likewise, given that you clear Old Harry Rocks and Handfast Point by a couple of cables. From the south, you should resist any temptation to pass inshore of the unlit red buoy off Peveril Point. The tide runs over Peveril Ledge like a millrace. There is a rip outside the buoy as well, but it is not nearly so dangerous.

Sound in and anchor in the vicinity of the pier head, ideally about a cable to the west-northwest in about 2m, keeping to seaward of local moorings.

Facilities

There are excellent hotels and shops. Early closing Thursday. Good sailing club, launching site at a slipway near to the pier with car parking adjacent. Buses.

Lulworth Cove

Tides

HW approx −0450 Dover

MHWS	MLWS	MHWN	MLWN
2·3m	0·3m	1·5m	0·9m

Double LWs are experienced in Lulworth. Predictions attach to the first of these.

Lulworth Cove.

Lulworth Cove. View from the southeast. Lulworth village in the centre.

Depths

5m in the centre of the entrance, then the bottom shelves gradually, leaving 2m LAT to within 100m of the beach. There are rocks inside the entrance on the east side (see plan), and a ledge on the shore side of the 2m line to the west of the entrance.

General

Lulworth is a well publicised beauty spot, and is of great interest to students of geology. The stratified rocks are fascinating even to the nonspecialist observer. The cove looks very sheltered on the chart, and in settled northerly weather a quiet night can be enjoyed. However, if the wind takes an onshore turn you should clear out without delay. Cases are on record of anchored yachts rolling their rails down, and horror stories are in plentiful supply. Your problems will be exacerbated if you have not left at the first sign of trouble, because if it really comes on to blow from a southerly or southwesterly quarter you may not get out at all.

Approach and entrance

It is not easy to identify Lulworth from seaward, though there are characteristic cliffs on either side of the entrance, and immediately to the west is a

LULWORTH COVE
2°15'W

sugar-loaf hill with an ex-coastguard hut. Fortunately, it is safe to steer fairly close to the cliff once in Lulworth's vicinity, and eyeball the gap in the rock walls. Keep slightly east of centre in the entrance to avoid the rocks off West Point (marked by an unlit red buoy in the summer months). The wind is fluky and squally, particularly in the desired northerlies, so sailing in may present something of a challenge. If you must beat in, remember the rocky shoals in the southeast corner inside East Point.

Anchorage

Anchor in around 2·5m about due north of East Point in clay with some sand and weed.

In southwesterly breezes use the northwest corner. Keep clear of local moorings, but try not to anchor in the fairway near the beach landing for Lulworth village, which is in this vicinity.

Facilities

Petrol and oil from garage. Small hotels, pub and simple shops. Early closing Wednesday and Saturday. Launching site at the beach at the end of the road. Frequent buses in the summer.

Lulworth Gunnery Ranges

There are two danger areas for shipping to the south of Lulworth and Kimmeridge. The one normally in use extends 6 miles out to sea, while the outer, which is seldom utilised, reaches out to 13 miles. Times of firing are published in local papers and notified to neighbouring harbourmasters and yacht clubs, who can supply leaflets giving the details. These can also be obtained from the Range Office, ☎ 01929 462721 ext. 4819 or 4859, or by listening to Radio Solent (96·1 kHz), who broadcast the information on their 0633 and 0745 forecasts.

When firing is in progress, red flags are flown by day. After dark, red lights are shown at the huts immediately east of the cove on the summit of Bindon Hill, and on St Alban's Head. Vessels may pass through the areas, but passage must be made as quickly as possible. Anchoring, fishing and stopping are prohibited.

When the range is active, fast patrol boats are on station to keep yachts clear of the area. Set watch on Ch 8 during firings. Portland Naval Base gives firing times on Ch 13 or 14 at 0945 and 1645. The ranges are not used during August.

Weymouth

Tides

HW approx −0440 Dover

MHWS	MLWS	MHWN	MLWN
2·1m	0·4m	1·4m	0·8m

Tides in Weymouth are eccentric, with 4 hours flood, 4 hours ebb and 4 hours slack around LW, subject to a small rise of around 0·2m (the Gulder) which creeps in around three quarters of an hour after LW.

Depths

The entrance, the fairway and the ferry-terminal area, including Berth No. 4 (adjacent to the Pavilion Theatre), are dredged to 5·2m. Depths alongside berths Nos 5 and 6 (opposite Weymouth lifeboat and slipway) are 4·8m. Between No. 7 Berth (by the yacht toilet facility at No. 13 Custom House Quay) and the bridge, depths are in excess of 3m. Berths in the Cove have at least 2m, and usually the best part of 3m. Above the bridge there is 2·5m in the channel and 2·5–1·75m in the marina.

General

Weymouth is a useful stopover for yachts bound east or west. It is also a strategic point to leave a

Weymouth Harbour. Berths for commercial traffic on right. Note leading marks low on left bank, downstream of sailing club. Proceed up-harbour leaving ships (if any) and 'large white yacht' to starboard. Yachts over 13m berth in this vicinity.

Weymouth Harbour entrance.

boat for a week or two in the safety of the marina above the bridge, as well as a practical destination for a weekend sail from the Solent. The pretty harbour is sheltered in all weathers and can be entered at any state of the tide, though easterly gales can make the entrance rough. The town itself is a delightful cameo of the English seaside holiday. As one strolls down the seafront, one expects to see Edwardian gentlemen in striped blazers and boaters escorting long-skirted beauties twirling parasols. Even in their absence, there are still real swingboats, donkey rides, a sand modeller and Punch-and-Judy shows.

Approach and entrance

From the west, the question will arise as to whether you should pass inshore or offshore of the Portland Race (see 'Principal headlands'), but in either event you will ultimately find yourself approaching from the vicinity of Portland Harbour breakwaters. These are left to port, giving sensible consideration to any traffic which may be about to appear through the entrances, and a course shaped for the South Pier of Weymouth with its conspicuous white lighthouse (Q.10m9M).

From the east, you will first discern the high ground of the Isle of Portland; as you come closer the wooded hill of the Nothe will become apparent immediately south of the entrance, with the buildings backing the perfect crescent of the beach showing up rather later. Note the conspicuous Jubilee Clock about half a mile north of the harbour mouth.

Various buoys will be seen between Portland and Weymouth Harbour. Some are lighted, marking the Outer Degaussing Range, but none is of navigational significance to yachts. The Mixen rocks which lie to the south of the South Pier cover at half-tide.

Apart from generally shoaling rocky water in towards Newton's Cove, which has little relevance to passage navigators, there are no dangers in the offing.

Give the South Pier half a cable clearance, watching out for fishing lines, and enter the harbour between it and the North Pier (2F.G). By night there is a useful transit of F.R leading lights on 239·5°. These have white posts with open diamond markers for daytime recognition, but in practice these are little noted by yachts. The harbour supports an active fishing fleet and is used by commercial vessels up to 130m LOA.

Attention to traffic signals shown from a mast midway along the South Pier is mandatory for safety reasons.

During normal working hours (summer 0700–2230) advice can be requested from *Weymouth Harbour Radio* on VHF Ch 16, working Ch 12.

RRR flashing – Emergency. Port closed
RRG – Entrance foul. Movement prohibited
RRR – Ship sailing. No entry
GGG – Ship entering. No departure
GWG – Move as directed by harbourmaster

If there are no signals, move at your own discretion.

Berthing

Visitors may be hailed from the upper windows of the harbour office opposite Weymouth lifeboat station adjacent to berth No. 5/6. Alternatively you can call *Weymouth Harbour Radio* as indicated above. This is advisable for larger vessels. Small craft may be directed by the duty berthing officer to berths in the Cove on the south side, either alongside pontoons or rafted to craft of similar size. The moorings along the south side of the fairway are private, and the pile moorings at the eastern side of the Cove area belong to Weymouth Sailing Club. Larger craft berth on the quays opposite the lifeboat station (Berths 5, 6 and 7) and, when the harbour is busy, spill outwards along the quay towards the ferry terminal. Expect to raft up alongside craft of similar size. Fender boards are available from the berthing master's office at No. 13 Custom House Quay, and all harbour users can avail themselves of the toilet and shower facilities beneath this office.

The new marina above the road bridge has well over 150 visitors' berths and they boast that nobody is refused. In summer, the bridge opens on even hours from 0800–2000, +2100. In winter, by arrangement, which creates no difficulties in practice. There is a clearly marked waiting pontoon immediately to seaward of the bridge on the north side of the harbour. Once through the bridge, turn to starboard and follow the signs. Call the marina on VHF Ch 80 and you will be met by berthing staff. The marina is run by the same firm as Haslar Marina in Portsmouth Harbour, whose showers and toilets have been described as the finest in the Channel. Similar facilities are available here.

Anchorage

In settled weather it is possible and economical to anchor northwest of the North Pier in varying depths. You must, however, lie to the east of a line joining St John's Church spire and the port signal station. There is a yellow can buoy marked 'foul' approximately 350m from the signal station and in line with the spire. Greater depths are available further to seaward. Holding is good, but the anchorage becomes untenable in easterly winds.

Facilities

Repairs of most descriptions at Kingfisher Marine, ☎ 01305 766595. Marine engineers at Rover Marine Services (☎ 781612), MPI Engineers (☎ 821862) and Cosens & Co (☎ 822922). Showers and toilets beneath the berthing master's office, 13 Custom House Quay, and at the back of the Royal Dorset Yacht Club bar on the North Quay – all welcome. Launderette in town. Water on quays, and some electricity, but it is not always convenient to run a hose. Diesel from a pontoon on the north side of the harbour near the entrance, or from a truck (minimum 25 litres, 0700–1900 daily) which delivers to your boat: call *Raybar Fuels* on VHF Ch 6, or ☎ 01860 912401. Petrol from garages. Launching from Wyatt's Wharf, adjacent to Weymouth lifeboat station. Good chandlery. All town facilities: banks, restaurants, etc. Excellent waterfront pubs, particularly on the Cove side.

Communications

Main line rail station with trains to London and Southampton. Buses also. High-speed passenger ferry to the Channel Islands.

Portland Harbour

Tides

HW approx −0430 Dover

MHWS	MLWS	MHWN	MLWN
2·1m	0·2m	1·4m	0·7m

Depths

Generally deep, but shelving towards its western boundaries – see plan.

General

Portland Harbour is far from ideal as a stopover for visiting yachts. It was built as a naval harbour in the mid-19th century of local stone using labour from the prison which still stands above it.

The Navy moved out in the mid-1990s, leaving the port facilities to commercial operators. There are some yacht moorings – all private – and limited anchoring possibilities. The harbour is large enough to be exposed in strong winds unless you are berthed under a weather shore. There have been numerous instances of yachts breaking free of their moorings and being wrecked on the stony breakwaters. A grim prospect.

Approach, entrance and berthing

There is no difficulty in identifying Portland, from whichever direction you approach. Note Portland Race (see 'Principal headlands') and the Shambles. Enter either at A head or between B and C heads. The lights are shown on the plan. Do not attempt the South Ship Channel. This is obstructed by the remains of the old HMS *Hood*, scuttled in 1914.

It may be possible to use a yacht mooring under the control of either the Castle Cove Sailing Club (☎ 01305 783708) or the Royal Dorset Yacht Club (☎ 01305 786258), but prior arrangement is strongly recommended. These moorings are in the Castle Cove area.

Alternatively, it may be possible to anchor to the east of Small Mouth, where a bridge joins the Isle of Portland to the mainland. Beyond Small Mouth is the East Fleet, the first of the lakes behind Chesil Beach. Depths to the east of the 2m line at this anchorage are adequate for all but the largest yachts; the recommended spot is likely to be 2 cables northeast of the *New Channel* beacon, which lies 4 cables east of Small Mouth Ferry bridge. There are no launching facilities here, and utilities are restricted, but you can walk to Weymouth from

Castle Cove. Whatever your intentions in Portland Harbour, you should contact Port Control on VHF Ch 13 between the hours of 0900 and 1700 when the office is manned. Outside these times, you are on your own, but don't be tempted to seek an alongside berth.

Portland Harbour looking towards Portland.

Bridport

Tides

HW −0500 Dover

MHWS	MLWS	MHWN	MLWN
4·1m	0·6m	3·0m	1·6m

The flood slackens after the first hour, then resumes its normal rapidity about 90 minutes later. HW stands for 1½ hours.

Depths

1·2m in the immediate offing, but the entrance channel dries up to 0·6m about halfway in. The eastern section of the harbour dries about 0·9m. The western varies from drying 0·7m in the centre to a drying height of 2·7m beside West Quay. There is a deep pool of about 3·3m at the coaster berth on the east side of the main run of the channel alongside the Quay.

General

West Bay, the port for Bridport, has little to offer yachtsmen. The entrance can be highly dangerous in strong onshore winds and there are few berths at which yachts may lie afloat. Nonetheless, the harbour has a strong character of its own, so for the brave and the adventurous it may prove worth a visit.

Approach and entrance

Apart from a 4m patch (the Pollock) about 7 cables south-southwest of the entrance, and a 3·7m patch inside this, there are no dangers in the offing. There is a lit yellow buoy (Fl.Y.5s) a cable southeast of the Pollock, marking a sewer outfall. Entry is only recommended within 2 hours of HW.

The best approach line is on a transit of 011°, which lines up the west pier head with Bridport town hall tower and flagstaff a mile or so inland. Enter between the pier heads. Beware of backwash from the walls and do not be surprised by the exceedingly narrow channel between the piers. It is around 12m wide.

Do not even think of sailing in, unless you are operating a quarter tonner with a following wind. Under power, do not be afraid to keep way on until you are well up the channel. If there is a surge, you will be glad of all the steerageway you can get.

Note that the harbour lights shown on the plan are only exhibited when a coaster is expected, so that night entry for strangers in small craft is a non-starter.

A black ball signal from the harbourmaster's office indicates that the harbour is closed.

Berthing

Consult the harbourmaster (*Bridport Radio*) on VHF Ch 16 or 11, or ☎ 01308 423222. A call in good time seems prudent in order to secure a berth in this tight little port.

Small yachts can dry out in mud at the west end of the harbour, or lean on the walls with their keels in mud, but the area is full of local moorings so space is severely limited. There is also a coaster berth, which is by the visitors' symbol indicated on the plan. This is scoured out by the river, which is released periodically through sluicegates. You may be given permission to lie here if the berth is unoccupied.

Bridport Harbour entrance near high tide.

Bridport.

Lyme Regis. Note the Cobb, lying to seaward of the true harbour entrance.

Facilities

Fresh water near the quay. There are shops (early closing Thursdays) and stores, but no notable repair facilities for yachts. There is a good slipway with a convenient car park.

Regular buses run to Bridport, a pretty West Country town 1½ miles distant.

Lyme Regis

Tides

HW −0455 Dover

MHWS	MLWS	MHWN	MLWN
4·3m	0·6m	3·1m	1·7m

The rate of rise is similar to that experienced at Bridport (page 112).

Lyme Regis. Entrance from the eastward.

Lyme Regis. Close to entrance. Sailing club on upper floor of building nearest entrance.

Depths

The whole harbour dries up to 2m, with around 0·3m drying height in the entrance. Berths along the sailing club wall dry from 0·3m to 1·3m. There is 1–2m of deep water a cable and more to the east of the harbour entrance, where the anchorage is to be found.

General

Lyme Regis is a fascinating town whose atmosphere derives from a unique mixture of fine old West Country buildings, which somehow do not quite dispel an exciting sort of 'outpost' feeling. This is particularly noticeable during periods of hard weather blowing in from the sea, when the harbour entrance becomes dangerous, and those drying out within its walls may experience prolonged heavy bumping. In settled weather, however, the anchorage outside makes for an attractive visit, and a berth inside by the warmly welcoming sailing club can be an experience to cherish.

Approach and entrance

Lyme Regis is to be found some 22 miles west of Portland Bill; the approach is straightforward. The harbour lies immediately south of a conspicuous green park, marking the scene of a landslip. It is protected from the west by a long stone pier known as the Cobb, which is forked at its eastern end. To seaward of the outer fork stands a post with a red can topmark marking a pile of large Portland stones covered at half flood. There is also rocky debris and shelves along the west and south sides of the Cobb.

The narrow harbour entrance lies between the inner fork of the Cobb and the southern end of the North Wall, a breakwater which affords partial protection to the harbour from the east.

Having done your tidal sums, steer for the post and topmark off the outer fork of the Cobb, leaving it about 50m to port, then stand on until the harbour entrance is open. Now steer in.

Leading lights

A transit of 296° leads up to the harbour entrance. It is formed by a rear F.G and an Oc.WR on the north arm of the Cobb, or south breakwater. Note that the cut-off point of the white and the red comes exactly on the transit, so if the light shows red and you are having trouble locating the F.G, come to port until the white sector hints at its presence. You are now on line. 'Too much white' at the inner end of the approach could place you uncomfortably close to the rocks.

Anchorage and berthing

If you decide to anchor outside, which is a fair proposition in calm weather with no onshore component in the breeze, sound in on a northwesterly heading towards a point to the north of the pier heads until you find a suitable depth. Shoal-draught craft can work well in, particularly on neap tides. Deeper boats may feel rather far out to seaward if proposing to pass a low water springs in their berth. The quality of the bottom varies, so be prepared to try again if your hook fails to hold at the first attempt.

There are 5 red buoys for visitors in the anchorage. They are clearly marked.

Vacant drying berths inside the harbour are likely to be few, as the harbour is much used, but there is room for a dozen or so visiting yachts to dry out on clean sand alongside the wall beside the sailing club (see 'Depths').

Whatever berth you may fancy, it makes sense to call the harbourmaster in advance on VHF Ch 16 (working Ch 14), or ☎ 01297 442137.

Facilities

Lyme Regis Sailing Club (☎ 01297 442800) is very hospitable, with showers and a bar which is open when a green light is shown.

Water at shoreward end of the Cobb. Fuel can be delivered for a small fee. Hotels and shops. Early closing Thursday.

Scrubbing can be arranged, and small yacht repairs. Launching site, slip and car park adjacent. Dinghy park.

Communications

Buses to all parts. Axminster station is 6 miles distant by road.

Axmouth and Beer

Beer

Beer is an open anchorage which should only be used in settled, offshore weather. In the right conditions it can be a delightful place. The nearest all-weather refuges are Torquay and Brixham.

The cove in which yachts may lie offers a little more protection than the chart might imply, and is first identified from seaward by Beer Head. This mighty, 130m headland is the last white cliff on the coast before chalk gives way to the red cliffs of Devon. The cove lies east of the headland.

Axmouth. Steer towards the end of the pier, then swing to port close to the wall, where the fairway is found.

Approaching from the west, round Beer Head then follow the cliffs northwards, skirting the rocks at their base, until abeam of the road running down from the village to the beach. The village church is conspicuous. The fixed white light nearby is not.

If you are coming from the east, give the headland to the east of the cove a wide berth as it has off-lying rocks extending for a cable to seawards.

Sound in and anchor as close to the shore as you reasonably can, clear of the fishing boat moorings. Landing is by dinghy on the steep beach.

Beer has the usual facilities of a moderate-sized village, plus Beer SC, an active club with both dinghy and lugger sailing. Early closing Thursday.

Axmouth

Eastward from Beer Roads, 1½ miles across Seaton Bay, lies the interesting haven of Axmouth. Axmouth was a flourishing small port until, after the advent of the railway which killed its trade, the harbour entrance works were destroyed in storms between 1869 and 1875. Inside, shelter is still excellent for bilgekeelers, yachts with lifting keels, or those equipped with legs. Visitors are welcomed, but the entrance is dangerous in more than moderate onshore winds.

The entrance is found at the end of a shingle spit where the Axe River runs out to sea, close to the west of Haven Cliff. The bar dries 1m and the unmarked channel shifts, though it normally runs east-northeasterly. Strangers are therefore recommended to anchor 2 cables west of the entrance, then either take local advice or sound the channel by dinghy. Enter half an hour either side of HW (Dover −0433), and note that the spring ebb, once running at full spate, can achieve 6 knots.

The channel is very narrow, but craft of up to 8·5m LOA and 1·5m draught which can take the ground can enter safely. Its position is denoted by a starboard-hand beacon (Fl.5s) on the pier. Immediately inside you must make a sharp turn to port, then keep over towards the wall, where the fairway is to be found.

The Axe YC (☎ 01297 20742) has moorings, a boat-hoist and slipway, also a bar and showers in the clubhouse. Boat builder and general marine services. Four hundred metres above the entrance, low bridges (2m) form an effective head of navigation.

The adjacent town of Seaton has most domestic facilities.

Exmouth

Tides

HW Exmouth Dock −0455 Dover
HW Topsham about ¼ hour later
Exmouth approaches

MHWS	MLWS	MHWN	MLWN
4·6m	0·5m	3·4m	1·7m

Streams
Streams run strongly in the entrance, with up to 5 knots past Exmouth dock gates on a spring ebb.

Depths

The sands around the approaches are liable to change, but the bar is often as little as 1m or less at LAT, giving a dubious 1·5m at MLWS unless you can be sure of the best route by virtue of local knowledge. Inside the river the bottom is uneven, with deep areas as well as the shoal patches which are notable to the west and north of Bull Hill Bank, where 1·5m LAT may be encountered.

Further up, the channel shoals intermittently to Topsham Lock, but you should not find less than 0·4m anywhere within its boundaries.

Above this lock, the river dries completely. The canal is very deep, but height is limited to 11m by the motorway bridge.

General

The River Exe is well worth a diversion during a West Country cruise. While the small tidal dock at Exmouth itself is closed to yachts, there are a number of useful anchorages, and there is the possibility of locking into the Exeter Canal at Turf Lock for complete shelter and a good pub. In shoal-draught craft, or others at the right tides, a visit to Topsham is fascinating for bird-watchers, or anyone who cares that galleons were built here that stood out to face the Spanish Armada.

The bar is not always easy to cross, with its shifting sands. Indeed, in the wrong conditions it is not a nice place to be. Nonetheless, on a reasonable day it presents no serious problems, being well buoyed.

Approach and entrance

The outer fairway buoy (east cardinal *East Exe* Q(3)10s) is to be found 6 cables southwest of Straight Point. This is a low promontory with two flagpoles on it, backed by red cliffs. It is not to be confused with Orcombe Point a mile to the west. Between these points there are high, red cliffs with rocky shelves at their feet.

Make for the *East Exe* buoy whatever your direction of approach, but if you are coming from Torbay be sure to give a good offing to the dangerous Pole Sands, which form the south side of the entrance channel by extending well to seaward. Do not attempt the entrance with strong onshore winds against the ebb. Ideally, a half-flood approach is recommended, but do not forget the powerful streams.

RIVER EXE

CONTINUATION TO EXETER

EXETER

Exeter Canal

Lower Wear

Retreat Boatyard
WC

M5 (11m Hm)

TOPSHAM

Topsham Lock

50° 41' N

30'   3°29'W

EXMOUTH

Exe SC

The Point

Dock 2

Swing Br

Q.12m7M

2F.G   Iso.2s6m7M

50° 37' N

Warren Pt No.12

36'·9

3°25'·5W   25'·3·0

41'

TOPSHAM

EBFORD

River Clyst

Viaduct

Exton

West Mud

Greenland

Turf Lock
2F.R(vert)7m3M

No.35
Q.G

No.20
Q.R

Powderham Sand

No.33
Q.G

No.31
Fl.G.3s

POWDERHAM

LYMPSTONE

No.29
Q.G

The Ridge

No.27
Fl.G.5s

Lympstone Sand

No.25
Q.G

40'

39'

50° 38' N

No.18
Q.R

No.21
Q.G

Cockle Sand

Starcross Sand

Starcross YC

STARCROSS

No.19
G

No.16
Fl.R.5s

Shelly Bank

EXMOUTH

No.17
Q.G

No.14
Q.G

Bull Hill

Cockwood

No.15
Fl.G.5s

No.13
Q.G

Bank

No.12

Q.12m7M
Iso.2s6m7M

Spire

Flagstaff (50)

Warren Pt

No.10
Fl.R.3s

No.11

No.9

No.8
Q.R

No.7
Q.G

No.5

No.6

No.3
Fl.G.2s

No.1
Q.G

No.4

No.2

Orcombe Pt

Fl.R.10s
34m7M

Straight Pt

E.Exe
Q(3)10s
BYB

Pole Sand

The Warren (3-5m)

DAWLISH

Langstone Point

37'

36'

Lts in line 305°

Caution
Depths and buoyage liable to frequent change.

Depths in Metres

26'   3°25' W   24'   23'   22'

River Exe approach. Note extensive shoaling to port.

Inside estuary. Exmouth on right, looking up-river. Main channel passes close round Warren Point (lower centre). Moored yachts in centre are *not* in channel.

Exe approach looking to Straight Point.

Exe approach. Passing *Checkstone* buoy with Exmouth seafront on right.

Because of the shifting sands, it is vital to follow the sequentially numbered red (even numbers) and green (odd numbers) buoys. Once in the vicinity of *No. 6* (red) you may come onto the leading marks on 305° (flagstaff on customs house at rear, black post on the sea wall in front), but they are difficult to spot. By night, the two leading lights tend to become lost in the town lighting. The port-hand buoys should be given a wide berth as they are often close to the dangers. The tide really picks up after *No. 10* buoy (Fl.R.3s) marking the treacherous Checkstone Ledge has been passed.

The River Exe

The channel takes a sharp turn to the southwest off Exmouth Dock immediately after *No. 12* unlit red buoy. This avoids the shoals extending east from Bull Hill Bank and takes you down past the Warren Sands. The main flood sweeps on northwesterly, so you must turn well before the dock opens, and make due allowance for cross-set, so as to get into the stream between Bull Hill Bank and Warren Point. This part of the river is called the Bight. It has two green buoys (Q.G *No. 13* and Fl.G.5s *No. 15*) to leave to starboard. On your port hand are moorings.

The channel now bends round northwards, past *No. 17* green (Q.G), left to starboard.

If you wish to anchor off Starcross you must pass west of Shaggles Sand, leaving the red *No. 16* buoy well to starboard, shaping up for the jetty as soon as green *No. 17* buoy is a cable or so abaft the beam, with depths of 0·9m to 2·1m as far as Starcross. The channel is unmarked save for a red beacon on your port side, but it can be readily discerned by following the line of deep-draught yachts on moorings.

From red buoy *No. 16* (Fl.R.5s) and unlit green buoy *No. 19* the main channel now trends north-northwesterly, past an unlit green buoy to starboard, with more moorings on your port hand.

St Clement's Church tower appears ahead as you pass Q.R buoy *No. 18* close to port and shape up towards *No. 25* (Q.G) buoy. Leave this and Fl.G *No. 27* to starboard before the channel bears round to the northeast, with *No. 29* (Q.G) buoy to starboard. Markers continue green (see plan) until the river curves round northwesterly once more towards the Q.R *No. 20* buoy. Follow the buoys to Turf Lock, and thereafter the buoys and perches up to Topsham.

Shelley Gut

There is an unmarked shallow channel on the east side of Bull Hill Bank, which offers considerable time savings to yachts bound up-river from Exmouth. The sands are steep-to on either side and the channel is intricate, so it is not recommended without local knowledge.

Anchorage and moorings

Exmouth

Anchor clear of the moorings (there is not much room) beyond the entrance to Exmouth Dock off the Point in 3m LAT if required, keeping clear of the lifeboat. This may be a rough berth when the wind blows against the tide, which can run at up to 5 knots.

Bull Hill

Anchor clear of the fairway in the Bight, between Warren Sands and Bull Hill Sands, or west of Bull Hill outside the moorings.

Starcross

Anchor southeast of the pier in 0·6 to 2·1m as required. The best positions are taken up with moorings; apply at the club if you see a vacant one you fancy. Starcross is well sheltered from the west and has a few facilities, such as a main line station.

Exmouth Harbour.

Turf Lock

Anchor in 1·5m south of landing stage, clear of the fairway.

Topsham

Anchor on the edge of the fairway north of the quay, opposite Trout's Boatyard. Here there is a landing which may be used by arrangement. Holding is poor, the bottom gravel, and there is 1m at LAT, so the berth may not suit you down to the ground.

It is possible, however, to lie alongside Topsham Quay, drying out at LW in soft mud. You are then conveniently sited for the Lighter Hotel, with its warm hospitality and excellent fare; if an on-board soirée is more in your line, fish and chips can be carried out from a nearby frier.

Exeter Canal

It is possible to lock into the Turf Lock basin, but you may not like the price. This is not a problem if you intend to lay up in the canal, but may deter the casual visitor. Nevertheless, boats with an air draught of under 11m can make the 5-mile trip up to Exeter. To enter the lock, speak to the lock-keeper, ☎ 01392 74306, or call *Port of Exeter* on VHF Ch 12.

The pub at the lock has considerable character and is worth a visit.

Facilities

Mainly at Exmouth and Topsham. Boat builders and repairs. Showers at yacht clubs. The usual town benefits.

Yacht clubs: Exeter Sailing Club. Starcross Yacht Club at Powderham Point. Starcross Fishing and Cruising Club. Topsham Sailing Club. Lympstone Sailing Club.

Water taxi at Exmouth. Call *Conveyance* on Ch 37.

Topsham with Exe Canal in foreground.

Fuel from The Retreat Boatyard (☎ 01392 874 720) near the M5. Accessible around HW.

Rail and bus services on both sides of the river, with Exeter Airport near at hand.

Teignmouth

Tides

HW −0450 Dover

Heights in the approaches

MHWS	MLWS	MHWN	MLWN
4·8m	0·6m	3·6m	1·9m

Depths

0·3m on the bar, but this is easily missed, and a drying height of 0·3m surrounds both passages. Inside there is at least 2·7m as far as Old Quay. Thereafter, gradual shoaling to an LAT depth of 1·5m just below the road bridge.

General

Teignmouth is a working port with coaster traffic as well as fishing boats. There is only one designated trot for visitors in deep water, so if you want to stay over a tide and this is full, you will have to dry out on 'The Salty'. Shelter is good inside the harbour, but the bar can be nasty with onshore winds and a swell, particularly on the ebb. Daylight entry is easy enough with a good rise of tide, but night entry is not recommended for strangers, even though the river is lit. The town is pretty. Shaldon is notably so, and quieter as well.

Approach and entrance

The Ness is easy to identify. It is a red cliff with pine trees at its summit. The point is much lower. It is wise to approach the entrance from well offshore, taking up a line of around 254° on the distinctive white Philip Lucette Beacon (Oc.R.5·5s2M) on the north side of the Ness. Cross the shallow water, which changes frequently, with the greatest caution because without local knowledge you may find less water than you had hoped. When the beacon is 50m or so ahead of you, come slowly round to starboard and head for the green beacon with triangular topmark (Oc.G.5s and F.G vertical) off The Point.

Teignmouth at low water, with the bar clearly showing. The Ness
at the extreme left-hand side.

Torquay Marina.

Teignmouth. Close to the Bar on west-southwesterly course. *Philip Lucette* beacon centre. Shaldon to its right. Cliff to the left is the Ness.

Rounding up to the moorings of Teignmouth. Note green beacon off the Point and pier to seaward.

The stream runs hard here. After leaving the green beacon clear to starboard, you should alter course to 021° and head for New Quay (2F.G vertical), leaving the three red buoys to port. These mark the Salty, a drying bank which occupies much of the harbour. The starboard side of the channel is largely steep-to. Once round the corner into the east-west part of the channel, the deep water is best found by observation of the moorings.

You may notice a number of small orange buoys with ∎ topmarks in the vicinity of the bar. These are used by pilots, but you will not be privy to their meaning unless you are lucky enough to be able to follow a ship or a pilot boat in. (Beware if your draught is deep. You may need more water than the pilot boat.)

Anchorage and mooring

There is a pair of large red mooring buoys with a 15m spread, in front of the town before the channel swings westward, to which visitors secure fore and aft, up to four abreast. The harbour office (VHF Ch 12 when a ship movement is expected) can advise as to availability. Otherwise, tie up and report to the office (☎ 01626 773165). The only viable alternative, short of picking up a vacant private mooring, is to sound in through the moorings off Shaldon, anchor (indifferent holding) and dry out in front of the village on sandy shingle. A ferry runs from the village to Teignmouth.

Upper reaches

The road bridge is so low that it is effectively the head of navigation for most craft. Dinghies can pass it, however, or cruisers able to negotiate its 3·5m clearance. It is then possible to reach Newton Abbot, given knowledge of where the channel may lie.

Facilities

Fresh water from New Quay. Fuel from garages. *Calor Gas* exchange at chandlery in Shaldon. No showers. Launderette in Teignmouth. Engineers and electronic repairs. Plenty of pubs, restaurants, fish and chips, etc. Good shops. Teign Corinthian Yacht Club in Dawlish Road, Teignmouth.

Communications

Buses. Main line railway.

Torquay

Tides

HW −0500 Dover

MHWS	MLWS	MHWN	MLWN
4·9m	0·7m	3·7m	2·0m

Depths

4·2m inside the entrance. For other depths, see plan, but note that visitors' berths have at least 2m LAT. The inner harbour mostly dries up to 1·5m.

General

Torbay is a fine big-ship anchorage in westerly weather. Indeed, it was the favoured bolt hole for the fleets blockading Brest during the Napoleonic Wars. In strong easterlies it was never the place to be. Today the new marina in Torquay gives all-weather protection, but even now some discomfort may be felt in southeasterly gales. The town is well known for its riviera atmosphere. It is, it must be said, overcrowded at the height of the season, but many will enjoy a visit here nonetheless.

Approach and entrance

As it was in Nelson's day, Torbay is still easy to approach. Torquay itself presents no difficulties either, except in strong southeasterly winds, when backwash from the harbour wall may render the entrance dangerous. During the summer months, a green conical buoy (Q.G) is established 75m southwest of Haldon Pier head. Leave this to starboard and enter between Haldon Pier (Q.G.9m6M) on your starboard hand and Princess Pier (Q.R.9m 6M) to port. It is only 80m or so from Princess Pier head to the marina, so there is less room than you might imagine, but there is still enough space for most yachts to be able to drop their sails in the sheltered water inside.

Each of the eastern pontoons of the marina, which are the visitors' berths, show 2F.R lights from the seaward ends.

Marina

There are berths for 60 visitors, clearly indicated by notice boards.

As you approach the port, call *Torquay Port* on VHF Ch 14. Then call the marina on VHF Ch 37, or tie up and report to the office.

Alternatively, telephone the harbour authority on ☎ 01803 292429 (out of hours ☎ 01803 550405), then the marina on ☎ 01803 214624. Subject to circumstances, pontoon berthing may be available on Haldon Pier.

Those more interested in historical authenticity than in present luxury may choose to anchor outside in westerly weather. The holding is good off Princess Pier in at least 3·6m. Do not be put off after dark by the creaking of ghostly oars and the muffled sound of 4in-diameter hempen cables running out after the splash of a wooden-stocked anchor.

Facilities

The marina (☎ 01803 214624/5) has water, showers, and launderette. Water on marina berths. Fuel and water are conveniently obtainable alongside South Pier of the old harbour. Repairs, with lifts up to 20 tons can be organised. Chandler, and all the facilities of a major seaside town. Customs, if required, on ☎ 01752 662091.

The main line railway station has frequent Intercity services.

The Royal Torbay Yacht Club (☎ 01803 292 006) welcomes visitors to its bar, restaurant and showers.

TORQUAY HARBOUR

Paignton

Tides
As Torquay.

Depths
The approaches dry progressively to a height of 1·8m on the visitors' berths alongside the East Quay, giving up to 3m at MHWS, 1·9m at MHWN.

General
Once a fishing and small commercial harbour, Paignton, with the exception of one crabber who will not give up, is now officially designated a leisure port. The town is part of the Torbay resort complex. It is quieter than Torquay, but still bustles with summer activity.

Approach and berthing
Paignton harbour stands on the north side of Roundham Head with its prominent red cliffs. A rocky outcrop extends to the east from the entrance, so approach from the northeast is best. The East Quay outer end exhibits a light Oc.R.3M.

Berth inside the East Quay, drying out if required on firm sand. The quay is not lit as such, but the street lighting is bright, illuminating the scene clearly. There are three drying visitors' moorings in the harbour, but whether lying on these or alongside, a maximum LOA of 8·2m (27ft) is adhered to.

Facilities
Fresh water at either end of the East Quay slipway
Toilets at the northwest corner of the harbour
Good beaches and the usual range of summer resor
activities.

Brixham

Tides
HW −0505 Dover

MHWS	MLWS	MHWN	MLWN
4·9m	0·7m	3·7m	2·0m

Depths
Up to 6m in the outer harbour (see plan), with 3m and more in the Prince William Marina. The deep-water fishing harbour is prohibited to yachts, and the inner harbour with its scrubbing grids dries 0·6m (plus the height of the grid sleepers).

General
Brixham's fame and fortune rest firmly on its fishing fleet. From the days of its innovative and highly successful sailing trawlers, the town has fed the nation with its deep-water catches. Today, after a serious recession in the early 1970s, the port is once again one of England's foremost fishing stations. With fish come the incontinent Brixham seagulls, infamous throughout the West Channel for their gross behaviour. Never mind. Brixham remains a pretty town and an exciting port of call.

The port is also an important station for the Channel pilots who embark and disembark from here. So long as you stay out of their way and do not impede the fishing fleet, you will be little troubled by the business of the town.

The outer harbour and the marina are accessible at all states of tide and in virtually any weather, though northwesterlies can make things uncomfortable.

Approach and entrance
The long Victorian breakwater with its white lighthouse (Oc.R.15s9m6M) lies just over a mile west of the prominent silhouette of Berry Head. There is a safe water red and white vertically striped lit buoy (Morse code A) a cable off the end of the breakwater. For safety, this should be left to port, unless the harbour entrance is very quiet. Proceed up the fairway, keeping green buoys close to starboard and the reds well off to port. Entry into the marina is straightforward, but you are recommended to call ahead (*Prince William Marina*) on VHF Ch 16, 37 or 80, or ☎ 01803 882929.

Berthing, mooring and anchorage
Anchoring
Do not anchor in the fairway, or close under the breakwater, as this is an unmarked fairway for the lifeboat.

In offshore winds, a better bet is to anchor in Fishcombe Cove, immediately west of the outer harbour. It is a pleasant spot, and lack of dues will suit the yachtsmen of frugal pocket.

Mooring

There are three pontoons moored off the yacht club for the use of visitors. The club landing is only a short row.

Drying berths

In the inner harbour there are a number of scrubbing berths for craft drawing up to 3m. These are available by arrangement with the harbourmaster (☎ 01803 853321, or VHF Ch 14 or 16).

Prince William Marina

Brixham's marina, named after William of Orange, who landed here to take over his new kingdom in 1688, is a large, modern establishment protected from the northwest by a wave screen. There are 30 visitors' berths. The reception berth is immediately inside on your port hand, but ideally you should call ahead on VHF Ch 37 or 80.

Facilities

All town facilities. Banks, pubs, restaurants, etc. General repairs and a sailmaker. Fresh water at the marina or from New Pier (see plan) where diesel is also available.

Launching sites can be found at public slipways on both west and east sides of the outer harbour.

Brixham Yacht Club welcomes visitors. It has an excellent restaurant, as well as showers, etc. Launderette in town and at the marina, where you can, of course, also have a shower.

Communication

Buses to Torquay and Paignton; thence main line trains.

Brixham Harbour. Above approach, below showing the docks.

Dartmouth

Tides

HW −0510 Dover

MHWS	MLWS	MHWN	MLWN
4·8m	0·4m	3·6m	1·8m

Depths

Deep water up to Dittisham, with the exception of a 4·5m patch a cable southwest of Higher Noss Point. Thereafter depths are variable, with only one drying patch to cross before Totnes.

General

Dartmouth is the archetypal West Country harbour. The lower reaches of the river are dominated by the pretty town of Dartmouth itself, with Kingswear climbing up the hill opposite on the east bank. The Royal Naval College stands proudly overlooking the anchorage. Further up lies the idyllic village of Dittisham, readily reached by yacht at all states of the tide. Beyond, a number of interesting creeks and villages are passed before fetching up at the fascinating town of Totnes – on the tide.

Dartmouth harbour is remarkably beautiful; it is well sheltered and can be entered by day or night at any state of tide. There is always room for visitors.

Approach and entrance

Dartmouth entrance is by no means obvious from seaward, but the 24m daymark (elevation 170m) on the hill behind Froward Point east of the entrance is unmistakable, as is the craggy Mewstone Rock (35m).

The entrance is deep and well marked, but there are a number of dangers. Rocks lie to the west of the Mewstone as follows: the Verticals (dry 1·8m), and the West Rock (with a depth over it of only 0·9m) is nearly 3 cables west-southwest of the Mewstone. The Bear's Tail (dries 0·6m) is 175m off Inner Froward Point, while 2¼ cables west is Old Castle Rock (with 1·8m over it), marked by the green conical *Castle Ledge* buoy (Fl.G.5s). For about three hours either side of HW the stream sets towards these dangers, which should be given a wide berth.

Approaching from the east, keep the East Blackstone Rock (a smaller version of the Mewstone half a mile east of it) well open of the Mewstone, until *Castle Ledge* buoy comes in line with Blackstone Point on the west side of the entrance.

On the west side there are drying rocks a cable off Combe Point; three cables east of this point is the Homestone (with 0·9m) with its red can buoy. Further in are the Meg Rocks, which dry 3m, and the 2m-high Western Blackstone Rock.

Dartmouth.

Mewstone from the southwest.

Dartmouth day beacon from 1 mile offshore.

Castle Ledge buoy, 6 cables SSE of entrance.

Between these dangers the approach is easy, except when strong south or southeast winds send a heavy swell into the harbour, sometimes as far up as the lower ferry. This can give rise to an ugly sea for small vessels, particularly on the ebb.

In the narrows you must avoid the Checkstone (0·3m over it) and the Kitten rock (1·8m), west-southwest of the red can *Checkstone* buoy (Fl(2)R. 5s), which lies off the ledges on the western side. Both rocks lie opposite Kingswear Castle. The Kitten rock is on the edge of the fairway, so when approaching the narrows keep east of it and give a good berth to the *Checkstone* buoy.

In the dark, stay in the white sector of the Iso.WRG.3s9m8M light shown from a squat white tower on the Kingswear side. Past the two castles and a cable beyond the *Checkstone* buoy, come round to 293° in the middle of the river in the white sector of the Bayard's Cove light (Fl.WRG.2s5m 6M), on the Dartmouth side. The light's position is emphasised by day with a white stripe on the foreshore.

When the river is well open, proceed up the harbour in mid-stream. Note that there is a directional fixed white light just up-river of Kingswear Castle, shining across the deep water between it and Bayard's Cove, which is of assistance to outward-bound traffic.

Berthing in Dartmouth and Kingswear

All berthing is controlled by the DHNA (Dart Harbour and Navigation Authority). Wherever you berth, you will have to pay them dues.

Anchorage

Anchor off Kingswear between the row of large free-floating pontoons occupied mainly by fishing boats, and the line of big-ship moorings in mid-stream. The holding is pretty good, but wind against tide can cause some notoriously chaotic situations with dissimilar craft lying too close to one another. The aspect pleases, however, and it is a beautiful spot in good weather. It is also perfectly safe in all weathers for vessels properly equipped with good ground tackle. Just keep an eye on the neighbours and beware fouling the bracing chains and anchors stretching E–W from the big ship buoys.

Pontoons and moorings

DHNA maintain a number of useful visitors' pontoons. A long one is on the Kingswear side just below the position of the Dart Marina, once again inshore of a trot of big-ship mooring buoys. This provides a snug berth, from which you must take the dinghy or the water taxi ashore. There are also pontoons on the Dartmouth waterfront (max. LOA 35ft) clearly marked 'Visitors'. Larger vessels can berth on the Town Jetty pontoon by arrangement between 1700 and 0900, when the tripper boats go off watch. It may be possible to lie on the inside of this pontoon over the full 24-hour period.

There are also a number of visitors' buoys. DHNA can be called on VHF Ch 11, or ☎ 01803 832337

Marinas

Darthaven Marina is on the Kingswear side just upstream of the railway station (prominent steam locomotives in season). Call them on VHF Ch 80. If you arrive after the berthing master has gone home, tie up in a vacant berth and check the dock office, where vacant berths are chalked on a board. Move directly to one of these.

Dart Marina, immediately above the upper ferry, maintains up to 36 visitors' berths in which you may

Dartmouth and, on right, Kingswear.

Dittisham. (A) Greenway Quay. (B) Landing jetty and dinghy pontoon. (C) Galmpton Creek. (D) Flat Owers.

be invited to raft up, sometimes to ten or more deep. Rouse out your longest lines and call them on VHF Ch 80.

Embankment

Yachts can tie up to the Dartmouth embankment in front of the town, tide permitting, for short stays. There is a good scrubbing grid here, bookable through DHNA.

Up-river

Continue in mid-stream about two miles up-river as far as Dittisham, leaving the Anchor Stone with its ■ topmark firmly to port. 2½ cables above the stone you come to the village on the west bank with its waterfront pub and passenger ferry running to the impossibly picturesque Greenway Quay. On the Dittisham side there are a number of DHNA visitors' moorings. You will probably have to raft up in the season, but ask the harbour launch if in doubt, or call on VHF Ch 11. The buoys are an easy dinghy trip to a pontoon on the village jetty.

Upper reaches

Proceeding up-river from Dittisham to the east of Flat Owers Bank, keep the mooring buoys close to starboard to avoid the mudbank. Drying heights in Galmpton Creek, where many fine Brixham sailing trawlers, including *Provident,* were built, vary from 0·8m to 1·5m. Galmpton is not set up for visitors.

When there is sufficient water to work to the west of Flat Owers Bank, steer 024° for the boathouse at Waddeton until the red buoy is abeam to port, then swing round steadily to port and steer for the upper Sandridge boathouse on a heading of around 310°. When the upper Sandridge boathouse is half a cable in front of you, alter smartly towards Blackness Point, keeping it just open on your starboard bow until High Gurrow Point is fairly close to port. Now come up to head for Blackness Point. When it is close at hand, alter for Pighole Point, and leave all moorings close to starboard after you have passed it. Enter Stoke Gabriel creek, if desired, by rounding the green beacon, then follow the short channel marked by port-hand beacons with orange topmarks up to the landing pontoon, where there is also a tiny quay. Above here is a tidal weir submerged at HW, so any attempt to go higher up the creek will result in disaster.

If proceeding beyond Stoke Gabriel, bring Mill Point abeam, then come to starboard for the middle of the wood on the south bank of the river. Off the entrance to Bow Creek there are red and green channel buoys. After passing close to the wood, steer to pass between these, then come round to starboard for the red buoy off Duncannon. The following bend should be taken wide, after which the river is marked with buoys and beacons to the end of the Fleet Mill Reach. Above here, the best water is in mid-stream up to Totnes.

Obtain advice on berthing facilities at Totnes from River Officer or Dartmouth Harbour Office prior to arrival there.

Facilities

Totnes

An extremely attractive historic town with a castle, shops, hotels, a quaint High Street and numerous interesting pubs and restaurants. Boatyard. Chandlery.

Dartmouth, Kingswear and Dittisham

A water taxi is on watch on VHF Ch 16 and 8.

Fresh water by arrangement at harbour office, or at any marina. At Dittisham, from a tap in front of The Ferry Boat Inn. Floating rubbish skip. Simple provisions up the hill. Diesel only, no petrol, at both marinas and from a barge moored in the middle of the river between the upper and lower ferries. Hotels and restaurants, good shopping centre. Early closing partly Wednesday, partly Saturday. Yacht yards, chandlers and all facilities. Travel-hoist at Darthaven Marina. Yacht clubs: Royal Dart Yacht Club (Kingswear), Dartmouth Yacht Club, Dittisham Sailing Club. Launching sites: public slipway at Kingswear next to Royal Dart Yacht Club, except near LW. Slipway at Dartmouth dinghy basin two hours each side HW, or slipway alongside upper ferry slipway at any tide, provided ferry is not obstructed.

Communications

The nearest rail connection is at Paignton, seven miles away. You can reach this by steam train in season from Kingswear, and a jolly fine trip it is too. If your luck is in, you could be hauled by none other than the *Flying Scotsman* herself. For the older at heart, there are buses to all parts.

Salcombe

Tides

HW approx −0523 Dover

MHWS	MLWS	MHWN	MLWN
5·3m	0·7m	4·1m	2·1m

Depths

The bar has a minimum depth of 1m on the transit, with 0·7m immediately to the east. These depths may vary. Inside the bar, a deep-water channel leads as far as Tosnos Point in the Bag. Above here to a point northwest of the Salt Stone there is 2m to be found with care. Thereafter depths shoal steadily, but craft drawing 2m can navigate as far as Kingsbridge from ¾ flood. For depths in the creeks, see plan.

General

Despite its appearance on the chart, Salcombe is not technically an estuary. No river debouches through its arms to the sea. It is, however, an excellent harbour, with minimal fishing activity and no commercial traffic. The village is extremely crowded in high season, but it is always a joy to lie on a mooring and watch the lovely Salcombe yawls racing around one's yacht. The entrance is spectacular and there are secluded anchorages available well away from the sea. The bar can be very dangerous in strong onshore weather, particularly on the ebb tide. Indeed, a lifeboat has been lost here. No attempt should be made to enter in these conditions, especially with the wind in the southeast.

Approach and entrance

With sufficient tide on the bar and in settled weather Salcombe presents few problems to the visitor.

The entrance lies just to the east of Bolt Head, an unmistakable promontory with a spiky silhouette. The Mewstone (19m) and Little Mewstone (5m) lie conspicuously southeast of the point.

The sea is often disturbed in the stretch from Prawle Point towards Bolt Tail. Mariners approaching Salcombe must bear this stoically in the knowledge that things will improve once they have gained the harbour. Strong southerly winds meeting the ebb by Bolt Head can set up overfalls, but these may be avoided by approaching from further east.

Salcombe entrance. The leading beacons nearly in transit with left-hand side of conspicuous red-roofed house with twin gables on the left of the picture. At this point you should come to starboard on to 042° transit for going up-harbour.

The only sunken dangers on the west side of the approach are rocks near the Mewstones, Cadmus Rocks, off the northeast corner of Starehole Bay and, much further in, Bass Rock, off Splat Point, about 100m to the west of the transit. To the east side, do not turn in too soon after passing Prawle Point. Rickham Rock, 4 cables short of the bar, has 2·7m over it.

The simplest answer is to alter course northward about a quarter of a mile east of the Bolt, then sail past Starehole Bay where lie the remains of the wreck of the barque *Herzogin Cecilie* under the high cliffs. Continue past the submerged Cadmus Rocks and the Great Eelstone, leaving this about a cable to port. The bar is now 2 cables to the north.

The front leading mark stands on Pound Stone Rock (dries 4m). The rear one is a red and white beacon with a ◆ topmark on Sandhill Point (DirFl. WRG.2s27m10/7M). This is not always easy to spot, but can be discerned by virtue of its situation in front of the left-hand edge of an unmistakable red-roofed house with two gables. If you still cannot make out the marks, a compass bearing on the left-hand edge of the house should suffice. By night, remain within the 5° white sector of the light. The dangerous nature of the bar in the wrong conditions of strong onshore winds against an ebbing tide cannot be over-stressed.

North of the bar, continue on the leading line, leaving to starboard the Wolf Rock (dries 0·6m), marked by a green conical buoy (Q.G.3s). As the *Blackstone* beacon light (Q(2)G.8s) comes abeam to starboard, swing to starboard, leaving to port the Pound Stone and two red and white beacons off Sandhill Point, then proceed on 042° up the middle of the wide fairway.

By night, there are leading lights to indicate this change of course and your subsequent heading. The front light is a quick flash, as is the rear one, which is sited on a stone column at 45m elevation. Both stand near Scoble Point on the east side of the Bag, and lead as far as the port-hand ferry landing light (F.R). You can continue on the transit to the Bag by bringing the rear light just open to the right of the front one when passing Snapes Point, provided there is sufficient moonlight to be sure of avoiding moored vessels. Note that the *Blackstone* beacon and *Wolf Rock* buoy keep the departing mariner off shoaling water on the eastern bank.

If you are proposing to sail up to Kingsbridge, leave the Salt Stone well to starboard, then look out for a series of red and white poles to be left to port which will lead you the 2 miles or so up to the quay. The first of these is about 1 cable northeast of Heath Point. Do not be tempted by a line of unlit red buoys beginning to the northwest of Charleton Point. These lead up to Balcombe Lake, where you do not want to go. Leave them well to starboard and concentrate on the red and white posts instead.

Anchorage and moorings

If the weather is settled, **Starehole Bay**, immediately north of Bolt Head, is a pleasant stop, but

SALCOMBE
ESTUARY

KINGSBRIDGE

N

50°
16'·5
N

*Channel
marked by bns*

3°46'W

*Balcombe
Creek*

High
House
Pt

Park Bay

Collapit Creek

Gerston Pt

Rawden Pt

Blanksmill Creek

Heath Pt

Charleton
Pt

Salt
Stone Bn

Halwell Pt

Tosnos Pt

Frogmore Creek

Ham Pt

Wareham Pt

N

See inset

Lower
Batson

Higher
Batson

Batson Creek

Island CC

SALCOMBE

2F.R

F.R.3M

Marine
Hotel

*Woodville
Rks*

White Ho

North
Sand
Bay

Sandhill Pt
DirFl.WRG.2s
27m10·7M

Moult Pt

*South Sand
Bay*

Pound
stone
Bn
RW
Q(2)G
8s4m2M

Q.G

Splatcove Pt

Black
Knob
Pt

Scoble
Pt
Q

Snapes
Pt

Smalls Cove

Mill Bay

Biddlehead Pt

Sunny Cove

Limebury Point

·106

Lower
Batson

Higher
Batson

SALCOMBE

50°
14'
N

North
Sand
Bay

Sandhill Pt
DirFl.WRG.2s27m10·7M

Pound
Stone
Bn
RW
Q(2)G.8s
4m2M

Bass Rk

*Wolf
Rk*

Black
Knob Pt

Ox Pt

*The
Bag*

Q.45m
8M

Q.5m8M

V

Scoble Pt

Snapes
Pt

*Fuelling
Barge*

*Dredged
Channel
(1m)*

2F.R

F.R.3M

Bn

Ferry

Bn

Smalls Cover

Mill Bay

Biddlehead Pt

*Sunny
Cove*

Limebury Pt

3°46'W

45'·5

N

Sharp
Tor

Great Eelstone

Wk
*Cadmus
Rks*

Red

Wh

*Starehole
Bay*

Bolt Head
CG

Mewstone
(19)

Little Mew
Stone

The Range

*Chapple
Rks*

Green

Bn and Lt 000°

Ldg Lts 042°30

*Seacombe
Sand*

Pig Nose

Ham Stone

16

3°45'W

46'

3°44'W

Depths in Metres

50°
14'
N

50°
16'
N

50°
15'
N

50°
13'
N

Salcombe Harbour. Leading beacons in view at left-hand edge of picture, together with the twin-gabled house. Central in the entrance is the Blackstone with its beacon.

beware of the wreck of the barque *Herzogin Cecilie*, marked by a red and black isolated danger buoy, in the northwest corner.

Sunny Cove, on the east side of the entrance inside the Blackstone, gives access to a clean sandy beach and has 2m at LW. Settled weather only.

No anchoring immediately northeast or southwest of Mill Bay because of undersea cables. **Smalls Cove**, however, is a popular anchorage when the sea is calm. Otherwise you may still feel the scend here. You can find about 2m at LW opposite the Marine Hotel. You can also anchor off the beach west of Ditch End on the edge of the shallow water which deepens rapidly into the channel.

If you are in search of peace, you will find it, subject to sailing schools and racing activities, in the last of the deep water in the vicinity of the Salt Stone. A good all-weather anchorage is to be had off Halwell Point with the Salt Stone beacon bearing north magnetic. Here there is water a-plenty.

The creeks offer seclusion and perfect shelter to those whose draught and sometimes readiness to take the ground permits them.

There are visitors' moorings on the **Salcombe** side of the channel off the Marine Hotel just below the town. Thereafter, a number of such buoys will be seen. The harbour staff will direct you from their launches, or call them on VHF Ch 14, *Salcombe Harbour*. There are three moorings between Ditch End and Scoble Point which can accommodate craft of up to 100 tons by arrangement.

In **The Bag** there is a visitors' pontoon opposite Ox Point.

At **Kingsbridge**, do not try to berth at New Quay or on the private pontoon off the Quay on your port hand. Continue right up to the end, where there is a visitors' pontoon for bilgekeelers to starboard and a good wall for deep keels of up to 12m LOA to lean against on the west side. Both are well marked.

Facilities

Salcombe is supplied with most marine requirements. Fuel from barge (VHF Ch 6 and ☎ 01836 775644). Fresh water on short-stay visitors' pontoon and on Whitestrand Quay, around which most facilities are congregated. Showers and toilets at Salcombe Yacht Club, or by arrangement at the Island Cruising Club in Island Street. Garbage skip on a barge off the town. There is a launderette in town, but it is overcrowded in summer. All normal provision requirements in town and at Kingsbridge (no fuel at Kingsbridge except by portage). Various chandlers, repairers and engineers, both mechanical and electronic. You can even have your liferaft serviced here. For a water-taxi service, call the Harbour Patrol launches on Ch 12 (if no response try 14). Salcombe Yacht Club and the Island Cruising Club both welcome visitors.

Salcombe town. Snapes Point is central in the picture with the Bag running away to the left behind it. Visitors are tied up to pontoons in the Bag, or at buoys off the town.

Communications

Salcombe is not the easiest place to approach by public transport. However, regular buses run to Kingsbridge, with ferries an attractive alternative when tide permits. Thence to main-line trains, via a connection at Totnes.

River Yealm

Tides approx −0522 Dover

MHWS	MLWS	MHWN	MLWN
5·4m	0·7m	4·3m	2·1m

Depths

0·3m on the leading line south of the bar, but up to 3m immediately south of the transit, between the red buoy and the starboard-hand beacon on the foreshore. Sands are liable to change. Variable depths in the region of 1·5m at MLWS on the second leading mark as far as Misery Point. Thereafter, 2·5m or more to Yealm Pool. Newton Ferrers Arm dries – see plan – while the Yealm itself carries variable depth for a further mile or so.

General

The Yealm is an extremely beautiful river with good shelter in all but strong onshore winds. Visitors should take note, however, that it is crowded with moorings and that at peak times the Harbour Authority has reluctantly had to limit visitors' numbers to 90 boats per night. Problems of space sometimes arise in settled weather at holiday weekends, so these times should be avoided if possible. The Authority stresses that notwithstanding this provision, no boat will be refused shelter from hard weather.

Approach and entrance

The entrance can be rough in strong onshore winds from the southwest, but otherwise presents no difficulties. Approach across Wembury Bay, noting

RIVER YEALM

WEMBURY

NEWTON FERRERS

Depths in Metres

that from Wembury Point rocks and ledges extend towards the conspicuous Great Mewstone Island (59m). The little Mewstone Rock (15m) lies on the southwest side of the Mewstone. If you are cutting close around this you must give a good clearance to the rock 50m off it, which is awash at low water. Further rocks or shoals extend 2 cables southwest of the Mewstone, and there are tide rips when the wind is across the stream. The Inner (dry 3m) and Outer Slimers (1·5m) lurk a quarter of a mile eastward of the Mewstone, and while these are unlikely to bother the rhumb-line navigator, an inbound yacht beating to windward should take care to be well clear of the Mewstone on her starboard tack.

Once the entrance to the river is opened up, look for a white cottage between trees near the summit of Misery Point on the south side of the river, and below it, above Cellar Bay, for a pair of leading beacons at 089°. These are topped by white triangles with a vertical black line. Bring these into line and, after leaving Mouthstone Point to starboard, move across to about 40m south of the transit, steering near the rocky shore on the starboard hand. In season a red buoy (Fl.R.5s) is placed to mark the outer end of the bar. A green beacon with triangular topmark on the south foreshore delimits the starboard edge of the channel, which is around 40m wide. By moonlight, the line of the hedge immediately south of the transit is readily identifiable and runs parallel to the line of the boards.

Approaching from the south or east, give Gara Point at least 3 cables' clearance to stay outside the Eastern and Western Ebb rocks (awash). Keep St Werburgh's Church (about a mile east of Wembury Point) bearing 010° and the Ebb Rocks will be left safely to starboard. Hold on until the black and white leading marks in Cellar Bay have been identified, then alter onto their transit.

When you have brought the green beacon abeam, alter to port to 047°, onto the next leading beacon. This will be seen to the northeast on the hillside to the right of a clump of trees about 3 cables east of Season Point. It is a white board with a red vertical line which leads up the first bend in the channel. Keep on the correct bearing, because an arm of the bar with only 0·6m at MLWS is close to port.

Hereafter, the river is clearly defined. Keep near mid-channel, leaving to port the red can buoy on the north side of the Pool. The deep channel is very narrow (50m) off the eastern extremity of Warren Point, with only 0·3m on its western side and 0·4m on the eastern (see plan).

The Newton Ferrers Arm opens out up the east side above Warren Point. Although wide, it dries out at low water. Above Warren Point, the Yealm itself continues first in a north-northwesterly direction before bearing through north to northeast. Depths vary from 3·4m to 1·8m for over half a mile, but with shallower patches as far as Shortaflete Creek. Note that anchoring is forbidden north of Madge Point.

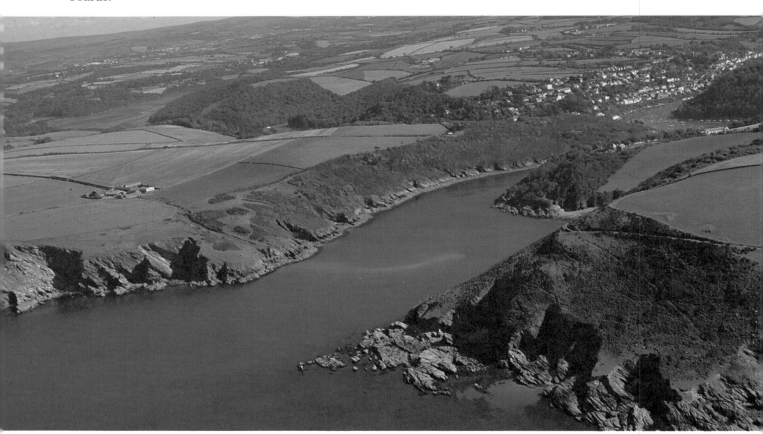

River Yealm entrance, with sand bar showing clearly.

The Mewstone from the southeast with Rame in the distance to the left.

Approaching the river Yealm entrance from SSW, keeping Wembury church open on starboard bow.

Cellar Bay leading marks on 089° pass south of the bar. Note very conspicuous line of hedge to the right.

Anchorage and moorings

The first visitors' moorings are encountered shortly after Misery Point comes abeam. These are for large craft, with the outer one being able to accommodate up to LOA 25m. Two cables further in on your starboard hand is a 46m (150ft) visitors' pontoon. Rounding Warren Point brings you to a series of fore-and-aft trots on the west side of the river which are also reserved for visitors. You may raft up on these. You may also pick up any vacant buoy that does not have a dinghy or a note on it. If it is inappropriate for you to remain there, the harbourmaster will advise when he visits you in his launch. Should you fail to make contact, report to the harbour office, in the driveway of the Yealm Hotel (convenient dinghy pontoon).

You will be charged dues if you anchor, so little will be saved and much anxiety may be caused, as space is so limited outside the fairway.

Shoal-draught craft able to take the ground can dry out by arrangement on reasonably firm foreshore off Newton Ferrers or Noss Mayo. Above Noss Mayo is a public quay at Bridgend with 2m at high water springs. There are drying berths alongside here (by arrangement with harbourmaster).

Facilities

Fresh water from hose at Yealm steps pontoon (Yealm Hotel). No fuel. *Calor Gas/Camping Gaz* refills from Village Fayre, Newton Hill. No cash point. Toilets and showers at the Yealm Yacht Club. Good hotels and pubs. Meals at yacht club (weekend only). Six buses per day to Plymouth (fewer at weekends), where all services are available, as well as onward transport.

Plymouth

Tides

HW −0540 Dover

Devonport

MHWS	MLWS	MHWN	MLWN
5·5m	0·8m	4·4m	2·2m

Depths

Deep-water big-ship harbour. River Tamar fairway carries 2·4m as far as Neal Point, 1¼ miles above Tamar Bridge. Thereafter the river is navigable on the tide up to Gunnislake, 16 miles above the breakwater. Note, however, that there are some height restrictions: the Tavy Bridge is 7·6m, pylons cross the Tamar at Weir Point (19m), and 1½ miles further up is a 16m power line. The spectacular Calstock viaduct has 24m.

General

Plymouth, with its associated creeks and rivers, forms one of the Channel's greatest natural harbours. For centuries its fame has rested with the Royal Navy. From the days of Hawkins and Drake to nuclear submarines, the city has found a large part of its prosperity in the business of war. Great fishing fleets have sailed from here, as have voyages of discovery and colonisation.

Only in recent years has the haven become of any general use to the casual yachting visitor. Now, in addition to the possibilities of pushing up-river, or roughing it out with the fishing boats, there are three modern marinas. The city, rebuilt after the Blitz, is still fascinating to all seafaring people, and the rivers and creeks have much to offer the explorer.

SUTTON HARBOUR

Queen Anne's Battery Marina
RWYC
DirOc:WRG. 7.5s14m3M
Oc:G.8s
Fl(3)R.10s
2F·R
Fisher's Nose
4°08'W
50° 22' N
Sutton Harbour Marina
2F·G
Fl.G.3s
Q.R
2F·R
Lock
Fl(2)G.5s
2F·R
Barbican
Fl.R.3s
Fl.R.2s

A NW Winter Q(9)10s
B S Winter Ql(6)+LFl
C S Mallard VQ(6)+LFl

Clovelly Bay Marina

N

River Plym
Oreston
HOOE
Hooe Lake
2F·G 2F·G
DirF·
F·WRG
Cattedown
2F·R Dir
2F·R Q.R
Clovelly Bay Marina
Turnchapel
Dunstone Pt
Jennycliff
Withyhedge
DirWRG.13m13·5M&
Fl(2)Bu.5s10M
Ramscliff Pt
Bovisand Bay
Crownhill Bay
Bovisand Pier
2F·G(vert)17m3M
Staddon Pt
Andurn Pt
Whidbey
Oc(2)WRG.10s29m8/6M
Renney Point
Wembury Bay
Wembury Pt
Great Mew Stone
Range B
Fl.Y.10s
Range C
Fl.Y.5s
Queen Anne's Battery Marina
Sutton Hbr
The Hoe
STONEHOUSE
Mill Bay Marina Village
Inner Basin
RWYC
Smeaton's T
Oc.G
Q.WRG
Q.G
Ash Fl.G
A Q.R
B
Asia
Fl(2)R
N. Drakes I
Q.G
Drakes Island
Marked by 8
The Bridge
Fiour Lt Bns
Fl(2)Bu.5s
Melampus
Fl.R.4s
Duke Rock
VQ(9)10s
Mount Batten
Fl(3)G
Smeaton Pass
349°
Cattewater Channel
EASTERN CHANNEL
Fort LFl.WR.10s9m8/6M
PLYMOUTH BREAKWATER
Oc.WRG.10s5m8·5M
Red
W Tinker
VQ(9)10s
W Tinker Fl.G.10s
E Tinker
Q(3)10s
Shag Stone
Oc.Y.10s45m
DEVONPORT
Mt Wise
DirWAG.13·5M
Mayflower Marina
2F·R
The Narrows
Cremyll
Fl.R.2s
Wilderness
Cremyll
Mt Edgcumbe
Battery
Fl.R
DirWRG.13·5M
Raveness
Raveness Pt
Redding Pt
New Ground
Fl.R.2s
WESTERN CHANNEL
Knap
Fl.G.5s
OSR North
Fl.Y.2s
OSR South
Fl.Y.2s
S. Rubble
Fl.G.3s
West Mud
Q.R
Inswork Pt
Millbrook
Q.WG.11m11/3M
Maker
Fl(2)WRG.10s16m11·6M
Queens Ground
Fl(2)R.10s
Fl.WR.10s19m12/9M
Iso.4s12m10M Horn 15s
Picklecombe Pt
Sandway Pt
Cawsand Bay
Penlee Pt
Draystone
Fl(2)R.5s
Iso.W.
Sango Pt
Q.0.8m5M
Insworke
Millbrook
Millbrook Lake
ST. JOHN'S LAKE
Cawsand
Kingsland
Whitsand Bay
Rame Head

PLYMOUTH SOUND

PLYMOUTH SOUND

Depths in Metres

Approach and entrance

Plymouth Sound lies with Penlee Point to the west, and Wembury Point and the Mewstone on the east. The north part of the Sound is protected by a long low breakwater built in the centre, with channels each side of it. Yachts may pass through either.

From the west a vessel will first round the unlit but unmistakable Rame Head, an almost conical promontory with the ruins of a chapel at its summit. Penlee Point, also unlit, a mile and a quarter further in, is a low headland with a turreted beacon. Note the Draystone rocks (over most of which there is 1·8m), extending ¼ mile to the southeast of Penlee Point, marked by a red can buoy (Fl(2)R.5s).

A conspicuous 23m white tower (Fl.WR.10s 12/9M) marks the western end of the breakwater, now 1½ miles ahead. The lighthouse also has an LFl.WR.10s light shining 4° either side of 035°, which is a safe course for big ships from *Draystone* buoy to the western entrance.

Drake's Island now lies conspicuously to the north. The main fairway leads northeast towards Plymouth Hoe, marked on the port hand by the red *New Grounds* (Fl.R.2s) and *Melampus* (Fl.R.4s) buoys, and thence through the Asia Pass (see plan). Yachts need not keep to this, and can pass any side of the buoys by reference to the chart.

There is a short cut to the Hamoaze, between Drake's Island and the Mount Edgcumbe shore, known as the Bridge. This channel has a least depth of 2·1m and is marked by two lit red and two green posts (S pair is Q.G and Q.R; N pair is Fl(4)R and Fl(3)G). The safest way to approach it is on a course of 332°, on a transit of Devil's Point and a conspicuous house with three chimneys on the skyline, which clears certain underwater obstructions. Continue for a cable or so past the posts, after which you are back in deep water. In most tidal conditions and reasonable weather the channel is the logical route for small vessels in daylight.

Approaching Plymouth Sound from the east, it is important to note the firing range at Wembury Point. Firing may occur from 0930 to 1630 local time on Tuesdays to Fridays. Two large red flags are flown on the point when firing is in progress. Call *Wembury Range* on VHF Ch 16 (they work on Ch 10 and 11) or telephone the range officer on ☎ 01752 862799 (☎ 553740 extension 77406 out of office hours). If you are entering the sound during firing, you should pass to the west of the Eddystone Lighthouse, which lies 10 miles from the breakwater on a heading of 204°.

From the east, the Mewstone (57m) and the rocks extending 2 cables southwest of it will be left to starboard. Next the Shagstone, off Renney Point (a nearly square rock 1·2m high, marked by a black and orange beacon surmounted by a cone), should be given a good berth, as the tide may be setting across the rocks between it and the shore. Continue northward, passing between the eastern end of the Breakwater (Iso.WR.5s) and Staddon Point, and passing either side of Duke Rock lit west cardinal buoy. Now steer for the wide channel between Drake's Island and Mount Batten. From here, if proceeding towards the Hamoaze, you may leave Drake's Island well to port by day, or take the well lit Asia Pass by night. If bound for Queen Anne's Battery, Sutton Harbour or the Cattewater, hold on to Mount Batten breakwater end (Fl(3)G.10s), leaving it to starboard, and the lit south cardinal *South Mallard*. If, as will usually be the case, the 3·6m Mallard shoal is of no consequence, you may pass either side of the cardinal buoy and ignore the green *West Mallard* (Q.G) a cable or so to its north-northwest. Should you be concerned about the depth, leave both to starboard before swinging up the Cobbler Channel. By night, there is a white sector to the Oc.WRG light on the wall of Queen Anne's Battery which indicates the position of the Mallard. The red sector clears it on your starboard side.

Anchorage and moorings

Cawsand Bay in the Sound has good holding ground and its gently shelving floor makes an excellent anchorage in weather from southwest through northwest.

Northeast of the pier on the north side of *Drake's Island* is historically exciting, as legend has it that here Drake lay in 1580 after his circumnavigation in the *Golden Hind* while he sniffed the political wind. Despite this, it can be an uneasy berth; the holding is good, but it may be exposed in poor weather.

Anchor well in towards the shore in **Barn Pool**, south of Wilderness Point and due west of Drake's Island. Sound in with care to the northern end of the bay, inside a large mooring buoy. Buoy your anchor, as the bottom may be foul. Expect tidal eddies. You will be well sheltered from the west, and may walk from here to Cremyll, whence a ferry runs to Stonehouse. Cremyll has Mashford's famous yard and a pub.

The Sir Francis Drake pub at the west end of the Hoe maintains a few visitors' buoys. Land at the small boat harbour nearby and 'sign on' in the bar.

The Royal Western Yacht Club, the Royal Plymouth Corinthian Yacht Club and Queen Anne's Battery run a few moorings in the Cattewater – available on application.

Marinas

Mayflower International Marina

Approached either up Drake Channel and through the Narrows or, if conditions of tide and weather are suitable, through the Bridge, passing west of Drake's Island. Once through the Narrows, the marina's location is obvious. Call them on VHF Ch 80 for a berth, or tie up to the outer pontoon's reception berth between two striped flags, and report to the marina office. There are 30 visitors' berths, and this has proved a good place to leave boats for a period. All facilities are here, including a clubhouse with bar which welcomes visitors. There is a courtesy bus to Plymouth centre in the season. Security is first-class.

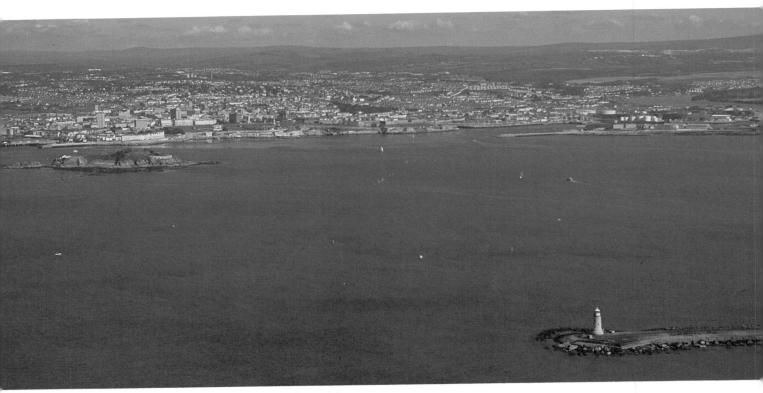

Plymouth Sound – Western Channel. Breakwater lower right,
Drake's Island at left and Mount Batten to the right. The green
Hoe is just left of centre.

The Cattewater looking west. Sutton Harbour and Queen Anne's
Battery on the right.

Sutton Harbour – Queen Anne's Battery on the right.

Mayflower Marina. Below the Hamoaze and River Tamar.

Plymouth Sound. *Panther* north cardinal buoy and the west entrance to Plymouth Sound.

Plymouth Sound. *Melampus* buoy with Drake's Island beyond.

The Hoe showing from right Smeaton tower, the Naval War Memorial and the Royal Western Yacht Club with flagstaff.

Approach to Sutton Harbour with *South Mallard* buoy off Mountbatten close to port.

Queen Anne's Battery

Approach between the *South Mallard* buoy and the end of the Mount Batten breakwater (Fl(3)G.10s), then shape up on around 030° to leave *Fisher's Nose* (Fl(3)R.10s) with its notice 'Speed Limit 8 knots to the east' to port. Queen Anne's Battery Marina is protected by a wall of vertical piling. Keep to starboard and follow this in. At night, you will be interested in the Oc.G light on the corner of the piling which effectively forms the entrance to the channel. Shortly after it, a Q.G indicates the end of

the marina breakwater, which you leave to starboard, swinging round to head for the visitors' berths on the southernmost pontoon. You can call ahead on VHF Ch 80. You may have to raft up, but do not enter a vacant finger jetty without permission. They are reserved.

The marina has all facilities, including launderette, clubhouse and café. The Royal Western Yacht Club of England has its clubhouse here, and from it many of the great long-distance races are organised. The club very generously makes its premises available to visitors.

The marina water taxi solves the otherwise messy problem of how to get to town, neatly circumventing a long, uninspiring walk. It drops you off at Mayflower Steps by the Barbican for a sensible fee. Sadly, 'QAB' is not a comfortable berth in heavy weather from a southerly quadrant. The snubbing of lines and general crashing around of pontoons can disturb even the most exhausted reveller.

Sutton Marina

Sutton Marina, whose approach is dredged to 2m, keeps a number of visitors' berths, mainly for vessels of under 10m LOA. The harbour is entered through its lock, which exhibits standard traffic signals. The lock will open at any time, day or night, 365 days a year. Free flow is established in the top half of the tide.

To port on entry is the Barbican, with its active fish market and salty atmosphere. Ahead is the marina. Always call the lock on VHF Ch 12. Their call sign is *Sutton Harbour*.

There are showers, toilets and a launderette, with fuel and water available seven days a week in summer, from 0730 to 2100 local time. There is a comprehensive boatyard close by, and the general facilities of the Barbican are also handy.

The Cattewater

Above Queen Anne's Battery this becomes highly commercial. Anchoring is prohibited and it is not recommended for pleasure craft.

Facilities at Plymouth

Plymouth offers everything any vessel could require, be she a dinghy or a man-of-war. There are many yacht yards. The marinas offer all services and there are a number of yacht clubs. The city council has a dinghy park with a launching site alongside the Mayflower Sailing Club, Barbican. *Calor Gas* and *Camping Gaz* exchange at all marinas.

Communications

Ferries to Roscoff, etc. Main line trains, buses, car hire. All you could ask for.

Beyond Plymouth

St Germans or Lynher River

Spring tidal range is 0·5m less than Plymouth, with all LWs about 20 minutes later.

This is the first major tributary to the Tamar, opening on the west side north of the old Devonport Dockyards, now privately run, and beyond the warship moorings. The river dries extensively, though there is good water in the channel for the first 1½ miles or so. Thereafter, shoal-draught yachts can comfortably work the tide up to St Germans.

Leave the first red buoy (*Lynher* Q.R) to port, or close to starboard, then leave the smaller (*Beggars*) definitely to port, before swinging to port to pass between small-craft moorings and the green *Sand Acre* buoy (Fl.G.5s) to starboard.

The next red is inshore off St Antony Passage, where you can anchor, row ashore and find a pub.

ST GERMANS
RIVER

Depths in Metres

N

SALTASH

Coombe
Bay

Viaduct

Henn Pt

Lynher
Q.R

Beggars I

Carew
Point

Sand
Acre
Pt

Sand
Acre
Fl.G.5s

Passage
Antony
Pt

Antony Passage

Forder
Lake

Viaduct

Jupiter
Pt

Bn

Bn

Bn

Shillingham Point

Bn

Bulland
Quay

Ince
Point

ST GERMANS RIVER

Wivelscombe
Lake

Ince
Quay

Ince

Black
Rock

Clift
Quay

Tredown Lake

Wacker
Lake

Redshank
Pt

Dandy Hole

Warren Point

Quay

Lynher   River

Viaduct
21mHm

Erth
Island

Jetty

Channel marked by posts

Markwell

Viaduct
21mHm

St
Germans Quay

ST GERMANS

Seaton Lake

Polbathick Lake

Polbathick

River Tiddy

Morvah Quay

TIDEFORD

27'

50°
26'
N

25'

4°18'W

19'

17'

15'

14'

13'

RIVER TAMAR

Depths in Metres

To Gunnislake

Morwellham

Quays

Harewood

Brickworks
(disused)

Quay

Quay

Railway

CALSTOCK

Quay

Viaduct
Hm 24m

Cotehele
Quay

South
Ward

BERE
ALSTON

Greenbank

North
Hooe

Halton
Quay

South
Hooe

Hole's Hole

Old
Limekiln

Weir Quay and
Boatyard

Pentillie
Quay

Clifton

Moorings

Hm 16m

Liphill
Jetty

Hallodene

Bere
Ferrers

Bn

Quay

Bn

Railway

Gas pipeline

Bn

Thorn Point

Pennards Pt

Cargreen

Quay

River Tavy

Warleigh
Barton

Quay

Weir Point

Lime
Point

Hm 21m

14'   13'   4°12'W   10'

30'

50°
29'
N

28'

27'

26'

In the next half-mile a power cable and gas line cross the bed of the river, so do not anchor here. Work towards Shillingham Point, noting that the deep water is about a cable offshore, then proceed on a heading of around 220° until Ince Castle bears a few degrees west of north. Now alter for the diminutive green *Ince* buoy, hard by the shore at Black Rock Point. Anchoring off Ince Point has much to recommend it to the seeker after solitude, but care must be taken over soundings and one's tidal height calculations.

After leaving *Ince* buoy close to starboard, pass on to the isolated red can in mid-stream, sounding with care. Leave this close to port and swing gently down onto 220°, sounding for the channel, to take you on into the steep, tree-lined narrows between Redshank and Warren Points. Here, on the south side, you will find Dandy Hole, with 4m and more at LAT. It is a wonderful anchorage, with absolutely no facilities except those provided by Mother Nature, who will always show her generosity given a chance.

Stay in the middle, slightly favouring the south side as the river turns northwesterly, then pick up the red and green posts which lead through the drying mud-flats to the private quay at St Germans. Speak to the club, upstream of the quay, about an overnight drying berth. There is a tap on the quay and basic facilities in the village half a mile away. The mighty rail viaduct peers down at you, but this, in its way, almost adds to the charm.

The Shell Channel Pilot makes no recommendations concerning the other creeks off this river. They are there to be explored by those with big hearts and small draughts.

River Tamar

Above St Germans River the Tamar continues under the Royal Albert and Tamar Bridges, and thence northward by a gradually shoaling, but well marked channel past Weir Point and on to Cargreen.

If you intend to proceed more than half a mile above the bridges, you must consult the tide tables and the plan. There is a shoal which dries 0·6m east-southeast of Neal Point. This is best avoided by passing very close to the 3 conical green buoys opposite Kingsmill Lake, beginning with *E Tamar N* (Fl.G.5s). The next two are smaller and unlit. You should thus leave the shoal to port.

Above the red beacon (leave to port) and the yellow buoy (leave to starboard) off Weir Point, the best water is found on a line which leaves the chimney at Cargreen close to port. There is deep water at Cargreen. Anchor clear of the moorings and land immediately above the Spaniards Inn close to the Cargreen Yacht Club.

Below Cargreen, Tamerton Lake and the River Tavy are non-starters for yacht navigation because of their bridges.

The stalwart spirit can now work the tide upstream, but the channel is largely unmarked after the green pile a couple of cables above Cargreen. The deepest water is on the outside of the various

bends, and sounding will reveal some pools deep enough for anchoring afloat throughout the tide for craft drawing 2m and more. Bear in mind, however, that this is a fairway and that excursion boats may not be amused by your presence in the middle of it.

Calstock has a line of moorings in just over 1m of water. There may be a spare one. Deep-draught vessels can dry against the quay. Fuel and water are available. Anchoring is not recommended below the viaduct, but a cable above it there is a 2·5m pool where yachts are reported to have lain.

Shoal-draught craft may manage to explore even further, and the river does not dry until a shoal patch just above Morwellham. Navigable water has been reported all the way up to Gunnislake, but you are advised to keep to the left-hand channel at Weir Head and use the redundant lock in order to avoid weirs (!) in the main channel.

Looe

Tides

HW −0538 Dover

MHWS	MLWS	MHWN	MLWN
5·4m	0·6m	4·2m	2·0m

Depths

Looe harbour and its entrance dry, with heights alongside of 2·4m (West Looe) and 1·8m (East Looe).

General

The important fishing port of Looe provides good shelter for craft able to take the ground. In offshore winds it is possible to anchor outside in depths of your choice, additional shelter being provided by Looe Island. The entrance is dangerous in strong onshore winds.

The town is picturesque in a workaday sort of way, but crowded in summer. Historically, its luggers, which were famed for their speed and power, have provided an archetype for numerous transom-sterned yachts.

Approach, entrance and berthing

Looe is readily identified by the conspicuous Looe Island (St George's Island) off the entrance. Approaching from the west the principal danger is the Ranneys rocks, which extend southeast and east from the island. These must be given a wide berth, but can be cleared in good visibility by keeping the beacon on Gribbin Head open of the cliffs at Nealand Point, west of Polperro, until the pier head (Oc.WR.3s) bears 305°. Steer straight for the pier head on 305°, staying in the white sector of the light after dark. A transit of the church spire in West Looe 'on' with the pier head will keep you clear of trouble by day, and it must be said that for the

Berth

There is one berth for visitors among the fishing boats. It is at the south end of the quay in West Looe, and is marked with a 'Visitors' sign. The bottom is firm sand and gravel. Report to the harbourmaster on arrival.

Off East Quay there is a reverse eddy on the flood, but you are urged not to try to berth on the east side, which is reserved for fishing boats.

Facilities

Fuel, repairs, engineers. Gas from chandlers. Diesel from lorry (ask at harbour office). Petrol by portage from garage. Pubs, restaurants, and all small-town facilities. Toilets and one shower.

Polperro

Tides

HW −0554 Dover

MHWS	MLWS	MHWN	MLWN
5·4m	0·6m	4·3m	2·0m

Depths

Polperro harbour dries up to about 2·3m, giving rise to depths of 3·3m at MHWS and 1·5m at MHWN. The anchorage outside shoals from 4·6m up to the drying harbour entrance.

stranger night entry is not recommended. It is better to anchor off and await the morning tide, but don't forget your riding light. Fishing boats may be moving whenever there is water to float them.

The overfalls south of Looe Island may be avoided in bad weather by keeping further to seaward. There is no passage suitable for strangers between Looe Island and the mainland.

Approaching from the east, keep Looe Island on the port bow until picking up the entrance. Then use the transit described above to keep clear of the rocks. Some of these are marked, but for a stranger the 'wide-berth' course is recommended.

Any safe approach must assume a sensible rise of tide to give a safe depth of water. Bear in mind that tides may run strongly in the entrance, so that entry under power is recommended.

Looe Harbour entrance dried out at low water between pier head (white band) and Chimney Rocks (left).

Looe Harbour and, below, Polperro.

General

The classic Cornish village of Polperro saw its finest hours many years ago when smuggling was its principal occupation. It is still active as a fishing community, with tourism supplying an important income supplement.

The harbour lies at the head of an inlet open to the southeast, with the outer pier about 1½ cables in from the sea. The harbour entrance is less than 10m wide, and in hard weather it is closed by a hydraulically operated gate. The current harbour chart is based on an original survey by Captains Williams and Bell RN in 1857. Trawlermen confirmed 120 years later that little had changed. Shelter on the outer moorings is good in moderate airs from all but the south or southeast, or at times of heavy swell, when the berth can be exceedingly uncomfortable. The inner harbour offers an excellent berth with comfortable drying-out in all but the latter wind directions in heavy weather.

Approach and entrance

Approach is made from a southeasterly direction when the harbour piers open up. As is shown on the plan, the Raney (dries 0·8m) lies off the headland on the west side of the entrance, with further rocks at the foot of Spy House Point on the eastern side. There is deep water up to the entrance of the inlet except for a rocky patch named the East Polca which lies half a cable south-southwest, clear of Spy House Point. This is only 1m down, but causes no problems in good weather with sufficient rise of tide. Another rocky patch about 30m northeast of the Raney can also be disregarded by many vessels of a size to make Polperro a serious option, as it has 2·5m over it. Entry is dangerous in fresh southeasterly or southerly winds, or when a swell is running in, though the inlet is protected from southwest through west to northeast.

Keeping the west pier head 'on' with the end of the outer pier on 310° will maintain your position in mid-inlet, clear of all dangers, passing north of the shallowest part of the East Polca.

Leave the outer pier well to starboard and steer midway between the inner piers. The west pier head shows a black ball when the harbour is closed (F.R by night). When it is open, the light is white. Strangers should not attempt entry by night.

Anchorage and berthing

There is just room for a small yacht to anchor outside. The deep water is only 25m wide, so if this doesn't attract you, try to pick up one of the moorings laid outside the outer pier for boats to await the tide. Moorings inside the harbour are for locals, but you may secure and dry out alongside the east quay wall just inside the entrance. It is a good idea to report to the harbour office, which is to be found in the fish market on the west side.

Facilities

Provisions, banks and pubs. Toilet opposite east quay. Fresh water on the quay. Petrol in cans from garage, and a smugglers' museum to explore while you wait for the tide to float you out. The Blue Peter 'one block back' from the west pier purveys real ales of global quality. These can be enjoyed while peering through low windows at the 'Pirates of Penzance' scene outside and listening to excellently canned blues music. Two or three hundred metres up the main street lies the Cottage Restaurant.

Here, first-class local seafood is served by staff who understand about pleasing their customers.

Fowey

Tides

HW −0540 Dover

MHWS	MLWS	MHWN	MLWN
5·4m	0·6m	4·3m	2·0m

Depths

There is deep water throughout this harbour and up the River Fowey as far as 3 cables above Wiseman Point. There is less water on the Polruan side, but still plenty for most yachts. Pont Pill is dredged for the moorings to 2m, as is Mixtow Pill. Above Wiseman's Reach the river shoals, but with sufficient rise of tide dinghies and other small craft can navigate as far as Lostwithiel.

General

Fowey is a fine, active port featuring a powerful mix of serious commercial shipping and almost equally serious yachting. In the Middle Ages it was relied upon to supply more ships and armed men to support the monarch of the day than any other harbour in the West Channel. Later, it became famous for privateering, piracy and smuggling. It has inspired many great writers, among them Sir Arthur Quiller-Couch, Kenneth Grahame (*The Wind in the Willows*), and Daphne du Maurier, whose first novel, *The Loving Spirit*, is said to be styled around the old Slade's yard in Polruan, still successfully building

Fowey Harbour. Polruan on right.

FOWEY

CONTINUATION TO LERRYN

N

23'

To
Lostwithiel

Boat Ho

Lerryn

River Lerryn

Mendy
Pill

2.6

River Fowey

Manley
Pill

0.1

2.8

Quay

0.6

Quay

Cliff Pill

2.6

50°
22'
N

St Sampson

Golant

2.7

1.8

Small Craft
Moorings

Quay

Hay Pt

St Cyrics
Creek

Quay

1.4

3.9

5

Penpoll Creek

Bodmin
Pill

4°38'W

See continuation

3.2

Wiseman's Reach

1.7

Moorings

4

1.4

Mixtow
Pill

Wiseman Pt

Mixtow

2.7

Pontoons

8.4

Mixtow
Reach

6.1

1.2

V

7.3

China
Clay Quay

Upper Carn Pt

Lew Roads

6

Lower Carn Pt

10.8

Ferry

BODINNICK

Caffa Mill
Pool

Pottery Corner

4

Prime Cellars
Boat House

7

Albert
Quay

Visitors' Moorings

Moorings

3.1

V

O Mont
(conspic)

St Fimbarrus Ch

0.9

Town Quay

Pont Pill

FOWEY

0.6

7.3

Penleath
Point

Swinging
Ground

Dredged 1985
2m

1.2

50°
20'
N

Hotel
(conspic)

2F.R(vert)

Iso.WRG.3s11m8-11M

Whitehouse Pt

2.3

V

Brawn Pt

N

Old Castle

3.6

Ferry

Moorings

0.3

Neptune Pt

Polruan
Pool

7.5

1

Readymoney
Cove

Mundy Rks

1.7

St Catherine's Pt

0.6

(1.8)

6.2

2

Town Quay

Fowey Lighthouse
L.Fl.WR.5s28m11/9M

Lamp Rk

Castle (ruins)

YC

Bns O

CG FS

POLRUAN

Coombe
Haven

2.4

0.6

Punch
Cross Rocks

Bn

Tr (59)

White House

3

7

6.4

Red

3.7

1.2

4.9

0.3

Wellake

3

7.3

0.6

Red

5.2

White

Light obscd N of line

2.7

Red

12.5

10.7

9.1

1.2

White

Green

39'

4°38'W

Depths in Metres

37'

19'·5

Fowey approach. *Cannis Rock* south cardinal buoy ½ mile southwest of Gribbin Head with its red and white tower on skyline. Fowey lies 1½ miles to the northeast.

heavy timber fishing boats under the ownership of Tom's. Transpose the name of Slade, and you will find many of du Maurier's characters still lying in Lanteglos churchyard above Polruan, as fine a walk as you will discover to enjoy on a long summer's afternoon.

Shelter is good, and Fowey is an all-weather entry, though this can be rough in an onshore gale on the ebb. In hard south or southwesterly weather a scend runs in, which can make lying in the lower harbour very uncomfortable, though quieter berths can often be found further up the harbour.

Approach and entrance

Fowey is easy to identify from seaward thanks to the unmistakable daymark on Gribbin Head 1¼ miles southwest of the entrance, a red and white tower 25·6m high standing on a base 71m above sea level.

Approaching from the east, the resident danger is the Udder Rock (dries 0·6m) 3 miles east of the entrance, marked by an unlit south cardinal bell buoy. By night, if you can see the red sector of Fowey lighthouse (LFl.WR.5s28m11/9M) you are south of the rock. The light cuts off to the north of the safe line.

The only dangers between this rock and the entrance are drying rocks immediately off Pencarrow Head.

The Cannis Rock (dries 4·3m) lies some 4 cables southeast of Gribbin Head. There are dangers south of the head as far as the rock, marked by a lit south cardinal bell buoy. To be safe, keep the cross on Dodman Point open southward of the 8m-high Gwineas Rock. If you have failed to see the *Cannis Rock* buoy after dark, the white sector of Fowey lighthouse (above) keeps you clear of it, with the western red sector opening immediately east of the buoy.

Arriving from the west, you can alter for the entrance once past the *Cannis*, but as there are rocky ledges off the west shore, give this side a good berth until close to the entrance. Within the narrows, the only dangers are the Punch Cross ledge on the east side, marked by a white beacon which should be given a berth of at least 60m, the Lamp Rock, marked with a white beacon nearly a cable beyond it, and the Mundy Rocks opposite on the west side.

At night, once clear of *Cannis* buoy, the white sector of Whitehouse Point leading light (Iso.WRG. 3s) will bring you safely through the entrance. Night entry is perfectly possible, but a stranger would need to be sure of where to go once inside. There are no further effective lights apart from two fixed reds (vertical) marking the end of a short jetty for the Polruan ferry east-northeast of Whitehouse Point.

Anchorage and moorings

The harbour and river come under the control of the Fowey harbourmaster. His office can be contacted on ☎ 01726 832471, but in any case call either *Fowey Harbour Radio* on VHF Ch 12 (office hours) or *Fowey Harbour Patrol* (0900–2000) on VHF Ch 12.

Short-term pontoon berthing is available at Berrill's Yard a cable or so upstream of Albert Quay, where the harbourmaster maintains a pontoon. Here, you can stay for up to 2 hours free of charge. The harbourmaster encourages yachtsmen not to abuse these free facilities.

Upstream of Pont Pill on the east side there are a number of clearly marked yellow or white visitors' swinging moorings, as well as a 30m pontoon. A similar pontoon is established in Pont Pill, where there are also a number of fore-and-aft visitors' moorings where you may raft up.

At the entrance to Mixtow Pill above Bodinnick is a further visitors' pontoon, and while lying here does involve you in a dinghy or water-taxi trip, you will be in calm water when things are livening up lower down the harbour.

All vessels over 12·5m LOA should seek advice from the harbourmaster or the harbour patrol before berthing.

Anchoring is not encouraged but, subject to the need for large vessels to use the Swinging Ground off Pont Pill, it is sometimes possible to anchor here by permission on the edge of the moorings.

Wiseman's Reach, once a favourite funk-hole in bad weather, is now largely taken up with moorings, some administered by FHC (including one visitors' mooring), but bilgekeelers can still slink away to discover a secluded berth somewhere in the mud up-river.

Facilities

Water taxi (VHF Ch 6). Fresh water on the pontoon at Albert Quay, or tap at Polruan. Fuel from *Fowey Refueller* (VHF Ch 10, 16), or in cans from the garage in Lostwithiel Street, Fowey. Outboard fuel and diesel from Polruan Quay. Outboard repairs at J A Marine. *Calor Gas/Camping Gaz* from Upper Deck at Albert Quay in Fowey. *Camping Gaz* also from chandler on Polruan Quay. Banks in Fowey. Post office in Fowey or at Polruan. Heavy repairs or hauling at Tom's (☎ 870232), Polruan, who are also marine engineers. Otherwise Fowey Boatyard, Passage Street. Nearby is the launderette. Oily water/dirty oil disposal facilities at FHC's Brazen Island yard in Polruan. Sewage pump-out facilities are available at Berrill's Yard pontoon, operated by the Commissioners. At this site, FHC will be developing further facilities including washing, showers, dryers, etc., plus a further pontoon system with fresh water.

Simple provisions in Polruan. Most of what you need in Fowey. Good pubs and restaurants on both sides of the river. Escape the mob at the pub at Bodinnick, just above the ferry.

Scrubbing by arrangement with harbourmaster at Brazen Island, Polruan. Royal Fowey Yacht Club welcomes members of affiliated clubs. Launching by arrangement at Tom's Yard, or at Caffa Mill. Rubbish skip in Pont Pill.

Communications

Buses to Par and main line railway.

Charlestown

Tides

HW approx −0555 Dover

MHWS	MLWS	MHWN	MLWN
5·1m	0·6m	4·0m	1·8m

These tidal heights are for the neighbouring china-clay port of Par. Charlestown is similar, but may not be identical.

Depths

Approaches dry 0·9m, with a drying height of 1·2m immediately outside the outer basin. Depths inside are adequate for small commercial vessels.

General

Charlestown is a privately owned artificial 19th-century harbour. It is austere, yet it is almost classically unspoiled and so is of great interest. It is still used commercially to a limited extent by vessels in the china-clay trade. The entrance and approach dry out, but a wet basin is maintained by a tidal lock. Shelter inside is total, but the entrance should not be attempted in any sort of onshore wind and sea, which will turn the outer basin into an untenable swirl of broken water.

Approach and entrance

On entering St Austell Bay from the southwest, Charlestown can be identified to the eastward of St Austell itself. Ideally, the entrance is approached on 287°, lining up a white patch on the west wall of the outer basin with the right-hand edge of a row of cottages which can be seen through the pier heads. This clears the rock shelves to both sides. Inside the outer basin, turn to starboard for the lock gate. If you wish to enter the inner basin you should either telephone the harbourmaster on ☎ 01726 67526 or call on VHF Ch 14. The lock will open on request

from HW ± 2 hours approximately, but if more vessels are expected you may be asked to wait for a short while.

Do not attempt night entry, even though the south jetty carries a fixed red light and the north jetty a fixed green. Note signals as follows:
Green light at night or red ensign by day – harbour open.
Red light at night or black shape by day – harbour closed.

There are a few alongside berths for visitors, but if you don't want to have the full experience, try anchoring off immediately east of the piers and come in by dinghy. There is a pub, and various other benefits.

Mevagissey

Tides

HW −0600 Dover

MHWS	MLWS	MHWN	MLWN
5·4m	0·7m	4·3m	2·0m

Depths

Alongside the outer end of the South Pier depths exceed 2m. Even at the inner end there is at least 1·5m. From an entry depth in the region of 2·5m, the outer harbour shelves to its rocky edges, and dries inshore of a line from the lifeboat slip to 25m from the outer end of the East Pier.

The inner harbour dries, but is not available to visitors.

General

Mevagissey is the perfect Cornish fishing village. As such, it is inevitably heavily populated with tourists in the summer months. The commercialism which goes with this has not, however, spoiled the picturesque nature of the place, which still operates a considerable fishing fleet. This is the harbour's main

Par.

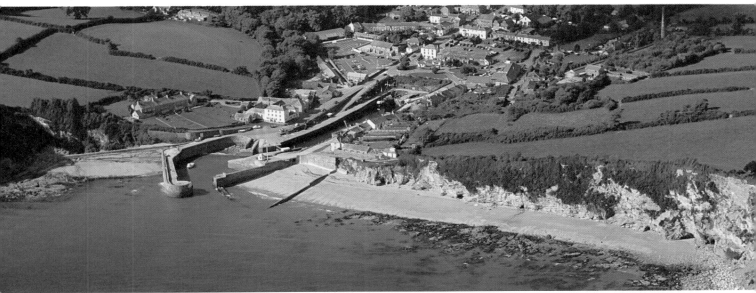

Charlestown. Lock can be seen at the right of the outer harbour.

Mevagissey.

function. Depending on draught and tide, the outer harbour is also available to visiting yachts, but there is no particular encouragement in the way of copious visitors' berths. It is well sheltered by the land from winds from south-southwest to north-west. The North Pier offers some shelter from the north except in rough weather, but easterly winds bring in a surge. The harbour is poor in strong onshore conditions, and entry may well be dangerous.

The nearest ports of refuge are Fowey (7 miles) and Falmouth (14 miles).

Approach, entrance and berthing

There are no dangers in the offing, save Gwineas Rock to the south-southeast. While it is safe to pass inshore of this, strangers who are not expert pilots in possession of a large-scale chart are advised to pass to the east of the lit east cardinal buoy marking the group.

On arrival off the port, steer for the white lighthouse on the South Pier (Fl(2)10s9m12M). Do not come in from north of northeast on account of Black Rock Sand (dries 0·3m), which extends to the east from the North Pier. Enter between the piers and seek a berth, usually alongside the South Pier, sometimes rafted up to another yacht, or to a fishing boat by arrangement. Anchoring is not permitted within the harbour, but a spare mooring may occasionally be made available. Because space is so limited, the harbourmaster may direct vistors to anchor in the offing if the weather suits. If you do not raise the harbourmaster on the radio, report to his clearly marked white-painted office on the North Pier. The harbour office can be called on VHF Ch 16, or telephoned in advance on ☎ 01726 843305 (842 406 out of hours).

Facilities

A fuel and water service is now available for yachts on the South Pier. There is an excellent traditional boatyard, shops, launderette, banks (with limited opening in summer months only), pubs, cafés, restaurants and a remarkable small fishing museum.

Communications

Buses to St Austell and its railway station.

Portmellon

Half a mile south of Mevagissey lies the small bay of Portmellon, which affords a good temporary anchorage between its headlands. Sound in to find your best berth. It should only be used in settled weather and offshore winds.

Falmouth and Falmouth estuary (including Truro, St Mawes and Penryn)

Tides

HW −0558 Dover

MHWS	MLWS	MHWN	MLWN
5·4m	0·6m	4·3m	2·0m

General

Falmouth is one of the finest all-weather harbours in the British Isles. It can be entered in any conditions, and the inner harbour is sheltered in everything but hard easterlies. Even when these arrive, Falmouth Yacht Marina is still protected, and a good lee can be found in St Mawes. The River Fal itself is virtually a string of hurricane holes where all manner of ghastly gales can be ridden out in peace and tranquillity.

The town of Falmouth and its associated creeks and villages have a long history of seafaring. Foreign mail was dispatched from here for hundreds of years, and the local newspaper still enjoys the colourful title *The Falmouth Packet*. More recently, great sailing ships came from every corner of the world to anchor in Carrick Roads and await instructions from their agents as to where their cargo was to be landed. It could have been bought and sold two or three times while they were on passage, bound towards 'Falmouth for Orders'.

Falmouth maintains a flourishing commercial port. Amongst its other delights is a fleet of oyster dredgers which still work under sail. Indeed, any traditional boat enthusiast will be thrilled by his visit, for here he or she will be able to enjoy the sight of some of the best sailed gaffers in Britain racing several times a week in the summer months.

The harbour is a favourite jumping-off point for ocean voyagers, as well as those whose aims are less grand. A 100-mile reach to Ouessant is a joy to the Solent-based sailor, more usually faced with a 250-mile slog to windward.

Approach and entrance

Falmouth approaches are well sheltered in even the hardest westerly blow. Note, however, that after prolonged easterlies the sea lumps up very unpleasantly. It is safe enough to navigate, but there is little pleasure in it. The entrance lies between Pendennis Point, with its conspicuous castle, and St Anthony Head (19m white tower, Oc.WR.15s22/20M). From the south and west there are no dangers in the offing once the *Manacles* buoy (east cardinal) has been left to port. Should the buoy prove difficult to spot, the Manacles are also covered by the red sector of St Anthony Head lighthouse. From the east, overfalls may be found up to 1½ miles off the Dodman, breaking over the 6 or 7m-deep ledges of the Field and the Bellows. Up to 3 cables south-

TRURO RIVER

TRURO

Truro River
(buoyed)

2_3

Tidal Barrage
2F.R(vert)   2F.G(vert)

1_5

Calenick Creek

1_5 1_9

3

Malpas

2_5

St Clement

2_7

2_7

Tresillian River

Malpas Pt

V

Woodbury Pt 1_6

Lambe Creek 1_4

Parson's Creek

Church Creek

Maggot Bank 0_7

1

Devoran

4_3

Restronguet Creek

1_2

2_7

1_8

0_9

Restronguet Pt

FALMOUTH HARBOUR

Restronguet Passage

Moorings 0_2

Weir Pt

Restronguet

0

Mylor Bridge

3

Mylor Creek

1_5

Mylor Pool

0_5 G   (May-Sept) 1_1

R 0_4

V

Mylor

2_4

Penarrow Pt 1_8

Northbank
Fl.R.4s

3_4

22

Cliffs

Trefusis Pt

Penryn Harbour

2_1

Penryn

1_2 Channel marked by buoys 0_6

Falmouth Marina

Fl.R.2s
Greenbank Quay 0_6

4

6_1

Flushing

Inner Harbour   Q.19m3M

2F.R(vert)   Eastern Breakwater

4_9 2F.R(vert)

4_3

3_7

Governor
BYB

East Narrows
R

West Narrows
Fl(2)R.10s

S_4

St Mawes
R
YB

Castle
Fl.G.10s 5_8

ST MAWES

St Mawes V

2_1

St Mawes Harbour

Amsterdam Pt

Carricknath Point

0_9

FALMOUTH

2F.R(vert)

Falmouth Yacht Haven

1_8 5_8

Port Pendennis

Castle (69)

Black Rock
Q(3)10s
BYB

6_4

Pendennis Point

0_4

4_1

5

Swanpool Pt

3_5

2_9 0_8

1

3_1

Pennance Pt

8_6

12_9

Falmouth Bay

15_5

12

R. Fal

10_5

14_1

6_7

8_9

12

8_8

White

Red

White

St Anthony Head
Oc.WR.15s22m22-20M
Horn 30s

Zone Pt

7_7

8

11_4

11_6

17_4

Church Ck

Truro River

2_5

Visitors' pontoons

1_6

Ruan Creek

2_4

R. Fal

2_7

Cowlands Creek

1_5 5_8

Lamouth Creek

14_9

King Harry Passage

Trelissick Ho   Ferry

River Fal

1_4

Channals Creek

2_4

Visitors' pontoons V

Turnaware Bar
Fl.G.5s

Tolcarne Creek

Turnaware Point

Pill Ck

Pill Pt

Pill
Fl(3)G.15s 1_2

0_8

Ch marked by buoys

1_2

0_6 0_8

Carick Carlys Rock 16_8

BY

Carick
Fl(2)G.10s

0_4

14

22   **Messack**
Fl.G.15s

St Just Creek

62

1_8

St Just

Messack Pt

24

2_8

29

St Just Pool

2_4

St Just
R

22

2_2

Carclase Pt

Trethem Mill

Trethem Creek

2_1

Percuil

0_6

North Hill Pt

Percuil River

4_3

The Vilt
Fl(4)G.15s

21

2_1

1_5

4_9

Carrick Road

5_8

25

2_1

3

Castle Pt

FALMOUTH YACHT MARINA

Small Craft Moorings 0_6

1_2 Fl.Y.2s 0_1 VQ(3)5s 3_4

Mud   2F R 6_3

3_1 2_1

0   1   Cable

N

southwest of Gull Rock (38m high, just east of Nare Head) lie the Whelps. These dry 4·6m. 2½ miles northeast of St Anthony Head, the Bizzies (3·7m and 4·6m) lie up to 1 mile east-southeast of Greeb Point.

The entrance is clear of dangers except for Black Rock, inconveniently sited just west of centre. This uncovers at LW and is marked by an unmistakable black beacon with two globe topmarks. Yachts can pass either side of this, giving it a respectable berth, but note that its shoal water extends for ½ cable north and south, and that 2·1m LAT extends almost a cable to the east. Those wishing to chance nothing to judgment can ensure success by leaving the associated lit east cardinal buoy to port. This is in any case prudent for strangers after dark, as Black Rock is unlit. Thereafter the deepest water is indicated by various main channel markers, shown on the plan.

If you are entering St Mawes, leave *Castle* green buoy (Fl.G.10s) well to port and look for the smaller *St Mawes* unlit south cardinal. This marks Lugo Rock (0·6m), and should be left to port according to your draught and the state of tide.

Most visitors enter the inner harbour of Falmouth by leaving the *Governor* east cardinal buoy to port, though for any but the deepest draughts this is not strictly necessary.

Thereafter, round the East Breakwater (2F.R) and the North Arm of Queen's Jetty (Q). Now proceed on a westerly heading until the inner harbour opens up around the west end of the Queen's Jetty. From here, steer southwest towards your chosen berth.

If you are headed for the Penryn River (for the Falmouth Yacht Marina), round the East Breakwater and North Arm as before, then continue west-northwest, keeping the bulk of the town moorings on your port hand, towards Greenbank Quay. This is rendered conspicuous by the Greenbank Hotel sign painted in large letters on the wall, as well as the Royal Cornwall Yacht Club immediately to the south. Stay in mid-channel between Greenbank and Flushing, and pick up the red and green channel markers which lead up-river.

Entry into the River Fal is easy for most yachts after half flood, for none of the large area of the upper harbour dries, outside of the creeks. Watch out for Carick Carlys Rock (dries 0·8m) 3 cables east of Restronguet Point. It is marked with unlit north and south cardinal beacons which are not always easy to see. The buoyed fairway has deep water at all states of tide, so deeper-draught vessels can follow it up from Carrick Road, confident that they can proceed all the way up-river as far as Maggoty Bank. Whether using the channel or not, all yachts should be sure to leave the small green buoy northwest of Turnaware Point to starboard in order to avoid the drying shoal between it and the Point. Above Turnaware Point, stay in mid-stream as far as Ruan Creek. Thereafter, favour the east side until *Maggoty Bank* buoy is identified. Leave this to starboard, then swing back to the centre of the river once more. Just south of the buoy is the minimum depth thus far at 2·1m (LAT).

Above Maggoty Bank, depths vary as far as Malpas. Between Malpas and Truro depths are very slender, but shoal-draught craft can work the last of the flood as far as the city by following the buoys. Truro is accessible two hours either side of HW. For those desirous of the city's benefits (including a large supermarket hard by the waterfront) but unwilling to chance their keels, a dinghy trip on the tide to Truro from an anchorage below Maggoty Bank is entirely feasible and can offer a welcome diversion for a gale-bound crew.

Anchorage and moorings

In Falmouth, anchor off Custom House Quay, keeping at least a cable clear of the commercial docks. You may be asked to clear out temporarily for shipping movements, but this is otherwise a secure and comfortable berth in all but strong east or southeast winds, though northerlies can sometimes funnel down the harbour. Depths vary from 1·5 to 2·5m LAT. It is deeper closer to the docks. If in doubt, call the harbourmaster (*Falmouth Harbour Radio*) on VHF Ch 16, working 12, or ask his launch. There is a small town marina here (Falmouth Yacht Haven) for 40 visiting yachts of up to 12m LOA, with a maximum depth of 1·8m. Call the harbourmaster to check availability.

Dinghies may be left on the inside of the yacht haven.

There are a number of visitors' moorings between Greenbank and Prince of Wales Pier. *K1* to *K6* and *T3* to *T5* are marked *FHC*. A further 7 or 8 are marked *RCYC Visitor* and are administered by the club, which has a good slipway for landing and a launch (1000–1900) which listens on VHF Ch 37.

There is also a pontoon island for visitors' use, situated beyond the moorings approximately east of the Royal Cornwall YC. In the right conditions this can be a quiet berth for vessels of up to 12m LOA.

Falmouth Marina

70 visitors' berths. Approach up the Penryn River, taking care to stay in the buoyed channel, and identify a black and yellow pole with ♦ topmark (VQ(3)5s). Leave this to starboard, and two fixed red lights beyond the north end of a private pontoon to port, then proceed to the reception berth beside the conspicuous fuel berth for instructions. Alternatively, call on VHF Ch 80, particularly if over 13m LOA. Note the black and yellow pole with diagonal cross topmark (Fl.Y.2s) beyond the fuel berth. This indicates the northwestern extremity of the dredged water. Keep it open to port of the east cardinal for your final approach after dark.

There is enough water on the outer berths for craft with draught of 2·4m or more.

St Mawes

Anchor on the north side off the beach (covers at HW), keeping clear of the moorings and the ferry fairway. St Mawes Sailing Club maintains three visitors' moorings up the Percuil River, but depths

Flushing. Landing pier on the left.

Mylor Yacht Harbour and moorings on the west bank of River Fal 2 miles from the entrance.

Approaching St Mawes from the southwest. *Castle* buoy on left, *St Mawes* south cardinal buoy to the right of village.

are uneven, so without local knowledge apply to the club (☎ 01326 270686). St Mawes harbourmaster (☎ 01326 270553) may also be able to help out with a mooring. Generally speaking, Percuil River holds considerable attraction for the shoal-draught boat prepared to anchor and take the ground, though care should be taken about oyster beds.

Mylor
Mylor Yacht Harbour, on the south side of the entrance to Mylor Creek, has some visitors' moorings off the pontoons. The entry from the deep water is marked by seasonal red and green buoys. Call *Mylor Yacht Harbour* on VHF Ch 80 during working hours, or tie up to the outside pontoon clear of the fuel berth and enquire ashore. The upper creek dries.

Restronguet
Deep-draught yachts anchor west of Restronguet Point in about 3m, but you must work the tidal height to approach safely. Whether you pass north or south of Carick Carlys Rock you will find less than a metre of water at LAT. Shoal-draught craft can work the tide up to the pontoon off the Pandora Inn on the south shore (dries about 1m). The upper creek dries, and the deep pool in the entrance is full of local moorings.

St Just
In easterly weather, anchor immediately south of the entrance to the creek or south of Messack Point, clear of the moorings. Land at the head of the inlet on the starboard hand. There is a shingle beach near Pascoe's Yard. The place is extraordinarily beautiful in summer.

River Fal
Once past Turnaware Point, with its small green buoy well to the north (which *must* be left to starboard), craft of any reasonable draught may anchor at the mouth of Channal's Creek, with a spectacular view up the lawns to Trelissick House. Shallower vessels may find a drying berth in the entrance to Tolcarne Creek, and a deep-water visitors' pontoon is located off Turnaware Bar.

A mile or so beyond Tolcarne, above King Harry Ferry, amongst a series of apparently permanently mothballed merchant vessels, the river swings 90° to the eastward at the entrance to Cowlands and Lamouth Creeks. Both offer delight to the dinghy explorer, and the yacht can anchor on the northwest bank clear of moorings in sensible depths by sounding in. Buoy your anchor. The ground chains from the merchant ships are serious tackle, and run close to the shore.

Falmouth, looking up-river to Penryn. Inner harbour on extreme
left. Greenbank Quay just right of centre.

St Mawes.

A quarter-mile further up, on the south bank, is the Smugglers Cottage Restaurant and Tea Shop. Here, visitors' moorings are maintained immediately upstream of a pontoon used by tripper boats. Secure to one, then settle up at the Cottage.

Ruan Creek is undeveloped, and a shoal-draught yacht could lie sweetly in the mud, undisturbed by much except the waterbirds.

The next reach runs northward to Maggoty Bank. Anchor at will in this stretch, or tie up to one of the midstream visitors' pontoons at its lower end, sounding towards the shoaling west bank.

Maggoty Bank buoy must be left to starboard. Above it is ample water for most boats to anchor until ½ mile short of Malpas, where depths begin to reduce considerably. There is a conspicuous pontoon below the yard at Malpas where shoal-draught craft can sometimes find a berth.

Malpas Visitors' moorings can be found here, marked *V1*, *V2*, *V3*, etc.

If you choose to go on up to Truro, the channel is fully buoyed. The Authority are keen to encourage visitors and would be pleased to assist a larger vessel in making the passage from lower down the river. The harbour office listens on VHF Ch 12 (*Carrick One*). At the top of the river, you will find three branches – all navigational dead ends. Berth on the quay, where the harbour office is located. The harbour office is in the western arm, and you should report there before drying out in soft mud. A boat of modest draught may float for a couple of hours either side of HW.

Facilities

Falmouth and Penryn have all the facilities any yachtsman could conceivably require.

Fresh water is available at both marinas, and at Mylor Yacht Harbour, Town Quay, Truro, St Mawes and Malpas. *Calor Gas* and *Camping Gaz*

exchange at Falmouth Marina and Falmouth Chandlers, in Commercial Road, Penryn. Also at Mylor Chandlery. Fuel from the Falmouth Yacht Haven, summer only. Also from *Ulster Industry* barge moored opposite Trefusis Point, Falmouth Marina (0700–2200) and Mylor Yacht Harbour in season. Falmouth Marina has showers and toilets, which are also available at the Royal Cornwall Yacht Club and St Mawes Sailing Club. Basic unisex showers could be had on Custom House Quay, but the Authority advises that these will be upgraded in time , on a new site on the North Quay close to the yacht haven. Launderettes in Falmouth town centre, Falmouth Marina, Truro and Mylor Yacht Harbour.

There are a number of excellent chandleries and numerous fine boatyards. All town facilities.

Facilities at Truro include fresh water, garbage disposal, shower, toilets, chemical toilet disposal, mail delivery, an excellent restaurant, cinemas and all shopping.

Communications

Trains to Truro, thence connections to everywhere. Coach services.

The main road from Exeter to Falmouth is now first-class. The car journey can be executed rapidly with fine moorland scenery to enjoy for much of the way.

Helford River

Tides

HW −0613 Dover
Entrance

MHWS	MLWS	MHWN	MLWN
5·3m	0·6m	4·2m	1·9m

Helford River. Mawnan Shear on the right.

Helford River. Helford Passage and the Pool. Visitors' moorings centre. Anchorage extreme left.

Depths

Deep water in the approach, shoaling inside to 3·4m half a mile west of Mawnan Shear, then variable depths, with a deep pool off Helford Point. Between here and Frenchman's Creek the plan or chart should be read carefully for depths. Above Frenchman's Creek the bottom shoals steadily into the drying mode within a mile, but it is possible for craft drawing 2m to work the spring tide up to Gweek Quay.

General

Helford River is as beautiful a stretch of water as the South of England has to offer. Despite being developed in its lower reaches, the river is still itself, with woods and enchanted creeks to explore by dinghy, if your draught does not permit your yacht to venture so far. To visit Helford without first reading Daphne du Maurier's *Frenchman's Creek* is to sell yourself short. Romantic it may be, but so is the place. She has caught it to a nicety.

Shelter in westerly weather is complete, but do not expect too quiet a night in a strong easterly unless you are well upstream.

Approach and entrance

When coming from Falmouth, be sure to clear the dangerous Gedges Rocks, marked by a green conical buoy (Fl.G.5s), which lie south of Rosemullion Head on the northeast of the entrance. This buoy must be left to starboard. The buoy may be taken up out of season. If so a transmit of Mawnan Shear and the wooded point immediately W of the pool just clears the danger.

Approaching from the east, stay in the middle of the entrance and be sure to leave Voose rocks to port. They are marked by an unlit north cardinal beacon some 4 cables east of Bosahan Point. Proceed through the narrows, avoiding the shoal marked by a green buoy on the north side opposite Helford Creek.

When coming from the west and south keep well clear of Nare Point and Dennis Head. If you are tempted by Gillan·Harbour, note that the rock in the entrance lies further inshore of the east cardinal beacon which guards it than you might expect. Note also the large rock shelf (dries 2·6m) which extends in all directions to seaward of Men-aver Point. Unfortunately the best water is taken up with moorings, so only shoal-draught craft able to pass on into the drying water will benefit from the harbour's not inconsiderable delights.

Pressing on up Helford River above Frenchman's Creek, just over a mile beyond Polwheveral Creek the water divides. The south fork goes to Mawgan. You want the northern branch, which is marked by red posts with can topmarks to port, and by green posts with triangular topmarks to starboard. From here up to Gweek the channel dries completely at MLWS.

Anchorage and moorings

Anchorage can be obtained in calm weather in the bight on the north side of the entrance, off Porth Saxon.

In the pool off Helford village there are a number of visitors' moorings with green pick-up buoys. Do not try to anchor. Either pick up a spare buoy, call the mooring officer on VHF Ch 80 or 37, or, better still, look out for him in his launch.

If you prefer to anchor, the only feasible deep-water site is further upstream, approximately opposite Porthnavas Creek. Immediately west of its entrance on the south side of the main river are some deep pools with over 3m, and sometimes as much as 6m in small areas. This is a beautiful place, and you are well sited to *row* round the corner into Frenchman's Creek. Truly a magic place in fair weather and foul.

Shoal-draught yachts may just find room to anchor around the edge of Abraham's Bosom, the 2m pool at the entrance to Porthnavas Creek. The pool itself is full of moorings. In a small creek on the west shore is Porthnavas Yacht Club, where you may lie alongside and even dry out by arrangement. The club welcomes visitors, and has a bar and restaurant. Further up-river, Polwheveral Creek has more water, or rather less drying height, than Frenchman's Creek, and can produce some wonderfully secluded spots for the bilgekeeler ready to avail herself of her full potential.

Up at Gweek you will find a quay and a boatyard where you can dry out alongside for a modest fee.

Facilities

Helford River Sailing Club welcomes visitors and has excellent facilities. There is a landing-point on the west side of the creek at Helford Point, where the boatyard has a shop, restaurant, fuel and boats for hire. Helford village has a post office, shops, provisions and the thatched Shipwright's Arms. It also has a gourmet restaurant. A ferry runs from Helford Point to The Ferry Boat Inn at Helford Passage, which is a hotel and restaurant.

There are boatyards at Helford, Porthnavas and Gweek. Launching site by the inn, which owns the car park.

The club at Porthnavas welcomes visitors. It has a bar, restaurant, dinghy landing and limited cranage. It can supply diesel and has the only petrol pump on the Helford River with the exception of Gweek. Minor repairs can be arranged. Provisions can be bought, and local oysters are available from the warehouse at the jetty.

Communications

Buses to Falmouth from the top of the hill at Trebah, behind the inn.

Coverack

Tides

HW +0607 Dover

MHWS	MLWS	MHWN	MLWN
5·3m	0·6m	4·2m	1·9m

Depths

The harbour dries completely, but has a minimum depth at the pier of 2·4m MHWN, or 3·5m at MHWS.

General

Coverack lies a little over 1 mile north of Black Head and the same distance south of Lowland Point southwest of the infamous Manacles rocks.

The tiny harbour with its small, colourful fishing village, is formed by a picturesque 18-century wall, built out and then extending westward from the north side of Dolor Point.

Approach and entrance

Coming from the north, round the Manacles east cardinal buoy, then give Lowland Point with its offlying rocks (½M to seaward) a wide berth before shaping up into the Cove. From southwards, beware of the Guthers, 2 cables off Chynhalls Point, halfway between Black Head and Coverack.

If rounding the end of the wall at a 'touch-and-go' state of tide, the best water will be found by hand-railing about 10m off. In any event, keep fairly close to the wall, because rocks on the west side of the entrance extend well out.

Berthing

Yachts can dry out inside the wall in suitable conditions, and shelter in settled weather or moderate offshore winds is surprisingly good.

If no berth is available, or you do not fancy taking the ground, there are a number of moorings in the offing. These are laid for local craft, but there should be no complaint if you take a free one. There is no guarantee as to the state of the tackle and you should rely on your own judgement. Charges are modest. Alternatively, anchor in a clear space.

Landing from the dinghy is easy. There are ladders on the pier and a slipway.

Harbourmaster is Mr Carey, ☎ 01326 280583.

Coverack.

Facilities

Lovely cliff walks.

The Paris Hotel pub standing above the quay sells beer, meals and rooms. Toilets close by. Basic provisions and a memorable ice cream shop whose rum and raisin special rejoices in the name of 'Yo-ho-ho'. No water, and no fuel, unless you enjoy lugging your cans 2 miles from the nearest garage.

Porthleven

Tides

HW +0551 Dover

MHWS	MLWS	MHWN	MLWN
5·5m	0·8m	4·3m	2·0m

General

The harbour at Porthleven was built originally in 1811. It maintains a few fishing craft and has a famous history of boat building, with pilots coming from as far away as Wales to commission sailing craft of 15m (50ft) and more, noted for speed, seaworthiness and beauty. The harbour, which lies about 8½ miles northwest of the Lizard, dries and is wide open to the southwest. As a result, it is rarely visited by yachts, but it is not crowded and suffers little from tourism.

Approach and entrance

Porthleven is entered between the Little Trigg rocks off the south pier head and the Deazle Rocks on the northwest side. It is a difficult entrance because it is only 60m wide and the Deazle Rocks are not marked by buoys or beacons, nor are there clear leading marks to the centre of the entrance. It would be unwise to attempt the entrance without local advice except by day under particularly favourable conditions in offshore winds. For a visitor to attempt entry by night would be madness.

Approach should be made on a course parallel with the long inner side of the pier, but about 20m northwest of it. This course crosses a bar formation (which is liable to change). At the entrance there are ledges of rock extending about 75m or more off the pier. The entrance lies between these rocks on the east side and the Deazle Rocks on the west. There is 2·4m at the entrance, followed by 4·1m after which shoaling begins rapidly.

The outer harbour dries 0·9m to 1·8m, and there are rocks fringing the foot of the pier. The inner harbour also dries out completely, and is closed with baulks of timber in bad weather and in winter.

By arrangement with the harbourmaster (☎ 01326 574270) yachts may berth alongside the quay with about 3m at MHWS in the deepest berth. The bottom appears firm for drying out purposes. In the absence of a prior arrangement, tie up to the wall in the inner harbour as convenient, then try to contact the harbourmaster, whose office is on the east side of the inner harbour.

A F.G light is shown about 30m from the pier head when traffic can move. A second light of similar characteristics shows when required over an arc 033°–067° for craft entering. This is sited on the east side near the entrance to the inner harbour.

Facilities

Fresh water by angling centre on west side of harbour. Fuel by portage from garage 50m from quay. Toilets, modest supermarket and off-licence. Pubs and cafés. Bus service to Penzance and Falmouth.

Launching sites: trailed boats of any size from ramp, slipway at the head of the inner harbour near high water for smaller craft only.

Porthleven. Dried out in the inner harbour with the gate closed for the winter. Note the clock tower visible from seaward.

Porthleven.

St Michael's Mount

Tides

HW +0550 Dover

MHWS	MLWS	MHWN	MLWN
5·6m	0·8m	4·4m	2·0m

Depths

Harbour dries from 1·5m to 3m, but the anchorage has at least 2·5m LAT.

General

The tidal island of St Michael's Mount makes a remarkable landmark, with its romantic, turreted skyline. It was of great importance as a commercial port from Roman times, when it was a base for tin trading, through the long centuries until the civil war. It then provided a perfect centre for Royalist gun-running. The harbour was rebuilt in 1727, and its prosperity continued until Penzance finally eclipsed it with its better facilities. The isle has been the home of the St Aubyn family for over 300 years.

Approach and entrance

Do not approach the east or north sides of the Mount. They are foul with shoals. Instead, come in from Penzance Bay with Gear Rock astern (black beacon with cage topmark) and the north end of the

St Michael's Mount.

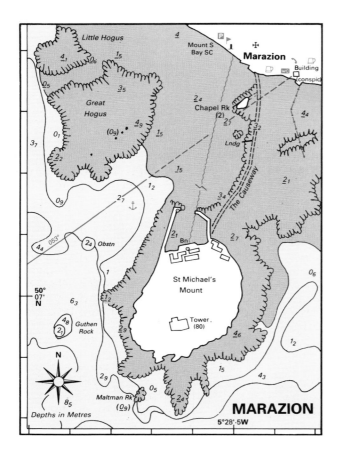

harbour wall on 074°. This will clear the unmarked Outer Penzeath Rock (awash at LAT) about ½ mile east of the harbour entrance, and the Great Hogus Rock, an extensive shoal area which dries 4·9m.

If you prefer to round the isle to starboard, beware of Maltman Rock (dries 0·9m) nearly a cable south-southwest of the south point. To the east of this, a shoal drying 2·4m extends from the island. These dangers are unmarked, and so the point should be given a wide berth.

The approach shelves gradually to 2·7m a cable west of the entrance, after which depths reduce to the drying heights of the harbour itself. Hogus Rocks lie 1 cable north of the pier head, so do not pass far off this.

If approaching from the south, after giving the south point a good berth (see above) follow the west shore at a distance of about a cable. You may cross a rock (2·1m) and an obstruction (2·4m), but if you are intending to enter the harbour itself you will have sufficient tide for these to pose no problem. Be careful if coming to anchor around LW. Alter for the anchorage when the pier head bears 060°, or ideally when the right-hand side of Chapel Rock comes into transit on 053° with a grey truncated clock tower about 100 yards east of the root of the causeway.

Night entry is a non-starter for the stranger.

Harbour and anchorage

There is a pleasant anchorage a cable or so west of the west pier, in depths of around 2·7m. This is usable in settled weather with breezes from north to southeast through east. Anchor to seaward of lobster pots. Entering the drying harbour, berth on the west wall (firm sand bottom) and report to the harbourmaster, whose office is on the opposite side. The East Quay is used by ferries and launches.

Facilities

Little on the Mount itself, but most requirements can be met in Marazion, half a mile northward across the causeway at LW or by dinghy at HW. Fresh water can be found; there is also no shortage of shops. Early closing Wednesday, though many stores remain open regardless in summer. Launching site on beach at west end of Marazion, with car park adjacent.

Buses run to Penzance, 3 miles distant.

Penzance

Tides

HW −0635 Dover

MHWS	MLWS	MHWN	MLWN
5·6m	0·8m	4·4m	2·0m

Depths

1·8m to seaward of South Pier. The outer harbour dries from 1·6m to 2·1m, except for a channel 0·6m deep leading up to the lock gates close along the South Pier. The gates open HW −2 to HW +1; the depth inside is 1·5m below datum, giving a depth at neaps of 5·8m.

General

Although its commercial importance has diminished since its early 19th-century heyday, Penzance re-

mains an attractive option for the visiting yacht. The tidal basin, open 3 hours out of 12, gives complete shelter, and a warm welcome is extended by a harbourmaster who is a well known West Country yachtsman. Yachts can be left here safely for a period at sensible rates, so during prolonged bad weather Penzance has much to recommend it. Be careful of approaching in strong southerlies or southeasterlies, however. The shoaling water and lee shore of Mount's Bay can render it dangerous.

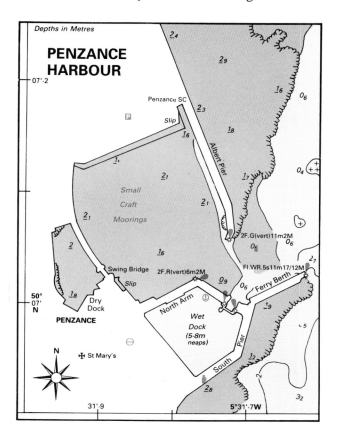

Approach and entrance

If approaching from around the Lizard, give the point 2 to 3 miles clearance in rough weather, then pass outside the Boa, 3 miles further west. Now pass southward of the unlit south cardinal *Mountamopus* buoy to clear all the shoals off Cudden Point. Thereafter, shape up for the harbour entrance, clearing Gear Rock with its isolated danger colouring (black and red with ‡ topmark). By night, the white sector of the light on South Pier (Fl.WR. 5s11m17/12M) clears all inshore dangers, including Gear Rock and the rocky ledges between Penzance and St Michael's Mount.

From the westward, leave the *Runnelstone* south cardinal buoy to port and continue a mile or so offshore past St Clement's Island. *Low Lee* lit east cardinal buoy is situated just under a mile northnorthwest of St Clement's Island and marks shoals of 1·5m and 1·8m. If in doubt, leave the buoy to port, but a suitable tide rise may well allow you to ignore it. A heading of 345° for the head of the

Penzance Harbour entrance from the east. Lock gates and dock are under church tower.

South Pier will clear Gear Rock (see above) and Battery Rocks, which lie just east of south from the entrance. 4 cables east-northeast of the entrance lie the Cressar Rocks, marked by a south cardinal beacon.

Anchorage and berthing

If waiting for the lock to open in settled or offshore weather, you can anchor safely enough in modest depths a cable or more east-northeast of the end of Albert Pier (2F.G). The inside of South Pier is used by the Scilly Isles ferry, but the berth is usually clear from 0930 to 1830 on weekdays. It is used on Saturday lunchtimes and all day on Sunday, when the ferry does not sail. If using this berth, lie by the ladder, not the steps near the lock, as these are in constant use. Contact the harbourmaster either personally or on VHF, call Ch 16, working Ch 12, or ☎ 01736 66113. Sometimes the harbourmaster will allow you to dry out alongside Albert Pier, but the generally preferred option is to enter the wet dock through the locks, which open from HW −2 to HW +1. The berthing master will direct you, and will also issue a key to the showers and toilets beneath the berthing office by the lock gate.

Lock signals

Shown from a flagstaff at the north side of the dock gate, these are not always exhibited for yachts.
2F.R vertical lights – Dock open
R over G light – Dock shut

Facilities

Fresh water and diesel by arrangement with berthing master. Petrol from garage. *Calor Gas* and *Camping Gaz* exchange through berthing master on the harbour side. A launderette will be discovered by railway station. Engineers, electronics and sailmakers all in town. 8-ton crane, but repair facilities limited. All the usual town facilities, with a wide selection of pubs. Also fish and chips. Various restaurants, some very reasonably priced, including the Bosun's Locker and the Waterside, both of which are on the harbour side.

Communications

Ferry to Scilly Isles. Bus and rail to all mainland destinations.

Newlyn

Tides

HW +0600 Dover

MHWS	MLWS	MHWN	MLWN
5·6m	0·8m	4·4m	2·0m

Depths

A minimum of 2·1m in the entrance and alongside the west side of Mary Williams Pier, where visiting yachts generally lie. Greater depths (see plan) in Gwavas Lake, and south-southeast of the South Pier, either of which may be used to anchor.

General

Newlyn is approachable in nearly all weathers, subject to the same provisos as Penzance concerning hard onshore blows. If it is blowing stiffly from south or southeast, then the nearer to HW you can time your arrival the better. Inside shelter is good except in strong southeasterlies, when a swell rolls

Penzance.

Mousehole.

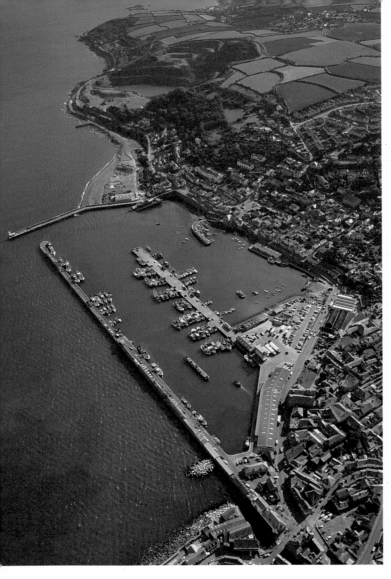

Newlyn. Mary Williams Pier in the centre of harbour. If in doubt, raft to a fishing boat well in on the west side.

in, but the harbour is not set up for yachts. It is commercial, with fishing its overriding concern. However, short-stay visitors and overnight shelter can usually be arranged with a good grace.

Approach and entrance

Follow the instructions given for Penzance; alter for Newlyn when the South Pier head (Fl.5s9M Siren 60s) bears due west. Swing in between it and the North Pier (F.WG) and shape up to leave the head of the Mary Williams Pier (2F.R) to starboard. On your port bow is an unlit red spar buoy marking the end of a slipway. Note that the western part of the harbour dries out, but that there is a dredged channel (2·1m or more) alongside the pier.

Anchorage and berthing

Yachts can lie to anchor in moderate offshore weather in Gwavas Lake, or south-southeast of the South Pier head. Show a riding light. Depths to suit most tastes.

Inside, tie up to a fishing vessel towards the northwest end of the Mary Williams Pier, on the southwest side of the pier. In this vicinity the boats

may well be laid up for repairs. Report to the harbourmaster, who will do his best to accommodate your vessel. He can be telephoned on ☎ 01736 62523, or called on VHF Ch 16, working on Ch 12 or 9.

Facilities

Fresh water from quay. Diesel in quantity by arrangement with harbourmaster. Petrol from garage. Showers and toilets for both sexes at the Royal National Mission to Deep Sea Fishermen, on the North Pier. Repair yards are largely fishing boat oriented, but may help in an emergency. There is no yacht club, but there are plenty of pubs and eating places. A launderette can be found on the Penzance road. All town facilities.

Communications

Bus to Penzance, thence onward by bus or rail.

Mousehole

Tides

HW +0550 Dover

MHWS	MLWS	MHWN	MLWN
5·6m	0·8m	4·4m	2·0m

Depths

Shoal in the north passage round St Clement's Isle, though with care 2·1m can be found at low water halfway between the mainland and the island. Ample depths on the south side of the island, drying out progressively to 1·3m in the immediate offing from the entrance, and 1·9m inside the outer ends of the piers.

General

Mousehole (Pronounced Mowzle) is a classic Cornish fishing harbour with massive, well maintained granite walls, a narrow entrance and water to float in from around half-tide onwards. Though long past its great days as a mackerel and pilchard centre when a man could walk across the harbour on moored boats, it has not lost its independent spirit and still retains great charm. In settled weather, a night at anchor between St Clement's Island and the south pier can repay your trouble, while for those prepared to dry out on its clean sandy bottom, the harbour offers good shelter in all but east or southeast blows. Winds from the east have so evil a reputation in these parts that back in the days when fishermen had no weather forecasts, it was well known that if slugs and snails in the garden became inactive, the wind would soon blow up from the east. This meant that the fish in the sea would also lose interest in life. As a result, easterly weather was a good time for gardening.

Speed boats are not allowed in Mousehole by the harbourmaster, but sailors should beware of children who still swim in the harbour as in days long gone by.

Approach and entrance

Mousehole is distinguished from seaward by St Clement's Island with its obelisk daymark. Note, however, that the height of this, given as 7m above MHWS, includes the island itself. The 'obelisk' is really more of a modest cairn. Approaches round the north side of the island should only be made with the greatest care, eyeballing to keep halfway between the land and the isle. This will ensure a minimum of 2·1m at LAT. Both sides of this passage are rocky.

Leaving the island to starboard presents no difficulty so long as you keep more or less halfway between it and the mainland. When Shag Rock (divided from the island at all states of tide) is in line with the end of the southern pier head, turn in and keep the rock astern. There are now no dangers at all, save the rocks close in around the piers themselves (see plan). Enter round the south pier head. There are 2 F.G vertical lights on the north pier, but night entry is not a good idea for strangers.

Anchorage and berthing

The anchorage mentioned above has good holding ground. It is open to south and southeast winds and even westerlies can hook in a swell. Settled weather is therefore desirable if a quiet night is what you are after.

Inside the entrance, berth on the south pier as tide, draught and space allow. There is a reasonable depth in the harbour from half-flood onwards.

The harbourmaster will make himself known in due course.

Note that from November to April the harbour entrance is closed with baulks of timber. A F.R light indicates 'Harbour Closed'.

Facilities

All town facilities. Fresh water. Toilets on the quay. Garage. Good pubs, cream teas and various restaurants including the Lobster Pot. Buses to Newlyn and Penzance.

Isles of Scilly

Tides

HW approx +0607 Dover
St Mary's Roads

MHWS	MLWS	MHWN	MLWN
5·7m	0·7m	4·3m	2·0m

Depths

2·1m in St Mary's Pool, with increasing depths further from the shore. 3m if required in Porth Cressa. 0·8m at Crow Bar on the northern passage round St Mary's, but deep water if approaching south-about via St Mary's Sound. Depths in New Grimsby Sound between Tresco and Bryher vary from 11m outside Hangman's Island to 3·6m inside, diminishing to drying heights further into the passage. Tresco Flats from New Grimsby Sound towards St Mary's and points south can safely be taken as drying 1·4m on the recommended route.

General

The 48 Isles of Scilly are a marine wonderland. Half-sea, half-land, they lie out in the ocean, a paradise for sailors in fair weather, an interesting stop-over when the breezes are moderate, but a place for the stranger to avoid vigorously when the spume rises over the rocks and the gales blow hard.

The inhabitants of the islands are true sea people, taking to boats as naturally as mainlanders do to their cars, so that it seems most families have some nautical connection. Historically the sea was all, and outside the usual fishing, trading and smuggling of other West Country folk, Scillonians were able to make a substantial contribution to their annual budgets by profiting from the steady parade of ships piling up on their outlying rocks. Of these, some of the most distinguished belonged to the Royal Navy battle fleet under the command of Sir Cloudesley Shovell, which ran ashore under sail in a grand spectacular with colossal loss of life and property.

Only five islands are inhabited, all very different from their neighbours: St Mary's, St Martin's, Tresco, Bryher and St Agnes. St Mary's is the biggest and most populous, with Hugh Town serving as the 'capital'.

It is possible to spend a considerable time exploring this fascinating archipelago. A shoal-draught

boat able to take the ground and in no hurry could spend a summer here. However, the detailed information required for this lies beyond the scope of *The Shell Channel Pilot*. There are a number of specialist books available, including Robin Brandon's *Isles of Scilly Pilot* and *A Yachtsman's Guide to Scilly* by Norm which, if not available 'from all good bookshops' on the mainland, is conspicuously for sale in Hugh Town. Buy a copy and read it. Not only does it keep you off the rocks, Norm's asides about local customs and characters leave you in no doubt about where you stand socially as well...

The Shell Channel Pilot will therefore confine its interest to Hugh Town, Porth Cressa (its backyard in certain conditions) and New Grimsby Sound at Tresco/Bryher. Between them, these anchorages can offer shelter to most vessels in all reasonable conditions. You may be safe, but you will not always be comfortable, because the swell of the ocean is never far away. Scilly is for sailors, and for them its rewards can be great, provided they come equipped with proper ground tackle. If you want a guaranteed quiet night, stay on the mainland.

Off-lying dangers

These are all well charted and tend to rise steeply from deep water. Because of their isolation in the extreme west, the Crim Rocks (2m) and others near them lying about 1½ miles north of the Bishop Rock are worthy of special mention. The others are too numerous to note, and mariners are warned to carry a detailed chart of the area and to study it assiduously.

Sailing into these islands in thick weather is extremely dangerous, and the greatest caution is needed when the distant leading marks cannot be positively identified. Choose your weather carefully for a first visit, and if in doubt, lie off.

Approaches to St Mary's from the east

The generally recommended approach to St Mary's Road from the east is by way of St Mary's Sound which is deep and adequately marked, though approach can be made, given suitable weather and state of tide, via Crow Sound. At night it may be helpful to note that Peninnis light (Fl.20s36m17M) becomes obscured on a bearing of about 231°, but island navigation after dark is not recommended in the absence of local knowledge.

Crow Sound

The flood tide tends to set onshore in this vicinity, so, having given the Eastern Isles and their associated rocks a berth of at least half a mile, one should leave the unlit south cardinal *Hats* buoy close to starboard to put the rock off Innisidgen Island (8m high), which dries 1·6m, clear to port. From the *Hats* buoy steer 289° with Green Island, a 4m-high rock off the nearest corner of Tresco, ahead. When Bar Point (the northernmost point of St Mary's Island) comes abeam, alter to 260° and leave the red and black beacon (⁑ topmark) marking Crow Rock well to port. Charted soundings on the Crow

Bar Sands, formerly 0·9m, are likely to be unreliable, so allow plenty of clearance. Entry should not be atttempted without ample tide. The best water will often be found where sand and weed meet; this can be eyeballed in the clear water. Once round Crow Rock, it is safe to alter to the southwest and the deep waters of St Mary's Road.

St Mary's Sound

The greatest danger approaching St Mary's Sound is the Gilstone (dries 3·9m), which lies a touch under 4 cables from Peninnis Light on a bearing of 095°. So long as you keep south of this clearing line on your approach, the rock will not trouble you. The recommended leading marks for Transit A (see plan) may prove difficult for the stranger to identify, but there is plenty of water close to the south of Peninnis Head, with its white pepper-pot lighthouse on a black trellised base (Fl.20s36m17M). Leave the unlit *Spanish Ledges* east cardinal bell buoy to port, also the unlit red can buoy on Bartholomew Ledges. Do not get too close to the south cardinal *Woolpack* beacon south of Garrison Hill, as there is a 0·6m patch half a cable west of it.

After leaving the *Bartholomew* buoy to port, swing steadily round to the north-northeast. Deep-draught yachts arriving around LW may want to take Transit C, widely clearing Woodcock Ledge, with 2·7m over it.

Approaches to St Mary's from the west

Broad Sound

Transit B on 059°, leaving Bishop Rock Lighthouse to starboard, will bring you in all the way to St Mary's Road, but the leading marks are over 7 miles away and may not be identifiable. Fortunately, the channel is buoyed with unlit cardinal marks. Leave the Bishop half a mile to starboard, followed by the *Round Rock* north cardinal buoy north of Great Crebawethan. The *Gunner* south cardinal is left well to port, after which a heading of around 060° will clear the ledges northwest of Annet, and the Old Wreck Rock. The *Old Wreck* north cardinal buoy should be left fairly close to starboard in order to keep clear to the southeast of the Jeffrey Rock (0·9m). The leading marks should now be picked up, but if they are still invisible, steer 059° towards the left-hand edge of St Mary's. It is important to remember the danger of cross-sets at all times.

North Channel

Transit D 130°. Once again, be on your guard for cross-tide. Here, however, the leading marks are readily spotted in reasonable visibility. The most significant danger is Steeple Rock (0·1m). Lying a touch over 6 cables southwest of Mincarlo, it is also less than 2 cables to port on the transit. Maintain your heading on the transit until you come onto the Broad Sound Transit B, which you will see easily at this range in reasonable visibility. Now alter course to 059° into St Mary's Road, in deep water all the way.

TRESCO

Abbey Pool

Bn Y

Skirt I

Diamond Ledge

Green I

Bounty Ledge

Crab's Ledge

Figtree Ledge

Tobaccoman's Ledge

CROW BAR

Quay

Crow Pt

Yellow Ledge

Conger Ledge

Mare Ledges

(2) The Mare

Round Rk

The Pots

Great Ganinick

Little Ganinick

Cadedna

Boiler

HATS

Hats

YB

CROW SOUND

Crow Rk

BRB

Bar Pt

Bn

Y

Innisidgen

(8)

Helvear Down

Block House Pt

Bant's Carn

TV TR (119) (R Lts)

(R Lts)

Toll's Porth

TELEGRAPH TR (63)

Carn Morval Pt

Higher Trenoweth

Watermill Cove

Trenear's Rk

Vinegar Ledge

Toll's I

Pelistry Bay

Dry Ledge

(3·7) Creeb

ST MARY'S ROAD

The Calf

The Cow

Taylor's I

Bacon Ledge

Newford

Porth Thomas

Saint Mary's Pool

F.R Bn

F.R Bn

ST MARY'S

WINDMOTOR

Normandy

(R Lts)

Gap Pt

Deep Pt

Little Britain Rk

Great Britain Rk (8)

Jacky's Pt

Porth Hellick Pt

Porth Hellick

Woodcock Ledge

Newman

Rat I

HUGH TOWN

Star Castle Hotel

Garrison

(3) Steval

Conger Ledge

Wk

Serica Rk

Woolpack Pt

Wras

Biggal

The Chair

Control Trs (F.R)

Aero RC

Airport

(R Lt)

Old Town

Tolman Pt

Old Town Bay

Carn Lêh

Gull Rk (1·5)

Inner Tolman Ledge

Church Pt

Church Porth

Church Ledges

Newfoundland Pt

Porth Loggos

Dutchman's Carn

Peninnis Head LtHo

Fl.20s36m17M

(15) Inner Hd

Pollard

Gilstone Ledges

Carrickstarne

Gilstone

Approach clearing Gilstone

Depths in Metres

Fl.R.5s

Bartholomew Ledges

St MARY'S SOUND

Spanish Ledges Bell

BYB

Spanish Ledges

GUGH

The Bow

Bow Ledges

Little Ledge

Dropnose Pt

Cuckolds Ledge

The Hoe

ISLES OF SCILLY
St Mary's

ST.MARYS HARBOUR
6°18'·5W

Newford I

Boat Houses

Porth Thomas

Mt Flagon

F.R W

F.R W

E Bns in line 097°

Lifeboat

Saint Mary's Pool

Porth Mellon

Boat Houses

Rat I.

The Bodnic

Quay

Old Quay W mark

Small Craft Moorings

Carn Thomas

Star Castle P Hotel

Customs

Shelter (W Mark)

Hugh Town

House with truncated roof and curved windows

Garrison

Buzza Hill (37)

Chy (48)

Tr

VC

49° 55' N

St Mary's. Hugh Town from the south. Anchored yacht in Porth Cressa in the foreground. Tresco and Round Island in the background.

Entrance to St Mary's Pool and Harbour

There are two main dangers between St Mary's Road and the pool: Bacon Ledge (0·3m) and the Cow (dries 0·6m). The most commonly used entry is Transit E on 097°, which lines up two white beacons north of Porth Mellon. There is a triangular topmark on the front one and a cross on the higher rear one. Each has a F.R light. Transit F leads you in from the northwest on course 151°, between the Cow and Bacon Ledge, bringing the squat Buzza Mill tower on the high ground behind Hugh Town into line with a small shelter on the esplanade, with a white roof and white vertical stripes on either end of its front elevation.

There are 38 strong visitors' moorings laid in St Mary's. They will be found inshore of the moored lifeboat. The outer two lines are for larger yachts up to 18m (60ft) LOA. If the buoys are full, anchorage is still available outside the trots, but beware of anchoring amongst the moorings themselves. They are laid on long ground chains and you may well foul your tackle.

Drying berths are often available well inshore on the harbour wall.

Whatever your intentions, you will be better received if you first call the harbourmaster on VHF Ch 16, working Ch 14.

Always leave plenty of room for the *Scillonian* ferry and remain aware that the quay and harbour are much used by large, powerful launches carrying on the islands' business.

Porth Cressa

St Mary's Pool is extremely uncomfortable in winds from north of west, and may become untenable. Porth Cressa, immediately south of the Hugh Town isthmus, then offers good shelter as well as easy access to the town. If coming from St Mary's, leave the *Woolpack* unlit south cardinal beacon well to port and *Bartholomew Ledges* red can buoy to starboard, then steer to give Biggal Rock (0·4m high MHWS) a sensible berth to port. After rounding Biggal, swing onto a heading a touch west of north and work into the anchorage leaving the 3·4m-high Wras rock on your port side, paying due heed to the large rock shelf (dries 4·9m) which clutters the eastern half of the bay. The Raveen rock (4·6m high) is conveniently sited just inside the southwestern extremity of this reef. Porth Cressa offers depths to suit most vessels and is sheltered from west-northwest through north to east. The bottom is sound and the holding is adequate, given a good scope of cable. Facilities are the same as for Hugh Town. Land on the clean sand beach at the head of the bay.

Alternative anchorage

If a blow from the southwest is imminent, large yachts are said to be able to anchor in Crow Sound southeast of the *Hats* buoy off Watermill Cove in the northeast of St Mary's Island. This will not be at all comfortable, but may be safe.

Facilities

Hugh Town on St Mary's offers most facilities, including post office, chemist, hospital, provision stores, banks, hotels and bistros, with the Mermaid a notable mecca for seafaring men and women. Water and fuel on the quay. Good showers in the Quay Building hard by the harbourmaster's office. There are chandlers, boat repairers, a sailmaker and an active customs service. Also daily helicopters to Penzance, with connecting bus services. Ferries leave every afternoon in the summer for Penzance. The harbourmaster is on ☎ 01720 422768. Yacht club: Isles of Scilly Yacht Club.

New Grimsby Sound – Tresco/Bryher

In spite of its appearance of being open to the north-northwest, New Grimsby Sound is probably the best all-weather harbour in the islands. Except in strong northerly weather it is a perfectly viable first port of call, approached from seaward. Its other entrance is entirely dependent upon rise of tide. The anchorage is beautiful and atmospheric.

Approach and entrance

From the northwest or west, simply leave Shipman Head to starboard and shape up towards Hangman Island, an unmistakable pile of rocks 16m high. It is surmounted by a well maintained gibbet, now patronised only by visiting yachtsmen whose patience with their crew has expired. Leave the island to starboard and stand on into the anchorage.

From the east, leave White Island and Lion Rock (8m high) with their associated dangers well to port. Now head past Round Island, the same shape as its name, surmounted by a classic white lighthouse (Fl.10s55m24M Horn(4)60s). Tide Rock (dries 2·3m) and Black Rock (6m high) lie halfway between Lion Rock and Round Island. Deep Ledges, with only 0·6m and 2·7m over them, lie up to a cable to seaward, so the stranger should aim to stand at least half a mile north of Lion Rock to be sure of safety.

Pass round the mighty Men-a-vaur rock, then steer about west-southwest, keeping on or north of the transit of the north edge of the rock and the north edge of Round Island. This clears all further dangers. The transit recommended on the Admiralty chart for entering New Grimsby is difficult for the stranger to identify. It is therefore preferable to stay on the Men-a-vaur/Round Island transit until Cromwell's Castle (18m round tower, not to be mistaken for the ruined King Charles' Castle on the hilltop behind it) is well open of Gimble Point, then swing in to your final approach, favouring the Shipman Head side so as to clear a group of rocks immediately north-northwest of Gimble Point. Once the Point is abeam, stay in the middle, leaving Hangman Island to starboard. Tides in the channel run at up to 2 knots. Their direction is controlled by the uncovering of Tresco Flats.

Tresco Flats

The passage from St Mary's to Tresco is not nearly so difficult as the chart makes it appear. The sands dry approximately 1m along the route, but if you allow for 1·4m instead you will have more confidence.

Leave St Mary's, avoiding Bacon Ledge (see St Mary's), and shape a course towards Nut Rock. At 1·5m high at MHWS, this is easier to identify than you might imagine. Leave the rock about 50m to port, then steer 340°, bringing *The Hulman* (a platform with a balustrade topmark) onto your starboard bow. (Distance about 4 cables.) Leave *The Hulman* at least 10m to starboard, and swing around to starboard so as to leave Little Rag Ledge with its red topmarked beacon 15m to 20m to port. Now steer 340° with Merrick Island 'on' with the Hangman until, approaching Merrick Island, the root of Tresco Quay (gable end of Quay Shop

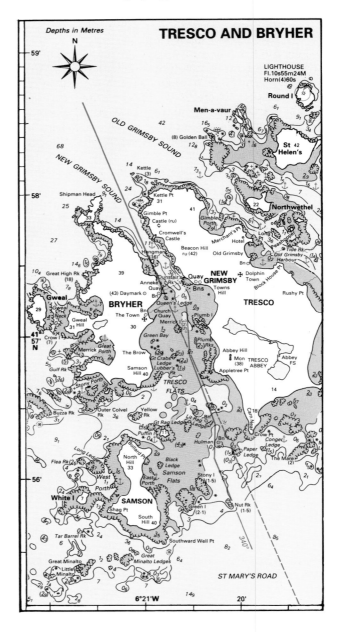

conspicuous) lines up with the left-hand edge of Plumb Island. At this point you should steer half-way between Merrick and Plumb Islands on about 355°. As Plumb Island comes abeam, shape up towards the visitors' moorings on the east side of the 'fairway'. This will clear Queen's Ledge, which dries 2·5m.

Anchorage and moorings

In settled weather, deep-draught yachts can lie to seaward of Hangman Island and south-southwest of Cromwell's Castle. Better shelter is available south-southeast of the island, sounding in to find a suitable depth (see plan) in good, sandy holding. A series of visitors' moorings is established on the Tresco side of the channel, administered from Tresco. A boatman will call for your dues.

Land on the quay (do not leave your dinghy near the end) at Tresco, or on the wooden jetty on Bryher. Launches use both, so ideally you should take advice before leaving your dinghy unattended.

Fresh water is available on the quay at Tresco, which also has a useful village store, up the hill from the New Inn, and a direct helicopter service. Diesel, by can, from Tresco estate workshop (ask at the estate office). There is a slipway with easy HW dinghy landing only 50 metres from the pump. Bryher has no pub, but a shop of surprising excellence is hidden away just north of the landing place. Local produce is for sale by the laneside. Buy some bulbs for your garden and keep your holiday for years.

This is a fine place for dinghy voyages. If you run short of outboard fuel, it can be purchased by arrangement on Tresco from the estate workshop. In the same complex is an efficient laundry.

One of the best nights out on offer in the English Channel is to take the local support boat from Tresco Quay for the evening gig racing in St Mary's. Enquire locally about which evenings and what time. The cost is modest, and seeing a fleet of six-oared gigs, some over a century old, striding out into a serious seaway makes coming to Scilly worth the trip by itself.

II. The French Coast
Dunkerque to L'Aber-Wrac'h

Principal headlands

With two notable exceptions, the headlands of northern France are of less importance than their English counterparts. The reasons for this are two-fold. East of the Cherbourg peninsula, the coast runs in general without salient promontories. West of the root of the peninsula, the shoreline is often beset with off-lying dangers and islands. These make coast-hugging a proposition which, while feasible in parts, does not fall within the scope of *The Shell Channel Pilot*. Nonetheless, the two great headlands at the northeast and northwest corners of this crucial landmass are of great significance to navigators. They also produce some of the most spectacular tidal effects in the Channel.

To avoid inaccuracies, tidal stream data are given with relation to the times of high water at Cherbourg or St Malo. For reference:

HW Cherbourg is −0308 HW Dover
HW ST Malo is −0506 HW Dover

POINTE DE BARFLEUR

Tidal streams in the offing
Northwest-going stream commences 3 hours after HW Cherbourg and runs until 3 hours before HW.

Spring rates can approach 5 knots in either direction. Inshore, there is an early turn of up to two hours on both east-going and west-going streams. This is particularly noticeable on the end of the west-going, with an easterly eddy creeping further and further offshore as the main Channel tide comes up to the turn.

Pointe de Barfleur can throw up a very nasty race indeed, particularly on the northwest-going tide, when dangerous seas may be encountered in strong westerly or northwesterly winds. These are caused not only by the seabed, but also by the north-going stream running up from the direction of St Vaast meeting the more general westerly stream in the main Channel. You will be well advised to give the whole place a wide berth under such conditions.

The headland is low-lying, and the grey, black-topped light tower (Fl(2)10s29M), at 71 metres high, is the most prominent feature. It stands close to the shore, to which it is joined by a causeway. Close north of the lighthouse stands the flat-topped grey tower of the signal station, surmounted by a mast. There is a fog signal (Reed(2)60s), and the light is obscured when bearing less than 088°.

CAP DE LA HAGUE

Tidal streams
These must always be considered in relation to the neighbouring Race of Alderney, where streams can achieve over 8 knots.

Close inshore, streams run at an almost unbelievable speed, with 10 knots and more being recorded. The northeast-going stream begins an hour before HW St Malo, the southwest-going 5 hours after, with a strong eddy to the west up to two hours earlier along the north shore.

Cap de la Hague is possibly the most stream-lashed headland in the Channel. Portland Bill comes close, but its dangers lie more offshore in the Race. Cap de la Hague is beset with rocky inshore dangers, over which streams set with a strength that may render useless any attempt to escape by a small yacht, even under power in flat-calm conditions. The area must therefore be given a wide berth when the streams are in full spate or in hard weather, and treated with the utmost respect at all other times.

The lighthouse stands immediately offshore on a rock called Gros du Raz. The French pilot book records a passage inside the rock which can avoid the worst of the tide, but offers no details concerning its access. *The Shell Channel Pilot* therefore makes mention of it and no more. We have no information as to how it may be passed, and the compiler, whose yacht is very dear to him and draws 2·44m (8ft) of water, makes no apology for not having ventured in to take a look.

The light is exhibited from a grey, white-topped tower, 51m high (Fl.5s48m23M Horn 30s).

Making landfall on Cap de la Hague from the north in good visibility, you will probably first see the huge square building and associated chimney etc. of the nuclear power station. This stands on high ground southeast of the light tower not far from a radio mast. By night, these exhibit F.R lights at 3·8M and 4·5M to the southeast of the light.

5 AFTER HW DOVER

4 AFTER HW DOVER

3 AFTER HW DOVER

2 AFTER HW DOVER

6 AFTER HW DOVER

Harbour pilotage

Dunkerque

Tides

HW +0050 Dover

MHWS	MLWS	MHWN	MLWN
5·8m	0·7m	4·9m	1·4m

Streams

Streams run hard in the offing, up to 3½ knots at springs.

ENE-going begins −0140 Dover

WNW set starts +0415 Dover

Depths

Dunkerque is a deep-water harbour with locked basins to float ships. In the tidal Port de Plaisance there is 2m at LAT, while the locked-in Bassin du Commerce has 4m.

General

Dunkerque will always be famous for the evacuation of the British Expeditionary Force from its beaches in 1940. Without this miracle, it is said that there would have been no British Army, no Battle of Britain, and no survival. Today, a visit to Dunkerque's beaches and breakwaters can do a little to recapture in the mind the heroic deeds that were performed more than 50 years ago in weather that the gods kept fair. Particularly remembered are the Little Ships which, together with their low-profile crews, have passed justifiably into legend.

Dunkerque. East jetty showing red lights along the breakwater (A) and main lighthouse on the right (B). Entrance for yachts is between these points.

Sizeable keelboats in the Bassin du Commerce, only accessible through a lock and two swing-bridges (see harbour plan).

Today, Dunkerque is a major industrial town and a port capable of handling all but the largest ships. It is a bustling centre of population which still maintains some residual charm, and boasts the unusual benefit on this coast of an all-tide entrance which is approachable in any reasonable weather.

Approach

From the east, clear Nieuwpoort Bank and take departure from *Nieuwpoortbank* lit west cardinal buoy. A track of 235° leads 4 miles further on to *E12* and *E11* buoys. *E12* is a lit south cardinal and *E11* is a tall green buoy (Fl.G) which the channel leaves to port. (Note that the red/green channel orientation runs from west to east, NOT towards the Dunkerque entrance.)

From here, steer approximately south-southwest past the unlit red can buoy *E10* on your starboard hand, down to the next pair of lit buoys: *E8* (red pillar Fl(3)R whistle, leave to starboard) and *E7* (green pillar, Fl(3)G, leave to port). A mile or so further on is *E6* (Q.R), to be left to starboard, after which a course along the coast leads to *E4* (Fl.R), and thence to the green *E1* buoy (Fl(2)G, leave to port). Off on your starboard bow is the lit south cardinal *E2*, from which the entrance is 1¼ miles on a southwesterly heading.

From the west, shape a course to the red and white Dunkerque fairway buoy (*DKA*, LFl.10s); proceed thence on an easterly heading to *DW6* (red pillar buoy, Q.R) and *DW5* (green pillar buoy, Q.G). After passing between these, follow the buoyed channel (reds to port, greens to starboard) as far as *DW30* (Fl(3)R) and *DW29* (Fl(3)G), then carry on to the harbour entrance on a southeasterly heading.

Entrance

Note that the really big lighthouse, 59m high (Fl(2)10s26M), stands *inside* the harbour, 8 cables southeast of the entrance. The west jetty, to be left to starboard, has a 35m lighthouse (Oc(2+1)). It is conspicuous from a distance by virtue of the 3 unmistakable flanges which protrude beneath the lantern. It sounds a fog signal Dia(2+1)60s, and exhibits standard light traffic signals.

The eastern jetty has a white lattice tower, painted red on the top (Fl(2)R.10s16M Horn(2)20s), only 11m high.

Note the violet leading lights with intensified sectors (see plan), established to assist pilots bringing in big ships on a heading of 179° to 185°. These can be useful to check your set and drift, as can two occulting white leading lights on 137°, sited at the entrance to the Wateringuet canal immediately opposite the big lighthouse. Unless you are proposing to lock in, these give your course inbound from the harbour mouth towards the marina in the Port d'Echouage, run by the Yacht Club de la Mer du Nord (☎ 03 28 66 79 90). Secure on the outside pontoon and be ready to move if so advised. There are berths for 70 visitors of up to 13m LOA. The pontoons upstream of the marina are not for visitors.

A second marina is operated by the Yacht Club de Dunkerque (☎ 03 28 66 11 06). Visitors are welcome. Enter through Trystram lock after first calling on VHF Ch 73 or 12, or blowing your horn, or simply circling in front of the gates, which are manned 24 hours a day. Once inside, follow the most direct route to the Bassin, which leads through 2 swing bridges in addition to the one at the lock. The marina is private and usually unmanned. If this proves to be the case, fees should be posted through the office's letter box in an envelope bearing the yacht's name. The first night is free, and rates are up on a board in English.

Facilities

Boatyard and scrubbing berths. There is a crane for masts at the Bassin du Commerce, where there is also a 24-ton fixed crane. Slipway in the Port de Pêche. Power, fresh water, showers and toilets at marinas. Launderette in town, where you will find bars, restaurants, banks, and all the amenities you would expect from a community of 200,000. Communications other than by road are surprisingly awkward.

Port Ouest

This tempting-looking harbour 7 miles to the west is for commercial vessels only. It may only be used by yachts in dire emergency.

Gravelines. Conspicuous old lighthouse at Petite Fort Philippe on east bank at harbour mouth. Its light is extinguished.

Gravelines

Tides

HW +0045 Dover

MHWS	MLWS	MHWN	MLWN
5·9m	0·4m	4·8m	1·7m

Streams
Streams run hard in the offing. See Dunkerque for details, which are similar.

Depths

Entrance channel dries 1·5m. Lock sill admits craft drawing up to an absolute maximum of 2m to the Bassin Vauban where they can lie afloat in certain areas. Only 1·1m is really guaranteed. The gates open ±¾hr at neaps, ±1½hr at springs. There is a depth gauge.

General

Gravelines, onto whose off-lying shoals Drake once chased the Spanish Armada with fireships, is now a suburb of Dunkerque. While the place had little to offer the Flower of Spain, it holds a touch more to tempt the yachtsman, with its small but ancient, moated town and excellently preserved Vauban fort. A massive nuclear power station has risen on the featureless shoreline to the immediate northeast, but despite having declined in the last hundred years, the port still operates a useful fishing fleet said by the late Captain Coote RN to take its catches from the shoals feeding around the rotting timbers of the Armada.

If Gravelines attracts you, do not consider it in more than a moderate breeze onshore. The entry is very dangerous in strong winds from west to east through north.

Approach

By day, starting from a safe position well in the offing, align the redundant lighthouse in Petite Port Philippe on the east side of the harbour with a conspicuous water tower to the left of the church steeple on 142°. The lighthouse is painted in black and white spirals and cannot be missed. By night, steer in on a sensible heading in the white sector of the light on the west breakwater, the outer end of which may submerge at high water. If coming from the west, stay well clear of the green sector (078°–085°) which covers inshore shoals. The light is set on a white steel tubular structure 9m high, with a red drum on top surmounted by a light, (Fl(2) WG.6s), wind instruments etc. The eastern breakwater, which also covers at its outer end, has a less ambitious pedestal for its light (Fl(3)R.12s).

Entry and berthing

Enter towards high water down the long narrow channel between the breakwaters, favouring the west side. Once inside the shoreline, the less shoal water is well marked by day. Nearly 2 miles inside the entrance the channel turns to starboard and there, 4 cables or so ahead of you, are the lock gates of the Bassin Vauban. There are various drying pontoons in the channel, on which 40 berths are for visitors. The bottom is believed to be mud. The pontoon on the east side of the Port d'Echouage outside the lock is a waiting pontoon for visitors wishing to lock in. It is often recognisable by the green and yellow lifeboat, labelled *SNSM*, moored alongside.

The locks open as stated above ('Depths'). They can be called on VHF Ch 9 around the time of high water, but note that the lifting bridge has been known to refuse duty in heavy weather. It is, however, generally open in July and August and at weekends. If shut, contact the lock-keeper or the Post Office (close at hand).

Beware of sluicing water in and around lock gates.

Facilities

Fresh water on pontoons and quay. Flandres chandlery. Showers and toilets. The town has 20,000 inhabitants and facilities to match, with a pleasant square; launderette, restaurants, banks etc. 3-ton crane in Bassin Vauban and 14-ton mobile available on request from port office. Scrubbing grid and boatyard. No fuel. Service station only.

Gravelines. Waiting pontoon outside Bassin Vauban on extreme left.

Gravelines. View from the west bank showing numbered channel tripod beacons (A). Old lifeboat station (C) is right. Conspicuous water tower (B) on far horizon forms daylight entry transit with old lollipop lighthouse.

Communications

Sally Line ferries from Dunkerque West to Ramsgate. Entry to the French Canal system is possible from the Bassin Vauban, but you will need to divest yourself of your mast.

Calais

Tides

HW +0048 Dover

MHWS	MLWS	MHWN	MLWN
7·1m	1·0m	6·0m	2·0m

West-going stream of up to 3 knots begins at HW Dover +3 hours. East-going starts at HW Dover −3½ hours.

Depths

The Ridens de la Rade shoal, running parallel to the shore half a mile north of the entrance, varies in depth and may, in parts, dry up to ½m. The Avant Port is dredged to 9m, but depths decrease to 0·5m in the approach to the lock for the Bassin de l'Ouest, where the Port de Plaisance is situated. The basin itself is dredged largely to 7·8m, with berths for craft drawing from 2·5m to 5·0m.

General

Until what some might say was an error of judgment by Good Queen Bess in 1558 Calais was a part of England. In 1588, Drake panicked the Spanish Armada, who were anchored offshore here, by running a flotilla of fireships into them at night. The rest, to cruise along with the old cliché, is history. In World War I Calais came uncomfortably close to the front line but was never taken, while in 1940 a sacrificial rearguard action in the area by the Green Jackets kept the Panzers from outflanking Dunkerque to the west until most of the British Expeditionary Force had been evacuated. Now, up to 140 shipping movements per day maintain the close links Calais has always had with England, just 21 miles away across the Dover Strait.

Given sufficient rise of tide to enter the lock of the Bassin de l'Ouest, Calais would be an all-weather harbour, except that it must be clearly understood that in gales from any northerly direction the entrance can be very uncomfortable indeed, with a 1·5m swell running into the Avant Port. Under such circumstances, entry in a small vessel must be considered imprudent.

Approach and entrance

In reasonable weather the Ridens de la Rade sand can safely be crossed in the top half of the tide, to the west of *CA 10* red buoy (Fl(2)R). To be absolutely safe, leave *CA 8* buoy, a mile west of the entrance, to port, or if you really don't like the look of the seas, go right down west to *CA 6* (VQ.R) buoy, which lies in deeper water a further 2 miles to the west.

In the centre of town is a mighty Fl(4)15s light 59m high with a white octagonal tower. This can just be seen from the English coast, and a steady bearing of 114° brings you straight in to *CA 8* from Dover west entrance. Peel off the entrance channel by day when the west breakwater comes 'on' with the big lighthouse mentioned above, on 138°. By night, shape up towards *CA 10* from *CA 8* until the intensified sector of the F.R.14M light at the Gare

Calais. (A) East breakwater light. (B) West pier head. (C) Main town lighthouse.

Maritime lines up with the west breakwater (Iso.G.3s12m9M). By day, the west breakwater is marked by a white tower with a green top. It has a bell fog signal. The east breakwater has a green tower with a red top, 12m high (Fl(2)R.6s12m 17M). In fog, the west breakwater light shines Iso.3s white.

Enter between the pier heads, giving a good berth to the west wall which has a knuckle at its root, and head for the Arrière Port. The mooring buoys inside in depths from 0·5m to 3m can be used by those awaiting the lock, but they are liable to be uncomfortable. The ineptly named Bassin du Petit Paradis dries completely and is foul with diverse creatively placed obstructions. Try, therefore, to coincide with lock-opening times. These are from 1½ hours before HW to ½ hour after, except Saturday, Sunday and public holidays, when they open from 2 hours before to 1 hour after HW.

By arrangement, yachts can enter the Bassin Carnot, remove masts and enter the canal system.

Berthing

In the marina, lock into Bassin de l'Ouest (☎ 03 21 34 55 23, VHF Ch 12). There are numerous berths for visitors, who are welcome. Maximum length without prior arrangement is 20m. Draughts as described under 'Depths' above. Berth initially on your starboard hand inside the lock, then report to the office. Waiting-buoys, as described, have depths of 0·5m to 3m (maximum 24 hours).

Traffic signals

Full code International Port Traffic Signals are shown from the Capitainerie, on the Quai de Marée near the Gare Maritime. In addition, white over red over green lights indicate absolute priority to harbour traffic.

Lock gates for Bassin de l'Ouest:

F.Y – 10 minutes before opening

F.R – All movements prohibited

F.G – Movement authorised

4 blasts – 'I request permission to enter'

When leaving, it is useful to tell the bridge operator of your intentions.

Facilities

Showers, toilets, fresh water and fuel at marina. Launderette at Calais Nord (Rue de Thermes). All repair facilities, but no sailmaker. Boatyard and scrubbing grid drying 3·2m above chart datum for craft of up to 26m LOA. Enquire at Capitainerie. Chandlery. Plenty of good bars, but restaurants of distinction reported to be in short supply in the immediate vicinity of the dock. There is a 3-ton crane.

Communications

Fast and moderate-speed ferries to Dover and Folkestone. SNCF to Paris, etc.

Boulogne

Tides

HW is the same as Dover (UT), but do not forget you are in Zone −1, so the 'clock time' will differ.

MHWS	MLWS	MHWN	MLWN
8·9m	2·25m	7·2m	2·75m

Depths

Entrance channel inside the harbour dredged to 5m minimum. Visiting yachts berth in Port de Marée where there is also a minimum of 5m.

General

Boulogne is France's most active fishing port. Historically it has been the site of various preparations for the invasion of England – under Napoléon Bonaparte and G. Julius Caesar, to name two of the better candidates. A 13th-century walled town dominates the city, and the prominent dome of the 19th-century cathedral of Notre Dame is a feature of the skyline. The building was erected to replace a predecessor laid waste by the revolutionaries. Napoléon's legacy to the town's silhouette is a 143m-high column dedicated to his Grande Armée.

The harbour can be entered regardless of tide in nearly all weather and is thus important on a coast where such benefits are not liberally bestowed. The outer harbour (Rade Carnot) is over 4 square miles in area. The north part is largely shoal and the south is given over to commercial traffic. Visiting yachts head for the Port de Marée where shelter is good and the water deep.

BOULOGNE

Boulogne entrance. Digue Carnot on right. End of Digue Nord (largely submerged) left of centre. Harbour entrance in background.

Approach and entrance

The offing is free of significant dangers to small craft and yachts. From the north, the breakwaters stand out well. Coming along the coast from the south, you will not see them until you bring Cap d'Alprech abeam. Eight miles to the north is the mighty light of Cap Gris Nez (Fl.5s72m29M), and Cap d'Alprech at Fl(3)15s62m24M is no slouch either in the 'illumination stakes'. Note that Cap d'Alprech still has a radiobeacon; call sign *PH* on 294 kHz. If still in doubt about the whereabouts of the entrance, watch for ferries.

Do not be confused by the fact that the outer part of the north mole is submerged. You cannot miss the rectangular 'box' structure on its extreme end carrying the small light structure (Fl(2)R.6s6M). Received wisdom is that no matter what you may see locals doing, you are best advised to leave this light to port, turning your back on any temptation to cross the obstruction.

The south mole carries a conventional white light tower 25m above the water (Fl(2+1)15s19M). This is obviously left to starboard on entry, and in fog you will hear its 2+1 horn once every minute.

As soon as you are through the pier heads, steer 170° or so for ½ mile to be sure of missing the shoal water on the north side of the Rade. Once the inner entrance is fully open (leading lights at night on 123° – DirF.R behind on Quai Gambetta, and F.G in a triangle in front on the end of the jetty north of the Gare Maritime) steer in through the inner pier heads. The southwest one (F.G Horn 30s) carries a signal station. The northeast one carries a F.R light. Continue down the jetty on your port hand to the yacht harbour in the Port de Marée. There is plenty of water as far as the last pontoon. Thereafter, rocks await. When the river Liane is in spate there can be some lively currents hereabouts.

Traffic signals

These must be observed. International Port Traffic Signals, plus:

Green over white over red – No entry or exit, with the following exceptions:

F.G – vessels with special permission to enter

F.R – vessels with special permission to leave inner or outer harbour

2F.R – vessels with special permission to leave inner harbour only

Berthing

The marina is not the most salubrious in the Channel, but it carries 114 berths of which 17 are for visitors, maximum LOA 10m. You can call on VHF Ch 9 if you wish (harbourmaster is on ☎ 03 21 31 70 01). In season (May to September) a further pontoon 100m long is established just downstream of the marina on the opposite (east) side, opposite the Gare Maritime. Here up to 30 extra visitors can be accommodated, including craft of up to 20m.

In the marina, berth on one of the outer berths or up to 5 fingers in on pontoon 1; 7 in on pontoon 2; the last 2 on pontoon 3; and outside only on pontoon 4. Harbour officials are there to help you during working hours.

Facilities

Toilets, showers and fresh water during office hours only. Automatically dispensed fuel by banker's card on the quay. Launderette conveniently close by. 50-

Boulogne. Entrance to Port de Marée, shared by ferries and yachts. (A) Notre Dame cathedral. (B) Casino. (C) Traffic signals.

ton crane on demand. Scrubbing grid immediately upstream of marina. Most boatyard facilities for repairs, including chandler and engineers. *Camping Gaz* exchange.

Communications

First class. Fast trains to Paris (2 hours). Ferries to Folkestone and Dover. Flights from Le Touquet.

Le Touquet/Etaples

Tides

HW −0010 Dover

MHWS	MLWS	MHWN	MLWN
9·6m	1·2m	7·7m	3·0m

The tide in the offing runs north from 2½ hours before HW Dover, turning south 3½ hours after. Rates can rise to 3 knots.

The Canche estuary at lower water. (A) Le Touquet airport terminal.

Depths

The river Canche dries to a trickle for up to 2 miles offshore, but within an hour of MHWS 3m has been reliably reported as far as the small marina at Etaples. More is claimed locally. This will reduce to 1·2m at neaps. Le Touquet dries completely, but there is likely to be 1·5m up to it at MHWN, with considerably more at springs.

General

The Canche looks an attractive proposition at high water, but at low it would curdle the blood of all but the most optimistic ditch-explorer. Le Touquet, with its reputation for high life and casinos, holds many attractions for some, but sadly its drying foreshore features patches of quicksand which can render the pleasure-seeking yachtsman's stroll to the esplanade more adventurous than he might have wished. Nevertheless, the yacht club is a friendly place, ¾ mile from town.

Etaples, with a drying pontoon marina in the centre of a pretty little town, is a better proposition for the visitor in a smallish yacht. Each *pêcheur* has his own fish stall on the waterfront, and across the street is a gourmet's delight of small seafood markets. *The Shell Channel Pilot* failed to sample the restaurants, but did extraordinarily well on a DIY seafood bonanza meal. The Coquilles St Jacques, 'cleaned while you wait', were Olympian.

Le Touquet. Etaples pontoons.

Approach

Try to time a first visit before the top of springs, just in case you fail to find the channel near HW.

Look out for the 54m orange octagonal lighthouse with the brown band and green and white top (Fl(2)10s25M) situated about a mile south of the Pointe du Touquet. You may also be able to discern the red pylon of Camiers light on the east side of the river. By night this has a white sector which will place you north of the most recent (1993) position of the channel, but strangers are emphatically advised to give the place a resounding miss after dark.

The outermost buoys of the channel are found 4 cables south-southeast of an unlit west cardinal buoy which marks a wreck on the edge of the drying line. The buoys are a lit red pillar, *Canche No. 2*, and an unlit green cone, *No. 1*. Thereafter, the buoyed channel meanders northeast towards the shore. Observe the buoys with great care. After a mile or so the channel swings to starboard, towards a light structure (Fl.R.4s) northeast of Pointe du Touquet. Further up towards Etaples, buoys stop and red and green beacons begin. Upstream of the yacht club the channel runs straight. Do not stray from it because it is bounded by training walls which will be submerged if you are afloat. The outer part of this channel is liable to major changes at any time. The important thing is to locate *Canche No. 2* buoy and then follow the others slavishly.

Berthing

As you come up to Etaples you will pass the shipyard with its slipway on the left bank and the long town quay reserved for fishing boats. Immediately downstream of the bridge are the five pontoons of the simple drying marina. The current runs very hard towards the bridge before HW, so be ready to take appropriate action. There is little space to turn, but once alongside you should 'wind ship' so as to breast the young flood when it arrives after low water, sometimes with bore-like ferocity. You are also then ready to depart. The bottom is soft mud.

Facilities

The smart modern Capitainerie and clubhouse are immediately beside the pontoons, and there you will find toilets and showers. The shipyard can handle yacht repairs and there is an 8-ton crane. Fuel may be brought to you by arrangement (☎ 03 21 94 66 96). The town has good provision shops and, as noted above, seafood is a speciality. Small boats can be launched near HW from a concrete slipway. The Capitainerie listens on VHF Ch 9 from 2 hours before to 2 hours after HW, ☎ 03 21 84 54 33.

Le Crotoy

Tides

Tidal heights and times are similar to those at St Valéry-sur-Somme, across the estuary (see page 192).

Depths

Approaches similar to those at St Valéry-sur-Somme, with 1·5 metres in the floating dock at low water.

General

Le Crotoy is a charming fishing village (population 2,500) which boasts a casino, a beautiful bathing beach, a number of useful restaurants and a well sheltered dock where craft of modest draught can stay afloat.

Approach and entrance

The immediate approach begins at the left-hand fork in the general channel into the Somme which divides, as described in the St Valéry-sur-Somme notes, at a west cardinal buoy. The channel up to Le Crotoy shifts dramatically, so you must be on your guard over the buoys, whose numbers are prefixed *C*. Nevertheless, you should find 2m on a

Conspicuous Le Hourdel lighthouse.

mean tide an hour or so before HW. Try to come here for the first time a few days before the top of springs to avoid any possibility of being neaped.

When the buoys run out you are nearly there, so steer for the quay (where there may well be a fishing boat or two) and thence along the wall and around the corner up to the Bassin à Flot, where access is limited to HW ± 1½ to 2 hours on a mean tide ('Coefficient 90'). There are 130 berths, all technically filled by yachts owned by members of the local sailing club. However, at any given time at least ten boats are usually away, so these berths become available to visitors. Call by phone, ideally.

Le Crotoy. Keep near to the wall on your port hand to avoid the shoal.

The harbourmaster's number is ☎ 03 22 27 81 59 and the club is on ☎ 03 22 27 86 05. Shelter is excellent. Do not be confused by a sluicegate a short distance upstream of the harbour entrance.

Facilities

Fresh water on the pontoons. No fuel. A repair yard and a 3½-ton crane. Good restaurants and bars, and the cheapest mussels in northern France for the galley gourmet.

St Valéry-sur-Somme

Tides

HW −0020 Dover

MHWS	MLWS	MHWN	MLWN
10·0m	No data	8·0m	No data

Depths

2m at HW neaps in the approaches. There is a minimum of 2m in the marina.

General

The 20th-century history of the Somme is too well known to be mentioned here. It is not common knowledge, however, that Duke William embarked at St Valéry for his adventure to 'put the breeze up the Saxons', or that St Joan of Arc was brought there from Le Crotoy by her English captors.

Le Hourdel, immediately inside the south point of entry to the river, has a tortuous channel, no room

for visitors and little to recommend it. Le Crotoy (see page 191) is an interesting little town, while St Valéry itself is positively attractive as well as being good value both historically and topographically, with its steep slopes and fine views.

The channels in the Somme dry in a big way, but nevertheless are deeper and less fraught than the neighbouring Canche river.

If you are bent on exploring this coast, you are advised not to tackle the Authie, 9 miles north of the Somme. The drying bottom is notoriously uneven in consistency and there have been unpleasant instances of bilgekeelers coming seriously to grief on drying out.

Approach to the Somme

There are no dangers in the offing, save the generally shoal nature of the shoreline. The critical mark is the north cardinal buoy very approximately 4 miles west of Pointe du Hourdel, marked *AT S0*. Local information stresses that to find this mark is imperative. The buoy is lit and lies within the red sector of Ault lighthouse, Oc(3)WR.12s95m18/14M, though as with the Canche, night entry is not a realistic possibility for strangers.

Give not a thought to entering the Somme in strong onshore winds. To do so would be an enterprise of dire folly for the stranger. In fair weather, however, matters are simple enough for those with good eyes and an understanding of the tide tables. An hour or two before HW is the ticket to peace of mind.

From *AT S0* buoy, try to identify the entrance channel. If the buoys are not visible, steer east until you are in 5 or 6m of water, by which time all should become clear. The first buoys are *S1* lit green and *S2* unlit red can. The channel now works its way inshore past Pointe du Hourdel until it divides at a conspicuous though small west cardinal buoy.

From the west cardinal buoy, the channel to St Valéry-sur-Somme is the right-hand option. It is also the deeper of the two, with over 2m at HW neaps. Follow it carefully to the lit green beacon (Fl(3)G) marking the beginning of the starboard-hand training wall. This ends at Cap Hornu. From here there are more green beacons, plus the occasional buoy, followed by small-craft moorings. A second training wall is set up to port in the last ¾ mile to the entrance. It is marked with red posts and, like the other one further out, is often submerged. The tide positively roars up and down this channel. At the end of the eastern harbour wall is a red light (Fl.R.4s) on a slender white structure. Follow on down the middle to the marina, where berth depths are 2m at LW and boats of 15m can be accommodated. There are 30 visitors' berths. The Club Nautique Valéricain runs the marina (☎ 03 22 26 91 64 or VHF Ch 9). The passage from the outer approach buoy will take a little under 2 hours at 5 knots through the water.

Facilities

Fresh water on pontoons. Fuel by portage. Noble toilets and free showers open 24 hours per day in the club. Entry to Canal de la Somme (lock ☎ 03 22 60 80 23). 6-ton crane, boatyard with engineer, chandler, etc. Bars and restaurants. The town is very interesting and there are a number of riverside walks, both up into the medieval town and along the esplanade to view the Somme.

Le Tréport

Tides

HW −0025 Dover

MHWS	MLWS	MHWN	MLWN
9·4m	0·7m	7·4m	2·4m

Depths

The entrance channel is dredged to a drying height of 2m. The Port de Plaisance is situated inside the locked Bassin de Pêche, with up to 3·7m depths. There are a number of berths for larger craft of up to 4m draught.

Le Tréport.

General

Le Tréport is a fishing town halfway between Dieppe and the Somme, at the mouth of the Bresle river. Local industry is supplied by coastal vessels drawing up to 4·5m, in spite of the outer harbour's drying out to over a cable to seaward of the breakwaters. The shingly beach on the eastern side of the town (Mers-les-Bains) is for some reason popular with holidaymakers camping in the district. The scene used to be discouraging to visiting yachtsmen, especially as they were obliged to berth nearly ½ mile away from the civilised part of the town. Now, however, with the Bassin de Pêche open to visitors, the place does have a certain gutsy appeal.

About 4km inland is the ancient town of Eu, with its 12th-century abbey curiously dedicated jointly to Notre Dame and St Laurent O'Toole, sometime primate of Ireland.

Approach

The approaches to Le Tréport are free of dangers. The entrance appears as a gap in high white cliffs 4 miles southeast of Ault Light (Oc(3)WR.12s95m 18/14M). Immediately south of the entrance is a prominent crucifix at an elevation of 91m, while the square church tower in the town centre also stands out well.

By night, the 20M light on the western breakwater (Fl(2)G.10s15m20M) is conspicuous. It is a white tower with a green top; its foghorn is Morse code N every 30 seconds. The eastern jetty light (Oc.R.4s6M) is mounted on a 7m white column, beside which stand the traffic signals. Watch out for cross-sets.

The lock into the Bassin de Pêche opens ±3 hours HW. Try to arrive during these times. If you do not, you may have a sticky time in the drying approaches, and the 'waiting' buoys in the Avant Port are not recommended. In strong onshore winds the water in the Avant Port becomes agitated, and approach in these conditions should not be attempted by strangers.

Berthing

Upon entry into the Avant Port, shape up for the southernmost lock, which may be obscured from you initially. Do not try to enter the northern lock to the Bassin à Flot, which is reserved for commercial traffic. As you approach the lock gates (call on VHF Ch 72, ☎ 02 35 50 63 06), watch out for a sluice immediately to the south, which sometimes debouches at considerable velocity.

The yacht berths are at the far end of the dock on your starboard hand, with 20 reserved for visitors. This situation was new in 1993/4 and outdates any previous information.

Facilities

Fresh water on the pontoons; toilets, showers. There is no fuel on the dock, but petrol by portage is at 200m. Diesel in quantity comes by lorry, ☎ 02 35 86 15 33 – 'SHIPP'. Launderette nearby in the town. Chandler, engineer. Ice from the fish market. There is a 6-ton crane at the Yacht Club de Bresles on the Avant Port, and various mobiles are available on request.

Launching of small craft (up to 6m) is possible from the stony beach.

The Capitainerie can be reached on ☎ 02 35 86 17 91.

Dieppe

Tides

HW −0011 Dover

MHWS	MLWS	MHWN	MLWN
9·35m	0·85m	7·35m	2·65m

Depths

Entrance and Avant Port dredged to 5m. Bassin Duquesne has 4m. Considerably more in the Avant Port de Plaisance.

DIEPPE

Dieppe, with new ferry terminal (centre).

General

Over the centuries the English have maintained considerable interest in Dieppe. It was occupied by them from 1420 to 1435, Henry II started the building of the church of St Jacques, Oscar Wilde, Aubrey Beardsley, Sickert and Whistler came here to write and paint, and many others ended their days in the war-graves plot during World War II.

Unfortunately, of all the ways to get to Dieppe and its many delights, taking a yacht is not necessarily the most enjoyable. The harbour entrance funnels in a nasty swell when it blows from the northwest, and the Avant Port tends to scoop in all the oily garbage and flotsam which onshore winds pile into it. However, all that will change in 1995 when the ferries move to their new berths alongside reclaimed land to the east of the entrance. The entrance has now been widened, the fairway made deeper and the breakwater extended 250m to the north, giving better all-round protection than that experienced in the past.

Approach

The approach to Dieppe is free of dangers except for a wreck with 1 metre over it. This is marked by a lit north cardinal buoy, 1½ miles off the prominent Point d'Ailly with its white square tower lighthouse (Fl(3)20s95m31M). Point d'Ailly light also has a 50M-range radiobeacon (*AL*) on 305·5 kHz.

Dieppe's gap in the 30m-high white cliffs is fairly wide. The church of Notre Dame de Bon-Secours, with its blunt spire, stands on the cliff top on the east side of the entrance. Close to it is a signal station. Call the port on VHF Ch 12 if you feel the need, but in any case obey the traffic signals as follows:

3 reds flashing – serious emergency, all vessels stop
2 greens over white – free passage
3 reds – vessels may not proceed
3 greens – one-way traffic from the direction lights can be seen
green/white/green – only proceed when authorised specifically

Leave the west breakwater to starboard (Iso.G.4s 8M) and steer in to the south. Pass the east jetty (Iso.R.4s8M) and the end of the old west jetty, now extended by the breakwater mentioned above. As you enter the narrows you will leave a flashing violet light to port. Head on through into the Avant Port. The new marina is on the site of the old ferry berth in the northwest corner, the ferries being due to move in 1995 to the new Terminal Multivrac outside. If the marina is open, take a suitable berth and report to the office. If not, the gates to the Bassin Duquesne will open at 2 hours before HW and remain open until an hour after HW. Proceed into the dock and find one of the 20 visitors' berths, immediately to starboard on entry. These berths are associated with the Cercle de la Voile de Dieppe hard by the lock gates and have the advantage of complete shelter. The tranquillity of the new berths remains to be tested.

Facilities

Showers and toilets in the clubhouse. Water on the quay. Launderette in the town. Fuel by portage, but diesel in quantity of 500 litres or more can be delivered by lorry: ☎ 02 35 82 79 79. There is a 6-ton crane at the club. Chandler, *Camping Gaz*, engineer, sailmaker, etc. all to hand. Ice can also be purchased, and the friendly club will always advise on repairs, etc. (☎ 02 35 84 32 99).

The town of Dieppe has long been famous for its restaurants, many of which are found close to the Quay Duquesne. Provisions etc. are readily available.

Communications

Ferries to Newhaven. Some flights to Shoreham. Trains to Paris and Rouen.

St Valéry-en-Caux

Tides

HW −0044 Dover

MHWS	MLWS	MHWN	MLWN
8·8m	1·0m	7·1m	2·4m

Depths

The entrance and the approaches dry out (2·5m) up to a cable to seaward of the breakwater ends. The Bassin à Flot carries over 3m in the visitors' berth, with a controlling overall depth of 2m.

General

St Valéry is a very attractive little town of 5,300 inhabitants. Its buildings are largely modern, the centre having been flattened in the early days of World War II when the 2nd French Cavalry and the 51st Highland Division made a heroic last stand against the Wehrmacht. Nevertheless, the place has great character and a warm atmosphere as it nestles between its cliffs. A former fishing port, the harbour is now almost totally given over to yachting. There are 580 berths in the long, narrow locked basin.

Approach and entrance

There are no dangers in the approach, but the entry should not be attempted in strong northerly winds, with northeast the worst. The tide sets at up to 2·8 knots across the approaches. To aid recognition of the narrow gap in the cliffs from seaward, note the power station 3 miles to the west and a conspicuous brown and blue building on a hill which bears 180° with the harbour ahead of you. By night the Oc(1+2)G.12s light on the western breakwater head should be visible, followed later by its Fl(2)R.6s counterpart on the eastern jetty.

Proceed up the entrance according to the plan, favouring the east side to avoid the bank of shingle which has built up on the west harbour wall. This is

cleared by leaving the 3 red posts marking a ramp at the outer end of the eastern jetty close to port.

Having negotiated the entrance, you can now steer up the middle to the lock. If you should arrive early, there are a number of waiting-buoys outside. There is 2m of water in the channel at half-tide, so if you are in any doubt about conditions, enter nearer to HW. The waiting-buoys are untenable in strong onshore winds.

Berthing

The entrance is available to most yachts from half-tide onwards, and the lock opens ±2½ hours HW during the daytime. By night it is available from ±½ hour HW. The bridge inside the lock opens every half-hour by day. By night it opens on demand.

The Port de Plaisance can be telephoned on 02 35 97 01 30, or called on VHF Ch 9 from 0800–1800 or at 'tide times'. Instructions to visitors are displayed in English on a board on the lock-keeper's house, which is also the Capitainerie. Your berth is initially immediately to starboard inside the lock. If you want to stay more than 24 hours you may be invited to move further up the basin, in which case watch out for the clearly marked remains of an old bridge halfway up. Depths reduce, so if in doubt advise the harbourmaster of your draught. The amount of water in the basin may fall while the gates are closed. There is a tide gauge at the lock gates.

St-Valéry-en-Caux. Note build-up of shingle in right side of
entrance.

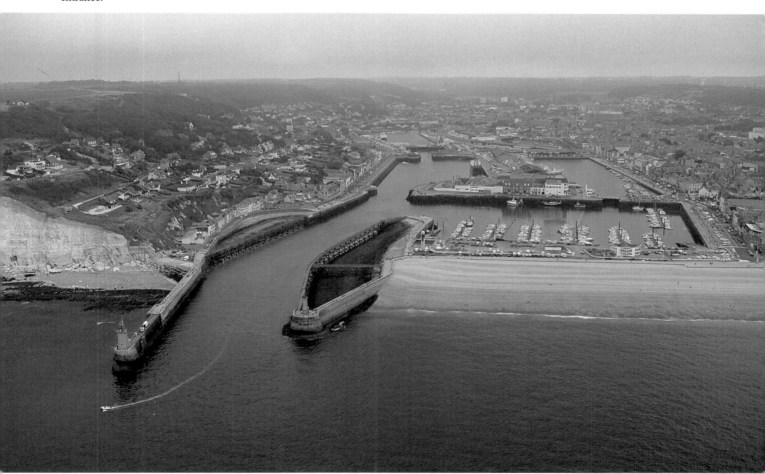

Fécamp.

Facilities

All fuel available, but only from the local service station, though consignments of above 500 litres of diesel can be arranged by lorry. Toilets and showers at the new yacht club building. Launderette situated very conveniently. Mobile cranes up to 6 and 10 tons. Chandler, engineer, ice, and *Camping Gaz* exchange. All small-town facilities, including provisions, bars, restaurants and bank. The Caves du Port were recommended by a serious connoisseur in 1990.

Fécamp

Tides

HW −0044 Dover

MHWS	MLWS	MHWN	MLWN
8·4m	1·2m	6·85m	2·95m

Depths

Minimum 1·4m at LAT in the entrance. The Avant Port was dredged to 1·5m in 1991, but parts of it are subject to some silting. The locked Bassin Bérigny has depths of 5m and more.

General

Fécamp made its name as the home of a major fleet of deep-sea trawlers. Today this is in some decline, but the town is still famous for being the fountain-head of Bénédictine liqueur. A visit to the museum in the ex-monastery is well worth the time.

Fécamp has a tradition of friendship to English yachtsmen. It can be entered at most states of tide, but note that onshore weather can make the entrance awkward or even dangerous. If in doubt, arrive near high water; in a whole gale, go somewhere else.

Approach and entrance

Apart from a rocky shelf extending up to 1½ cables from Pointe Fagnet there are no off-lying dangers. The town can be recognised from seaward by the prominent water tower on rising ground southwest of the entrance, in proximity to the churches of St Etienne and La Trinité. On high ground to the east stands the church of Notre Dame du Salut, surmounted by a fine gilded statue.

Approach from the west (the leading lights shown on the plan give a line of 085°), keeping to starboard on entry between the pier heads. If you are well before high water, be ready for a northerly set.

The north breakwater has a grey tower with red top (Fl(2)10s16M). The south wall shows a green tower with a Q.G.9M light. This light lines up on 085° with the Q.R Feu des Pilotes on the north side of the entrance immediately inside the harbour. The north breakwater has a reed fog signal, 2 blasts every 60 seconds.

Note the traffic signals shown on the south jetty as follows:

Green over white over green – passage with permission

White – harbour open

Red over red over red – no passage

The harbour may be called on VHF Ch 9.

Whether you intend to berth in the Avant Port at the main marina or lock into the Bassin Bérigny, you must turn hard to starboard as the Avant Port opens up.

Berthing

There are 40 visitors' berths on C pontoon (fourth on the right) in the Avant Port. These in theory accept a maximum LOA of 10m and a draught of 2m (considerably more at neaps), though bigger yachts can sometimes be accommodated. The bridge for Bassin Bérigny listens on VHF Ch 12, or ☎ 02 35 28 25 53. Larger craft can lock into the Bassin during the last 2 hours before HW.

The Avant Port is subject to surge in strong onshore weather. The Bassin Bérigny is not only perfectly sheltered, it is also cheaper.

Facilities

Fuel. Fresh water on quays and pontoons. Basic showers and toilets at the Capitainerie. Launderette in town.

There are mobile cranes to cope with anything up to 35 tons, chandlers, engineers, *Camping Gaz* exchange, ice and general repairs. Restaurants, bars and the rest up to normal French standards. Slipway in the Avant Port.

Communications

SNCF to Le Havre, Rouen and Paris.

FECAMP

Depths in Metres

Le Havre

Tides

HW −0103 Dover

MHWS	MLWS	MHWN	MLWN
7·9m	1·2m	6·6m	3·0m

Depths

Deep water in approaches. Port de Plaisance is dredged to 3m (LAT) on visitors' pontoon.

General

Built as the 'Havre de Grace' on the orders of King Francois I in 1517, Le Havre is still the third most important port in Europe, serving major commercial interests with container ships of up to 260,000 tons, and handling 500,000-ton tankers at the neighbouring terminal of Antifer. The city was almost totally destroyed with 4,000 civilian deaths in 1944, and is now largely a modern urban development. It carries ferry traffic, and has an all-weather, all-tide entrance to its deep-water marina.

Le Havre also provides entry to the Tancarville canal, 25km along the 115km to Rouen, with Paris a further 235km. This entrance avoids the passage up the somewhat exposed Seine estuary.

Approach and entrance

Cap de la Hève light structure (Fl.5s24M) is a white octagonal tower with a red top, 32m high and 123m above the sea. Nearby is a prominent communications pylon with a dish aerial. Inside the port near the head of the entrance channel (107°) are tall chimneys 247m high.

Yachts of less than 19·8m LOA are specifically forbidden to use the 10M-long entrance channel. Cross it if you must, under power if necessary, at right angles. This instruction is important if approaching from the southwest. From anywhere north of west it makes sense to home in on Cap de la Hève, then slide southwards to the vicinity of *LH14* (Q.R) or *LH16* (VQ.R) red buoys. From here you can round the Digue Nord with its 15m white tower (Fl.R.5s21M Horn 15s). Next, leave the short breakwater attached to the Digue Nord to port (Fl(2)R.6s) and make a turn to the north to leave the end of the south breakwater of the yacht harbour to starboard. This has a weak light (Q(2)G.5s) on a metal pole.

After rounding this breakwater, steer to starboard and berth on the outside of the first pontoon you come to. This is O pontoon. If there is no free berth, either call the Capitainerie on VHF Ch 9 (☎ 02 35 21 23 95) or find a vacant berth and then report. Protection is excellent.

Le Havre. Yacht harbours in foreground to the left and conspicuous chimneys (centre).

Conspicuous St Joseph's Church overlooks Anse de Joinville yacht harbour.

Harbour Control at north entrance of Bassin de la Manche leading to Tancarville Canal for those bound for Rouen or Paris.

If you are making a first approach by night, French authorities recommend that you study your charts carefully. There is a multitude of lights which must be carefully dealt with. This apart, no problems should be experienced.

Facilities

Le Havre is less convenient for shopping than you might imagine. The shops are there, all right, but you need to take your hiking boots. Some other facilities are more proximate. Fresh water and fuel in the yacht harbour. Showers and toilets in office hours. Launderette, sadly, is in town. Chandlery, engineers, repairs and a 4-ton crane on site. There is a scrubbing grid in front of the clubs which dries up to 3m at mean springs, and a launching ramp in the Anse des Régates. There is also a 30-ton slipway. Ice can be obtained. *Camping Gaz* exchange.

The Sport Nautique de Havre is a friendly club with a bar open each evening except Mondays (all day weekends). The Société des Régates du Havre (the westernmost club building) is more formal, and visitors must dress accordingly. Its restaurant is first-class, so it is reasonable for the members to expect you to wear a tie around your neck.

Two blocks inland from the esplanade is the Rue Augustin Normand. Here, from Nos 114 to 120, are a sailmaker (☎ 02 35 43 16 70), an engineer (☎ 02 35 42 00 41) and a chandlery.

Communications

Ferries to Portsmouth. Trains etc. to all continental destinations – Paris 2 hours. Le Havre/Octeville Airport has flights to London and Brussels as well as domestic ones.

Tancarville canal

As noted above, this can allow you to avoid bad weather in the Seine estuary. Nonetheless, it has problems of its own. You must lower your mast, but you'll need to do this anyway if proceeding up the Seine as far as Paris. There are also a number of bridges and locks which will need to be opened.

Ask at the Société des Régates or at the Capitainerie for more details.

River Seine caution

Ships using this busy waterway maintain comparatively high ground speeds when navigating in the same direction as the tide. Near LW this can generate an unusually steep wash which can be very dangerous to small craft.

Honfleur

Tides

HW −0135 Dover

MHWS	MLWS	MHWN	MLWN
7·9m	1·2m	6·6m	3·0m

Currents can run at up to 5 knots outside Honfleur, up-river or down-river in accordance with HW and LW. Lock opens any time. Enter on the hour, exit on the half hour.

Honfleur – Vieux Bassin lower right.

Depths

At least 2m in the Vieux Port, and more in the Avant Port. Least depth in approach to the lock is approximately 1m at MLWS.

General

Honfleur is perhaps the most picturesque of all Norman ports. You lock in to the new big lock at any state of tide and, if there is room, lie in the middle of the medieval town. The town has known many famous days, with both Champlain and Jacques Cartier sailing west from within its walls. The 16th-century Lieutenance building, which now harbours the port office and was once the governor's seat, is immediately by the old lock into the Vieux Bassin. The church of St Catherine, also 16th century, was built by shipwrights and is composed entirely of wood. At the top of the town are excellent views over the Seine estuary.

Approach and entrance

Honfleur lies on the south bank of the Seine estuary. To approach it, the main channel to Rouen is used. This is defined on the north side by the buoyed Digue Basse du Nord, with which you should take no chances. Three quarters of a mile west of the entrance stands the white square tower of the Falaise des Fonds lighthouse (Fl(3)WRG. 12s). Its white sector leads loosely into the outer end of the channel, while the green covers the Banc du Ratier to the south.

Pick up *No. 4* red buoy (Oc(2)R.6s) about half a cable southeast of the colourfully named lit west

cardinal buoy *Duncan Clinch.* From here, the channel is clearly buoyed (plenty of them lit) as it runs east-southeast, then a degree or two south of east, for the 7½ miles or so total to the entrance. This is found on your starboard hand immediately upstream of the lit *No. 19* green buoy. The west corner of the entrance is lit by a Q.G light, the east side by a quick white with a Horn(5)40s fog signal.

The lock is visible as soon as the entrance is rounded. The keeper listens on VHF Ch 73, *Honfleur Radio*, switching to Ch 9 to pass messages. Enter the lock, then proceed, ideally to the Vieux Bassin. The bridge into the Vieux Port opens to coincide with the lock at 0730, 0830, 0930 and 1030. It does not open again until 1730, 1830, 1930 and 2030. Tie up outside the bridge on or near the waiting jetty if necessary.

Berthing

Visitors' pontoons are maintained on the eastern part of the northern wall of the Vieux Bassin (see plan). Boats of significance which appeal to the harbourmaster's aesthetic sense may be invited to lie immediately to starboard on entry, against the eastern end beneath the Lieutenance. This plum berth is more likely to be available in August when the fishing fleet is away at sea.

Yachts too large for the joys of the Vieux Bassin may be berthed on the northwest wall of the Avant Port, or they may lie in the Bassin de l'Est. See the harbourmaster for details.

A new clubhouse and Port de Plaisance are to be built in the Bassin Carnot at the south end of the Bassin de l'Est. This will be a poor substitute for those arriving too late for the guinea seats in the Vieux Bassin, but the place will still be worth a visit. The walk to the action is not long. The only real sufferer will be the photographer, who will no longer be able to take shots of his yacht under the most colourful buildings in Normandy. Harbourmaster's ☎ 02 31 89 20 02.

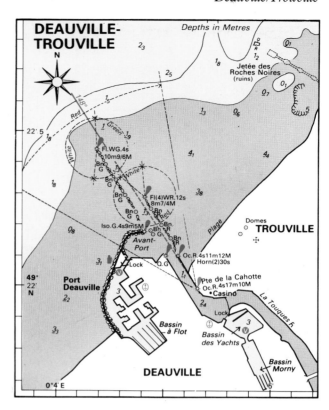

Facilities

Fresh water on the quays. Showers and toilets were basic (beneath the Lieutenance), but improvements are promised (1994). Diesel in quantity can be trucked in by Taupin (☎ 02 31 88 09 43). There is a chandlery and engineers, and a good boatyard by the eastern basin.

The old town is charming in the extreme, with shops, restaurants and the rest to match. Tourists love the place, so do artists and so does every yachtsman who visits it.

Communications

There is a railway station. Buses to Le Havre and Deauville which, incidentally, can often be reached from Honfleur (or vice versa) whilst both locks are open, though with the new deal at Honfleur this will no longer be of the notability it once was.

Seine estuary traffic control tower.

Deauville/Trouville

Tides

HW −0130 Dover

MHWS	MLWS	MHWN	MLWN
7·75m	1·1m	6·4m	2·8m

Depths

The entrance channel crosses shifting sands and generally dries up to 1·8m. Once you have locked in, depths in excess of 3m are promised in all the yacht harbours.

General

Deauville and Trouville are a long-standing pleasure resort for people of quality, which definitive has at times been stretched to include British yachtsmen. The twin towns are separated by the Touques river, which virtually dries. The Trouville foreshore is reserved for fishermen and consists of a long fish market with a fine selection of restaurants and shops to back it up. The river entrance is dominated by the baroque casino, featuring both thalassotherapy and cult movies.

On the west side of the river, Deauville is a favourite watering hole of the jet set. Here you can escape the horrors of yacht cruising or racing and lose your shirt among the rich and infamous at either the tables or the race track. Walk *les planches* on the edge of the beach and elbow your way into Ciro's Beach Bar for a swift bottle of Dom Perignon. Captain Coote advised shrewdly that sailors should take care not to be trampled by 'Tory landowners, inside traders accoutred by Gucci, or dishevelled pop stars with their expensive doxies'.

Berths may be available in Port Deauville or the old port of Deauville/Trouville. The former is a typical modern marina development with designer flats. It is a half-mile hike from the action, but has the advantage of being open from two hours either side of low water. Since no boat of stature could traverse the shoaling entrance any closer than this to the bottom of the tide, this effectively means it is open whenever you can get there. The older harbour is much handier, but lock openings have been reported to be unreliable. Charges and depths are the same in either basin, but even on a good day the old lock is unlikely to open more than 2½ hours before or after HW.

Deauville at low water. Above, approach showing half-tide wall.
Below, Port Deauville.

Approach and entrance

The entry can be dangerous in strong onshore winds. It is perfectly feasible at night in good weather, but all entries should have a good rise of tide.

The casino is readily spotted from seaward, and the rear leading light (Oc.R.4s10M) is situated immediately to its right-hand edge on a white metal tower. The front leading light stands on the end of the east breakwater (Fl(4)WR.12s7/4M) on a white red-topped tower. The west breakwater extends almost 2 cables to seaward of its eastern partner and terminates in a black pylon on a dolphin 16m high (Fl.WG.4s9/6M). Both breakwaters cover before half-tide and are marked with red or green piles. Try to come in on a heading of around 148°, as indicated at night by the leading lights, the forward one of which is showing its white sector for some distance either side of the transit.

If you are coming down from the north or east, you must keep well clear of the shoal water – Banc du Ratier and Les Ratelets – which extends well offshore.

Wherever you are sailing from, pay particular attention to the lit east cardinal buoy 2 miles north-northwest of the entrance and within 3° of the leading transit. It must be left to starboard, as it marks wrecks somewhat to seaward of its position which are virtually awash at LAT.

Berthing

Port Deauville

This lies on your starboard hand, inside the western breakwater 'proper' with its Iso.G.4s light on a green pole. Be sure to leave to starboard the green posts off this breakwater. Further in are unlit buoys – reds to port, greens to starboard. The lock will open when the rise of tide is at least 4m, but note that it is a full, 2-gate affair with no free flow except near HW. Visitors' berths are on the long pontoon on your starboard hand. Larger yachts may berth on the wall before this is reached. The lock listens on VHF Ch 9. There are red and green traffic lights.

Bassin des Yachts and Bassin Morny (Le Vieux Port)

Go straight on past Port Deauville between the east and west inner breakwaters (Oc.R and Q.G). Once you are past the casino, the lock for these basins is in front of you. This opens and shuts automatically when the height of tide reaches 5·5m which, on exceptional neaps, may mean it does not open at all. Traffic lights on the mast on the southwest side of the lock indicate what you should do. The favoured berth is on the pontoons in the southeast corner of the Bassin des Yachts. By arrangement with the warmly hospitable Deauville Yacht Club you may be able to pass through into the Bassin Morny.

Facilities

Water on pontoons. Diesel by pump at Port Deauville, otherwise by portage. There is an 8-ton crane near the yacht club. Showers and toilets at Port Deauville and the Bassin des Yachts, also at

the club. There is a launching ramp in the Avant Port, a 100-ton slipway. All repair facilities, including sails. Chandlers, *Camping Gaz* exchange and ice. Two good restaurants are reported close to the footbridge by the yacht club. These are L'Ocean, opposite the Bureau du Port, and L'Esperance, in the Rue Victor Hugo, 1½ blocks westward.

Communications

Very fast train (2 hours) to Paris. 1¾ hour bus ride to Le Havre. Thence ferry to Portsmouth. Alternatively, Ouistreham is not far, also with regular ferries to Portsmouth. St Gatien airport (7km; ☎ 02 31 88 31 28) has flights to Nice, London and Jersey in season.

Dives/Port Guillaume

Tides

HW −0135 Dover

MHWS	MLWS	MHWN	MLWN
7·45m	0·85m	6·1m	2·4m

River Dives. Channel at half-tide swinging clockwise from seaward. (A) Houlgate Church and (B) Starboard-hand beacon.

Depths

Entrance channel dries up to 2·6m and deep water disappears a mile to seaward of the entrance. Port Guillaume itself has at least 2·5m.

General

This port, now gaining a modest significance as a yacht harbour after many years as a drying river mouth, was of great importance to Duke William. He not only established his independence of the King of France here in 1059 during a notably nasty battle, but is also said to have massed his ships and troops here to invade England seven years later. Whilst such ports in Normandy are almost as common as 'King Charles slept here' signs in English pubs, it does seem that Dives may have a genuine claim.

During the 19th century Dives developed as a resort around its casino, and much of the bizarre architecture of that period survived the last war. Now, property developers are having their wicked way and Dives' character is being watered down. The new harbour of Port Guillaume has realistically opened the place up to visiting yachts for the first time.

It will be apparent to sensible observers that this entrance is emphatically not an all-weather push-over, though from half-tide on shoal-draught craft can enter in fair conditions, with deeper-draught craft coming safely to haven nearer the top of the tide. The entrance is reported to be dangerous in winds from northwest to northeast of force 5 or more.

Approach and entrance

By day, look out for the gap between Houlgate (wooded and hilly, with a conspicuous church standing on the seafront) and Cabourg, where high-rise apartments terminate a half-mile or so of sand dunes to the west. By night, enter the 5° white sector of the lighthouse (Oc(2+1)WRG.12s) on a heading of around 160° while still well to seaward.

About a mile offshore in the white sector you will find the red and white (LFl.10s) safe water buoy *DI.* Halfway in from this is the pair of unlit green and red buoys *No. 1* and *No. 2.* Thereafter, the green beacon *No. 3* (Q.G) and the unlit red buoy *No. 4*

are followed by green beacon *No. 5* (Fl.G.4s) and *No. 6* unlit red buoy. Finally, you will find *No. 7* green buoy (Fl(2)G) and a last unlit red, *No. 8.* By day, the lighthouse structure itself is a reddish-brown hut with a prominent white stripe. By night, from *No. 3* beacon onwards you must leave the white sector and follow the green lit markers, though night entry is not recommended for a first time.

Approach the shore close to the 'light hut', then swing round parallel with the land and quite close to it, running beside the railway and the road, which is brightly lit with a row of street lamps. Now steer to leave the fish quay close to port, ignoring the two green posts indicating a channel to the north. This is the river Dives, with its drying moorings. You should watch for the small green buoy, to be left to starboard, followed by a red post (leave to port). There are two further green posts (leave to starboard on a west-southwesterly heading) leading to the lock gates. On the south side of the lock is the prominent eight-sided Capitainerie building with its conical grey roof. To starboard is a red and white windsock.

Berthing

The lock opens with a rise of tide of 4·5m, giving 2m on the sill. This is generally around half-tide. Boats drawing in excess of 1·5m can often enter from HW ± 2½ hours, but attention is emphatically drawn to the requirement for careful calculation of an individual tide. Berth inside the locks on either side. Call VHF Ch 9 or ☎ 02 31 24 48 00.

Facilities

All good marina facilities, including repairs, fuel, chandler, etc. Showers, toilets 24 hours, and all-night launderette on site. Launching ramp by the fish quay and 30-ton slipway. 1·5-ton mobile crane on quay accommodating 2·5m draught.

Shoreside facilities are not exciting, but there may be further scope for exploration of the town.

It is reported that there is 3m of water at springs in the river channel up to Cabourg. There they will find a firm bottom to dry out on and a welcoming yacht club.

Approach to the River Dives, showing all buoys and beacons.
Below, Port Guillaume.

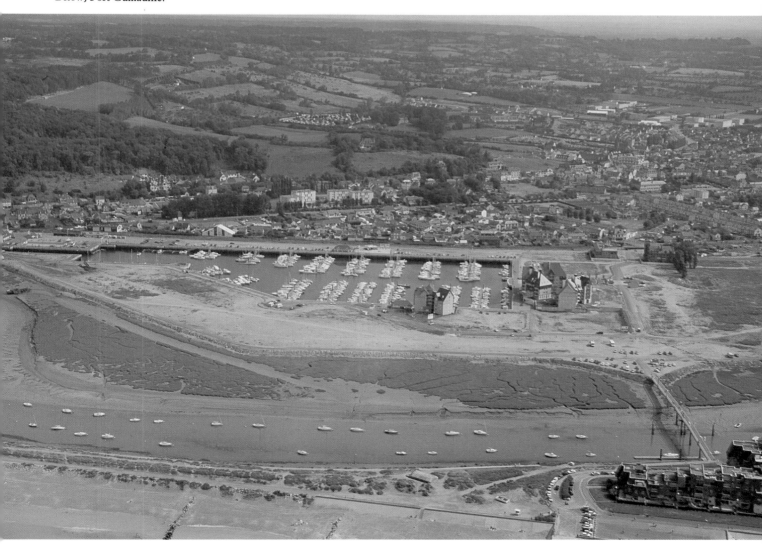

Ouistreham/Caen

Tides

HW −0118 Dover

MHWS	MLWS	MHWN	MLWN
7·6m	0·95m	6·35m	2·75m

Depths

Entrance channel dredged to 6m as far as ferry terminal. Thereafter 3m as far as yacht lock and waiting pontoon. Depths inside marina are 3·5m. There is 8m in the Caen canal, and 4m in the visitors' berths in the city.

General

Ouistreham is best known today as a major ferry port, though often under the name of Caen, the cathedral city lying at the end of the 8-mile canal running parallel to the river Orne.

The area was the scene of bitter fighting after the D-Day landings in 1944. The British airborne drop secured Pegasus Bridge, 4km up the canal, and it carries the name to this day. There is a museum next to the pub on the west side of the bridge itself.

The port of Ouistreham has little to offer the pleasure-seeker unwilling to walk 1½ miles to civilisation, but it is approachable as far as the waiting pontoon at all states of the tide and in most weather except strong northwest to northeast winds.

Approach and entrance

Approaching from the west, it is important to maintain a good offing of at least 3 miles to keep clear of the Plateau du Calvados, watching for the two unlit spar buoys, *Roseberry* (E cardinal) and *Essarts de Lagrune* (N cardinal). In the northwestern approaches to the *Ouistreham* (E cardinal) buoy there are a further 2 spars (*Luc* and *Lion*, E cardinals), which must be left to starboard as they mark wrecks with little clear water.

The only distinguishable feature on the foreshore is a line of beach huts at Riva-Bella, to the west of the entrance. These end abruptly near the west bank of the canal. There is also a white 37m-high lighthouse (Oc.WR.4s) hard by the lock itself.

From the *Ouistreham* (E cardinal) buoy it is just over a mile on a southerly heading to the first pair of buoys in the entry channel. These are *No. 1* (Q.G) and *No. 2* (Q.R). From these you should come onto the leading lights on 185°. These are Oc(3+1)R.12s and are visible well to seaward from their lattice red towers.

The channel is also well buoyed (see plan). Note that the breakwater ends are both submerged. The port-hand one (St Medard) is marked by a red tower beacon 16m tall (Oc(2)R.6s). Its opposite number is *Barnabe No. 5* (Iso.G.4s). Note the white-painted tower at the *visible* end of the west breakwater (Iso.G.4s7M). This sounds a 10s horn

when required. Keep well clear of all ferries, especially when they are berthing or unberthing on the west side.

If you are early or late for the eastern lock (the only one available to yachts), there is a waiting pontoon with deep water something over a cable beyond the ferry terminal on the east side. It is not salubrious, and can be crowded with craft whose line discipline may be poor, so stand by for squalls. Beyond this are the drying Port de Pêche and the locks.

Depending on tide range, the lock opens ±3 hours HW, but do not try to force a passage too near to the end of the period as the lock fills slowly, particularly in times of drought. The lock listens on VHF Ch 68 at tide times. The Capitainerie is also on VHF Ch 68, or ☎ 02 31 85 85 85.

Note the lock traffic signals: entry is permitted by green over white over green with a further white alongside the group.

The yacht harbour entrance lies a cable above the lock on the port side. Visitors' berths are well marked, to port of you or straight ahead. You may have to raft up if the harbour is busy.

Facilities

Fresh water on pontoons. Fuel at marina, open 30 minutes before locks. Toilets and showers at yacht club; also public facilities with combination locks. There is no launderette. All chandlery and repair facilities you could wish for. There are various cranes and a slipway near the Port de Pêche. About 2 miles up the canal towards Caen is another boatyard with many facilities, including a serious slipway.

Caen

The 15km canal to Caen is free of difficulty, except for the various bridges. Reasonably enough, the authorities are unwilling to open these for individual yachts, so convoys are arranged, free of charge. These normally leave Ouistreham in the afternoon and return from Caen in the morning. Ask at the lock for times of ascent, and at the Capitainerie in Caen for coming back to the sea.

After the last bridge you will find yourself in a cul-de-sac which forms the arm of a 'T' across your passage. Turn to starboard and berth on the marina. There are good toilets and showers in the Capitainerie, water on berths, and a convenient launderette.

Caen was largely flattened in World War II, but a number of ancient buildings survived. Fuel is available, as are most back-up facilities. As you would expect, there are restaurants and other city attractions to suit everybody.

The harbourmaster can be contacted on ☎ 02 31 95 24 47 or VHF Ch 12 and 68.

Caen yacht club (S.N. de Caen et du Calvados) is at 132 Rue Basse.

Communications

From Caen there is a regular train service to Bayeux, a remarkably lovely town where the famous tapestry can be viewed. It is stunning. The station is only 500m from the marina. Ouistreham has ferries to Portsmouth.

Caen. La Fonderie swing bridge leading into Bassin St Pierre. Turn to starboard for yacht pontoons.

The first house to be liberated in France (June 1944). Airborne Forces' Museum is next door to the pub.

Pegasus bridge at Bénouville, 2½ miles upstream. Wait alongside wall on east bank, just out of picture (left).

Canal de Caen, Ouistreham. Note waiting pontoon on left-hand side of entrance, then the Port de Pêche and the lock.

Courseulles-sur-Mer at low water, showing half-tide training wall.

Courseulles

Tides

HW −0300 Dover

MHWS	MLWS	MHWN	MLWN
7·4m	1·1m	6·15m	2·85m

Depths

The entrance channel dries up to 2·6m as far as 0·8M offshore. There is 3m in the Bassin Joinville, and berths for yachts of 1·5m (not visitors) in the Bassin de l'Ile de Plaisance. This is reached via a sill which dries 3m. The short-approach river up to it beyond the swing bridge dries 2·8m.

General

Courseulles is built around the river Seulles as it reaches the sea. The adjacent beaches were 'Juno Beach' during the 1944 Allied landings. The town is now a quiet holiday resort still taking advantage of its sandy foreshore. It has a remarkable *château* whose history already dated back more than half a millennium when it was stormed by Henry V. There are berths for 750 vessels, including at least 30 for visitors. The entrance is dangerous in strong north or northeast winds.

Approach, entrance and berthing

By night you will see the mighty Pointe de Ver light (Fl(3)15s42m26M), but its low tower is not conspicuous by day. Instead there are 3 unmistakable churches, which perspective causes to appear equidistant from one another. The entrance seems to lie to the west of the westernmost church, about as far from it as the next place of worship.

The landfall buoy (red and white, Iso.4s) lies 9 cables at about 346° from the west jetty. By night, the white sector of the Iso.WG.4s light on the end of the west jetty clears the worst of the rocky ledges adjacent to the shore. Lined up with the Oc(2)R.6s light on the eastern jetty well inshore, it gives a good lead in. Leave the western jetty light to starboard and steer for the Oc.R, keeping it on your port hand as you come to starboard into the Avant Port.

By day, note that, as is so often the case in Normandy, the outer breakwaters cover. In this instance the outer light on the west jetty therefore appears as an isolated dolphin surmounted by an open tower. This must be left to starboard. Beyond it, both walls are marked by red or green perches with topmarks. From the approaches, the inner lighthouse on the east jetty mentioned above appears as a white tower that can be lined up with the western dolphin to find acceptable water in the offing. The deepest approach is with the Oc.R lighthouse 'on' with the red beacon at 198°, but it cannot be over-stressed that the vicinity of Courseulles is strewn with off-lying dangers which just dry or are awash at MLWS, so adequate rise of tide and a good clearance are vital if you are to remain afloat.

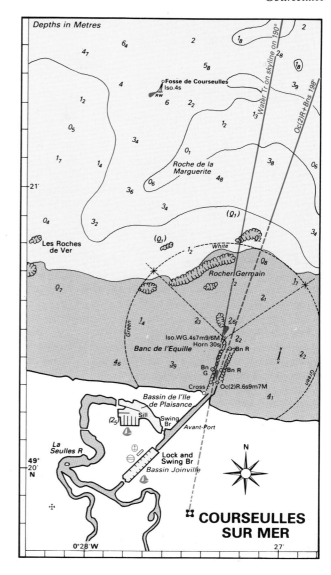

Once inside, proceed up the Avant Port to the lock for the Bassin Joinville. This opens two hours either side of HW, together with its attendant bridge. Call port control on VHF Ch 9 for instructions, or find a berth and report.

The newer harbour of the Bassin de l'Ile de Plaisance has no visitors' berths.

For obvious reasons, you should time your approach to coincide with lock openings.

Facilities

Fresh water on pontoons. Fuel by portage from Citroën garage. Launderette in town square. Good showers and toilets at the Capitainerie.

There is a useful yacht yard (Chantier de la Seulles, ☎ 02 31 37 42 34) close by which can tackle most repairs. It also sells chandlery. The yacht club welcomes visitors.

All the facilities in town that you would expect from a rather upmarket resort, including a fine fish restaurant and various hotels.

Transport is by taxi (☎ 02 31 96 54 07, or 02 31 37 15 15) to Caen railway station, etc.

Arromanches

Tides approximately as Courseulles.

General

Arromanches lies 6½ miles west of Courseulles and represents a remarkable piece of modern history. There is no harbour in this crowded village, but artificial protection of the foreshore was created in 1944 by the sinking of a large number of 60m concrete barges, or caissons, in a ring offshore. This bold Allied enterprise permitted stores of war to be landed, thus keeping supply lines open for the invasion troops who had landed on the beaches, but had not thus far secured a major port for supply ships to enter.

Approach

Paying full heed to various off-lying spar buoys and giving the Rochers du Calvados a respectful berth, it is perfectly feasible to enter the harbour between a pair of small, unlit red and green buoys. The green lies almost due north of the red, despite the basically east-west disposition of the 'harbour wall', so you will have to enter on a southwesterly heading.

Anchorage

The 'official' anchorage is in 6m or so immediately inside the caissons west of the entrance, but you may find more shelter closer in. Pay the greatest heed to the plan, and buoy your anchor, because there is still considerable debris on the seabed.

Arromanches can make an atmospheric overnight stop in calm weather, but winds must be light and settled. As a lunch break en route from Courseulles to Port-en-Bessin it would be a 'must' for the student of history, or for anyone else with an interest in why we are all here and still free to go yachting.

Facilities

Few. Only those of a small village dedicated to informed tourism. The museum is fascinating.

Port-en-Bessin

Tides

HW −0215 Dover

MHWS	MLWS	MHWN	MLWN
7·2m	1·1m	5·9m	2·6m

Depths

The outer harbour dries up to 2m. There is up to 3·5m in the first locked basin and 2·5m in the second.

General

Port-en-Bessin is one of the few harbours in Normandy to have escaped the flood of yachts. It is purely a fishing harbour, but it is well protected and can accommodate a few visitors who do not outstay their welcome. There is an active market on Sunday mornings; there are also good restaurants, and the Pêche à Pied at LW springs is great fun. Here visitors can vie with canny locals as they scour the rock pools for any fruits of the sea unwise enough to have stayed around.

Approach and entrance

In gales from north or northeast, do not attempt the harbour. In lesser but still strong conditions, strangers are recommended to stick to an hour either side of HW.

There are no dangers in the offing. The leading marks are a white house, 42m up, behind a white pylon with a green top immediately behind the quay

Port-en-Bessin. Note half-tide jetty left of centre.
Below, Grandcamp-Maisy.

on 204°. Both are Oc(3)12s, and the tower boasts a siren (20s) when required.

The western breakwater has a sectored Fl.WG.4s light whose green sector covers the rocks west of the western mole. The eastern mole has a red tower (Oc.R.4s14m7M) on its outer end. Pass between these and shape up between the pier heads of the inner harbour. These are Fl(2)G.6s to starboard and Oc(2)R.6s to port. Note that the western half of the outer harbour is foul with dangerous rocks. Outside the eastern inner breakwater is a submerged jetty whose northern extremity carries a red beacon with a ■ topmark.

If the lock is closed, wait at the northern end of the inner western quay on the side nearer to the lock. The southern end is obstructed by a slipway whose outer limit is denoted by a painted strip on top of the masonry.

Traffic signals

Red over green (lights or flags) – basins closed.

There is also a F.R light in the middle of the lock gate when shut. The fixed reds on *either* side are not traffic signals.

Berthing

Taking the ground in the outer harbour on smooth mud is possible, but not recommended in any but the fairest weather, as a scend runs in.

The lock and bridge keeper listens on VHF Ch 18 at HW ±2 hours to advise on lock and bridge opening. He may also put you straight on where to berth. If you do not receive advice, berth as seems sensible – even alongside a fishing boat by arrangement – then report to the harbourmaster's office halfway up the second basin on the west side. Have nothing to do with the small section marked 'Plaisance', as this is used by diminutive local yachts. The harbourmaster is on ☎ 02 31 21 70 49, and the lock is on ☎ 02 31 21 71 77.

Facilities

Fresh water on the east quay. There are two boatyards capable of timber or fibreglass repairs, and there are at least two engineers at the dock. Electronic repairs can be arranged at L K Electronique on the inner basin. Rudimentary chandlery at Hutrel, 5 Rue le Fournier, one block west of the inner basin.

Real town facilities, little sullied by tourism. Some visitors in recent years have not been charged for a few days' stop-over.

Grandcamp Maisy

Tides

HW −0220 Dover

MHWS	MLWS	MHWN	MLWN
7·2m	1·3m	5·9m	2·7m

These heights are approximate, as Grandcamp is the site of some tidal anomaly.

Depths

The approach dries 2m from up to 2 cables to seaward of the lock. Inside is up to 2·5m, with at least 2m on the visitors' berths at HW, falling to 1·5m at LW.

General

Grandcamp Maisy is an undistinguished resort town with a considerable fishing fleet. The lock-in harbour is approachable in most conditions given a good rise of tide, but may be dangerous in strong onshore weather, notably from the northeast.

Approach and entrance

For some obscure reason, the rhythm of tides at Grandcamp follows the same hours as Dunkerque. The locks officially open about 3 hours either side of local HW, but this coincides almost exactly with the full period of the flood at Dunkerque. Thus, you will probably get in any time between LW Dunkerque (lock opens) and HW Dunkerque (when it closes).

Immediately south of the harbour is La Maresquerle light tower on its 12m-high white mast (Oc.4s28m12M). This transits on 221° with Perré light (Oc.4s8m13M), on a 7m green pylon set on a white hut on the foreshore. The transit is of no use close in, but may give you a good start if you are coming from the northeast. The best approach is from a point between *No. 5* and *No. 3* north cardinal spar buoys (unlit) which will place you on the transit of two quick flashing leading lights. These bring you in past the east and west jetties with their white light structures (see plan) to the inner jetty heads, where you must alter onto a heading of south by east for the lock gate. If you can't spot the leading marks by day, do not worry. Any approach heading between southeast and southwest is safe because Grandcamp rock ledge is as smooth as a billiard table. Note that the outer ends of both jetties cover, leaving only their light structures as salient features.

There is no satisfactory waiting place in the outer harbour, so you should be sure to arrive when the gates are open. The harbour authorities listen on VHF Ch 9 (☎ 02 31 22 63 16).

Berthing

Tie up in the outer twelve berths on either side of the northern long pontoon on your starboard hand inside the entrance. Lie alongside if you end up on the hammerhead, otherwise bows-to with your stern secured to the relevant mooring.

Facilities

The harbour office in the southwest corner of the port has toilets and showers. Fresh water is available on the pontoons and fuel at the eastern fish quay (Henri Chéson). Restaurants etc. are undistinguished, though La Marée on the east side of the basin, is reported to serve excellent fresh fish.

Some chandlery and repair facilities. There is a small yacht club open only at weekends. The large launching hard on the north side of the basin where local boats often lie is not available for visitors to dry out, which may discourage larger yachts.

Isigny-sur-Mer

Tides

HW −0225 Dover

MHWS	MLWS	MHWN	MLWN
7·3m	dries	6m	dries

Depths

Craft drawing 1·8m can creep up at HW ± 1½ hours at neaps. More water at springs. All berths dry.

General

Isigny is an undeveloped small Norman town. Its total unsuitability for all forms of *plaisance* have kept its rather rude waterfront free of the sort of aids to convenience without which some seem unable to live. For the intrepid explorer of creeks who is on the hunt for a chunk of 'real France', Isigny may therefore prove a satisfying port of call. It must be stressed, however, that the berths all dry and that the bottom, while fairly soft, is uneven. In an ideal world, it would be prudent to eyeball the bottom at LW before committing your yacht to it.

Approach and entrance

From the north, make for the red and white buoy *C1*, with its Iso.4s light. This is not always notably easy to spot, so be ready with your binoculars. If arriving from St Vaast, you must press on. It is too easy to take a cavalier attitude and find yourself arriving after HW. Now steer on to buoy *No. 7*, an unlit north cardinal. Here you will join up with any mariners arriving from the east, who will either have crossed the Grandcamp rocks (dry 2m) if bound

Isigny.

from Grandcamp Maisy, or skirted the other north cardinals stretching away to the east, north of the shoal.

From *No. 7* buoy, steer south-southwest and look for a pair of unlit channel buoys, followed by more of the same. These lead in a fairly straight line, coming ultimately to a green-topped beacon to starboard followed by a red to port, marking the outer ends of a pair of training walls. The channel now runs straight between these on 173° and is defined, for those locals prepared to give the channel a go in the dark, by intensified leading lights set up at the junction in the river, both of which are DirOc(2+1) 12s18M.

The front light is on a conspicuous white beacon which is left to starboard at the divide. From here, stay in the middle up to the town.

Berthing

The advised berth is on pontoons at, or just past, the yard on your starboard hand. These dry out at LW, so leave some slack in your lines so as not to strain your cleats. The bottom is soft but uneven.

If you are lucky you may secure a berth in the small 'dock' inset from the stream on your port hand, further up towards the town. Here you may dry out with some confidence on a shelving, hard bottom. There are walls on either side to lean on, and as depth diminishes away from the river, a bilgekeeler could dry out comfortably in the middle so long as she lay at right angles to the stream with her bows to the bank.

Further up near the bridge is not recommended, as the bottom may be foul and where it is not there are holes left by fishing boats. In the winter of 1993 there was a large pontoon jammed across the stream which had caused considerable shoaling of what water there is. Even if this hazard has been cleared, these upper berths are unsuitable unless first surveyed at LW.

Facilities

Good local shops and restaurants. The yard can handle some repairs. Fresh water at the yard.

Carentan

Tides

HW −0225 Dover

MHWS	MLWS	MHWN	MLWN
7·2m	1·3m	5·9m	2·7m

Depths

The approach channel dries completely, but craft drawing 1·5m can use it at HW neaps ±2 hours. An hour before or after a moderate spring can accommodate the needs of a boat drawing 2·4m, but in order to be sure, consult the tidal graph below. The lock sill has about 1·8m at HW neaps. Inside the marina basin there is plenty of water.

Note, if you are creeping up, heart in mouth and eyes on echo sounder, that the shallowest water is at the kink in the buoyed channel immediately before the canal. If you float through there, you've made it!

General

Carentan is a fascinating county town, seriously beaten up in the battles following D-Day, which now presents a delightful prospect for the cruising yachtsman. Shelter is perfect, facilities in the quiet marina are good, and the town has good shops and restaurants in addition to considerable recent historic interest.

Approach

Do not attempt either Carentan or Isigny for the first time by night. You are extremely unlikely to succeed if you do, because of the winding nature of

The lock will open from HW −2hr to HW +3hr and can be called on VHF Ch 9 (☎ 02 33 71 10 85). Once inside, proceed up the long, narrow basin. Work was in progress in 1993 on a new project which interfered with navigation, but the passage was kept open. There are at least 50 visitors' berths in the marina at the top of the basin, and room for plenty more. Either tie up in a vacant spot and report, or call the Capitainerie on VHF Ch 9 (☎ 02 33 42 24 44).

It is all too easy to dawdle on your way to Carentan, resulting in having to tackle the river and the channel as the tide is beginning to ebb. Since this can run strongly, you are then in a no-win situation. Try to arrive at C1 at least an hour before HW, and preferably 1½ or 2 hours.

Facilities

The church is 15th century, and some of the shops have medieval stone arcades which survived the serious bombardment following the landings. Middle-aged people still living in the town remember hiding in cellars while the battle raged in the streets above.

Fresh water, fuel and good chandlery at the head of the basin. Showers etc. in the Capitainerie. Launderette in town.

All provisions, restaurants, postal services, etc. from the town centre, which is 10-minutes' walk through the streets. There is a reasonable bar on the waterfront for a late night *café et Calvados*.

If it could be arranged with the harbour authorities, who are friendly and helpful, Carentan would be an excellent, secluded place to leave a yacht for a few weeks.

Carentan. Capitainerie is on the left in the branch of the 'T'.

the largely unlit channel. Such lights as there are are shown on the plan.

First, find the red and white safe water buoy *C1*. You are now abeam of Utah Beach. From here, steer approximately 215° for something in the region of 1¼ miles, until you come to the first pair of channel buoys, labelled *1* (green, Fl(3)G) and *2* (red, Fl(3)R). The water is now shoaling, and if the wind is powerful and blowing in, it may be prudent to abort. Otherwise, carry on up the well buoyed channel, which will not be described in detail because of its shifting nature. About 2½ miles in from *Nos 1* and *2* buoys you will arrive at a red and a green beacon to be left to port and starboard respectively. The course is now 210°, and you will in due course see the structures carrying the leading lights. As you pass the first of these, you will swing round to starboard and proceed up-river between gentle reedy banks in deep water marked by withies until the lock appears ahead.

St Vaast-la-Hougue

Tides

HW −0240 Dover

MHWS	MLWS	MHWN	MLWN
6·65m	0·9m	5·4m	2·3m

Depths

Approach dries up to a height of 1·8m north of the Grande Jetée. However, there is well over 2·5m inside at HW. At LW, depths inside the lock drain off to 2·5m on the official visitors' berth, where the bottom is hard, or 2·3m in the marina, where you may well be berthed.

General

St Vaast is a fine harbour, even if it is bound by tidal constraints (see 'Approach' and 'Entrance'). It is perfectly sheltered and, given a good rise of tide, can be entered in most weathers. The town is a fishing community and the influx of yachts since it was locked and dredged in 1982 has not spoiled it.

CARENTAN TIDAL GRAPH

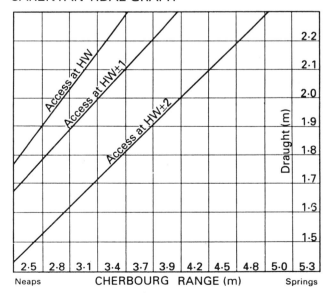

Caution. This data is approximate.

St Vaast-la-Hougue.

(A) Fort de la Hougue. (B) Morsalines lighthouse 1·7 miles inshore.

Rounding east end of St Vaast Grande Jetée to enter open gates. Note Chapelle des Marins at the landward end of the mole.

A walk across the causeway to Ile de Tatihou at LW springs reveals the oyster industry in full cry, the Saturday morning market is one of the best in northern France, and the waterfront bars and bistros are well up to standard.

The locals are extremely friendly, and St Vaast has become one of those ports where, if you loll on a bollard for long enough, you will meet every sailor you ever knew.

Approach

From the north, round Pointe de Barfleur with a 1½ mile clearance, being aware that if the wind is blowing hard against a spring tide this is one of the nastiest corners in the Channel. With the light abeam on a south-southeasterly heading, carry on for 6 miles until Pointe de Saire (white 10m tower, Oc(2+1)12s10M) is bearing 295° and in transit with Reville church. Now alter to 200° until Ile de Tatihou with its characteristic fort is well abaft the beam and *Le Gavendest* unlit south cardinal whistle buoy is on the starboard bow. Leave this to starboard and steer about 260° to round *La Dent*, a second unlit south cardinal.

By night, pick up the transit of Fort de la Hougue (Oc.4s9m10M) and Morsalines (Oc(3+1)WRG.12s 11·8M) on 267°. This will take you well clear of the dangers south of Tatihou. It should also be used when outward bound after dark. Once you are well into the white sector of the Grande Jetée light (see plan) you are safe to steer so as to leave it close to port. By day, you can turn in, given enough water, when a cable or so past *La Dent*, though the best water is said to be found by approaching the jetty end on about 335°.

From the south, by day, spot the Ile de Tatihou and the small, fairy-tale Fort de la Hougue. Keep the latter to port, the former to starboard until you are close enough to spot *La Dent* (see above) and *Le Manquet* east cardinal buoy. This should be left to port, as must *Le Bout du Roc*, just under half a mile north-northeast. From *Le Bout du Roc* you can steer for the pier head, giving *Le Creux de Bas* east cardinal daymark a healthy berth to port. By night, the white sector of the light on the breakwater clears all these dangers, as it does their opposite numbers around Tatihou.

Strangers are not advised to pass north-about round Ile de Tatihou, though at the right state of tide this is perfectly feasible with local knowledge.

Entrance

Round the Grande Jetée, then steer for the single lock gate, inside the two inner breakwaters. Priority is given to inbound vessels, but watch out for eddies and strong currents which can set you on alarmingly, both inward and outward bound. The harbour-master listens on VHF Ch 9, but he also displays a board at the Capitainerie on the right inside the gates which indicates which pontoon you should head for.

Berthing

Large craft berth on the big pontoon immediately inside on the starboard hand. Others as described above. When the gates shut there is about 2·5m depth on the big pontoon. As the last of the fishing boats charge in or out a deep-draught yacht may bump, but it isn't for long. Once the gates shut, all is peace. You can even take a short cut to town across the gates.

It is possible to dry out on the north side of the Grande Jetée, which dries 1·4–1·8m. The bottom is muddy.

Whilst waiting for the lock, or even simply for a quiet, economical night in settled weather, there is good anchorage on clean sand east or south of the *Bout du Roc* buoy. A riding light is essential because you are effectively in the fairway. You may find more peace on the line between *Bout du Roc* and *Le Manquet*.

Facilities

As already noted, St Vaast has nearly everything a sailor could ask for. Fresh water on the docks, showers and toilets in the yacht club and the Capitainerie, and a launderette *face au port*. There is a good shipyard where yacht repairs can be undertaken, *Camping Gaz* exchange and some chandlery. There are also engineers, diesel on the quay, a 15-ton mobile crane and a launching ramp beside the Capitainerie on the seaward side.

For the shopper after provisions the town is akin to heaven, with many small stores selling all the delights, plus the noble emporium of the famous M. Gosselin a block back from the Quai Vauban. Here you can buy anything in the delicatessen line, with one of Normandy's best wine stocks as a bonus. The fine wines are in the dark room at the back and if your French is less than perfect you can browse through the vintages without fear of embarrassment. Should your tastes be less sophisticated, M. Gosselin also bottles his own at popular prices.

On no account miss the Saturday morning market.

There are a number of waterfront bistros and bars of acceptable quality for a quick *moules et frites* lunch, but the serious diner is well advised to visit the Hotel des Fuchsias, where he or she will not be disappointed, unless of course *The Shell Channel Pilot* compilers have got there first and taken the last available table.

Fishing boats use old town quay to port inside gates at St Vaast.

Communications

St Vaast is not far from Cherbourg and its ferries and trains.

Barfleur

Tides

HW −0208 Dover

MHWS	MLWS	MHWN	MLWN
6·5m	1·2m	5·3m	2·6m

Depths

Deep water in the approaches, rapidly shoaling to an entrance which dries 0·6m and quayside berths which dry in the region of 2m.

Barfleur.

General

Except for deep water berths, Barfleur offers most of what the discerning cruising sailor could ask for. The town is quiet and little patronised by yachts because of its awkward berthing. As a result, one is something of a curiosity in the local fishermen's bars, but this need be no impediment to having a Good Time. The town is a classic grey-stone Norman fishing village, and seems little changed by time, except that the 2CV has now almost completely replaced the ox-cart with solid wheels.

The bottom on the northwest quay is clean for taking the ground and shelter is good in all but east or northeast winds, in which case you should not enter at all. If you are caught inside, you must clear out as soon as you float.

Approach and entrance

It is unwise for the stranger to enter Barfleur until about 2 hours before HW.

Note that tidal streams reach up to 3 knots in the offing (and far more off the notorious Pointe de Barfleur, a couple of miles north). North-going stream starts at HW Cherbourg +2¼; south-going at HW Cherbourg −4½.

Always consult the tidal stream atlas, and be sure you make no mistake at Pointe de Barfleur, where a wicked race develops east of the light.

Even in good weather, keep at least a mile offshore until you see the unlit green conical buoy with topmark, *La Grotte*. Round this, then steer southwesterly to pass between the green unlit buoy, depressingly named *Roche des Anglais*, and its red partner, *Le Hintar*. A course of 219·5° should make the transit of two square white towers which bear leading lights synchronised to Oc(3)12s. The front tower is in a roughshod car park on the down-market side of town, while its rear counterpart sits on the roof of a prominent house at the top of the harbour.

This transit actually passes to port of the end of the south jetty, but once you have passed *La Vimberge* (green buoy), *La Filleule* (ditto), *La Raie* (red daymark) and *La Grosse Haie* (ditto) you can shape up safely for the harbour mouth. The southern breakwater has an Oc.R.4s light, and the inner end of the north breakwater shows a Fl.G.4s; the outer end is very close to a small green beacon.

Berthing

In suitable wind conditions it is possible to anchor immediately outside the entrance to await sufficient tide to work up to a berth. The best berths are on the northwest wall, where you will dry out on clean sand or shingle. The wall is appropriately equipped with ladders.

The southwest wall is used by locals and partly encumbered with 'haul-offs'. The southeast wall is foul with rocks.

Facilities

Water, good shops and bars, and a marine mechanic (☎ 02 33 54 02 66). Toilets are basic. Fuel by portage. There is a workaday bistro by the waterfront and a good hotel with restaurant up the obscurely titled Rue de St Thomas à Becket (Archevêque de Canterbury). There is a further excellent restaurant (the Moderne) in the Place Charles de Gaulle, down the back streets towards the rear leading mark for the harbour entrance.

Like St Vaast, Barfleur is fairly handy for Cherbourg with all its onward travel possibilities.

CHERBOURG

Ile Pelée

B.n.Tr.

Red

La Truite

Green

Oc(2)WR.6s19m10/7M

Digue de l'Est

Passe Cabart Danneville

Fl(2)R.5M

Tromet

Fl(4)R.15s

Passe de l'Est

Fort de l'Est
Iso.WG.4s12/9M

White

White

Fort Centrale

Digue Centrale VQ(6)+
LFl.10s

White

Fl(3)WR.15s19m24/20
LFl(3)160s

Fort de l'Ouest

Oc.R.4s

Lts in line 141°

Passe de l'Ouest

White

Red

Green

Digue de Querqueville

Fl(4)WG.15s
8m6/4M

Baie de Ste Anne

Fort

Grande Rade

Arc of Vis.

Ldg Lts 124°

White

VQ
BY

Q.9

Dir.2Qthor117M

Dir.Q.G

Dome Naval Base

Dir Q.G

Digue du Homet

F.G.10M
Horn (2+1)60s

LFl.R.10s

Fl(2)G.6s
Fl(2)R.6s

F.G

F.R

Darse du Béton

Petite Rade

VQ.R

Pylon O

Iso.G.4s7M

Jetée des Flamands

Ft des Flamands
DirQ.WRG.12-10M

Oc.R.4s

Fl.G.2s
F.Vi

Quai Amiral Kniskern

DirQ.35m
19M

Avant Port

Scrubbing berth

Port de Chantereyne

Bassin à Flot

Hypermarket

CHERBOURG

Depths in Metres

**49
41
N**

PORT DE CHANTEREYNE

Fl.G.4s2m6M

Quai de France

O.R.6m6M

Gare Maritime

Oci(2)R.6s
3m3M

DirQ.35m19M

Quai de l'ancien Arsenal

Fl.G.2.5s

F.Vi

Oc(2)G.6s
7m6M

Fl(2)R.6s

Fl(2)G.6s

Yacht Club

Port de Chantereyne
**49
38.8**

1°37'W

1°40'W

N

Barfleur. Approach on 219°. The church's square tower is conspicuous by day.

Barfleur. Front leading light next to caravan park.

Cherbourg

Tides

HW −0308 Dover

MHWS	MLWS	MHWN	MLWN
6·35m	1·15m	5·05m	2·55m

Depths

Cherbourg is a deep-water harbour where any yacht but a total giant can lie at any state of tide. The approaches are also deep.

General

From the average British yachtsman's point of view Cherbourg is the most important port on this stretch of coast. It is strategically sited in the central Channel and, because of the northern-thrusting aspect of the peninsula, it is the closest of all harbours to the ports of central southern England. With its well marked, broad entrances and sheltered inner harbour, it is approachable in absolutely any weather and at any state of tide. Shelter in the Chantereyne yacht harbour is perfect, and for those unwilling to pay 'le price' and prepared to dinghy half a mile or so, the Petite Rade offers an excellent anchorage where space, for once, is not an issue.

Cherbourg's massive fortifications were conceived in Louis XVI's time, but not finally completed until 1853. There is now a military port on the west side of the Petite Rade and ferries at the eastern end, making use of the old transatlantic terminal from which the first scheduled service to New York began in 1869. Inside a further breakwater lies the Chantereyne marina and, further in still, the Avant Port where yachts used to lie in the heart of the city. Beyond this is the lock-in Bassin à Flot where, by arrangement, quite large craft can be left.

It is fashionable amongst old lags of the central Channel to be blasé about Cherbourg and its attractions. Why this should be, *The Shell Channel Pilot* cannot imagine. In foul weather the town has all anyone could wish for except pastoral scenes and nature in the raw. There is, it must be said, a half-mile walk from the marina to the action, but this is not unpleasant. If it is raining, as often seems to be the case, there is no law against taking a cab to the supermarket.

Finally, there is one overriding benefit if the weather never does get better and you run out of time: you could not be better placed for the ferry home. The yacht will be perfectly safe until next weekend, and by this expedient you can offset your costs by importing a double consignment of duty-free.

Approach and entrance

The tide positively gallops past the Cherbourg peninsula, so wherever you are coming from, you must have its movements uppermost in your mind.

Eastern entrance to Cherbourg. Light on the end of Digue Centrale, with Fort Centrale at right-hand edge. The west entrance is 3·7km distant at the far end.

Cherbourg. The eastern end of Digue du Homet. Everywhere immediately to the right of the beacon is forbidden. White buildings to the right are part of naval dockyard.

Entrance to Chantereyne yacht harbour, with the old transatlantic jetty to the left.

Approaching from the north, continue making tidal offsets to your course (or lock onto your 'cross-track error') until you reach the entrance; otherwise you will wish you had. Always shape a course towards a point a mile or two up-tide of the entrance. Simply to steer for it is the road to frustration.

In good visibility, Cherbourg is first seen as a dip in the land to the left of the high ground behind Cap de la Hague, whose massive nuclear power station is extremely prominent, particularly at night. Ferries from Poole or the Solent making a beeline for the harbour are also a reassuring confirmation of your whereabouts. There are no particular dangers in the offing except the various rocks off the coast (notably in the vicinities of Barfleur and Omonville), all of which are well marked with buoys or beacons. The Ile Pelée off the eastern entrance should be treated with respect.

The major lighthouse is on Fort de l'Ouest (Fl(3)WR.15s24/20M), but if you are approaching from the north your first light will be Cap de la Hague or Barfleur. Staying out of the red sector of Fort de l'Ouest gives a very safe clearance of the Pointe de Querqueville. There is plenty of water to within 60m of the fort and the breakwater, but be sure to leave the red buoy (Oc.R.4s), just inside it, to port.

If you are favouring the eastern entrance, the green sector of the Fort de l'Est light (Iso.WG.4s12/9M) indicates the position of the Ile Pelée, as does the red buoy (Fl(4)15s) in the entrance, which you must leave to port. The Oc(2)WR.6s Ile Pelée light, which shows red in any but the most westerly of approaches, will turn to white as you pass the buoy. Favour the western side of this entrance, but note that debris from the fort fouls the water for 100m or so around it. By day, give a wide berth to the unlit red beacon (*La Truite*) on the northwest extremity of the Ile Pelée rock shelf.

The southern edge of the Ile Pelée white sector now guides you to the entrance of the Petite Rade, though you may be better served by shaping up for

the F.G.10m8M on the end of the Digue du Homet and the red buoy (VQ.R) immediately off the unlit Jetée des Flamands on a heading of around 220°.

There are a number of directional leading lights and transits set up to assist ships making for both eastern and western entrances. These can be useful in checking set and drift. They are shown clearly on the plan and may well prove to be of value. However, Cherbourg is lit like the proverbial Christmas tree, and the stranger would be well advised to decide which lights are important to him and stick with them. The ones described above will serve well.

From Fort de l'Ouest, the track to the Petite Rade is beautifully clear. Simply line up the F.G on Digue du Homet with the DirIso.G behind it on 124°. This will take you past *La Tenarde* lit north cardinal buoy and clear up to the entrance.

In daylight, the whole entrance procedure is entirely unambiguous and can be negotiated by a beginner, provided always that current is borne in mind.

Once inside the Petite Rade, steer approximately 200° for 6 cables towards the unmistakable old transatlantic terminal, with, very likely, a ferry alongside. By night, you want the Q.R light, not the green flash to its left, which is for the ferry terminal. As you leave to port the red light on the big jetty end, you will see the breakwater for the marina, with its Oc(2)G light on a white pillar. Swing to starboard inside and make for the marina, which is well lit up at night.

If it is blowing hard, there is room for all but the largest yachts to round up inside the last breakwater to drop sails.

Berthing

Visitors' berths are officially on G pontoon, the second from the north end. Larger yachts may sometimes berth stern or bow-to on the north side of the northern pontoon, held off by moorings. The outer berths on pontoons J through Q running north from the south wall also sometimes accommodate visitors. There is a waiting pontoon island in the middle from which you may conveniently dinghy ashore. There are 300 berths here for visitors, including specials for multihulls and big yachts.

There is anchorage in the Petite Rade on the north side of the marina wall, with adequate depth and fair shelter. No charge is made. The marina is no longer as reasonably priced as it once was. No anchoring is permitted under any circumstances inside the marina breakwater.

Facilities

Absolutely everything you need. Toilets and showers are best in the marina Capitainerie building. The ones by the new berths on the south side are not desirable (1993). To reach the town, set course for the statue of Napoléon on his horse (conspic). Thence, carry on up the wide street running away from the water. At the top of this, take a left and follow your best instincts. Good luck.

The hypermarket is found by following the water down to the old Bassin de Commerce. Cross the bridge at its northern end. The hypermarket is on its eastern shore. It is conspicuous by the hordes of Brits staggering out behind trolleys piled high with booze and other benefits. You can take your dinghy up here to avoid the inevitable cab-full of bottles, but only at HW ±2 hours or so. *The Shell Channel Pilot* compilers failed to note this and were left with the embarrassing portage of a loaded punt across the zebra crossing. Fortunately, it was raining as usual (cf. *Les Parapluies de Cherbourg* – classic accordion music) and the boat slid sweetly across the greasy cobbles before the little green man on the traffic lights turned red.

Communications

Ferries to UK, and trains to the Continent.

Omonville-la-Rogue

Tides

HW −0330 Dover

MHWS	MLWS	MHWN	MLWN
6·2m	1·1m	5·0m	2·6m

Depths

Omonville dries alongside, but it has a number of moorings in over 3·5m (LAT).

General and facilities

The port of Omonville-la-Rogue is little more than a roadstead with a small stone breakwater. In fair weather, with no east in the wind (and little north) it can provide a strategic stop-over for the Race of Alderney. The village is very pretty, with small restaurants and shops. It is about 1 mile distant. There is a bar/bistro at the root of the pier, much frequented by locals, who enjoy the mussels. Close at hand is a first-class fish restaurant of no great appearance. Do not be put off by its workaday looks.

There are basic *sanitaires* and not much else, barring the freshwater tap. No fuel, even by portage. Beaumont-Hague is 5km inland, with all town facilities and buses to Cherbourg.

Approach and berthing

By night, keep well clear of the shore until you are firmly in the white sector of the Iso.WRG.4s light at the root of the bay. This will bear about 255° and will bring you in past *Le Tunard* green unlit beacon. When you have discerned this abeam to starboard, swing 40° or so to starboard and make up towards the moorings. This night approach is not recommended to strangers.

By day, from the east, keep a mile or so offshore, leaving the *Raz de Bannes* unlit north cardinal beacon well to port. You will see the 13th-century chapel of Omonville with its little steeple on rising ground above waterfront cottages. Line this up with a white lattice beacon (the light structure) with a

Omonville-la-Rogue.

red top in the southeast corner of the port on 257° until *Le Tunard* beacon is abeam to starboard. Now turn in to the moorings or the inner quay.

From the west or north, the safe transit is *Le Tunard* 'on' with an old fort at the south point of the bay, on 195°. The fort has a small block of flats on it. Jink to port around *Le Tunard*, then swing to starboard up to the moorings.

The inshore end of the breakwater has a clean bottom and dries about 1m. If there are no fishing boats you could dry out here, but this is emphatically not advised unless you are sure of the weather. A yacht could take a wicked pounding in an easterly scend.

The visitors' moorings are a safer option, because if conditions took a turn for the worse you could escape to seaward even after dark by using the white sector of the light. This has been done by a number of yachtsmen even after eating and drinking their fill in the fine restaurant mentioned above.

Alderney (Channel Islands)

Tides

HW −0400 Dover

MHWS	MLWS	MHWN	MLWN
6·3m	0·8m	4·7m	2·6m

Depths

Deep water in the approaches. Small-craft moorings are generally laid in 4m or much more. Anchorage in Braye Bay can be anything from 7m if you need it, down to drying berths on the sandy beach.

General

For most yachts, Alderney lies within a 12-hour passage from the Isle of Wight and is no more than an 'overnighter' from the West Country. The island is less than 6 miles square, and has a winter population of around 2,000. Like most islanders, the residents of Alderney are friendly to visiting sailors.

Alderney arrived under British rule as part of the Anglo-Norman package arranged by Duke William. It now exercises a moderate degree of independence on questions of tax on booze and other necessities of life. Licensing hours are dangerously flexible; there is no VAT, and, as the late Captain Coote was swift to point out, no hurry.

There are excellent visitors' moorings and a fine, stable water-taxi service that seems to work all civilised hours, so the 'closing-time shuffle' at the dinghy berth may be avoided by those bent on serious enjoyment of the island's varied facilities.

Braye Harbour is safe in all weathers except strong northeasterlies, but it can become uncomfortable with winds from northwest through northeast. With this proviso borne strongly in mind, it is otherwise an all-weather, all-tide refuge.

BRAYE
HARBOUR (Alderney)

Depths in Metres

Cap de la Hague from the north, a 51m grey tower well clear of the land. It marks the eastern side of the Alderney Race.

Alderney lighthouse at the western end of the Race, seen from the north.

Landfall approach

Alderney is all about the tidal stream. It sits off one of the most tide-swept of all headlands, and the race between this and the island is of international notoriety, achieving streams of over 5 knots on the tidal diamonds, but up to 9 knots in real life. *The Shell Channel Pilot* compiler recalls running 14 miles between accurately fixed positions in one memorable hour in a 32ft yacht whose log read 6½ miles for the hour's run. Nor was the spinner foul. We checked.

Slack water is half an hour before HW Dover. The tide then runs southwest for 5½ hours. It switches northeast 6 hours before the next HW Dover and doesn't slacken a lot until 5 hours later.

This intelligence is crucial to anyone coming from Cherbourg because if they are not careful they will end up in Guernsey. Arriving from the south, the most careful planning is also needed. Nor is the Swinge between Burhou and the north coast of Alderney, to be taken lightly. It is full of overfalls and beset with rocks, but can still be managed. Check the tidal stream atlas for the full story.

Making landfall from the northwest, you should arrive at an early decision – before reaching the Casquets ('whiter than white' lighthouse and associated buildings Fl(5)30s37m24M) – about whether to go for the direct approach north of Burhou or, if the tide is being awkward, to leave Alderney to port and approach south-about. It is only 3 miles more and can save a great deal of time, due to the west-running eddy along the top of the island on much of the east-going stream.

From the southwest (Guernsey way) in the last hour before the Race turns foul, you may be served by nipping up through the rough seas of Ortac Channel between Burhou and the Casquets to arrive from the north. Even if you end up having a hard time, it will be better than the alternative.

It is worth noting that the Alderney radiobeacon (*ALD* 383 kHz 50M) is still in operation (1994). If you are using Decca or GPS and are disinclined to believe the excesses of your cross-track error, think again.

Lights

Before you see the grey tower of Cap de la Hague lighthouse (Fl.5s48m23M), you will raise the square buildings of the nuclear power station on the high ground behind it. Coming from the Solent at night, the loom of this monster may be your first indication that there is life to the south.

Alderney light stands near the eastern extremity of the island. It is a round white tower with a black band, 37m high in all (Fl(4)15s28M).

Half a mile west of this big light is Château à l'Etoc light, a white column showing Iso.WR.4s. The white sector (111° to 151°) clears the outer edge of the submerged Braye breakwater; this clearance is underlined by lining the light up with the main lighthouse, also on 111°.

Alderney main lighthouse has a fog signal (Siren (4)60s), as does Casquets (Horn(2)60s).

The breakwater end now has a LFl.10s light.

Approach to Braye Harbour

In the daylight, line up St Anne's Church (squat steeple, not to be confused with a water tower to its right) with a white pyramid on the end of the old harbour breakwater on 210°. This clears all the rocks, also the wretched unmarked hazard of the outer breakwater debris. If you can't make out the marks, steer for the middle of the entrance, but be aware that the shoal off the breakwater extends 3 cables, has only 1·2m of water in places, and causes overfalls.

Braye Harbour. Visitors' moorings mainly on the left of the picture.

After dark, the leading transit is the Q.17M light on the old harbour breakwater with the Q.18M light behind it, on 215°. The lights show in a fairly narrow sector.

Berthing

There are well organised visitors' moorings all the way along the inside of the big breakwater. Note the green buoy (Q.G) – leave to starboard – inside the breakwater head, and the Q.R red buoy well up the harbour. Leave this well to port. Pick up a vacant yellow mooring (red ones are private), or raft up in fair weather. Fly a yellow 'Q' flag wherever you have come from. The harbourmaster will visit you shortly. The formalities are simple, but must be observed. The harbourmaster's representative will do the whole job for you in a very pleasant manner indeed.

Do not attempt to tie up on the jetties, which are commercial. You may anchor anywhere out of the fairway and clear of the moorings, but this is getting more difficult as moorings proliferate. To the east of the fairway is the favourite place for large craft (16m is the largest possible craft for the moorings, and this could be pushing your luck). Shoal-draught cruisers have been seen happily dried out on the beach, but if you are a stranger you should survey your site first. There are a number of isolated rocks.

Facilities

Fresh water, showers and toilets near the harbour office and the yacht club. Diesel and chandlery from Mainbrayce in Crabby Harbour (see plan). Draught 2m ±3 hours HW. Call on VHF Ch 80 first). *Calor Gas* reported in Braye Street. There is a dinghy pontoon near the entrance to Crabby Harbour, and a small supermarket nearby; also the famous Diver's pub, where you can meet your mates, and The First and Last Restaurant, justly well known in Channel waters. Also at Braye are excellent fish and chips, round the back – eat in or takeaway.

St Anne is a charming community with all small-town facilities. It is well worth the modest climb. The island is great for walks, full of reminders of the Nazi occupation 50 years ago, some of which housed activities that may be best forgotten.

Diélette

Tides

HW −0440 Dover

MHWS	MLWS	MHWN	MLWN
12·2m	1·6m	9·2m	4·3m

Depths

According to data published by the port in 1996, the new yacht harbour (1997) will be subject to the following depths: channel dredged to LAT, while sill level dries to 5·5m above datum. The threshold of the swing gate, when open, will be a drying height of 4·0m.

General

Diélette is a well established small port which has never been of practical use to yachts until the new marina, due to open in 1997, came on the scene. Like Carteret to the south, the new port with its promised space for visitors should be of considerable strategic value to yachts cruising the Channel Islands and the St Malo area. Its tidal accessibility is greater than Carteret, with the offing providing the same sort of straightforward approach, given reasonable weather and height of tide.

The town has undergone a series of historical changes governed by its commercial purpose, altering from a granite quarry to an iron mine and now to nuclear electricity. Its buildings reflect this and while the waterfront is underdeveloped at the time of writing, it seems likely that this may change with the new potential.

You cannot see the nuclear power station when you are in the harbour.

Approach and entrance

Having ascertained that the height of tide is suitable, and that onshore winds and seas are not rendering the approach too difficult, shape up for the pier heads on a heading of around 125° to clear all

Diélette. Marina under construction (1996/7). The excellent breakwaters are to remain in place.

dangers. Be aware of the prohibited area extending 5 cables offshore from Diélette to Cap de Flamanville.

The Jetée Ouest has a white tower with a green top (Iso.4s22m7M), while a red light structure (Fl.R.4s17m) appears on the end of the Digue Nord.

Once inside, either tie up on the waiting berths in the commercial harbour on your port hand or, if the tide serves, proceed to the entrance of the wet dock. At the time of writing (winter '96/7), no information was available as to traffic lights or tide gauges, but the compilers imagine that some such will be in existence by the inauguration of the dock in June '97.

Access to the outer, or 'commercial' dock for vessels drawing 1·5m should be permanent at mean tides or less and 10 hours or so at mean springs.

Access over the lip of the sill gate to the marina for 2m draught should be HW±2½hr, depending a little upon the tide, while for 1·5m draught, access is promised from HW±3hr, regardless of tidal coefficient.

Facilities

Currently, basic facilities in the village of Diélette itself, – a *charcuterie*, a bar and one sizeable restaurant in the hotel – though fuel, fresh water and a chandlery are promised in the marina. In the meantime, the village of Flamanville 1 mile up the hill has all domestic needs, plus a fine *château*.

Carteret

Tides

HW −0440 Dover

MHWS	MLWS	MHWN	MLWN
11·2m	1·4m	7·9m	4·0m

Depths

Approach dries up to 3·7m at the pier head. Berths alongside the harbour wall dry at around 5·5m. The channel up to the yacht harbour dries 5m. There is 2·3m dredged depth inside the locked marina. The sill dries 5·5m and there is 1·3m over the threshold when the gate opens at HW−2½hr.

General

With its massive drying heights, Carteret used to be a dubious proposition for most visitors. This situation has now been eased by the opening of the new locked marina. Entry is simple enough unless it is blowing hard from south or southwest, in which case, forget it. The town is quite pretty so if you are prepared to arrive an hour or two either side of high water, it can be considered as a worthwhile visit. In the old days, yachts were known to have enjoyed a peaceful tide dried out in a fisherman's berth, to leave when their host returned on the evening flood. This option still remains.

Approach and entrance

Carteret is easy to identify because of the prominent 15m square grey tower of Pointe Carteret lighthouse on the cliff immediately west of the breakwater. The lantern is 81m above sea level and shows a Fl(2+1) 15s, with a Horn(3)60s.

Apart from the generally shoal waters and the well charted offlying dangers, there are no special problems close in. The extended western breakwater (1993/4) with its hooked, 'semi-submersible' outer end stands north/south and is lit at the extremity by a white beacon with a red top (Oc.R.4s). A hundred metres or so inshore at the elbow of the jetty stands the small truncated tower of the now redundant lighthouse. About halfway along this jetty on the eastern side of the entrance is a training wall submerged at half-tide. This has a white beacon with a green top (only the green part is visible at HW) at its outer end, lit Fl(2)G.5s. On the best approach line, it may be possible to line up these red and green lights to form a useful entry transit.

Entry is not recommended to the stranger in strong onshore winds, particularly on the ebb. It is also worth noting that in a hard sou'wester rough seas have been noted on the 'red' side of the entrance, with easier water on the starboard hand when entering.

Once inside, continue straight along the wall to the pair of lit red and green beacons 900m inside the pier head. At the inner end of the quay is a beacon with a port-hand topmark indicating the beginning of foul ground extending up to 20m from the landward side of the harbour. Before the beacon, the wall is steep-to. After, it is footed with rubble as far as the conspicuous white hotel at the bend of the river. From the lit pair of beacons, swing steadily to starboard until you see the traffic lights for the marina ahead. The sill lies to the right of these and is marked by a flashing red and a flashing green beacon. Do not be confused by the berthed yachts on your port hand just before you reach the traffic lights. These are on drying trots and are nothing to do with the marina.

Carteret. Inside the entrance looking upstream with the fish quay in the foreground. The white hotel is conspicuous left of centre. Note the red beacon marking foul ground immediately left of the fishing boat and the lit red and green beacons left and right of the hotel. The marina is visible far right of centre.

Above: Carteret: the new marina now lies immediately to the
right of the old drying 'marina' to the right of centre at the top of
the picture.
Below: Portbail, showing training wall to be left to port.

Berthing

Drying berths may be had alongside the quay opposite the green beacon at the outer end of the training wall. These are somewhat exposed in all but the most settled weather. Make sure that you do not secure in the ferry's berth.

Enter the marina and continue to the farthest (easternmost) pontoon. There are alongside berths for 20 or so visitors on its eastern side. Raft up if need be.

Facilities

Passenger ferries to the Channel Islands.

Not a great deal specifically organised for the mariner, except for basic showers in the yacht club attached to the marina, to which visitors are invited. Town facilities are good for a place so small, with a choice of fish restaurants. The Bar du Port, hard by the Petit Port where lurk fishing boats, laid up and less laid up, serves Guinness to those stalwart souls who have penetrated as far as its doors.

Portbail

Tides

HW −0440 Dover

MHWS	MLWS	MHWN	MLWN
10·9m	1·1m	7·9m	3·9m

Depths

As at neighbouring Carteret, depths are nonexistent, with the whole port and its approaches drying to a great height. The entrance is reported to dry about 5m along the best approach. The river outside the 'marina' dries 6m, so there is a respectable amount of water for shoal-draught craft even at neaps. *The Shell Channel Pilot* has seen deep sailing craft of at least 1·8m draught lying against the inside of the harbour wall, but it is generally recommended that only vessels which dry out upright should attempt this because of the possibility of rafting up.

General

Portbail (pronounced 'Por bye') is definitely 'different'. Inside, shelter is fair, but it should not be attempted in strong onshore winds, when wall-to-wall breakers could well be your portion. The village, which is reached by walking across a causeway from the harbour, is unspoilt, and the possibilities for anchoring on the drying sands with the birds for company will appeal to more than a few yachtsmen equipped with suitable vessels. The harbour area has an 'outpost' feel which has a certain attraction.

Approach and entrance

The waters to seaward of Portbail are shoal, but entirely navigable when there is enough tide to contemplate entry. This should be within an hour

either side of HW, not only to ensure that you stay afloat, but also to avoid the excesses of flood and ebb, which can readily notch up to 5 knots at springs.

There is a prominent water tower immediately to the north of the entrance which bears very approximately 030° from the fairway buoy, *Portbail* (red and white, unlit). From the buoy, shape for the beacon (Q(2)R.5s5m1M) on the end of the training wall (see plan). Soon you will see the unlit red and green entrance buoys, between which you should steer. The training wall itself covers so that you will probably not see it, but it is marked with a line of poles. Come in a couple of boats' lengths from these, after favouring the green side of the channel for the first cable or so by steering straight for the white leading mark on the foreshore (see below) from the green buoy. From the next-to-last pole, steer for the end of the short pier, rounding it to enter. Be careful of the slipway on the end of the jetty, and the ferry pontoon (regular passages to Jersey as tide allows) immediately round the corner.

There are leading lights on 042°, consisting of a front light (Q) on a white pylon with a red top, and a prominent belfry in the town (Oc.4s). If you can discern this transit in the daytime it may prove useful.

Berthing

There is a visitors' pontoon on the inside of the quay wall beyond the ferry pontoon. The bottom here is smooth. The 'marina' has 200 berths, 15 of which are for visitors. Moorings here are on buoys. When you pick one up, you will find two forward 'risers' and two aft, one for each bow and quarter; each pair is seized together, leaving just two lines to come aboard, one forward, one aft. Secure accordingly. Maximum LOA is realistically around 9m (30ft). To enter the marina, steer straight for the end of the mole from the jetty head, thus avoiding a muddy bar which forms parallel to the jetty.

There is every possibility of finding a fine place to dry out in privacy up-river, but this is not recommended without prior low water survey, on account of a few isolated rock patches. If you fancy this, stay with the crowd to start with, take a stroll at low water, then move at the next high.

Facilities

Lovely village, after a short, unusual walk, with the regular shops, restaurant, etc. There is fresh water on the jetty, showers, toilets, and a payphone. There is also a bar/bistro within half a cable of the jetty.

Guernsey (Channel Islands)

Tides

HW −0449 Dover

MHWS	MLWS	MHWN	MLWN
9·0m	1·0m	6·7m	3·5m

Depths

Various – see below, and see plans.

General

Guernsey is the seat of government of the Bailiwick of Guernsey, which includes Alderney, Jethou, Herm and Sark. 55,000 make up its permanent population, which number is added to by almost half a million visitors annually, attracted by the romance of island life, the beaches, the hotels and the duty-free shopping.

There is usually room in St Peter Port, where you berth in the town centre, either on moorings or in a marina. The harbour is well sheltered, though it may become lively in an easterly. It is deep, well lit and approachable at all states of tide, day or night. By catching the Race of Alderney, it seems surprisingly close to the Needles, and it is actually only 65 miles from Weymouth.

The moorings are quiet in most weather conditions. Overspill is into Havelet Bay, where one can anchor in the absence of anywhere better. Safe you may be in westerlies, but life can be rough in here, with rolling as your reward 3 hours either side of high water in any but the calmest of conditions, and a poor time of it getting ashore. It is clearly a nonstarter with winds from the east, so you should then go elsewhere – the Grande Grève or Havre Gosselin, in Sark, offer joyous diversion if things are not too boisterous. Beaucette Marina at the north end of Guernsey is a further possibility.

Above all, St Peter Port is a fun place to be.

Approach

The island has the appearance of a flat plateau. With the sun in the right direction you may well see its light flashing off the 'Guernsey Tom' greenhouses before you ever see the beaches. There is a radiobeacon (*GRB* on 361 kHz) of 30M range situated 1 mile northeast of the southwest corner of the island. There is also an interesting radio device on

St Peter Port breakwater. This radiobeacon (*GY* 304·5 kHz 10M) works conventionally, but the long dash for homing in starts at exactly the same moment as the St Peter Port fog signal sounds (every 15s). Count the time in seconds between them, multiply by 0·18, and you have your distance off in miles. There is truly no end to the wonderful works of man.

From the Race of Alderney, the Little Russel Channel is the obvious and favourite route in. Avoid the Banc de la Schôle en route; it is very shoal indeed and can kick up a wicked sea. Tidal streams in the channel itself run largely 'fore and aft', but cross-sets can be expected to the north. The tide starts ebbing to the southwest 1½ hours before HW Dover. 6 hours later it reverses.

In the dark, your first mark will be Platte Fougère (Fl.WR.10s16M). This is a 15m black and white horizontally striped tower. Its red sector covers

Platte Fougère 25m-high white octagonal light-tower with black band to be left to starboard entering Little Russel, 1½ miles northeast of Beaucette. It has a WR.10s light and horn every 45s in fog. Red sector guards rocks to NW.

rocks to the northwest, and it features a racon call sign *P*. On your port bow you should see Tautenay beacon tower, a vertically striped black and white varde (Q(3)WR.6s) whose red sector (215°–050°) covers various nasties to the northeast. If you cannot do better on the way in during daylight, make sure it bears 215° or less.

The steel lattice tower of Roustel, 18m high (Q.7M), stands in mid-channel and can safely be left to either side. If you line it up with the 19m-high flat fort on Brehon (Iso.4s9M) on 198° you have an excellent safe line in through the dangers as far as Roustel.

Alternatively, line Brehon up with the lighthouse on St Martin's Point, south of St Peter Port, on 208°.

Brehon is left to port, and if on the latter transit you must do this in plenty of time, because rocks lurk nearly 2 cables to the west of it. Just before you reach Roustel (leave to starboard on this line) you will see the prominent Belvedere House, at 57m elevation south of the town, line up with a white patch on the east end of Castle Cornet, at the harbour entrance. Go for the transit on 223°, and

Brehon fort one mile SW of *Roustel* beacon, due west of Herm.

Les Hanois lighthouse at SW corner of island, 36m grey tower with helipad. View from WSW with Fort Saumerez beyond (left). Many off-lying dangers lurk to seaward of the lighthouse.

follow it until the entrance opens. If you are coming in leaving Roustel to port, simply head for Castle Cornet, having lined a part of it up with some prominent background feature of your own choosing. The home-made transit will serve you well.

All routes leave La Platte (NOT to be confused with Platte Fougère) to starboard. It is a 6-metre green varde (Fl.WR.3s7/5M) standing 8 cables east-northeast of St Sampson.

By night, in decent visibility, you simply cannot miss the leading lights. These excellent illuminations are on 220°, clear all dangers, and are: rear – Oc.10s61m14M – small tower with orange stripes, close by Belvedere House, and front – Al.WR.10s 14m16M. By coincidence, these lights, whose structures can be plainly seen in daylight, are almost in transit with two radio masts displaying red lights.

The north breakwater head shows an Oc.G.5s light visible for 14 miles, and the south breakwater is, of course, the front leading light (see above).

Do not be alarmed by looking at the chart of the Little Russel. It is wider than you might imagine, and in decent visibility is easy enough to follow.

The Big Russel channel, between Herm and Sark, is a safer option if visibility is in doubt. If the weather is or seems likely to become foggy, do not go to Guernsey until things improve. It is not an easy place to enter in fog. Should you opt for the Big Russel, head in towards the big light on Sark (Fl(4) WR.15s8M) until you can safely shape across to the lit south cardinal *Lower Heads*, or St Martin's Point. Round *Lower Heads* and shape across to the harbour.

From the south there is no problem. Leave St Martin's Point to port and shape up for the Castle Cornet.

From the northwest, if the tide serves, there is much to be said for leaving the awesome Les Hanois light (Fl(2)5s33m20M) to port and approaching south-about. Les Hanois needs a wide berth, not only because of the rocks to seaward of it, but also because it is one of the good old Channel's rougher corners. The lighthouse has a conspicuous heli-pad on top.

Note that the tide along the south coast shows a strong preference for running east-west.

Berthing in St Peter Port

You will probably be met by a harbour patrol launch and told where to moor. The choice is mooring to a buoy or a pontoon, with rafting up, or Victoria Marina, which has a busy waiting pontoon. You may well have to wait for the marina. The sill dries 4·18m, giving about a metre over it at half-tide. The entrance shows a tide gauge. Visits are limited to 14 days.

If you are not met in St Peter Port, move slowly in via the clearly buoyed channel, swinging round to starboard to where you see visiting yachts moored. If you cut the corner, you may well hit the mud.

Alternatively, for stays of more than 4 days or so, you can ask to be admitted to Queen Elizabeth II Marina (see plan), once called the North Beach Marina. This is a snug berth, though a slighly longer walk to town, but this is little hardship for a thirsty sailor. Depths are 4·5m just inside the sill and no less than 2m anywhere else. Approach on 270° from close to the south cardinal lit *Reffée* buoy, in the white sector of the DirOc.WRG.3s5m6M light. If the light goes green, nudge to port. If red, vice versa. By day, line up a yellow triangular board in front with an orange rectangular board to the rear.

Facilities in St Peter Port

Simply everything you could want, except possibly major repairs. These are undertaken at St Sampson 'next door'. Central Guernsey is equally good news for the family yacht or the 'rugby club trip', as either will be superbly catered for in civilised but relaxed surroundings. The only sadness is that whereas in the bad old days *The Shell Channel Pilot* used to call in at Guernsey to stock up with the best pullovers in the world at knockdown prices on the market, visitors must now pay the same as mainland customers. Never mind. You can save the difference by replenishing your essential rations at the best prices in the English-speaking world.

Channel Islands Yacht Marina, Vale

This converted flooded quarry at the northeast end of the island is more generally known as Beaucette Yacht Marina. The dynamited cut into the quarry gives access to a perfectly sheltered 200-berth yacht harbour.

Join the approach channel about halfway between Platte Fougère and Roustel (see above, under 'Little Russel'). The entrance is not easy for the first-timer

Depths in Metres

N

**ST PETER PORT
(Guernsey)**

Q.G

Panel
DirOc.WRG.3s5m6M

Q.R

North Quay

Sill &
Gates

Queen
Elizabeth II
Marina

Glategny Esplanade

(Locals)

South Quay

Reffeé
Q(6)+LFl

Sardrette

Boue
Gosselin Foul

Foul
Area

○ Victoria Tr
(36) PA

**49°
27'·5
N**

St Julian's Pier

Cambridge
Pier

F.G

F.G

New
Jetty

White
Rock
Pier

North Esplanade

Royal Channel
Island YC

Victoria Pier

North Pier

F.G

F.G
2F.G
(vert)

Fl.R

Oc.G.5s11m14M
SS(Port Control)

265°·

Arc of vis

Iso.R.2s22m3M

Victoria Marina
(Visitors)

Oc.R.5s10m14M

South
Pier

Fl.R

THE POOL

Lighthouse
Al.WR.10s14m16M
Horn15s RC

Spire

Albert Pier

Fl.G

Sill

Fish F.R.
Quay

F.R

Fl.R

Fl.R

Fl.R

Fl(2+1)G.10s

Cow Bay

Tremies

Spire

Albert Marina
(Locals)

Guernsey YC

Viaduct

Castle Breakwater

Castle
Cornet

Slip

Ferico

2°31'·5W

St Peter Port

to identify, but it lies about 2 cables south of the more conspicuous Fort Doyle.

The channel starts to the south of the unlit south cardinal beacon *Petite Caroupe* (which is tall, thin and hard to spot in daylight, with its tiny topmarks and its legend 'PC') with a lit green buoy (VQ.G), and is now well buoyed on a heading of 276°. There are also leading marks: front – a wide vertical red line and pole over a white background on the north side of the entrance, rear – mast on the white club-house bearing a white board with a red vertical stripe. Both carry F.R lights at night. The rear leading mark also picturesquely carries a windsock.

The sill of this marina dries 2·4m. There is a tide gauge in the entrance and a couple of waiting moorings. Best entry is ±3 hours HW, though even at half-tide the entrance is only 8m across. If this doesn't faze you, there will be 1·9m on the sill at ±2 hours on LW neaps. At springs, you will have to wait a little longer. Consult the tide gauge and do your sums.

A late jink to port is desirable to keep clear of rocks with a beacon. Leave to starboard the 'breakwater' of old tractor tyres and enter the basin, sure of at least 18m(!) of water inside.

There are at least 50 visitors' berths and harbour staff who are keen to fit you in.

The harbour listens on VHF Ch 80, 37 or 16. The harbourmaster is on ☎ 01481 45000.

Facilities include fresh water, fuel, provision shop, chandlery and a floating launderette. Some repairs can be arranged. The harbour also has one of the most famous restaurants in an island celebrated for its cuisine. St Peter Port and the airport are a long taxi ride, but the marina has a community of its own, and neighbouring L'Ancresse Bay is generally agreed to be the finest beach on the island – perfect for family bathing.

Beaucette Yacht Marina.

Beaucette Yacht Harbour. Entrance only 18m wide. Leading marks: orange board above tide gauge in line with flagpole and windsock at right-hand end of clubhouse.

Petite Canoupe south cardinal beacon outside Beaucette Yacht Harbour.

St Sampson

A commercial harbour which dries out beyond its entrance. Major repairs can be undertaken here. From a point equidistant between Platte and Brehon, steer 286° on the leading marks of the post on the south pier head (F.R.5M) and the 12m-high clock tower (F.G) on the south side, near the inner harbour entrance.

Communications

By air or sea to other Channel Islands or French destinations. Fast ferry to Weymouth.

Jersey (Channel Islands)

Tides

HW −0455 Dover

MHWS	MLWS	MHWN	MLWN
11·1m	1·3m	8·1m	4·1m

Depths (St Helier)

Deep-water approaches, then 2·7m on the leading line in the small road and 2·2m in the New Harbour. The marina sill dries 3·5m and there is 2·1–2·4m inside. La Collette basin is dredged to 1·8m.

General

Jersey is the largest Channel Island, at 10 miles by 5½. Its population of 80,000 copes with 800,000 visitors per annum. Money is the island's other industry, with *The Financial Times* a bestseller, but the island is also filled with history, from William of Normandy's time to the Nazi occupation of 1940–45.

Jersey is a mere 12 miles west of the Cherbourg peninsula, and 36 from St Malo, but until the deep-water marina was opened in the heart of St Helier it was little favoured by visiting yachts – hardly surprising, with a 10m range of tide and no deep-water harbour available in those days.

Approach to St Helier

Access to the main marina is usually around half-tide for most yachts, and there is a waiting pontoon in 2·2m for those who would cross the sill. La Collette Yacht Basin has 3·1m at MLWS.

From the north, round Point Corbière (Iso.WR.10s 36m18/16M), noting that the tide runs south from 3 hours after HW Dover (−4½ hours HW St Helier) and runs strongly eastward along the south coast until 5 hours before HW Dover, which is HW St Helier. This benefit enables the determined mariner to make St Helier in one tide from the Race of Alderney.

La Corbière lighthouse off the southwest corner of Jersey seen from the north. Note the causeway linking the shore.

Corbière is a nasty corner, like its equivalent in Guernsey, Les Hanois. Give its 19m white stone tower (36m up) a wide berth. Its foghorn sounds Morse C every 60 seconds and it has a 20M radio-beacon *CB* on 295·5 kHz with a distance-finding device (see your almanac for details). Its red sector slips you the wink if you are cutting too close to Grosnez Point by night, or are taking a flier with the buoyed channel past St Brelade's Bay.

The Pierres de Lecq are cleared at night by staying out of the red sector of Grosnez light (Fl(2) WR.15s50m19/17M). By day, if you keep Point Corbière open of Grosnez you are well to the west of danger. *Desormes*, a lit west cardinal buoy 4M north-northwest of Grosnez Point, will also be helpful.

After rounding Corbière, run parallel to the shore, about half a mile off, for 3 miles, passing close to seaward of the black and white hooped tower on Noirmont Point at 18m elevation (Fl(4)12s13M). To starboard you will see the lit north cardinal buoy, *Les Fours*, off the Grand Four shoal. Do not confuse this with the lit north cardinal *Passage Rock* buoy marking the entrance to the western passage you are now joining. You will leave this buoy well to starboard. You can now alter onto 082°, leaving an unlit red, then a lit red buoy (Fl(2)R.6s) to port, and a green buoy (Fl.G.3s) to starboard. You are now on the first leading line in, lit by front Oc.5s14M and rear Oc.R.5s12M. By day, you should see the white pillar and globe on Dogs Nest Rocks; line it up with the red vertical board on a white tower 20m high a mile or more beyond it.

Noirmont Point from the west.

Two cables your side of it is a lit green buoy (Q.G) marking East Rock. This is also on the transit.

Just before this buoy, alter to port onto 023°, which is the so-called 'red+green' transit up the final 7 cables to the entrance. The rear leading light is Oc.R.5s12M on a red structure and the front one is Oc.G.5s11M on a white daymark. You will pass the *Platte Rock* (Fl.R.1·5s) red lattice beacon on your port hand after first leaving the *Oyster Rocks* red and white beacon also well to port. Swing to starboard off the transit when two F.G leading lights (or the harbour entrance in daylight) come on, bearing 078°. Then either come to starboard again for La Collette or enter the New Harbour on your port side and make up for the sill or the waiting pontoon.

From southwest-about the Minquiers, head for *Passage Rock* lit north cardinal buoy off St Brelade's Bay. The mark is 2 miles from Corbière light on a bearing of 125°. Leave it to starboard and continue as for the western passage described above. Alternatively, steer for the Demie de Pas yellow and black light tower (Mo(D)WR.12s14/10M Horn(3) 60s).

Keep watching for the 'red+green' transit described above. You will come onto it 1½ miles short of Demie de Pas. When the lights or the daymarks come on, turn up them and you are in the guinea seats. Don't wander though; there are rocks to starboard. Note that this entry crosses a 1·2m patch (LAT).

From the east, or east-about the Minquiers, steer to leave Demie de Pas (above) two or three cables to starboard and make a track of 314° towards a black and white mark in St Aubin Bay. Leave the red can buoy *Hinguette* (Fl(4)R) to port, and keep going on 314° until you come onto the 'red+green' transit mentioned above.

Whichever pass you are using, remember the tide – up to 3½ knots at springs, 1½ knots at neaps. The harbour listens on VHF Ch 14, and appreciates a call.

ST HELIER HARBOUR

2₁

0₅

11'

1₈

2₄

La Vrachère

Local boat channel
(marked by beacons)
1₈

10₄

4

3₈

Causeway

New Marina
Works in progress

Harbour Office

Marina Shop
Toilets/showers
Telephone

0₉

3₄

2₁

Albert Pier

Waiting pontoon

North Quay

2₄

Rocquemin

0₃

Bn

1₈

2₄

Elizabeth
Castle

7

11

Buoyed channel

5₃

R Mark
Oc.R.5s12M

R Mark
Oc.G.5s
11M

St
Helier
Hbr

Old
Hbr

Yacht Club

Fuel

F.G   F.G

078°

3₁

Gros du Château

0₃

0₆

10₄

0₆

R

2₈

Port Control
Tower

Victoria Pier

5₂

Crow Rk

6₁

3₃

R

R

Chy
(95)

0₃

0₆

Hermitage Rk

4₆

Small

Q.R

La Collette
Yacht Basin

Toilets/showers
(Floodlit)

Pt des
Pas

2₇

Bn

0₃

1₂

Road

3

2₄

La Collette

(4)

Crabière
Rk

7

3₁

2₇

Breakwater
End

2₅

Tanks

1₈

Platte Rk
0₉   Fl.R.5M

3₅

0₁

Reclamation

2₄

3₁

1₈

Oyster
Rks

2₇

West Rks   2₄

5₅

2₁

6₇

4₆

3₇

5₂

1₅

Bn

Dog's Nest
Rk

1₈

3₄

Mondine

49°
10'
N

4₃

2₁

W La Cloche   2₇

8₅

East Rock
Q.G   G

4₆

2₅

E La
Cloche

2₄

Signal Mast in line with
Breakwater end 044°

N

Depths in Metres

5₈

9₈

5₂

7₃

Ldg Lts 023°

3₁

7

Nipple Rk   9₇

2₆

2₇

2°8'W

7'

La Grève d'Azette light on the waterfront one mile southeast of St Helier. Vertical orange board on pylon. By day it is the rear mark for 082° transit with *Dogs Nest* beacon. By night it is the front light on the same transit with Mt Ube light one mile ENE.

Entrance to Old Harbour at high water.

Berthing in St Helier

La Collette Yacht Basin Leave the dolphin to starboard and both red buoys to port, then make for either the waiting pontoon on your starboard bow or the permanent berths to port.

Traffic lights

Green – enter

Red – leave

Red and green – don't do either

Q.Y – craft under power of <25m may proceed against the signals

Find a berth, usually on F or G pontoons, the furthest ones from the entrance. Larger yachts than 12·5m LOA or 2m draught may be accommodated nearer the entrance on A. Harbour office ☎ 01534 885588, *Fax* 885599 (harbourmaster) or 885509 (marina). La Collette ☎ 885529. Most users of La Collette are waiting for a place/water to enter the new marina.

Facilities include toilets and fresh water. Diesel is near the yacht club by the South Pier elbow, as is *Calor Gas* exchange. La Collette is a hike from town.

St Helier Marina has a gate over the sill which closes with the tide, leaving only 0·8m of water. A Fl.R light means it is about to close. A F.R means it is closed. Take no chances with the flashing red unless you have no option, for reasons of manoeuvring commitment.

The visitors' berths in this first-class establishment are clearly marked, but in any case you will probably be directed to a suitable spot. All facilities you could want are here. Visit the friendly yacht club, but beware the weekend, with Saturday closing as well as Sunday an ever-present menace.

A new marina is planned to be built at the west side of St Helier, inside the outer breakwater and Elizabeth Castle. It seems likely that larger visiting yachts will be directed here, but that most of the berths will be for local boats. The channel east of Elizabeth Castle will be suitably buoyed. La Collette yacht basin will continue to be the holding area when direct approach is not possible for lack of tide rise.

St Catherine This rather open deep-water harbour lies at the northeast corner of the island. It is wide open between east and south-southeast, and you must anchor off. Ashore, facilities are thin on the ground. Approach from due east or a little north of it. Note that the only light in the vicinity is the Fl.1·5s18m13M on the end of the breakwater. Tuck in round this and anchor in 3·5m about a cable offshore. Be aware of Pillon Rock (0·9m), just under 2 cables east-northeast of the light.

Gorey lies 1½ miles south of St Catherine. It dries 4·9m, and has little room, but is very pretty as it sits under the floodlit castle of Mont Orgueil. There is plenty in the way of hostelries to entertain you ashore as your yacht dries out.

Whichever your direction of approach, keep half a mile to seaward until you find the leading marks on 298°. These are the light tower on the end of the pier (Oc.RG.5s) 'on' with Gorey church steeple (Oc.R.5s). Don't even think of entering at night as a stranger. Passage from St Helier is via Violet Channel, which could well be a test for 'extra-yacht-masters'. Find *Canger Rock* lit west cardinal buoy 2¾ miles south-southwest of the Martello tower on La Rocque Point (and 'rock' is the word for it!), leave the buoy close to starboard and make good 075° to the red and white safe water mark (L.Fl. 10s) two miles further on. Now alter to 010°, and be sure you pick up the 332° leading line of Verclut Point at the inshore end of St Catherine's breakwater 'on' with the turret on Coupe Point, the right-hand edge of the land half a mile beyond it. Stay on this 332° transit with the turret just open of Verclut Point for about 3 miles made good until you pick up the entry transit mentioned above.

On the way, you will leave to port *Le Giffard* unlit buoy.

St Aubin is the very attractive home of the Royal Channel Islands Yacht Club, and it also dries out – to half a mile from the entrance. The harbour is packed out, so do not just pitch up. If you feel you

Above: St Helier Harbour.
Below: Gorey Harbour.

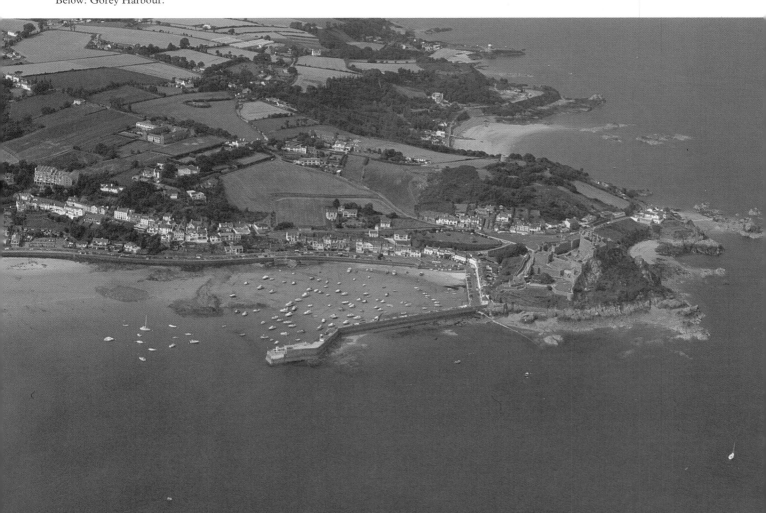

must go for it, wait for half-tide plus, then make good a course of north-northwest from *Diamond Rock* red buoy (Fl(2)R.6s) for something in the order of 1 mile. You should now pick up small channel buoys marking the way in. Dry out alongside the North Quay. The yacht club is very friendly.

Iles Chausey

Tides

HW −0500 Dover

MHWS	MLWS	MHWN	MLWN
12·9m	1·9m	9·8m	4·9m

Depths

Drying approaches from the north, and shoal water (0·3m) in the south part of the approach. It is, however, possible to lie afloat in the anchorage at all states of the tide in 2m or more (LAT).

General

Chausey is an impressive pile of rocks and reefs covering 12 square miles. Largely covered at HW, they poke out of the sea at LW springs in a sort of moonscape.

Grand Ile is inhabited by around 100 souls who 'do a spot of fishing' and milk the tourist trade from Granville. Cows do well here, and are reported to graze around the keels of grounded yachts at LW.

All the business of the island is transacted at its southeast end, which is also proximate to the moorings and anchorage. The charts make the place look horrendous, but with care and modest adherence to the tide tables the two main roads to the anchorage are simple enough.

Approach

If coming from the north for the first time, leave the lit east cardinal *Northeast Minquiers* to starboard and shape a course across the strong streams to pass well clear of the western rocks of the Iles Chausey. The *Cancalaise* south cardinal beacon near the southwest corner is your only mark. When this bears 110° it is safe to alter to leave it to port by at least a cable to be sure of clearing a rock (dries 1m) west-southwest of it. A track of 095° until the square 19m Pointe de

Iles Chausey near high water. (A) Lighthouse on Pointe de la Tour. (B) The Sound – deep-water anchorage opposite landing slip. (C) Hotel restaurant.

Lighthouse during approach from the southeast. Note line of east cardinal beacons to be left to port.

North cardinal beacon opposite the Crabière, with local moorings.

la Tour lighthouse bears 035° will clear all further dangers, after which you can track in towards the three east cardinal perches, all to be left to port, at the corner of the island. The first of these is 1½ cables south-southwest of the light. Bear in mind that you will cross a 2·3m shoal. If this is a problem, first open *La Crabière*, a lit south cardinal tripod beacon (Oc.WRG). If you bring it 'on' with the black and white tower on *L'Enseigne* at 332°, you have a transit good for all states of tide, except that just past the green buoy in the entrance a shoal approaches its line from the west. Stay a touch to the 'right' of the transit, therefore, until you pass the

Crabière beacon to starboard and enter the deep-water pool, with depths from 3–5m. Note, the N cardinal beacon 2·5 cables SSE of *La Crabière* is best treated as a W cardinal. The reef extends some little distance to the northward of it.

If approaching from south or southwest, join this approach plan in the vicinity of a point south of Pointe de la Tour.

The tide runs southwest at up to 3½ knots past the west end of Chausey from HW Dover −2½ hours, turning northwest 5 hours later. Close north or south of the islands the tide runs east from 2½ hours after HW Dover for 7 hours, then it turns

Granville

La Crabière Est. The best water for anchoring is in its vicinity.

west for 5. Within the anchorage the stream flows northwest at under 3 knots for 9 hours, then southerly for 3½ hours at most.

The Northwest Channel
This is best found for the first time starting from the moorings, and is therefore given here 'outward bound': note that the channel dries over 4m, and make the necessary calculations.

Leave the anchorage on 310° and proceed between the pair of east and west cardinal beacons a cable or so northeast of the north end of Grand Ile. From here, head 325° for 9 cables, with the east cardinal *Grunes de la Massue* beacon fine on your starboard bow and its white chimney beacon on your port bow, passing a west cardinal beacon 50m to starboard on the way. You will also notice another white chimney beacon, *Le Chapeau*, about 2½ cables to port.

Approaching *Grunes de la Massue*, swing to starboard onto 018° to bring the white beacon into transit with its fellow on *Le Chapeau*. This will leave the east cardinal beacon to port. 3 or 4 cables after the course change you will have the black and white daymark of *L'Enseigne* abeam to starboard. Keep on your transit until this lines up with the lighthouse tower on Pointe de la Tour. Now swing to port and sail clear out on this transit, heading 335°. You will pass a west cardinal beacon to starboard and an east to port. Thereafter, you are in deep water and can break open the drinks locker.

Berthing and facilities
Yacht Club Granville has some moorings in the pool. Tie up fore-and-aft on trots. Raft up if need be, but *note the depth.* The vedettes do not usually stay overnight, so their buoy may be free. Use a mooring if possible, otherwise anchor where you can find space north of the jetties. Do not attempt to lie alongside the jetty or the slipway, where you will not be welcome, and don't forget an extra-long dinghy painter. The spring range is 11·3m (37ft)!

Limited provisions from a small store, and a welcoming hotel with a decent restaurant.

Tides
HW −0510 Dover

MHWS	MLWS	MHWN	MLWN
13·0m	1·4m	9·8m	4·6m

Depths
Approaches dry up to 4·0m from *Le Loup* beacon onwards. The sill into the yacht harbour dries 5·25m and depths inside are maintained at 2·5m on the visitors' berths.

General
Granville is an ancient walled community built on a 50m-high promontory jutting westward from an otherwise straight stretch of coast. Some fishing craft remain, but the port is now noted for its yachting. The great days of the far-ranging 'Bisquine' three-masted luggers have been revived by the town's building of the full-sized replica, *Granvillaise.* Even a modern yacht has only to sail alongside this flying machine for a few minutes before being seen off. What hope can the poor British revenue men have had against smugglers of her calibre when they swept across the channel on moonless nights, loaded with contraband and sailed by characters straight out of *Frenchman's Creek*?

Approach and entrance
The first thing you will see on raising Granville is the 16m grey lighthouse on Pointe du Roc (Fl(4)15s 23M). 1½ cables northwest of it is *La Fourchie* red daymark, with a Horn(4)60s. Give the point at least 3 cables' clearance, heading southeast to pick up *Le Loup* isolated danger daymark (black/red/black, ⁞ topmark, Fl(2)6s8m11M). This is kept about a cable to your south as you line up the white tower at the seaward end of the Hérel marina breakwater (Fl.R.4s) with a small *château* on the hill with a lawn in front of it on 057°. With sufficient rise of tide, this transit is not critical.

If you have it in mind to dry out, you should turn in for the Avant Port when its breakwaters open up, paying attention to the plan. It is recommended, however, that you head for the marina.

The marina is kept full of water by a sill with a 'gate' in it. The sill dries 6m and the gate dries 5·25m. It does not open, however, until it has 0·65m over it. Thus, at the time of opening a vessel of draught 1·4m can scrape in. Thereafter the tide rises considerably, admitting larger vessels.

There is an illuminated display on the wall indicating the depth in the gate to both inward and outward-bound vessels. When the gate closes, this indicates zero. Its first reading on opening is likely to be in the region of 1·4m. It is strictly forbidden to cross the gate with the tide gauge reading zero, no matter what the circumstances.

To arrive at the gate, round the breakwater mentioned above and turn sharply to port. On your starboard hand is a short breakwater (Fl.G.4s), and ahead you will see two poles, one red and one green (Oc.R and Oc.G). They are 4m high at HW springs. Pass between them and shape up for the visitors' berths on F or G pontoons – see plan. The marina has 1,000 berths, including 150 for visitors. If desired, the marina can be called on VHF Ch 9 during office hours (☎ 02 33 50 20 06).

By arrangement with the harbourmaster, very large yachts can lock into the Bassin à Flot, which has 5m depth. The lock opens from 1½ hours before to 1 hour after HW.

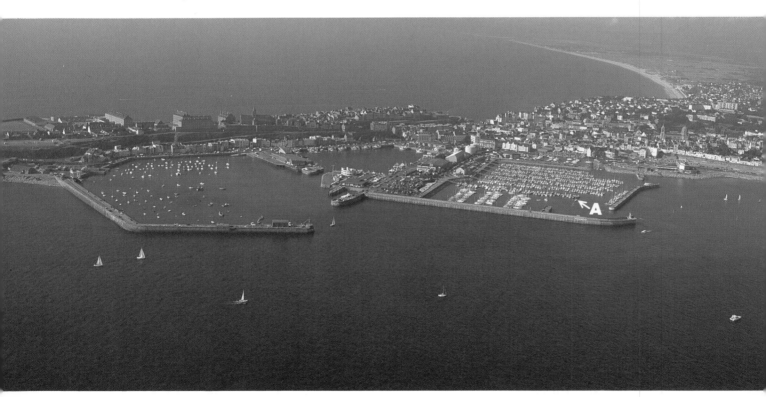

Granville. (A) Red and green poles on entrance to submerged sill.

Granville. *Le Loup* beacon.

Granville. Day transit for entry: 057° with beacon at end of Hérel breakwater in line with *château* between trees with conspicuous lawn.

Facilities

There is a splendid yacht club which caters for most bodily needs. Fresh water is on the pontoons. Fuel is also in the marina. There is a slipway (dries 7m) in the Avant Port, various mobile cranes, and a grid-iron. Excellent shops. Chandlery, mechanics and boatyard. For additional diversion you can always lighten your wallet in the casino, or take the kids to the aquarium. There are good restaurants in town and ferries to Jersey and the Iles Chausey.

Cancale

Tides

HW −0500 Dover

MHWS	MLWS	MHWN	MLWN
13·3m	2·0m	10·3m	5·1m

Depths

Dries extensively.

General

Cancale is famous for its oysters and, amongst sailors, for its three-masted luggers. The *Cancalaise* berths here, drying out tide by tide, so afficionados

of vessels of quality might feel inclined to make a pilgrimage to visit her, particularly if HW is around lunch time. They will then be able to anchor off, or tie up on the Môle (from HW ±2 hours), run ashore, and enjoy the benefits of the lovely restaurants and oyster bars on the seafront. With luck, the great lugger herself will be dipping to her mooring, itching to set to sea and beat up a few British cutters.

Afloat moorings owned by the Hotel Continental (good meals reported) can be found north of the town, but the tide runs hard, so getting ashore may prove problematic. Better to approach the shelter of the conspicuous Môle de la Fenêtre, sound in, then either anchor or tie up. Once round the Ile des Rimains with its old fort, giving it a half-mile's clearance, you can swing steadily to starboard and stand in towards the pier head – distance about 1½ miles. There are no further notable obstructions to your timely arrival.

Overnight stays are not recommended except in the finest weather with no hint of east anywhere to be seen in the wind. In such circumstances, drying out would be perfectly possible, either on legs, perhaps on the wall, or on bilge keels.

There are no facilities aimed at the cruising yacht, but if you want to buy oysters this is the place. You will never find them fresher.

St Malo/St Servan/Dinard

Tides

HW −0506 Dover

MHWS	MLWS	MHWN	MLWN
12·25m	1·5m	9·25m	4·4m

Depths

Deep-water approaches in the main channel. Bas-Sablons has 3m minimum depth on visitors' berths inside a sill which dries 2m. Port Vauban (main town) locks in to 7m depths; this marina is approached via a channel dredged to 4m (LAT).

General

Dinard and St Malo shelter behind a chain of rocky shoals and outcrops lying up to 3 miles offshore. The ports could not be more different. Dinard has all the opulence of a bygone age, when yachts used to roll their masts out at anchor as their owners played the tables.

St Malo, with its walled city (Ville Intra Muros), was flattened in 1944, but it has been faithfully rebuilt in a manner suited to the trading and buccaneering traditions of the city. It seems there is nothing you cannot buy there – or eat, if that be your pleasure. If you like cities, you'll love this one.

St-Malo. Anse des Bas Sablons on right. Lock for Bassin Vauban immediately 'above' end of pier.

ST-MALO APPROACHES

ANSE DES BAS SABLONS

Depths in Metres

Atterage S-Malo
LFl.10s
Whis

La Grande Hupée

Bunel
Q(9)15s
Bell

Chenal 16 de la Petite Porte
La Balue in line with Gd Jardin 129½

No 6
R

No.1
Fl.G.4s

Fl.(3)G.12s9M

Les Courtis
Vg

Le Sou
VQ(3)5s
BYB Bell

Le Gd Jardin
Fl.(2)R.10s
24m15M

Basse
du Nord

Les Buharats

No.2
Fl.(3)R.12s
Whis

No.4
R

089°

Chenal de la Grande Porte

Nerput
BYB

Chenal du Décollé 133°

Les Patouillets

I de Cézembre

La Pte. Conchée

Becher

La Plate
Fl.WRG.4s
11m11-7M

Les Pierres aux Normands

Chenal de la Bigne

Chenal de la Grande Conchée 182°

Chenal des Petits Pointus 202°

La Gde Conchée

Le Bouton

Les Petits Pointus

Basses des Rousses

La St Servantine
Bell

White

Red

Green

La Crolante

Les Letruns
Bell

Gd Dodehal

Roche aux Anglais
Q.G

Les Roches aux Anglais

No.14
Fl.R.10s

No.12
Fl.R.10s

Les Crapauds

Les Clefs

Le Buron
Fl.(2)G.6s

No.10
Fl.R.10s

No.8
R

Banc des Porceaux

Le Moville

Le Haumet

I. Harbour

Villa Hennessy

'Château'

Le Diamant

Roche Pelée

Bellefard

Pte de Roc'h Pelée

Le Grand Gemillet

Villa Lonick

Pte du Décollé

St Enogat

Baie des Etétés

DINARD

Anse de Dinard

Pte de la Vicomte

ST-SERVAN
Anse des Bas-Sablons

Les Bas-Sablons
Dir.F.G.20m22M

ST MALO

Le Fort National

La Cité

Rade de St-Malo

Le Pt Bey

Le Gd Bey

Paramé

Pte de Rochebonne

Pte de la Varde

Le Bénétin

Le Durand

La Petite Bigne

La Bigne

Rochebonne
Dir.FR.40m24M

La Balue
Dir.F.G.69m25M

Les Fiandais

Môle des Noirs

Avant Port

Saint-Malo Port Limit

Fl.R.5s11m13M
Horn(2)20s

Q(6)+LFl.15s
YB

VQ
B

Bassin Vauban

Bassin Duguay-Trouin

Ferry

F.R.

F.Vi

F.Vi

Avant Port

Sill

Fl.G.4s7m5M

Fort
(ru)

Pte Bechard

La Merciêre
BRB

Anse de Solidor

Dir.F.G.20m22M

Anse des Bas Sablons

Fl.R.5s11m13M
Horn(2)20s

Fl.G.4s7m5M

2° 2'W

2'W

48°
38'
N

It is hard to believe that 50 years ago it was a heap of ruins. Walking its alleys, it seems as though they have been there for ten times as long.

St Malo and neighbouring St Servan now furnish two excellent marinas. Dinard has sunk back to obscurity, at least as far as yachtsmen are concerned.

Approaches from the west

Chenal de la Petite Porte This is the main fairway. It holds no hidden nasties, except in fog, so even if you don't fancy the alternative approaches, this one should be no problem.

Navigate to the vicinity of the *St Malo* fairway buoy, or cut the corner to the next stage. Take note of *Le Bunel* lit west cardinal buoy, marking a 3·8m drying rock. Leave the green tower of Les Courtis to starboard (Fl(3)G.12s14m8M) and steer in towards Le Grand Jardin (Fl(2)R.10s15M) with its grey tower situated half a mile southwest of the prominent Ile de Cézembre. Leave this and its red beacon

Le Grand Jardin lighthouse, with red beacon immediately inshore.

Le Buron. A green tower halfway from Le Grand Jardin to the harbour entrance. Leave to starboard.

Les Courtis green beacon ½ mile NW of Le Grand Jardin – to be left to starboard. The red *Pierres des Portes* beacon beyond is a port-hand mark on the Chenal de la Grande Porte from the west.

a cable or so to port and, if it is dark, pick up the leading lights as shown on the plan on 129°. Note that the rear F.G light is intensified on the transit.

There are now various buoys (see plan), and *Le Buron*, a stubby, green 14m tower, lit Fl(2)G.6s8M. This is left to starboard, as are the green buoys and the north cardinal spar buoy marking the Plateau de la Rance, which you will pass 3 cables before reaching the main breakwater, the Môle des Noires. This is marked by its Fl.R.5s13M light, set on the top of an 11m white tower with red top. Whether by night or by day, be sure you are not set sideways towards the Plateau de la Rance, or its buoy.

Swing round the mole onto 070°, which takes you up to the lock for the Bassin Vauban. There are leading lights for the dark hours – see plan. Peel off to starboard for the Bas-Sablons marina – see 'Berthing' below.

Chenal de la Grande Porte Coming from the west, this saves a little time. Leave the red *No. 2* pillar buoy (Fl(3)R.12s) to port, followed by reds *Nos 4* and *6*. *No. 1* green pillar buoy (Fl.G.4s) is left to starboard. The whole while, you are steering 089° towards Le Grand Jardin (see above). By night, Le Grand Jardin lines up with Rochebonne light, away on the shore (DirF.R.40m24M). You will come onto the main leading lights for the Chenal de la Petite Porte as you swing to starboard onto 129° a cable before Le Grand Jardin.

Le Chenal du Décollé This is not easy for a stranger to eyeball, so it might be better starting outward bound the first time. Nevertheless, here it is; the channel is unlit.

From the vicinity of *No. 2* red buoy (see above under 'Grande Porte'), pick up two white beacons on 134°. The front one is on Le Grand Gemillet, a heap of rocks, and the rear one is the Roche Pelée, on a promontory ashore. Continue on this line until the islet off Pointe du Décollé is abeam, then alter to 105° and follow the marked route to the Pointe de Dinard, 2½ miles east-southeast. This will leave the green beacon *Le Petit Genillet* to starboard and the red, *Le Petit Buzard*, to port. You now pass over a 0·8m patch and swing to port onto about 094° to leave the green *Le Rochardieu* to starboard. Away to port ¼ mile later is *Le Mouillé*, which is red and sits on an extensive rock which dries 12m. When this is abeam, alter to 110° to pass down the channel between a red beacon, followed by a green, a further red and a green immediately off Pointe de Dinard. You may pass over the edge of a 2m-drying patch right at the end.

Approaches from the east

All these channels end up crossing the shoal of 0·5m northwest of the Petit Bey fort. They are all unlit and are not always easy to spot on first meeting them. Better to try them outward bound, though they can save up to 3 miles.

Chenal de la Bigne Leave *Basse aux Chiens* east cardinal buoy to starboard and line up *La Crolante* white beacon tower, off Pointe de la Varde, with the right-

Fort la Grand Conchée to be left to starboard at seaward end of Chenal de la Grande Conchée on course 182°.

hand edge of Le Grand Bey island, on 222°. You will see the fort on Le Petit Bey open to the right of this transit. This will take you past *La Petite Bigne*, a green beacon, left to starboard. Stay on the transit until the distant Villa Lonick, by the white-painted Pointe Bellefard, lines up with *Le Buron* (stubby green tower). This transit leads down past Pointe de la Varde and a green buoy (leave to starboard) ¾ mile further on. It is now safe to steer in a south-westerly direction to leave the red beacon of the *Grand Dodehal* to port and the lit green buoy guarding the Roches aux Anglais to starboard. Thence proceed to the main channel, leaving the unlit red *Les Crapauds du Bey* to port. Round Le Petit Bey and you are in with the main stream.

Chenal des Petits Pointus Leave the *St Servantine* green buoy to starboard, then *Les Petits Pointus* (red daymark) to port. Now line up the right-hand edge of Le Petit Bey fort with Point du Dinard. Join the Chenal de la Bigne in the vicinity of the Roches aux Anglais.

Chenal de la Grande Conchée Leave the fortified islet La Grande Conchée 3 cables to starboard on course 182°. Shortly you will pass *La Platte* beacon and *Le Bouton* south cardinal buoy to port. Still on 182°, make sure you leave the green beacon on Les Pierres aux Normands and the Roches aux Anglais green buoy to starboard, then join the Chenal de la Bigne.

If in doubt, use the Chenal de la Petite Porte, but when bound out to the east the Chenal des Petits Pointus is easy enough, provided there is enough water in the first mile or so.

Berthing

Port Vauban (VHF Ch 9, ☎ 02 99 56 51 91.) There is plenty of room here, and the harbourmaster is keen to accommodate visitors of all sizes. Large yachts in the Bassin Bouvet by arrangement with the harbourmaster. There are three waiting-buoys outside the lock, marked 'Vauban'. Diesel in quantity by telephone and lorry (☎ 02 99 81 30 71). Toilets and showers. Fresh water on the quay and pontoons. Small crane for masts etc. All repairs, chandlery and back-up. More restaurants in the

Intra Muros than you can count on a good evening walk.

Port Vauban is very handy for the town.

Port des Bas-Sablons (VHF Ch 9, ☎ 02 99 81 71 34.) All the facilities you would expect from a modern, purpose-built marina, including diesel on the pontoon (1000–1200 and 1600–2000). Fuel is also available from the quay at Dinard from HW±3hr. St Servan itself is a very pretty town, with a lovely waterfront opening onto La Rance. This includes the famous Solidor tower and numerous waterfront bistros etc. Very agreeable indeed, except in stiff northwesterlies, when the visitors' pontoon, being nearest the sill, has been reported as somewhat bumpy. The marina is a cab-ride from the Intra Muros, but maybe you won't want to go there. Don't try to walk it unless you are desperate.

La Rance

Depths

At least 2m as far at St Suliac. The next 6 miles partially dries up to the Chatelier lock, which opens usually at chart datum +8·5m. Port du Lyvet marina inside the Chatelier lock has 2m or a little more on visitors' berths. The Port Lyvet harbourmaster advises that from the Chatelier lock to Dinan there is a maximum of 1·4m in the canal, though up to 1·9m has been reported by other sources. In times of drought, there may be less than either. The suspension bridge at Port Hubert has 23m clearance, and the railway viaduct a mile above Mordreuc clears up to 19m. A power cable crossing the river just below Dinan has air draught of 16m.

It is worth noting that as a general rule, HW in the Rance will occur 2½–3hr after HW St Malo, but this is by no means reliable.

General

The hydroelectric barrage across the Rance, 1½ miles south of St Malo has a lock passable by yachts. This opens up an extensive cruising area

La Rance. Road bridge and lock gates at western end of barrage open for passage of yachts.

inside and permits access to the ancient town of Dinan, 12 miles above the lock, at least for shoal-draught yachts. There is one further lock at Chatelier.

The walled town of Dinan was saved in 1395 during a difficulty with the English by the local champion, one Du Guesclin, who gained a 'points' verdict from the judges in a single combat contest against Canterbury, the Duke of Lancaster's man. The port is now a picture-book Breton stone spectacular set in a deep gorge with the main town up above it. There is a beautiful view from the 'English Gardens' inside the ramparts, and from this port suitably shallow vessels with masts lowered can complete a passage to the Bay of Biscay via a further 47 locks.

Main barrage and entry locks

Because of the need to maintain a head of water to do its business, the barrage's opening times appear eccentric to the uninitiated. Check hours with the harbour office at one of the St Malo marinas. The Capitaineries at St Malo and St Servan issue tide tables from *Electricité de France*, but these may not be rigorously adhered to by the lock-keepers, whose job is to maintain a head of water for the hydro-electric arrangements. There is also a recorded message on ☎ 02 99 16 37 37, and times are published in *Ouest France*.

The above port authorities will advise as to Chatelier lock and its opening times, and they will issue you with the printed instructions you must have to be a legal operator inside the barrage. There is an English version available, but your attention is drawn to the excellent Carte Guide *Navigation Fluviale No. 12*, which also gives The Word in English. The power company are on ☎ 02 99 46 21 81 or try VHF Ch 13.

In short, the lock can open when the level is 4m above datum, giving at least 2m in the lock. Normally, it opens every hour when there is 4m in the Rance Basin at St Suliac, 3 miles further on. The lifting bridge will open at any time during the first 15 minutes of the hour. The lock works from 0700–2100 local civil time.

There are waiting berths on dolphins useful only near high water, and it is recommended by the lock-keepers to arrive here 20 minutes or so before 'opening time'. On no account be tempted to pass between the dolphins. They are joined together by a wooden paling which may well be submerged when you arrive. If you don't fancy the dolphins, hang around in sight of the gates.

Approach

Leave St Malo and push across to the west side of the river, picking up the red beacon on Bizeux, a rocky pile opposite Pointe de la Vicomté. Leave Bizeux islet to port, and continue to the south, leaving red buoys to port and *La Jument*, a lit green tower 6m high, to starboard. There are two unlit green beacons just before the lock, whose opening is signified by traffic lights.

Note that there are prohibited areas both upstream and downstream of the lock marked by round floats strung together on cables.

Approaching St Suliac, 3 miles from barrage. Note pagoda on headland.

Approach to lock in the Rance barrage. The building in the centre is the lock office with the lock immediately right of it. Note La Jument just right of centre, also various red buoys, including the lit one opposite La Jument. The prohibited area marks can just be discerned left of centre immediately below the barrage.

Continued from opposite

DINAN

Channel marked
by beacons

Canal de l'Ile-et-Rance

Overhead power

Pontoons

Low bridge

N
100
Metres
(Approx)
0

Ecluse de
Châtelier

Shop

Lyvet

N

2
Nautical Miles (approx)
3000
Metres (approx)

0

N

Pte Garo

Oyster
beds

0·4

1·5

2

Pte de
Châtelais

Pte du Grouin

Pte de la Haye

Continuation

Port St-Jean

Br 23m
Br Hm23m at MHWS
Port St-Hubert

Plouër-sur-Rance

Pte de l'Enclos

Buoyed channel

Mordreuc

Château

*Rance
Maritime*

Viaduc de Lessard
Hm 19m

Lyvet

Châtelier
Lock

See Continuation to right

LA RANCE
Scale on Continuation

N

ST-MALO

Anse des
Bas Sablons

Les Bas Sablons

DINARD

2·5

4·7

6·8

*

G
G

8·8

BY

*

3·8

BRB

Pte de la
Vicomte

La Jument
Fl(5)G.20s

4·5

Bizieux

Prohibited Area

See plan

Rance Tidal
Barrage

Tidal power
station

Lock

7

(11·2)

3

2·5
3

Zébres

Pte du Grouin

Ferry slip

Sea plane
Landing area

I. Chevret

Hotel

Pte de Cancaval

Anse de
Montmarin

Le Richardais

10·2

7·7

Ile Orteau

au Moine

Pte de
la Landrais

Le Minihic
-sur-Rance

Anse de
Gauthier

Pte de
Bay du put

St
Suliac

Les Echaudieres

Le
Chaudron

Pte du
Thon
Pte
Gare

La
Morne

Pierres
du Fil

2

1

1·8

Pte de
Trégondais

Depths in Metres

Rance Tidal
Barrage

2·01'W.

Tidal
Barrage

(2·)

*Prohibited
Area*

48°
37'
N

Lock
Fl.G.4s
Iso.G.4s

G
G

Fl(2)R.6s

Oc(2)R.16s

1·5

G

0

Once inside the barrage, observe the buoyage. There are many anchorages, but St Suliac is worthy of note. Anchor or moor (caveat – see 'Berthing').

At Mordreuc, you can sometimes muscle in alongside in 1·5m. Here you can buy fuel and enjoy the view of the small *château* opposite. The river now narrows seriously.

The channel up to the lock at Chatelier is well marked with unlit red and green beacons, but the lock should only be approached with 8·5m of 'rise'. See your local instructions for times. Even the harbourmaster at Port Lyvet will not commit himself far in advance as to what these may be. The lock-keeper is on ☎ 02 96 39 55 66 and VHF Ch 14 – worth a call to be certain.

Berthing and facilities

Note that when anchoring in the Rance, depths may vary and you cannot refer to your tide tables in the usual way. The hand-out may prove helpful, but if in doubt, reduce to soundings and assume the worst. Levels can drop alarmingly, particularly at night.

St Suliac is a delightful large village with limited facilities but at least one waterfront restaurant reported to be good. Anchor outside the moorings, or pick one up if you can find a suitable one free. There is a long stone slipway for landing and a rough beach.

Port de Plouer has a sill accessible with 8·5m water level (depth gauge in entrance) and a number of alongside visitors' berths. Facilities are thin on the ground here, but there is at least a bar.

There is a 250-berth marina at Port Lyvet immediately inside the Chatelier lock. Also moorings opposite. Here, there are showers, electricity, fresh water, a kiosk for basic provisions, and one or two bars and restaurants. 1km up the road is the pleasant small town of Viscomtes with all domestic facilities, though little for boats.

At Dinan, berth on the quay. There is adequate shopping. Fuel arranged via Bar des Vedettes. WC and showers on the quay. A selection of fine waterfront restaurants, including the Relais Corsaires beloved of Captain Coote, awaits the enthusiastic diner, all at the bottom of the hill. Do not be dismayed by the English subtitles on the menus, or the numbers of Brits toddling around the wharves. The fare remains top class.

De Lessard railway viaduct one mile upstream from Mordreuc with 19m clearance. Note fishing nets either side of well marked channel.

Chatelier Lock, 3 miles from Dinan.

Bridge at Port St Hubert with 23m clearance.

St Briac

Tides

HW −0515 Dover

MHWS	MLWS	MHWN	MLWN
11·2m	1·3m	8·5m	4·1m

Depths

Dries from 1·2m to something over 6m. No alongside berthing.

General

St Briac makes a convenient day-sail with a lunch stop-over for yachts based in St Malo. It is open to the northwest, but otherwise adequately sheltered. Its natural beauty and peace are somewhat disturbed by water-sports enthusiasts, but nonetheless it is a worthwhile picnic stop. If you want to stay overnight you'll have to be prepared to dry out in the middle on the sand bottom.

Approaches

From the east (St Malo), either creep round the Pointe de Dinard and follow the rock-hopping Chenal du Décollé, ultimately popping out past Pointe du Décollé and its various beacons on the 314° transit, or head down the main channel as far as Le Grand Jardin. With this abaft the beam and not before, steer west, between green *No. 1* and red *No. 6* buoys. Then leave *Nos 4* and *2* red buoys to starboard and the east cardinal *Nerput* daymark to port. Thence, leave *Ile Agot* and *Les Herplux* red beacons to port (it is easier that way) and shape up for the entrance on 125°. Give *Les Herplux* a wide berth if the tide demands. A rock (dries 5·3m) lies 1¼ cables north of the beacon. Leave *La Moulière* north cardinal beacon to starboard, then leave red beacons to port and greens to starboard as per the plan.

From the west, leave the unlit east cardinal buoy *Les Bourdinots* to starboard and steer for the Ile Agot until you pick up the entrance beacons on 125°.

Anchorage

To suit the weather, drop anchor on either side of the small headland on the north side, just beyond the last red beacon. Do not cut inside the beacons or approach the headland, for it is rocky. Alternatively, pick up a spare mooring. There are lots.

Facilities

Beach café and local yacht club with shower and toilet. There is a Vietnamese restaurant, a few shops and some hotels.

255

St Briac. Northwest entrance channel viewed from the dried-out anchorage.

Cap Fréhel lighthouse, 33m grey square tower 85m above sea level, as seen from the ESE off St Cast. It is often the first landfall on passage to St Malo from outside the Minquiers. RDF beacon on 305·7kHz, call sign FÈ (··—·/··—··).

St Cast

Tides

HW −0515 Dover

MHWS	MLWS	MHWN	MLWN
11·2m	1·3m	8·5m	4·1m

Depths

1·5m on the buoys or alongside the mole.

General

St Cast is a classy summer resort with a fine sweep of beach a mile long. There is little room to anchor, but the helpful harbourmaster seems always willing to assist with a mooring. Anchorage is possible either side of Point de la Garde where the yacht club can be found, but take care not to foul oyster beds with your tackle.

The place has a claim to fame of ambiguous joy for the British visitor. In 1758, 2,400 British invaders were apparently slain here. A monument has been erected to celebrate this locally satisfactory event.

It is expected that in winds of north through southeast this will be an uneasy berth.

Conspicuous semaphore station on Pointe de St Cast.

Approach

Watch out for Les Bourdinots rocks, marked by an unlit east cardinal spar buoy. Ideally this should be left to starboard, but there is plenty of water to pass between the buoy and the Pointe de St Cast. Just stay in the middle to avoid the rocks on both sides of you. In the dark, use the white sector of the light to clear the rocks. To anchor off Pointe de la Garde, sound in from the northeast.

As you leave the breakwater end to starboard, leave the *Bec Ronde* red beacon to port. Note also *La Feuillade* red/black/red isolated danger mark. Check the plan very carefully if arriving when these dangers are covered.

Berthing

The first two lines of buoys from the mole are fore-and-aft fishing boat moorings. Find a vacant yacht mooring. Ten are marked 'visiteurs'. Then ask the harbourmaster. There are waiting-buoys outside the Bec Ronde if you prefer to pick one up and then enquire from your dinghy about where you should be. The maximum LOA that can be accommodated is 13·5m. 2m draught presents no problems.

Facilities

Fresh water, petrol and diesel on the quay. Showers and toilets, small boatyard and chandlery. The town is about 1 mile distant, with the other facilities you would expect to find, including a launderette.

Dahouet

Tides

HW −0520 Dover

MHWS	MLWS	MHWN	MLWN
11·35m	1·25m	8·65m	4·05m

Depths

2·5m inside the basin. The entrance dries up to 5m. The sill dries 5·5m.

General

Dahouet is a quiet, unspoiled fishing village, made accessible by the wet dock with its marina and visitors' berths. The port can be entered 2 hours either side of HW by most yachts whose owners are on the lookout for a quiet stopover with simple food and pleasant cliff walks.

Approach

In strong onshore winds Dahouet is not recommended, on account of the breaking seas across its entrance. Otherwise, a boat drawing 1·5m can safely enter 2 hours either side of HW. Deeper yachts are readily accommodated towards the top of the tide.

Verdelet island is conspicuously conical and lies 1½ miles north-northeast from *Le Dahouet* unlit north cardinal buoy. Leave the buoy to starboard and steer about 115° towards *La Petite Muette*, a green-topped white varde bearing a sectored light (Fl.WRG.4s10m9-6M). By night, the white sector would see you through this far, keeping you off the Plateau des Jaunes to the north (red sector) and Le Dahouet shoal and others (green sector).

Leave the sprawling rock of *La Petite Muette* to starboard and a red stake well to port. By night, the green beacon in the entrance (Fl(2)G) opens as you pass clear of the *Petite Muette* and can be taken as your next mark. By day, steer for the green beacon when you are halfway between the *Muette* and the pagoda-shaped shrine of Notre Dame de la Garde. When the light structure is abeam a boat's length or two to starboard, swing to port and run along the quay until you see the entry to the sill at the western end of the marina, marked by a red and a green post. Enter with sufficient rise of tide.

Note that there are two transits in the entrance which are of no assistance. One is on the cliffs, a pair of white beacons now in disrepair, which probably defines the position of one of the offlying shoals. The other, which is made up of two small white posts right in the entrance, has been the source of some confusion in the past, not least to the compiler of *The Shell Pilot*. These appear to lead in through an entrance to the southwest of *La Petite Muette*. Such an approach is fraught with peril and you are warned against trying it by the locals as well as the *Pilot*.

Berthing

Berth in the marina on the westernmost pontoon ('O' pontoon – marked *'Visiteurs'*) or, possibly, dry out against the Quai des Terre-Neuvas east of the Capitainerie (dries 7m). There are numerous drying moorings in this area. The Capitainerie is on VHF Ch 9, or ☎ 02 96 72 82 85 during office hours.

La Dahouet. Beware of the sill across marina. Entry at its western end.

La Légué.

Facilities

Two or three waterfront bistros and a useful chandlery. Marina has toilets and showers. All other requirements modestly available in the old village which is just round the harbour, the sort of short stroll a determined yachtsman could execute while portaging a case of *vin ordinaire*. Fuel on the Quai des Terre-Neuvas (dries 7m). There is a scrubbing grid immediately outside the wet basin. It dries 6·5m and is thus not a favourite at neaps. There are 4-ton and 6-ton cranes, as well as engineers and some repair facilities. *Camping Gaz* exchange and ice are on hand.

Le Légué (St Brieuc)

Tides

HW −0520 Dover

MHWS	MLWS	MHWN	MLWN
11·45m	1·4m	8·7m	4·1m

Depths

Entrance dries up to 6m 2 miles to seaward and is highly dangerous in strong onshore winds. Local authorities put the absolute maximum as force 5 northeasterly for a small sailing yacht. Inside, however, there is at least 4m in the locked basin (sill dries 5m) and perfect shelter, though surroundings are not the most agreeable.

General

Le Légué is the port for the town of St Brieuc, across the river, which is the provincial capital. The quays give perfect shelter, but are noisy during the day, and in dry, windy conditions can cover your decks with a virulent grit. In the mid-1980s Captain Coote noted that the port was mainly for fishermen and coasters, but added that determined yachtsmen could penetrate its locks and find good shelter. There are now 20 visitors' berths in Bassin No. 2, and boats of up to 15m LOA are welcome. The sight of the entry channel at LW once you are safely inside can be a source of either satisfaction or ulcers, depending upon the balance of your humours.

Approach

The approaches to Le Légué can be dangerous in northeasterly winds of over force 5.

By day, come to the *Le Légué* red and white whistle buoy (Mo(A)10s). From close to this, steer about 200° for a couple of miles to *No. 1* green unlit buoy. Note the prominent folly on the south side of the estuary. Now follow all the buoys, greens to starboard, reds to port, until the lock appears ahead. Pte de l'Aigle (see plan) is an old-fashioned stone lighthouse with a green lantern built on the end of a very short, bullnosed pier. The beacon on Jetée de la Douane (Iso.G) is white with a green top. If you need to wait, tie up at the wall on the south side just before the lock. The lock is on VHF Ch 12, 16, and 9 towards tide times. It is also on ☎ 02 96 33 35 41. The lock opens at HW−2 to HW+1½, depending on the tide coefficient.

Night entry is not recommended, but if you must, try to place yourself on the line joining Pointe à l'Aigle (VQ.G.13m8M) and the VQ(9) *Rohein* west cardinal beacon 7½ miles to the north-northeast of it. This sets Pointe à l'Aigle on about 208°. As you close the land you should try to spot the unlit channel markers, but note that the Jetée de la Douane carries an Iso.G.4s light and that the red buoy before it (*No. 8*) is lit Fl(2)R. *No. 9* green buoy, immediately past the jetty against the shore, is Fl.G.2s. Thereafter the channel heads southwesterly to the left bank, and thence west by south to the lock.

Berthing

Once inside the lock, proceed according to the plan to Bassin No. 2. This is really a 'canalised' part of the Gouet river. The swing bridge does not open often and not at all between 2100 and 0700. Once through, if no one tells you where to berth, tie up on your starboard side in the vicinity of the viaduct. Beware of blowing sand and grit. You may have to raft up.

Facilities

All manner of repair and back-up facilities. Fresh water by tap on the quay west of the viaduct, fuel from service station on the quay. Public toilets and showers reported. One or two bars and restaurants, but a 7-minute bus ride (about every hour – times posted at bus stop west of viaduct on north side of quay) to St Brieuc will offer the bon viveur a greater variety of watering holes. Those of a more frugal turn of mind may elect to cope with a mile or so along the road towards Pte de l'Aigle, where a totally real coastal village will be discovered. Bars/*jeux*, *ménus ouvriers* at lunch-time for a genuine 55Fr including *boisson*, good chandler, etc., plus views of the entrance to make your hair curl.

Binic

HW −0525 Dover

MHWS	MLWS	MHWN	MLWN
11·45m	1·4m	8·7m	4·1m

Depths

The approaches dry 4·5m to a distance of ¾ mile. There is, however, from 1·4m to 2m in the basin generally, with deeper water (up to 3·5m) near the north end of the visitors' pontoon.

General

A sometime fishing harbour; now mainly *plaisance*, since the installation of the locked basin. The entry is dubious in strong winds from east to southeast. The lock only officially opens when the tide height reaches 9·5m. As a result, dead neap openings are very short or not at all. On mean tides or above, the lock opens an hour or so either side of HW. The port can normally be approached by craft of modest draught at any time in the top half of the tide.

Approach

The offshore approach to Binic is clear of dangers at the sort of tide height that will enable the user to come close to the port. Care must be taken, however, about the Roches de Saint Quay. These can readily be passed on either side by reference to the clear navigation marks (see plan, page 263). Indeed, the inside passage is the best part of half a mile wide at its narrowest point.

The first sign of the harbour may well be the 12m white tower (Oc(3)12s12M) on the end of the northern breakwater of Binic. A transit of this tower and the church steeple on 275° clears absolutely everything, even when the approach is dry, but is not really necessary for safe navigation. It may, however, be a useful guide to set and drift in the later stages of your approach.

There is no reason why a prudently navigated yacht should not come to shelter in Binic by night, using the easier (after dark) passage south-about round the Roches de Saint Quay. The white sector of *Roheim* west cardinal beacon (VQ(9)WRG.10s 13m11-18M) keeps you south of all the associated horrors, and you can keep this on a back bearing of around 060° until you pick up Binic light (see above).

Once past the breakwater, hang about for the lock, or tie up temporarily, watching your echo sounder. A green light means enter and a red means don't. There is no VHF at the lock, but the Port de Plaisance monitors VHF Ch 9 in office hours (☎ 02 96 73 61 86).

Berthing

The first pontoon you reach is officially designated 'visitors', though you may end up seizing the main chance of a berth. If over 10m LOA you may be directed to deeper water on the quay wall (still inside the gate) rather than a pontoon. You could be able to dry out on the inside of the breakwater (dries 4·5m – sand and mud).

Facilities

Showers and toilets reported. Fresh water on the pontoons but fuel by portage only. Good chandlery; also repairs, *Gaz* exchange and ice. For the pleasure-seeker, particularly one with a young family, Binic has all the facilities of a moderate-sized summer resort, with a well stocked, picturesque waterfront and glorious beaches to match. These are very convenient to the port, and when the tide is out, a sea-water swimming facility has been created right on the harbour wall. There is a handy supermarket.

All in all, Binic is one of the nicest of the North Brittany resort towns, and well worth a visit.

Binic.

Portrieux-St-Quay Yacht Harbour.

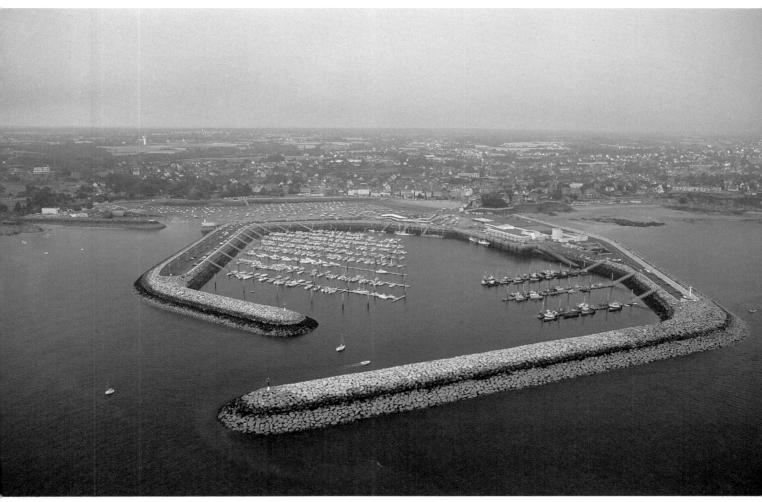

St Quay-Portrieux

Tides

HW −0520 Dover

MHWS	MLWS	MHWN	MLWN
11·4m	1·4m	8·6m	4·1m

Depths

Deep-water approaches to a deep-water marina, with berths dredged to 3·5m at LAT.

General

This is one of the few all-weather, any-tide harbours along this stretch of coast, and as such it is important. The place has beaches, restaurants and shops, a casino, and a string of rocky reefs 2½ miles long outside the front door where lobsters can fatten themselves up for the pot. The harbour is accessible at day or night, which goes some way to making up for its rather bleak, brand-new atmosphere.

Approach from the north

By day, start by sorting out *Madeux* west cardinal beacon and leave it well to port. Now find *Moulières de Portrieux* east cardinal beacon and steer a southerly course to leave this well to starboard. If the visibility is good, you will pick up a distant water tower. Line this up with the *Moulières* on 172° and you will have a useful transit to check your drift. When *Herflux* comes 'on' with the distant *La Longue* south cardinal beacon on 119°, steer down this transit for a third of a mile until the marina breakwater head bears south. Now peel off and go for it. Swing round hard to starboard to enter the marina. If you cannot discern *La Longue*, just make sure you leave the *Moulières* at least 2 cables to starboard if it is less than half-tide.

By night, come in on the white sector of Port de Pontrieux light (DirIso.WRG.4s15-11M). Keep an eye on the red sector of *Herflux* (DirFl(2)WRG.6s), and when it turns white steer towards it on about 120° until you enter the narrow white sector of Ile Harbour light (Oc(2)WRG.6s) behind you. You are now safe to alter for the Fl(3)G on the pier head. Round this to starboard, leave the Fl(3)R on the south breakwater to port, and you're in.

Approach from the south

By day, leave *Caffa* (lit east cardinal buoy), *La Longue* (south cardinal beacon) and *La Roselière* (west cardinal buoy) all well to starboard, then steer for the entrance on about 317°, making sure to leave a single east cardinal spar buoy to port. There are shallow patches of possibly as little as 0·3m on this line, but the best water (1·1m) is on the transit (317°) of *La Hergue* white beacon beyond the harbour, and the distinctive white summit of an islet called Le Pommier nearly 3 miles northwest of it.

By night, entry is easy. Round the *Caffa* (lit east cardinal) and *La Roselière* (lit west cardinal) buoys, giving a fair clearance, then home in on the white sector of the Portrieux light (DirIso.WRG.4s15-11M). This leads to the pier heads, Fl(3)G and Fl(3)R. Enter between them.

Berthing

There are visitors' berths on pontoon '7' for craft drawing up to 3·5m and up to 18m LOA. The port office monitors VHF Ch 9 day and night and is on ☎ 02 96 70 49 51. Alternatively, you can sound in and anchor south of the southern jetty, tide permitting.

Facilities

Fuel and fresh water in the marina, as are large-scale toilet and shower facilities as well as a launderette. All back-up requirements for your yacht are taken care of, including chandlers, engineers, *Camping Gaz* and ice. There is a 25-ton crane and a slipway in the old harbour. There you can also dry out if you have a mind to, after consulting the port office. The town is a lively resort, though some say less attractive than neighbouring Binic.

Communications

By bus to St Brieux, thence by train to your interior destination, or by plane to Paris from St Brieux airfield.

ST-QUAY-PORTRIEUX

Depths in Metres

Paimpol

Tides

HW −0525 Dover

MHWS	MLWS	MHWN	MLWN
10·95m	1·45m	8·35m	3·95m

Depths

The entrance channel dries for 2 miles to seaward from 3m to 4·6m. Inside the locked basin is 4m. The lock can handle 3m draught at neaps and 4m plus at springs.

General

Paimpol is a fishing town built around the deep-water Icelandic and Newfoundland cod industry. Until 1935, topsail schooners and ketches of the type known locally as 'Dundee' put out to sea from here in spring to spend the summer line-fishing in the sub-Arctic. They returned in autumn with holds full of salt fish and, as one may imagine, great was the revelry.

Today, the town offers an interesting visit for the cruising yacht. It is picturesque and maintains a strong interest in its past, having hosted in recent years one or two very successful festivals of the sea.

Approach and entrance

There are a number of secondary channels into Paimpol, none of which saves more than 4 miles overall, and most of which require delicate pilotage.

Some are indicated on the plan. The main road in is straightforward and is called the Chenal de la Jument.

First, identify *Les Charpentiers*, an east cardinal daymark to seaward of the Roches du Roho. Half a mile northwest of it stands a white pyramid, *La Cormorandière*. If coming from the east, you may first discern the Lost Pic lighthouse a mile south-southwest of it. This is a distinctive 20m square white tower with a red top (Oc.WR.4s11/8M). By night, you can come in initially in its northeastern white sector, which will turn red as *Les Charpentiers* comes abeam.

There is a useful daytime transit to take you as far as the *Gueule* red buoy. Line up the isolated white house on Pointe Porz-Don with a column on the skyline on 269°. Porz-Don light (Oc(2)WR.6s13m 15/11M) has a 3° white sector from 269°–272°. The northern edge of this, just in the red, corresponds to the transit. If you cannot identify this daytime transit, a white building on top of Pointe Brividic 'on' with Paimpol church spire gives 260° and will take you down to the *Gueule* buoy and *La Jument*.

The final leading marks on 264° are a 4·3m (14ft) truncated white tower with a red top labelled 'Kernoa', showing 2·4m (8ft) above the red-and-white painted bullnose of the jetty, and the back marker, which is a 9m white lattice tower, also with a red top. These show F.R lights at night, the rear one intensified in the safe sector. The last half-mile of the 30m-wide channel is marked with buoys and perches of which the final green is lit. If arriving

Paimpol approach.

Paimpol.

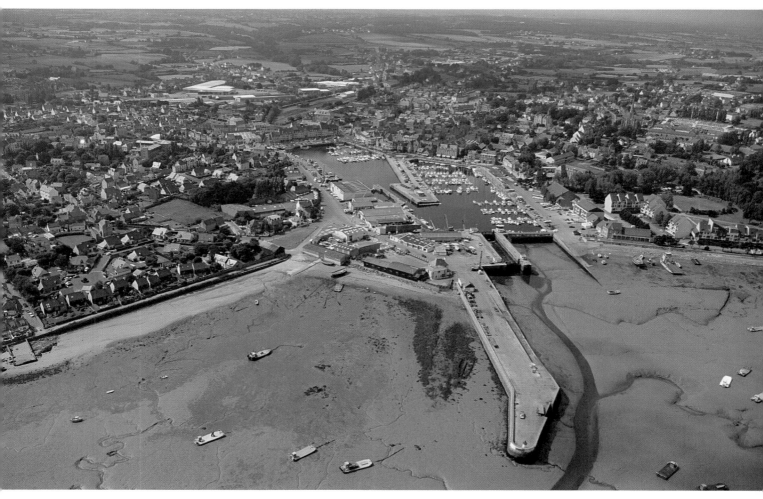

after dark without much water, note that this beacon is 70m off the transit and is in shallower water. The best depth lies in the middle of the marked channel.

Swing to port round the Jetée de Kernoa and make up for the lock. The gates open ±2½ hours HW springs, ±2 hours HW neaps. The lock-keeper listens on VHF Ch 9 at tide times. The berthing master is on ☎ 02 96 20 47 65. The lock works from 0600–2300 local time in season, 0700 to 2200 in winter.

Berthing

There are 300 pontoons and quayside berths inside Paimpol, of which 20 are reserved for visitors. The maximum length on fingers is 11m. The Quai Loti can deal with up to 15m, sometimes rafted up. More than 15m by discussion with the port officer – up to 50m can sometimes be accommodated. Visitors' berths for most yachts are in Bassin No. 2, but you may end up with a catch-as-catch-can situation. Always report to the office (Quai Neuf) on the divide between the basins after berthing. Yachts may safely be left here for short periods.

Anchorages

Off Porz-Even, with the isolated danger beacon (black/red/black, ⁑ topmark) bearing about 190° at around a cable distant, you can anchor in 2·7m just east of the moorings. This works well in suitable conditions. The whole of the Anse de Paimpol is potentially an anchorage, but you must look to your tide tables and read the chart carefully to discover the other good spots.

Facilities

Fresh water on pontoons. Fuel on the quay. Showers and heads (24 hours). Chandlery, yard facilities, sailmaker, *Camping Gaz* exchange and ice. Launderette at 4 Rue de la Benne. There is an excellent supermarket by Bassin No. 2 and all other town facilities, including the Librairie Maritime and restaurants to suit all tastes and bankrolls. L'Islandais serves an unusual menu whose wine list is sensibly salted with affordable bottles. You dine in surroundings of great interest beneath the ribs of an upturned *coque classique* under the velvet glove control of Madame herself. The bedrooms here are spectacular if you need a break from your cosy cabin.

Communications

Spectacular bus-rides to neighbouring coastal towns. Rail branch line connecting to St Malo or Brest.

Ile de Bréhat

Tides

HW −0525 Dover

MHWS	MLWS	MHWN	MLWN
10·4m	1·1m	8·0m	3·6m

Depths

Variable, from drying to deep water at LW springs. For details, see plan and anchorage notes below.

General

Bréhat is a rocky archipelago, popular with owners of shoal-draught yachts, artists, and the day-trippers who arrive in vedettes with what Captain Coote described as the regularity of the Gosport ferry. The area is also loved by those fed up with motor cars – none are allowed on the islands.

Approach

Any navigation in the vicinity of Bréhat should be taken very seriously. Streams can run at up to 5 knots, and it is therefore axiomatic that you are continuously aware of your position.

From the north, shape for a point one mile east of Le Paon lighthouse, which is a yellow framework tower (F.WRG.12-8M) 12m high at 22m elevation. Leave the Plateau de la Horaine with its various markers to port and the north cardinal daymark *Petit Pen-Azen* well to starboard on 168°. This will place you in the Chenal de Bréhat. Alter course if necessary to leave the unlit east cardinal buoy *Rc. Guarine* close to starboard and the east cardinal daymark *Men Garo* well to starboard. You now have the unlit north cardinal buoy *Cain-ar-Monse* ahead. 2 or 3 cables short of this, alter to a west-south-westerly heading to leave the south cardinal beacon *Lel-ar-Serive* to starboard. Now you can alter to 290° to pick up the south cardinal pillar due south of Ile Logodec for La Chambre, or to 278° for the west cardinal beacon *Men Joliguet*, bearing the sectored light at the southeast head of Port Clos.

The Chenal de Ferlas offers a further approach for craft coming out of Lézardrieux. In this case the west cardinal beacon *V. de Loguivy* is left well to port as you come onto a heading of 088° towards the isolated danger beacon (red/black/red, ⁑ topmark) *Rompa*. Leave *Rompa* to port and shape up on 078° to leave *Trebeyou* (south cardinal daymark) and the south cardinal beacon 1½ cables east-southeast of it to port. Continue on this track, leaving 3 south cardinal beacons at various distances as well as *Men Joliguet* to port and *Les Piliers* north cardinal daymark to starboard. You are now south of La Chambre.

Anchorages

La Chambre is marked with red and green perches with topmarks. There is deep water at the entrance if you can find room. Otherwise do your sums, then sound in. There is a dinghy landing.

APPROACHES TO LEZARDRIEUX

Ile de Bréhat. Port Clos looking S.

Port Clos dries out to its entrance and is the vedette terminal.

La Corderie is approached from the main Pontrieux river channel until you see the white pyramid daymark, Amer du Rosédo, on the westernmost point of the north island. Head in for this until the green *Men Robin* beacon is spotted and leave this well to starboard, steering south-southeast. Now leave red beacons to port and green to starboard until you are into the mouth of the bay. There is deep water north of the *Kaler* green beacon, but in order to escape the tides you should tuck right inside. Halfway in, it dries about 2·5 metres; at neaps it is an excellent anchorage. Row ashore to the south island for a pleasant walk to Le Bourg.

Facilities

Basically, there aren't any, but the place is none the worse for this. Better, some would say. Don't expect paradise unfound, because of the visitors, but it is still a fine spot where peace may descend in due season.

Lézardrieux/Pontrieux

Tides

HW −0510 Dover
HW Pontrieux lock is approximately −0505 Dover and is the same as HW St Malo

MHWS	MLWS	MHWN	MLWN
10·55m	1·35m	8·05m	3·8m

Depths

Deep water all the way to Lézardrieux. For Pontrieux, see its own section.

General

Lézardrieux has the great benefit of being only a little over a tide from Guernsey. It can be entered in any weather at any state of tide. Berths are absolutely sheltered. The town is delightful and is reached by a short walk up an unchallenging hill.

Approach

Coming from east or southeast with a reasonable rise of tide, enter the river by passing south of Ile de Bréhat (See 'Ile de Bréhat' notes, above). From points north, after negotiating the Roches Douvres, Barnouic, or the rocks stretching seawards from the mouth of the Tréguier river, fix your position using Les Heaux de Bréhat (Oc(3)WRG.12s48m17–11M) and La Horaine (Fl(3)12s13m11M). The former is a 57m-high grey tower and the latter a black octagonal tower of some 20m. You will also see Rosédo lighthouse (Fl.5s29m20M). This is a 13m tower at 29m elevation on the north part of Bréhat. The pyramid-shaped daymark (l'Amer de Rosédo) on

the western extremity of the north part of Bréhat was demolished by an over-zealous German defender, but has now mercifully been rebuilt and painted white. If this lot seems complicated, don't worry. It isn't in practice. Just study the chart and be grateful for plenty of navigational aids.

Leave La Horaine a mile or so to port (watch for the *N Horaine* unlit north cardinal buoy) and steer 225°. If it is dark, the red sector of Les Heaux de Bréhat will now have turned white, indicating your approach to the runway, and you should now be picking up the leading lights of La Croix (Oc.4s19M) beacon, a white tower with a flat, red top, and the DirQ.22M of Bodic, a squat white tower with a pyramid green roof on the skyline. These buildings are clearly visible in the daylight. The lights are intensified either side of 225°. As you pass La Croix tower a cable or so to port, pick up the second transit on 219°. This is defined by two white-gabled houses on the west bank. The front one is Coatmer (F.RG.9M) and the rear one is F.R. Both are narrow sectors, the front one ±25°, of course, the back one ±22·5°. Along this transit you will pass various beacons (see plan), including the west cardinal daymark *V. de Loguivy*, which is left to port if you wish to enter the channel south of Bréhat.

After dark, steer for Les Perdrix (Fl(2)WG.6s) white sector on 198° before the transit has run you into Coatmer. If Perdrix turns green while you are still on the transit, you must alter sharply to port to

Trieux River looking upstream.

Lézardrieux.

Les Heaux lighthouse 57m high on rocks 2 miles offshore, midway between the mouths of the Tréguier and Pontrieux rivers.

Le Paon lighthouse, a 12m high square yellow tower, 22m above the sea. It is the northernmost point of the Ile de Bréhat on the eastern side of the approach to the Pontrieux river.

At the NW corner of Bréhat, near the entrance to La Corderie anchorage, stands the white Rosédo pyramid (A). La Moisie channel from the NW is in transit 159° with the Chapel of St Michael (B).

La Croix light beacon on the east side of the estuary. The fairway is when it is in transit with Bodic on 225°.

Le Vincre red beacon ½ mile up-river from Le Croix.

The *Vielle de Loguivy* marks the junction between the fairway to Lézardrieux and the Ferlas channel to Port Clos.

Conspicuous Bodic lighthouse overlooking the west bank of the river.

regain the white sector, then steer for the Perdrix light. By day, look at the chart and the beacons. Entry is straightforward. From Perdrix, shape up for the marina.

Berthing

Anchor at will off the fairway anywhere you feel is suitable, but watch for moorings. Lower down the channel is fine. Visitors' moorings reported in Perdrix reach and off marina on trots. The marina has room for 80 visitors in season, on pontoons with up to 2·5m at MLWS, and listens on VHF Ch 9 during office hours, ☎ 02 96 20 14 22. If you fail to make contact, tie up on No. 3 pontoon and await instructions. Note that there are no longer any fixed lights on the pontoon ends. Instead, the area has been lit with powerful arc lights which show what is what far more clearly.

Facilities

Fresh water and fuel on marina. The fuel berth is inshore below the harbour office and has 1m at LW springs. Showers, heads and launderette at yacht club. There is a scrubbing grid at the Port de Commerce; also a chandler, repairs, *Camping Gaz* exchange, etc.

A pleasant *crêperie*/restaurant will be found just beyond the boatyard. Otherwise, it's up the hill to the town, where you will discover a modest but agreeable choice of eating houses, as well as traditional food shops.

There is a launching ramp (dries 2m).

Pontrieux

Pontrieux offers a peaceful and agreeable diversion from the hurly-burly of the sea. There is plenty of berth space alongside, good restaurants, shops and even a torch-light procession on the third Sunday in July, with a funfair and other benefits. The Château de la Roche-Jagu hosts a programme of cultural events from 1 June through August.

There is a minimum of 18m under the viaduct, and although the river is not officially charted there is good water for a respectable-sized yacht to pass on a rising tide. Common-sense pilotage can be applied on bends in the river, where the outside looks and usually is steep-to and the inside is shoal and muddy.

Near the top of the flood there is about 4m at springs and 3m at neaps. If you arrive early for the lock there is a mooring (raft up if necessary) in deep water just below the Château. Upstream of here, the bottom may be rocky and unsuitable for exploration before the tide is well up. The lock opens from 2 hours before to 1 hour after HW and the gates are 1 mile below the town. The river is buoyed for the approach to the lock. The sill is at 3·5m above chart datum. Do not be dismayed by the industry on your port hand soon after passing the lock. This is a 'one-off' and is soon forgotten.

Berth alongside the quay as far upstream as you can. The harbourmaster is on ☎ 02 96 95 64 66, also VHF Ch 12 and 16. The basin has all the usual yacht facilities, including fuel (from harbourmaster). Boats can be laid up here.

There are some good local cafés and restaurants, and much more in town, where all normal requirements will be met. The town is a pleasant, easy ½ mile walk from the berths.

Communications

Trains, with connections to Roscoff and St Malo for the ferries, or Paris for a good time.

Tréguier

HW −0540 Dover

MHWS	MLWS	MHWN	MLWN
9·8m	1·1m	7·5m	3·3m

Depths

Deep-water approaches. The river is also deep – at least 5m at MLWS – almost to the marina. The last 3 or 4 cables are dredged to 2m at LAT, but note that at MLWS this is 3·1m. The berths on the marina advertise at least 3m draught.

General

Tréguier is approachable by day and night in all weathers and at all states of tide. Its river is unusually lovely and offers anchorage in varied types of scenery. The town itself is a meandering medieval wonderland which contrives to be much less tourist-ridden than Vannes or Quimper, which have also retained their ancient buildings. It features a remarkable and ancient cathedral with a bizarre spire cut into hollows. It contains the tomb of St Yves, the patron saint of lawyers and, as a sideline, the protector of the poor. One day every May there is a procession in his honour, which would seem ideally timed for British yachtsmen, still on the ropes after paying their yard bills for the spring refit.

Approaches

By night, the various lighthouses are well charted and will provide good fixes in reasonable visibility. In thick weather this rock-bound coast cannot be recommended. Your landfall will ideally be at the brightly lit *Bs. Crublent* (Fl(2)R.6s) red pillar buoy,

but you may arrive first at *La Jument* north cardinal with bell. Leave *Bs. Crublent* to port and shape up on 137° for the Grande Passe. This is easier by night, as the lights are a good sight clearer to see than the notoriously invisible daymarks at 3 miles' range. These are: front Port de la Chaine (Oc.4s 12m11M), a white-painted house, and rear Ste Antoine (Oc.R.4s34m 15M intensified ±3° on 137°), another white house, this time with a red roof.

If you don't spot the transit in the daytime, watch your back-bearing on *Bs. Crublent* until you identify the red buoy *Le Corbeau* (leave to port) and its green starboard-hand partner, the *Pierre à l'Anglais*. You must pass between these, and then continue on 137°, still on the transit, to leave *Pen ar Guezec* green buoy to starboard, watching your drift all the way.

La Corne light beacon ½ mile upstream from Men Noblance is at the narrowest part of the channel.

Plougrescant church with its spire on the right-hand edge is a conspicuous mark by day when approaching from any direction.

Tréguier river approach. Passe de la Gaine on 242° brings into transit (A) Men Noblance with (B) a white wall with black vertical stripe. (C) Plougrescant church well to the left.

Tréguier river near low water.

Tréguier Marina. Inner berths may dry. Capitainerie is the large building lower right.

Roche Skeiviec ½ mile upstream from La Corne beacon.

RIVIERE DE TREGUIER

At night, course is now altered to starboard to head for La Corne, whose green sector (Fl(3)WRG. 12s) will by this stage have turned white. If it is red, you have gone too far. By day, keep the white, pepper-grinder La Corne tower just open to the left of *Skeiviec*, a white beacon tower half a mile or so further in, heading in the order of 215°. You will pass various beacons (see plan) before reaching La Corne, which is left to port. The green channel buoy is left to starboard as you hitch onto 235° (in the southerly white sector of La Corne by night). Pass the Fl.R buoy *Le Guarivinou* to port, swing onto 210° for the next red, and so carry on up the lit buoyed channel to your chosen anchoring spot or to the marina.

The last lit green buoy (*No. 17*) is within 50m of the pontoons. The penultimate green buoy (unlit) marks Le Grand Rocher, which dries 3·7m; don't cut inside it!

There is also a 'daytime only' inshore channel into the river from the northeast, the Passe de la Gaine. This saves about 1½ miles if you are coming from Lézardrieux or points east. It passes over a 0·5m patch, within a cable of various drying rocks, and is generally tight, so it requires favourable weather, some rise of tide and good visibility.

Outward bound, the channel can be picked up at the *Pen ar Guezec* turning mark (green buoy), when you swing to starboard onto 062°, with the *Men Noblance* black and white daymark on a back transit with a white house and a black-and-white-painted

wall 2 miles behind it. These carry you well beyond Les Heaux and past various self-explanatory beacons (see plan). With Les Heaux well abaft the beam you can come off the transit, after careful reference to the chart. Towards the end, you may require binoculars to see the transit.

Tréguier. Commercial quay downstream from the marina. The cathedral has the tomb of St Yves, who is reputed to smile on the poor while looking after lawyers!

Berthing

The river contains a number of moorings, and a suitable spare one can sometimes be picked up, subject to the usual international unwritten rules of lying to someone else's buoy. It is definitely preferable to anchor in this lovely river, and there are a number of sites which will appeal to the sharp-eyed mariner. On the west shore beneath the Château ¾ mile north of the town is a good spot, where the compiler of *The Shell Channel Pilot* rode out Hurricane Charlie in 1986.

The marina maintains 100 visitors' berths. Tie up near the outside and report. Watch out for strong streams along berths.

Facilities

Fresh water, showers and toilets at the marina. Laundry in the Rue St André, up in town. Fuel on the pontoon. There is a launching ramp and a 30-ton crane on the quay, with 5m of water at MHWS. One of the best chandleries in Europe is situated just over the river bridge above the marina. Worth a visit just for the atmosphere, even if you don't buy anything. Boatyards, engineers, *Camping Gaz*, ice, etc.

There are bars and bistros down by the quay – the pizzeria is the best value – and a plethora of delights up in the town. Don't miss it, or the market once a week, where, as Captain Coote remarked, you could buy anything from 1-day-old chicks to 10-year-old Calvados.

Port Blanc

Tides

HW −0550 Dover

MHWS	MLWS	MHWN	MLWN
9·4m	1·0m	7·0m	3·2m

Depths

Deep enough to anchor in the outer pool, even at LW springs, for any yacht small enough to be interested. At neaps shoal-draught yachts could get close enough in to stay the night – see plan. The quay, however, dries a staggering 9m.

General

Port Blanc is worth a visit, particularly a lunch-time stop in good weather, if only to marvel at the spectacular pink granite rocks. There is little ashore to tempt the fun-lover, but the sailor ridden with the guilt of his general excesses may find relief from his burden in the general *pardon* issued in the 16th-century chapel on 8 September. Those choosing to stay overnight in what can obviously be a very exposed place may be disturbed by the manifestation of a local story which alleges the periodic arrival

Port Blanc. (A) White daymark of Ile du Château Neuf guides approach from seaward on 150°. Deep-water anchorage off Run Glas on left.

Protected, if drying, anchorage will be found north of the slipway on Ile St Gildas.

Dried out alongside the quay at Port Blanc.

Perros Guirec

Tides

HW −0550 Dover

MHWS	MLWS	MHWN	MLWN
9·4m	1·25m	7·3m	3·5m

Depths

Channel dries 3·5m up to 1 mile from the marina. There is 2·5m inside.

General

Perros Guirec is a serious summer resort with wonderful beaches. Now that there is an artificial locked yacht harbour it has become a realistic possibility for the casual caller, who will find bars, discos and sports-gear shops in the marina area. The more traditional joys offered by hotels and restaurants tend to have stayed around the casino beside the north-facing beaches.

The bay dries to at least a mile offshore.

Approach and entrance

It is important before making a run in to Perros Guirec to establish that the lock will be open ready to receive you and that you have sufficient rise of tide to clear the drying shoals of the bay. In westerly weather you could wait for a while outside, but otherwise you will have an uneasy time of it hanging around in some very shoal and open water. The lock opens at springs from 2 hours before HW to 1½ hours after. At mean tides it opens from 1½ hours before to an hour after. At neaps it may only open for an hour before HW, and at dead neaps it may not open at all. If in doubt, call the harbourmaster on VHF Ch 9 (☎ 02 96 23 19 03).

There are two lines of approach, as follows.

From the northeast (Passe de l'Est) Leave the red can *Guazer* northwest of Port Blanc to port, and come onto a track of 224°. You now have 5 miles to go. As Ile Tomé comes abeam you should see the leading marks, Le Colombier in front (a white-gabled house 28m above the sea with a 15M light (Oc(4) 12s) and, 1½ miles inland, the white Kerprigent tower, 79m up, carrying a quick flashing light intensified close to the course. By night, this transit will carry you right in until the end of the breakwater (Fl(2)G.6s) bears west less than a cable from you. Turn in to round it, watching for the lit red buoy (Fl.R) which must be left to port on your way to the gate. By day the transit marks are clear, but if they are dimmed by poor visibility, pay due heed to the various marks on the plan. Leave reds to port, greens to starboard, with the large red and black *Pierre du Chenal* (⦂ topmark) to starboard, and you will be fine.

---

of a spectral woman at the head of a column of drowned sailors. All hands go ashore on the Ile St Gildas to water up, while their ships can be seen dimly riding in the offing.

Approach, entrance and anchorage

Navigate with care to half a mile northeast of the *Guazer* red whistle buoy. You are now 1·2 miles to seaward of the harbour entrance on the entry transit of 150°. This is defined at night (not recommended) by the white sector of the Fl.WRG.4s light (Le Voleur) which also forms the front marker for the day transit. The rear mark is the Moulin de la Comtesse windmill a mile or so inland, but this is reported (1991) as having fallen down. Therefore, unless it has been re-established by an opportunist developer, keep the white tower of the light structure on 150°, treating the conspicuous white beacon tower on the Ile du Château Neuf as a starboard-hand marker. Thereafter, you have the red beacon *Rc. Ruz* off to port. By the time you reach the green beacon *Run Glas* on your starboard hand you will be thinking of anchoring, if you have not already done so. There are a number of visitors' moorings.

The adventurous bilgekeeler may be able to work into a fine berth and dry out amongst the rocks, but this would emphatically need to be arranged first at LW from the 'afloat' anchorage.

Facilities

Nothing is set up for visiting yachts in the way of facilities, but rudimentary assistance may be found ashore in the form of simple shops. There are also a couple of hotels.

If you have need of the harbour office, it is in the local sailing school, as are showers, toilets and fresh water by portage.

Perros Guirec.

PERROS GUIREC

Depths in Metres

50'

I. Tomé

Passe de L'Ouest

143°

224°

Passe de l'Est

Pierre à
Jean Rouzic

Roc'h Bernard

Pierre
du Chenal

La Durante

Gribineyer

Pte du
Châteaux

TV mast

48°
49'
N

Port l'Epine

PERROS GUIREC

R
de Perros

Red

Green

Banc du
C'harou

L'Ost ar
C'hraou

Anse de
Perros

Gomenénou

Lifeboat
Slip

Gate

Sill

Fl(2)G.6s
4m7M

Fl(2)R.6s
4m8M

Nantouar

48'

Kerprigent

Le Colombier
DirOc(4)12s28m18M

DirOc(2+1)WRG.12s
78m15·13M

Kerjean 23'

26'   **3°25'W**   24'

From the northwest (Passe de l'Ouest) navigate into a position a cable or so southwest of the red daymark *Petit Bilzic*, on the end of the rock spit extending from Ile Tomé. If coming down from the north, be sure to leave the unlit west cardinal buoy *Les Couillons* to port. By night this position should put you in the narrow white sector of Kerjean (DirOc(2+1) WRG.12s78m15-13M). If it is red you must come to starboard, if green go to port. Follow this until you hit the leading lights for the Passe de l'Est, then swing onto them.

By day the pass is straightforward, leaving to starboard the *La Fronde* unlit green buoy and the *Roche Bernard* green daymark. When you are halfway from this to the *R. de Perros* red daymark you can swing round slowly to starboard, being sure to leave the green beacon *L'Ost C'hraou* to starboard before coming to the breakwater.

The lock-keeper may direct you to a berth.

Facilities

Fresh water on pontoons. Showers and toilets 24 hours a day (buy a token from the Capitainerie). Laundry on the quay. There are various launching ramps and cranes from 7 to 20 tons. Scrubbing is possible on the west mole, but ask first for a suitable berth. Fuel from a pontoon inside the lock – open to coincide with the lock.

There is a chandlery, and light repairs can be arranged. *Camping Gaz* exchange and ice. The town proper, with its 12th-century church, is a mile or so uphill. The casino and the best beaches are a short cab-ride away for all but the fittest gamblers and sand-castle builders.

Communications

Bus to Lannion, where there is a railway station.

Ploumanac'h. Mean Ruz square pink light tower set on pink boulders 26m above the entrance.

Ploumanac'h

Tides

HW −0550 Dover

MHWS	MLWS	MHWN	MLWN
9·0m	1·1m	7·1m	3·4m

Depths

Entrance dries 1·6m, and the sill dries 2·25m. The low water depth inside the basin is given as 1·5m, but the bottom is largely mud, so craft of greater draught can stay upright over low water. Greater depths have been reported inside.

General

Ploumanac'h is a rambly village with most small-town facilities. It is well equipped with bistros and bars, but has clearly been cleaned up from its days

Ploumanac'h. Entrance on course 214° is well marked and not as alarming as it appears here. Château Costaérès and beacon *No. 1* on starboard hand.

Anse de St Guirec is an anchorage between beacons *6* and *8*.

as a fishing community. It hides inside an entrance guarded on the east by outrageously sculptured rose granite rocks and on the west by the elegant Château de Costaérès, which has its own wooded rocky islet.

While its official size limit for the 20 visitors' berths is 10m, it has been known to extend a warm welcome to considerably larger vessels of the 'old gaffer' persuasion at times of *fête de mer*.

Shelter is excellent in all conditions, but entry may be unpleasant in strong northerlies and north-westerlies.

Approach

It is not recommended to make a first entrance in the dark. You will also have to calculate your necessary rise of tide for the sill (dries 2·25m). Having done this, the entrance is not complicated.

Identify the Pointe de Méan Ruz with its square pink light tower (Oc.WR.4s26m13/10M). Give Méan Ruz a healthy berth and shape up for the red (to port) and green (to starboard) unlit entry beacons, *Nos 2* and *1*. If coming from the northwest, steer for the light tower outside all dangers until the gap between the beacons bears about 165°, then turn in. Entry is now simply a matter of coming in between the beacons as per the plan. There are no nasty surprises, so long as you do not come too close to any of the beacons, some of which stand on ragged rocky bases. The sill is immediately after *Nos 7* (green) and *12* (red). The fourth port beacon (*No. 8*) carries a tide gauge, and there is a depth indica-

tor on the port-hand side of the sill, showing actual depth over the 'hump'.

If you need to wait for the tide, anchor near the mouth of the Anse de St Guirec by *No. 6* red pile. A few visitors' moorings can be found here, in minimum depth 1·5m. This berth will only be of interest to those vistors awaiting water for the sill, unless you intend to take the ground in tight circumstances. In any event, take care because of the proximity of numerous rocks. The village here is now set up for tourism, but the beach is sandy and there is an excellent series of easy cliff paths to explore.

Berthing

Buoys consist of two fenders joined by aluminium rods. Pick one up by its pick-up line and secure alongside it. The outer row is for visitors, but the best water (2m) was reported in 1991 to be at row C. The harbour office listens on VHF Ch 9 and 16, or ☎ 02 96 23 37 82.

Facilities

Dinghy landing near the sill after half-tide can be somewhat fraught. Seek a better alternative or wear your wellies and try the mud. Fresh water by cans from the Quai Bellevue. Showers and heads (24 hours) on the jetty by the sill. Laundry at the port. Launching slip on the Quai Bellevue. Chandlery and engineers available, but no major repairs. No *Camping Gaz* exchange or ice. There is an accommodating garage which does boat repairs.

There are spectacular cliff walks down numerous tracks in the direction of Guirec and beyond.

Ploumanac'h. Below, Château Costaérès.

Trébeurden

Tides

HW −0600 Dover

MHWS	MLWS	MHWN	MLWN
9·1m	1·3m	7·2m	3·6m

Depths

Depths in the offing, which dries, appear to coincide with or be greater than the depth on the sill. This has a mobile gate which has an 'open' drying height of two metres. Access to the port for a yacht of moderate draught is said to be at least 7 hours per 12-hour tide on a mean spring, and almost perpetually for a mean neap.

Alongside depths vary from 3·5m on the outer jetty to 3m in the central basin. There are ten yellow waiting buoys outside in a deep water pool. However, you are advised to reduce your depth to soundings when picking up one of these if intending to stay over LW, as depths here have not been personally checked by *The Shell Pilot* and all the charts contradict the advice of the harbourmaster.

General

The coast from the Morlaix river to Perros-Guirec is some of the most spectacular in the Channel. It is also highly popular with French holidaymakers for its camping among the pine trees, pony-trekking and surfing or sailboarding from the fine, sandy beaches which lie between the rocky headlands. With only Lannion, Ploumanac'h and Plougasnou offering

281

Trébeurden. Entrance to sill is hard by the breakwater end.

Trébeurden. The sill at low water. Note profitable pêche-à-pied in progress and best water indicated clearly by beacons.

limited access to yachts, it was natural enough that a new marina should be built at Trébeurden, between two small jetties linked by a massive breakwater. The town is an up-market resort featuring 3-star hotels and an 18-hole golf course. The major civil engineering work was completed as early as 1991, but political and economic uncertainty put off the grand opening until 1994. The well run marina now offers an excellent stopover, as well as a safe place to leave a yacht for a while.

Approach

This is possible by night or day, given a modest rise of tide. For details, see above ('Depths').

By day, work in so as to leave *Ar Gouredec* buoy (VQ+LFl) to port, then shape up on an easterly heading to pass between the first port-hand buoy and the northern extremity of Ile Milliau. This area is a good deep-water anchorage under the right conditions. Next, identify a green buoy on your starboard bow and a south cardinal beacon ahead or somewhat to port. Continue between these, then leave the next red buoy (*Roc'h Derrien*) to port. From here, take a heading for the end of the mole, where there are two green and one red unlit beacons close in. Take due action. On rounding the end of the mole, look for the green and red beacons (triangular and conical topmarks) indicating the position of the sill. Steer between these, according to the orders of the traffic lights, then make for the pontoon with blue pile-tops, where you should tie up and report.

Beware of the fixed retaining sill (dries 3·5m), which is marked by beacons.

When approaching from the north, do not turn in onto *Ar Gouredec* too soon, as the rocks surrounding the tiny islands of Ar Veskieg Vraz and Ar Veskieg Kriez are notorious yacht-munchers.

By night, home in on the Lan Kerellec light (Iso. WRG.4s), situated approximately 4 cables to the north of the sill. The white sector (064°–069°) leads in past the *Ar Gouredec* lit south cardinal buoy and clears Ile Milliau. Once past here, look out for the lit red buoy (Fl(2)R.6s) near the edge of the green sector. Leave this to port and swing to starboard off the sectored light, heading to leave the next buoy (Q(3)G.10s) to starboard. A few degrees south of

east from this is a red buoy (Q(3)R.10s) which is to be left to port. Now shape up to leave the end of the mole (Fl.G.2·5s2M) close to starboard, then proceed according to the daytime sailing directions.

Berthing and facilities

Contact the harbour office on VHF Ch 9 if at all possible between 0600 and midnight, or ☎ 02 96 23 64 00 (*Fax* 02 96 15 40 87). There are 560 berths in all (maximum length 16m), of which a good number are for visitors.

There are showers and toilets ashore. Shore power, fuel (0800–2000) and fresh water are available, with a crane and a local boatyard for repairs. Laundry in the rue de Trozoul. Restaurants and shops at all prices abound nearby.

Lovely sandy beach.

Transport

Flights from Lannion airport. SNCF to Paris in 3 hours. Taxi on ☎ 02 96 47 48 49.

Lannion

Tides

HW −0605 Dover

MHWS	MLWS	MHWN	MLWN
9·1m	1·3m	7·2m	3·5m

Depths

Outside its narrow channel, the river dries up to 2·5m or more as far as the anchorage off Le Yaudet where at least 3m can be found. Deep pools have been reported further upstream, where a carefully anchored yacht could float, even at LW. However, the bottom is reported as foul in parts, so the greatest care is required.

General

The pleasant country town of Lannion lies 4 miles up the Lannion river (or Le Léguer) at a modest elevation above the quays. The river is extremely pretty, but dries onto an often foul bottom. The quays are sadly no longer a serious proposition for

RIVIERE DE
LANNION

Depths in Metres

LANNION

cruising yachts to dry out (1996), being either foul or taken over by fishing craft, though a trip on the tide in yacht or dinghy may remain an option.

The entrance is dangerous in west-northwest and northwest winds, particularly on the ebb. It seems reasonable to assume that it would also break in a big swell from the west under similar tide conditions.

Approach

Night approach not recommended. Nor is entry before half-tide or on the ebb. Navigate to a spot a couple of miles south of *Le Crapaud* unlit west cardinal buoy. Now try to locate the white house that is the Bec Léguer light structure (Oc(4)WRG.12s) just north of the entrance. It is not conspicuous by day, but it may help to know that it stands 60m above sea level. Steer towards this on about 095°, but if you cannot see it, sag south of the line to be sure of avoiding Le Taureau (dries 9·7m), and look instead for the unlit green buoy *Kinierbel*, 8 cables west-northwest of Pointe de Dourvin. The direct route from this to the entrance passes over a rock which dries 0·1m, so you are better off on the official route, but from half-tide on most yachts will cross this safely enough in calm conditions.

If you have identified Bec Léguer, keep in on 095° until the two green daymarks on the south side of the entrance come into line, then steer in on about 122°, keeping just to the north side of their transit. Give both 50m clearance to miss the surrounding rip-rap. Now keep in on 122° until close to the south bank, then sweep round to port and steer over towards the red beacon on the north shore. The rock pile on the north bank halfway to the beacon is readily distinguished by the small dry island (3m) near its outer end. From the red beacon, stay in the middle until you pass the slipway at Le Yaudet on the south side, then anchor in 9ft (LAT) unless proceeding further. Above here, the river shoals progressively and may dry as much as 6m.

The anchorage at Le Yaudet is well sheltered and the village is most interesting. Well off the tourist route, it is reached by a stiff but not 'cardiac' climb directly up from the tiny landing place. The church, which is open to casual callers as well as those looking for a quiet place to pray, has a fascinating tale to tell and a remarkable altar piece of seemingly unique importance. The church also boasts a number of unrestored 'votive ships' suspended from its rafters. A great rarity in these tidy times.

Lannion. Le Yaudet.

Primel.

There are two hotels offering meals, the more up-market of which had the impertinence in 1996 to advertise that it refused to serve Boeuf Anglais, and thus missed the custom of *The Shell Pilot*. The other was willing and able.

Primel

Tides

HW +0620 Dover

MHWS	MLWS	MHWN	MLWN
8·5m	1·2m	6·7m	3·0m

Depths

Deep water in the approaches, 1·5m in anchorage northeast of Roc'h an Trez Braz. Between 0 and 1m (LAT) in the 50m-wide dredged area behind the outer part of the breakwater. There is about 2m alongside the outer projection of the breakwater near the lighthouse. The rest dries, is foul, or is not available.

General

Primel is an almost natural harbour, completed by its breakwater. The entrance is fairly easy and readily identified. It is dangerous in strong onshore winds, however. There is commercial fishing and some moorings for visiting yachts. The village is totally unspoilt and is in every respect a 'real' Breton fishing community.

Approach

By day, identify *Meloine*, the unlit west cardinal buoy marking Les Trepieds rocks. The entrance lies about 3 miles south from here. As you approach, pick up the conspicuous leading marks (white with red centrelines) on 152°. With Point de Primel abaft the beam you will pass Ar Zamegues rock to starboard, with a green patch painted on a white background, followed by a red and a green beacon. Keep on the line up to the breakwater.

By night, follow the leading lights in. Both are F.R and have a narrow visible sector. Note that the rear light has been reported dim (possibly as a result of a period of poor pruning of the surrounding trees), and the front one very bright. Both lights seemed fine in 1996.

Berthing

There are a number of visitors' moorings, some in fairly deep water, east of Roc'h an Trez Braz. There is plenty of room on these for small yachts. 40-footers (12m) would be OK, but larger than this may have to watch their extremities with care. If space permits, secure alongside the easternmost projection of the jetty (see 'Depths' above), but beware of fishing boats, which may appear at any

PRIMEL-TREGASTEL

time of day or night. Do not use the central projection of the jetty.

The moorings are moderately well sheltered, but some rolling may be experienced in strong westerly weather. Shelter is not ideal in onshore winds.

Facilities

Freshwater tap near fish market, where you can join the jolly Bretons filling their boots with *crustaces* and fresh fish of all sorts. There is a beach, an excellent chandlery in the fishing boat repair yard (where there is another fish shop), shops for simple provisions, a *crêperie* and a north-facing beach like a ghost seaside resort across the neck of land on the east side of the bay. You can land on either side, but for most purposes the 'pier' side is best. The Hotel de l'Abesse at the root of the bay has a public swimming pool, while the 'English Pub' with Guinness and 'jeux' will delight smokers exhausted by the excesses of the anti-smoking lobby, as they enter through a portal marked in large red letters, 'Bar Fumeurs'.

Morlaix

Tides

HW −0610 Dover

MHWS	MLWS	MHWN	MLWN
9·0m	1·3m	7·0m	3·5m

Note that low water figures may be variable

Depths

Deep-water approaches, fading out to a drying river (up to 5m drying heights). Inside the locks, there has been a great deal of silting. Yachts drawing 1·8m or more should now tie up on the west side as near to the lock as space permits, and in any case, north of the harbourmaster's office. Once secure, the harbourmaster will advise as to any recent developments. The visitors' pontoons just north of the office now have little more than 1·5m on them (1997), while further towards the town, there may be even less.

General

Morlaix is a 16th-century town at the head of the river of the same name. A new bridge carrying the N12 autoroute spans the river below the lock, while above the basin an old viaduct above the town dominates the view. The locked yacht harbour is perfectly sheltered. The marina is not the world's most picturesque, but it is safe and can offer a convenient spot to leave a yacht or change crew, only 60 miles from the Chenal du Four. Morlaix is only 28km by fast road from Roscoff and the ferry.

Approach

The trickiest part of the entrance is at the mouth of the river between Pen Lann and Barnénez. The Château du Taureau lies smack in the middle, having been built in 1542 to keep the Brits out, ten years after 600 marauders had been 'taken out' in their bivouacs just up-river. Once you are past this, there is a well buoyed channel between the oyster beds to take you on to the river.

There are two main channels.

The Chenal de Tréguier starts effectively at the green beacon (*La Pierre Noire*) 2 miles west-southwest of Pointe de Primel. It is straightforward, leaving green beacons to starboard and reds to port (see plan), and joins the Grand Chenal after swinging to starboard onto a southwesterly heading with *La Chambre* green daymark to starboard. If in doubt, keep *La Chambre* on a back transit with the red *Petit Arémen* until you are near *No. 1* buoy. Do not forget that this channel has one or two drying rocks of up to half a metre, so use it only with suitable rise of tide. Not recommended for strangers by night.

The Grande Chenal has a minimum of 3m of water and starts between the unlit red buoy *Stolvesen* and *La Vieille*, a green daymark, though care is needed in the offing to avoid the Plateau des Duons, further out to sea. The back marker for the leading line on 176° is the prominent square tower of La Lande (Fl.5s85m23M). The front mark is Ile Louet 1·7m square white tower with black top (Oc(3)WG.12s), sitting on its islet off Pen Lann. This line brings you safely between Ile Ricard, with its dangers, to starboard, and the various horrors to port.

When you have passed *Calhic* green daymark to starboard, swing onto about 160° to pass between *Le Corbeau* green daymark and its red opposite number just before the Château. Once the Château has been left to port, look for *No. 1* green buoy, *La Banc de Flot;* leave it to starboard and proceed onwards between the buoys.

The channel, then the river, is well buoyed all the way with buoys and perches. When they finally run out ¾ mile from the locks stay in the middle.

Ile Louet and Château du Taureau seen from the southwest. The Grand Chenal passes between these two.

The alternative channel (Tréguier) leaves Ile Noir tower clear to port before joining the main channel. Ile Stérec and the last red channel marker in the distance to the left.

APPROACHES TO
MORLAIX
AND
LA PENZE RIVIERE

after. By these times there should be at least 2½m over the sill. In winter, the lock works only from 0800–1700.

Inside the lock, berth according to your draught (see 'Depths'). Note that the official visitors' berths are on the transverse pontoons on your port hand just before you reach the harbourmaster's office on the dockside.

Berthing

Berth where you can, then ask. It is not recommended to anchor in the river, but you may be lucky at Dourduff, and the enterprising sailor may succeed in the lower reaches.

Facilities

Fresh water on the quay, also diesel. Toilets and showers at the Bureau de Plaisance. All repairs, chandlery, *Camping Gaz* exchange and the rest. The city has the usual benefits common to all centres of population, but this one has a plentiful supply of medieval buildings to offset any gloom which may descend.

There are one or two privately owned but sometimes vacant moorings in the Dourduff area near No. 7 buoy. You may be able to pick up one of these, or anchor nearby to await the lock, (VHF Ch 9 and 16, ☎ 02 98 62 13 14). This opens 3 times: at 1½ hours before HW, at HW, and at one hour

Morlaix town.

Communications
Buses and trains to Roscoff and the ferry, also to Brest and Paris. Trains connect to St Malo, but you have to change, so the experience is not speedy.

Roscoff – Port Bloscon

Tides
HW −0605 Dover

MHWS	MLWS	MHWN	MLWN
8·9m	1·3m	7·0m	3·45m

Depths
Roscoff dries out to about 3·2m along its north mole and to up to 5m on the inner harbour. The approaches also dry, but to a lesser extent.

Port Bloscon has deep water for a limited amount of anchorage.

General
Roscoff is known best today for its RoRo ferry terminal. In past times it was the point of departure for the Breton onion sellers whose striped shirts and bicycles festooned with strong onions were such a colourful part of British life. *The Shell Channel Pilot*, though it is technically none of its business, has not seen Johnny Breton in England these 30 years or more. Joyous to relate, however, 6 strings (excellent) were reported purchased in Hinton St George, Somerset, in 1994. The old port of Roscoff dries, but is well worth a visit nonetheless. It is pretty, with an agreeable aspect, a fine square and a number of points of interest, including the largest *vivier* in France, which you can visit.

The approaches to Roscoff can prove challenging, notably from the west, but Bloscon is comparatively easy of entry, and this roadstead, partly sheltered by the land, partly by the breakwater, gives a good lee in westerly weather. It is the ferry terminal, however, and yachts are only tolerated outside the swinging ground.

Approach
All approaches to Roscoff should be in the last 2 hours before HW.

From the west
From the west you have two choices. Either you pass outside Ile de Batz and award yourself an easy ride, or you save 3 miles and go for the Chenal de l'Ile de Batz, a rock-strewn, tide-scoured chamber of horrors which may yet be passed by day, given enough tide, fair weather and good visibility.

Inside To take the Chenal, first consult your tide tables, then keep the mighty tower of Ile de Batz lighthouse bearing about 070° until *Basse Plate*, a north cardinal daymark, bears about 100°. Steer to leave it about half a cable to starboard on a heading of around 106°. This will make good a transit of Le Loup, a steep rock with a white patch north of Pointe des Jacobins, and St Barbe, a distant white pyramid immediately to the right of a clump of trees. This transit carries you as far as *L'Oignon*, a north cardinal beacon to be left to starboard. You should now alter to a degree or two north of east and track east towards *Per Roc'h* north cardinal daymark.

Keep on this track until Ile aux Moutons ferry slip (lit south cardinal buoy off its end) a cable past *Malvoch* south cardinal daymark bears north. Now alter to 080° on Pen ar Cleguer, the right-hand edge of Ile de Batz. On this leg, the channel crosses a rock which dries 0·8m. Continue towards Pen ar

Roscoff.

ILE DE BATZ

ILE DE BATZ

ROSCOFF

Roscoff. Old lighthouse (A) on its transit with light on end of west breakwater. (B) Breakwater for Bassin de Vieux Port.

Cleguer until *Run Oan* south cardinal beacon comes 'on' with Ile Pigued white pyramid on 100°. Follow this transit, leaving *Per Roc'h* half a cable to starboard. When halfway between *Per Roc'h* and *Run Oan*, alter for the end of the Roscoff/Batz ferry pier (violet light), leaving this to starboard and *Duslen* south cardinal about 50m to port. *Run Oan* is also left to port by this course change. It is now safe to head for *Ar Chaden* south cardinal light tower a cable or so south of Ile Pigued, and thence to comparatively open water.

If you are headed for Roscoff, leave *Roc'h Zu* north cardinal beacon to starboard and continue with *Ar Chaden* on your port bow until the entry transit comes into line. This is the 7m white column (green top) on the end of the breakwater with the prominent square tower lighthouse (24m high) on the waterfront. The transit is 210°. For light characteristics, see plan.

Round the end of the breakwater and proceed to the inner, or Vieux Port.

Outside Give the Ile de Batz a comfortable berth to avoid its various off-lying dangers – 1½ miles clears all – until the lit east cardinal buoy *Bse Astan* bears southeast. You can then head to leave it to starboard in complete safety, so long as you monitor set and drift. From here, head south towards *Basse de Bloscon* lit north cardinal until the white pyramid north of *Duslen* south cardinal beacon is in transit with *Ar Chaden* south cardinal light tower on 277°. Now steer towards Roc'h Zu until the entry transit (see above) comes into line on 210°.

From the northeast
In order to keep off the Plateau des Duons, keep on a line joining *Men Guen Bras*, a 20m-high north cardinal light tower, with the bell tower of the church near the right-hand edge of the town. Come off the transit when *Ar Chaden* lines up with the white pyramid north of *Duslen* south cardinal beacon on 277°, as mentioned above ('Outside'). Then continue as per the 'Outside' instructions.

Bloscon
To enter Bloscon is a question of bearing in mind the information above, then steering round the end of the breakwater, paying sensible heed to the various buoys and beacons shown on the plan. Watch out for ferries, which have absolute right of way. Keep in the south part of the harbour, and steer somewhat south of east from the north cardinal buoy and sound in to the south of the breakwater. Shelter here is excellent in a strong westerly and, no doubt, in a southwesterly too.

Berthing
Anchor in Port Bloscon as described. As noted, a good passage berth in westerly weather, but a long walk to anywhere and not a place to visit ashore unless you have no option.

In Roscoff, dry out on the outer mole in the inner harbour. The outer harbour mole is much used by local commercial craft, whose skippers will tell you how things are.

Anchoring in Ile de Batz channel is a poor proposition on account of strong tides. Southeast Malvoch may look tempting and so it is, but should the wind come in westerly, as it once did on the compiler of *The Shell Channel Pilot*, a grisly time awaits you in the long, dark hours.

Facilities
Bloscon
Land on the small slipway at the root of the wall at the south end of the ferry-terminal car park. From here, it is 500m to the casino and the over-priced and poorly stocked tourist wine warehouse set up for road travellers bound home for Blighty with empty tanks. Roscoff is ¾ mile.

Don't be tempted by the sign inviting you to patronise the supermarket up the road. *The Shell Pilot* walked a mile in the rain with no sightings, before retreating to the snug anchorage for cheddar cheese and paté imported by can from the UK.

Roscoff
Water from hydrants by arrangement, or tap in the toilets. Incredibly, no fuel is available in Roscoff. The 'de-taxing' of fishing boat diesel means honest yachtsmen are debarred from filling their tanks with the French taxpayers' money. Municipal showers and toilets at the Gare Maritime on the Vieux Port – *jetons* for the showers from the Maison du Tourisme.

There is a chandler and a competent engineer, a sailmaker, etc., and various mobile cranes. *Camping Gaz* exchange and ice close by.

The town, as noted, is a winner, with good food and drink.

L'ABER-WRAC'H
APPROACHES

Depths in Metres

48° 38' N

4° 38' W

Chenal de la Malouine
Pt Pot de Beurre and W Bn in line 177°

Bns in line 136°
Chenal de la Pendante

Grand Chenal
Lts in line 100°

Dir Lt and Bn Trs in line 100°

Lanvaon
DirQ 55m12M

L'Aber-Wrac'h
Oysters
Oysters

Pte
Camelut

Perros

St Antoine
La
Palue
R Or W

L'Aber-
Wrac'h
Amer de
la Pendante

DirOc(2)WRG
6s13·11M

Tourin

Moorings

Roche aux
Moines

Ile
Longue

Anse de
Anges

Presqu'île Ste
Marguerite

Enez
Terc'h

Ile
Cezon

Breac'h Ver
Fl G 2·5s

Fl(2)R·6s

Ile Vierge
Fl5s77m27M
Horn 60s

RC

Ile Vénan

St Elio

Ile
Wrac'h
Q·R 20m7M

Ile
Stagadon

La Malouine

Karreg
R Brazil

Barr ar
* Bleiz
R

Plate Aber
Wrac'h

B de la
Croix
Fl(3)G 12s

Pt Pot de
Beurre BYB

Réun
Bras

Gd Pot
de
Beurre

La
Pendante

Ile de
la Croix

Petite
Ile

Trépied
R

Le Libenter

Libenter
Q(9)15s
YBY Whis

Petite
Fourche
YBY
37

L'Aber-Wrac'h

Tides

HW +0547 Dover

MHWS	MLWS	MHWN	MLWN
7·8m	1·05m	6·1m	2·85m

Depths

Deep water past La Palue and well on up-river to Paluden, where a road bridge forms the head of yacht navigation. Water becomes shoal at LW springs just above the last bend to the south, but it is possible for a yacht drawing 8ft to lie just west of this bend to a short scope and a weighted cable, even at LW springs. Near the bend, in the mud, lie

Ile Vierge lighthouse.

the dramatic remains of a Citroën which, *The Shell Channel Pilot* was once assured by a fisherman, was left there by a successful *suicé*. Perhaps this colourful wreck has now been cleared or, more likely, rotted away.

General

L'Aber-Wrac'h is famous for its strategic importance, good shelter and ready accessibility in all but strong northwesterly gales. Facilities are limited, but it makes an ideal place to gather one's wits for the Chenal du Four. Up-river, a pleasant soujourn can be passed in peace and tranquillity within easy reach of the raptures which await at Le Relais de l'Aber (see 'Facilities' below).

Approach and entrance

You simply cannot miss L'Aber-Wrac'h by day or night in decent visibility because of the colossal tower of Ile Vierge light (Fl.5s77m28M Horn 60s), 3 miles east-northeast of *Libenter* west cardinal buoy; Ile Vierge also has a radiobeacon (*VG* 314 kHz 70M), on which yachts innocent of more modern assistance can home on a safe bearing in poor visibility. Fog is not recommended for entering L'Aber-Wrac'h. It has been tried by sane and courageous navigators who have ended up amongst the rocks, saved only by kindly fishermen out stirring up the lobsters.

Grand Chenal This is by far the easiest entry, and the only option by night. Round *Libenter* lit west cardinal buoy on a southerly heading to be sure of missing the Libenter shoal and hold on until you pick up the transit on 100°. This consists of a white square tower with a gabled roof and a red top on Ile Wrac'h (Q.R.20m7M), and the conspicuous though distant Lanvaon light 2 miles inshore. This looks like a Venetian campanile, 27m high, square-sided, and 55m above sea level. The side you are interested in is white. (Q.12M intensified 090°–110°). Further on still, bang on the transit, stands Plouguernou belfry.

Follow this easy transit as far as the *Petit Pot de Beurre*, a prominent east cardinal daymark. Leave this to port, then alter to 128°, leaving the green beacon *Breac'h Ver* (Fl.G.2·5s) to starboard and picking up the transit of two less than conspicuous red and white beacons in the vicinity of the lifeboat shed something over a mile ahead. By night you have an obvious sectored light to guide you in (white – straight ahead, green – turn to port, red – turn to starboard). By day, if you cannot make out the leading marks, do not worry. Following *Breac'h Ver*, you have a red buoy (*Ile d'Ehre*) to leave to port, then the green beacon *Roche aux Moines* to starboard. Immediately after this, leave the next unlit red to port and shape up for the moorings or the pontoon, leaving *Touris* red daymark to port.

La Palue, L'Aber-Wrac'h. Lifeboat slip lower left. Visitors' buoys above and to the right.

Le Passage. Anchorage is possible on the last bend (top left), Left-hand white house (bottom right) is the Relais de l'Aber.

L'Aber-Wrac'h approach. (A) Ile Wrac'h on 100° transit of Grand Chenal. (B) *Breac'h Ver* is a green tower beacon to be left to starboard. (C) L'Aber-Wrac'h. Chenal de la Pendante on 136° leaves *Grand Pot de Beurre* and *Petit Pot* (both red beacons) to starboard, Grand Chenal leaves both to port on 100°. (D) Chenal de la Malouine on 177° has the *Petit Pot* and a white pyramid on Petite Ile, immediately southeast of Iles de la Croix, in transit until it joins the other two channels.

La Palue seen from the north bank, with (A) *Le Touris* port-hand beacon (B) lifeboat slip (C) boats stored ashore while pontoons are removed for the winter.

Chenal de la Malouine lines up the *Petit Pot de Beurre* on 177° and a white pyramid on Petit Ile, immediately southeast of Iles de la Croix. The pass is very narrow and can easily pass over a 0·6m patch. It must therefore be treated with great respect and suitable tide rise. It can, however, save 3 miles, joining the Grand Chenal at the *Petit Pot de Beurre*. The channel is best spotted by looking south through the gap between the two large rocks, La Malouine and La Pendante. From the outside you will normally be approaching this channel from the east or northeast. Do not be dismayed if the white pyramid is slow to appear. Both features of the transit do not show themselves until you are almost on, and you should check them with a bearing (177°) to make sure you have got the right ones. The transit line takes you very close to the rocks immediately south of Réun Bras which may well be breaking. Stick rigidly to the transit and do not be alarmed.

Chenal de la Pendante passes northeast of the Libenter shoal. It lines up a white beacon on Ile Cezon with a further white beacon 3 cables south of La Palue lifeboat station on a heading of 136°, joining the main channel at the *Petit Pot de Beurre*.

Up-river

Follow channel markers as far as they go, then keep to the middle. When choosing an anchorage, watch out for moorings, of which there are many.

Berthing

On visitors' buoys off La Palue, or on the pontoon bows-to (11m maximum LOA). Raft up on buoys, if necessary. Alternatively, go up-river and anchor.

Facilities

Basic. La Palue still feels like a summer station rather than a year-round town. Nevertheless, a certain amount can be achieved. There is a small bistro, some chandlery and basic repairs. If in doubt, consult the sailing school. Diesel on the quay from ±2 hours HW. There is a launderette at the small yacht club by the Capitainerie at the base of the pontoon. A good walk will take you to the little town of Landéda, where basic provisions can be purchased.

The yacht club can provide showers at a price. Takeaway oysters from Belon des Abers.

If up the river, do not miss the opportunity of a meal at Le Relais de l'Aber, by the bridge. It isn't cheap, but for a proper French meal, unsullied by the word 'tourist', it cannot be beaten. Book early to avoid disappointment. The place is full of locals . . .

Appendix

I. Charts

ENGLISH COAST

Harbour	Admiralty	Imray
Ramsgate	1827, 1828	C8
Sandwich	1827	C8
Dover	1698	C8
Folkestone	1991	C8
Rye	1991	C8
Eastbourne	2154	C9
Newhaven	2154	C9
Brighton	1991	C9
Shoreham	2044	C9
Littlehampton	1991	C9
Chichester	3418	C9, Y33
Langstone Harbour	3418	C9, Y33
Portsmouth	2625, 2631	C3, C9, C15
Bembridge	2022, 394, 2050	C3, C15
Ryde	394	C3, C15
Fishbourne	2022	C3, C15
Cowes	2793	C3, C15
Hamble River	2022	C3, C15
Southampton	1905, 2041	C3, C15
The Beaulieu River	2021	C3, C15
Newtown River	2021	C3, C15
Yarmouth Harbour	2021	C3, C15
Lymington	2021	C3, C15
Keyhaven	2021	C3, C15
Christchurch	2219	C4
Poole	2611	C4, Y23
Swanage	2172	C4
Lulworth Cove	2172	C4
Weymouth	2172, 2255, 2268	C4

Harbour	Admiralty	Imray
Portland Harbour	2255, 2268	C4
Bridport	3315	C5
Lyme Regis	3315	C5
Axmouth and Beer	3315	C5
Exmouth	2290	C5, Y45, Y43
Teignmouth	26	C5, Y43
Torquay	26	C5, Y43
Brixham	26	C5, Y43
Dartmouth	2253	C5, Y47
Salcombe	28	C6, Y48
River Yealm	1613	C6, C14
Plymouth	30, 1901, 1902, 1967	C6, C14
Looe	147	C6
Polperro	148	C6
Fowey	31	C6, Y52
Charlestown	31	C6
Mevagissey	147	C6
Falmouth	32, 154	C6, Y58
Helford River	147	C6, Y57
Coverack	154, 777	C7
Mullion Cove	777, 2345	C7
Porthleven	777, 2345	C7
St Michael's Mount	2345	C7
Penzance	2345	C7
Newlyn	2345	C7
Mousehole	2345	C7
Isles of Scilly	34, 883	C7

FRENCH COAST

Harbour	Admiralty	Imray	SHOM	Navicarte
Dunkerque	1350, 323	C30	7057	1010
Gravelines	1350, 323	C30	7057	
Calais	1352, 1892, 323	C8	6474	1010
Boulogne	438, 1892, 2451	C8, C31	6436, 6682, 6795	1010, 1011
Le Touquet/Etaples	2451	C31	6795	1011
Le Crotoy	2451	C31	7084	1011
St Valéry-sur-Somme	2451	C31	7084	1011
Le Tréport	1352, 2147, 2451	C31	5928, 7083, 6824	1011
Dieppe	2147, 2451	C31	5927	1011
St Valéry-en-Caux	2451	C31	6794	1012
Fécamp	1352	C31	7207	1012
Le Havre	2990, 2146, 2613	C31, C32	6796, 6736, 6683	526, 1012
Honfleur	2994, 2146, 2613	C31, C32	6796, 6736, 6683	1012
Deauville/Trouville	1349, 2146, 2613	C32	6928	526
Dives/Port Guillaume	2146	C32	6928	526
Ouistreham/Caen	1349, 2613	C32	7055, 6927, 6928	526
Courseulles	1349, 2613	C32	5598, 6927	527, 528
Port-en-Bessin	2613	C32	7056	527
Grandcamp Maisy	2613	C32	7056	527
Isigny-sur-Mer	2073	C32	7056	527
St Vaast-la-Hougue	1349	C32	7090	527, 528

Harbour	Admiralty	Imray	SHOM	Navicarte
Barfleur	1349, 2073	C32	7090	528
Cherbourg	2602	C32	7068, 7092	528
Alderney	60, 2845	C33A		
Carteret	3655	C33A	1014	
Portbail	3655, 2669	C33A	7133-6966	1014
Guernsey	807, 808, 3140, 3654	C33A		
Jersey	3278, 1137, 3655	C33B		
Iles Chausey	3656, 3659	C33B	7134, 824, 4599	534
Granville	3672, 3656, 3659	C33B	5897, 824	535
Cancale	3659	C33B	5644, 824	535
St Malo/St Servan/Dinard	2700, 3659, 2669	C33B	5645, 824	535
La Rance	2700, 3659	C33B	4233, 5645, 844	
St Briac	2700, 3659	C33B	4233, 5645, 844	
St Cast	3659, 2669	C33B	5646, 844	535
Dahouet	3674, 2669	C33B, C34	833, 6966	536
Le Légué (St Brieuc)	3674, 2667	C34	5725, 833	536
Binic	3674, 2669	C33B	5725, 833	536
St Quay-Portrieux	3672, 3674, 2669, 2668	C33B, C34	5725, 833	536
Paimpol	3673, 3670, 2668	C34	3670, 832	537
Ile de Bréhat	3673, 3670	C34	2845, 882, 832	537
Lézardrieux/Pontrieux	3673, 3670, 2668	C34	2845, 882, 832	537
Tréguier	3672, 3670, 2668	C34	973, 972, 967	537, 538
Port Blanc	3672, 3670, 2668	C34	973, 972, 967	537, 538
Perros Guirec	3672, 3670, 2668	C34	973, 972, 967	537, 538
Ploumanac'h	3672, 3670, 2668	C34	974, 967	537, 538
Trébeurden	3669	C34	7124, 967	538
Lannion	3669, 2668	C34	7124, 967	538
Primel	2745, 3669	C34	7095, 7151	538
Morlaix	2745, 3669	C34, C35	7095, 7151	538
Roscoff – Port Bloscon	2745, 3669	C35	7095, 7151	538
L'Aber-Wrac'h	1432, 2644, 3668	C35	7094, 7150	539, 540

II. Conversions

Feet	Metres	Metres	Feet	Nautical miles	Kilo- metres	Gallons	Litres	Pounds	Kilograms
1	0·3	1	3·3	1	1·9	1	4·5	1	0·4
2	0·6	2	6·6	2	3·7	2	9·1	2	0·9
3	0·9	3	9·8	3	5·6	3	13·6	3	1·4
4	1·2	4	13·1	4	7·4	4	18·2	4	1·8
5	1·5	5	16·4	5	9·3	5	22·7	5	2·3
6	1·8	6	19·7	6	11·1	6	27·3	6	2·7
7	2·1	7	23·0	7	13·0	7	31·8	7	3·2
8	2·4	8	26·2	8	14·8	8	36·4	8	3·6
9	2·7	9	29·5	9	16·7	9	40·9	9	4·1
10	3·0	10	32·8	10	18·5	10	45·5	10	4·5
20	6·1	20	65·6	20	37·1	20	90·9	20	9·1
30	9·1	30	98·4	30	55·6	30	136·4	30	13·6
40	12·1	40	131·2	40	74·1	40	181·8	40	18·2
50	15·2	50	164·0	50	92·6	50	227·3	50	22·7
100	30·5	100	328·1	100	185·3	100	454·6	100	45·4

Conversion tables

An approximate method of converting metres to feet is to multiply by 10 and then divide by 3. The answer will be too great, but only by one part in 60, which can usually be neglected.

III. Distances tables

Distance table for passages between harbours on the south coast (in nautical miles)

The shortest navigable distances on the rhumb line between harbour entrances or bars

	Ramsgate	Brighton	Chichester	Portsmouth	Cowes	Lymington	Poole	Weymouth	Dartmouth	Salcombe	Plymouth	Fowey	Falmouth	Penzance
Ramsgate														
Brighton	78													
Chichester	112	34												
Portsmouth	119	41	7											
Cowes	125	47	15	8										
Lymington	132	56	24	17	9									
Poole	152	74	42	35	27	19								
Weymouth	173	97	64	57	49	40	27							
Dartmouth	212	135	107	100	92	84	70	52						
Salcombe	220	144	117	110	103	95	81	64	17					
Plymouth	241	165	135	132	123	115	96	82	35	14				
Fowey	255	178	152	144	139	129	116	96	48	36	20			
Falmouth	271	194	168	160	152	143	130	113	63	50	38	20		
Penzance	295	219	190	183	176	168	155	135	88	74	64	48	32	
Scilly	322	246	218	211	204	195	183	163	116	102	92	76	60	37

Cross-Channel distances

Safe navigable routes between breakwaters and/or estuary entrances (in nautical miles)

	N Foreland	Dungeness	Beachy Head	Nab Tower	Needles	Anvil Point	Portland Bill	Berry Head	Rame Head	Lizard	Bishop Rock
Boulogne	39	25	51	97	125	137	157	196	227	269	318
Dieppe	90	58	58	91	115	126	144	182	211	246	294
Le Havre LtV	130	96	75	76	88	94	106	140	165	198	246
Grandcamp	158	122	94	78	80	82	89	116	140	175	223
Cherbourg	164	128	98	66	60	57	60	84	106	141	188
Alderney	180	144	114	74	61	53	49	65	85	118	167
St Peter Port	201	165	134	96	83	73	65	70	90	112	157
St Helier	219	183	151	113	101	94	87	94	108	130	173
St Malo	245	209	178	140	127	120	113	117	138	145	183
Lézardrieux	243	207	175	134	123	113	102	92	100	108	146
Morlaix	274	238	206	169	149	138	124	106	100	92	123
L'Aber-Wrac'h	300	264	231	195	171	159	146	117	103	84	104
Le Conquet	325	289	252	216	192	179	161	136	120	98	110
Brest	342	306	269	233	209	196	178	153	137	115	127

	Ramsgate	Dunkerque	Calais	Boulogne	Le Touquet/Etaples	St Valéry/Le Crotoy
Dunkerque	39					
Calais	27	20				
Boulogne	37	41	20			
Le Touquet/Etaples	48	51	32	12		
St Valéry/Le Crotoy	66	69	50	30	19	
Brighton	81	96	78	65	97	71

Distance tables for passages between principal headlands along the south coast (in nautical miles)

The shortest navigable distances on the rhumb line between safe distances off each headland

	N Foreland	Dungeness	Beachy Head	Owers	St Catherine's	Anvil Point	Portland Bill	Berry Head	Start Point	Bolt Head	Rame Head	Dodman	Lizard	Runnel Stone
N Foreland														
Dungeness	36													
Beachy Head	66	30												
Owers	101	65	35											
St Catherine's	125	89	59	24										
Anvil Point	150	114	84	49	25									
Portland Bill	170	134	104	69	45	20								
Berry Head	210	174	144	109	85	60	40							
Start Point	218	182	152	117	93	68	48	13						
Bolt Head	224	188	158	123	99	74	54	19	6					
Rame Head	242	206	176	141	117	92	72	36	23	17				
Dodman	263	227	197	162	138	113	93	57	45	39	24			
Lizard	282	246	215	181	156	132	111	75	62	56	44	22		
Runnel Stone	300	265	234	200	175	151	130	94	81	75	63	42	19	
Bishop Rock	330	294	263	229	204	180	159	123	111	105	93	71	48	32

Distances around the Channel Islands

Distances shown are safe navigable routes between breakwaters and/or estuary entrances (in nautical miles)

	Cherbourg	Alderney	St Peter Port	St Helier	Chausey (S)	Granville	St Malo
Cherbourg							
Alderney	21						
St Peter Port	41	23					
St Helier	57	40	26				
Chausey (S)	77	60	48	24			
Granville	83	66	53	29	9		
St Malo	83	66	52	30	15	21	
Lézardrieux	81	65	41	41	47	56	7

Safe navigable distances between yacht berths, outside Ile de Bréhat and Ile de Batz (in nautical miles)

	St Malo	Binic	Paimpol	Tréguier	Perros-Guirec	Morlaix	Roscoff	L'Aber-Wrac'h	Le Conquet
St Malo									
Binic	33								
Paimpol	38	19							
Tréguier	57	39	26						
Perros-Guirec	62	64	31	20					
Morlaix	92	71	59	48	32				
Roscoff	85	64	52	41	26	13			
L'Aber-Wrac'h	117	96	84	73	58	46	33		
Le Conquet	133	112	100	89	74	61	48	23	
Brest	150	129	117	106	91	78	65	40	17

IV. Radiobeacons

V. English–French Glossary

General
yes *oui*
no *non*
please *s'il vous plait*
thank you *merci*
excuse me *pardon*
it's nothing *de rien*
where? *où*
when? *quand?*
how? *comment?*
today *aujourd'hui*
tomorrow *demain*
left *à gauche*
right *à droite*
big *grand*
small *petit*
open *ouvert*
closed *fermé*
goodbye *au revoir*
good morning *bonjour*
good afternoon *bonjour*
good evening *bonsoir*
good night *bonne nuit*
I understand *je comprends*
I don't understand *je ne comprends pas*
OK *d'accord*
How are you *Comment allez-vous/Ça va?*
Fine, thanks *Très bien, merci*
Excuse me, do you speak English? *Pardon, Madame/Monsieur, vous parlez anglais?*
one *un*
two *deux*
three *trois*
four *quatre*
five *cinq*
six *six*
seven *sept*
eight *huit*
nine *neuf*
ten *dix*
twenty *vingt*

fifty *cinquante*
one hundred *cent*
one thousand *mille*
Sunday *dimanche*
Monday *lundi*
Tuesday *mardi*
Wednesday *mercredi*
Thursday *jeudi*
Friday *vendredi*
Saturday *samedi*

Shopping
apples *pommes*
apricots *abricot*
aubergine *aubergine*
bakery *boulangerie*
beans *haricots*
beef *boeuf*
biscuits *biscuits*
bread *pain*
butcher *boucher*
butter *beurre*
carrots *carottes*
cheese *fromage*
chicken *poulet*
chocolate *chocolat*
coffee *café*
cucumber *concombre*
eggs *oeufs*
fish *poisson*
flour *farine*
grocer *alimentation*
honey *miel*
jam *confiture*
lamb *agneau*
lemon *citron*
meat *viande*
melon *melon*
milk *lait*
oil *huile*
onions *oignons*
oranges *oranges*
peaches *pêches*
potatoes *pommes de terre*

rice *riz*
salt *sel*
sugar *sucre*
tea *thé*
tomatoes *tomates*
water *eau*
wine *vin*

French names and terms found on charts
anse bay, creek
avant port outer harbour
baie bay
balise beacon
banc bank
barre bar
basse shoal
bassin basin
blanc white
bouche mouth of river or channel
calanque fjord-like inlet
canal canal, channel
cap cape
capitainerie port/harbour office
château castle
chaussée causeway
chenal channel
col mountain pass
colline hill
côte coast
darse basin
digue mole
écueil shoal, reef
est east
étang lake, lagoon
fleuve river, stream
fosse ditch
golfe gulf
grand(e) great
grau channel
gros large
haut-fond shoal
île island

îlot islet
isthme isthmus
jetée jetty
lac lake
maison house
marais swamp
marine marine
mer sea
môle mole
mont mount, mountain
montagne mountain
mouillage anchorage
neuf(ve) new
noir(e) black
nord north
nouveau new
ouest west
passe channel
petit(e) small
pic peak
plage beach
plateau shoal
pointe point
pont bridge
port port
presqu'île peninsula
quai quay
quai d'accueil arrivals/reception quay
rade roadstead
rivière river
roche rock
rocher above-water rock
rouge red
sable sand
saline salt works
sommet summit
sud south
torrent stream, torrent
tour tower
vieux, vieil, vieille old

Index